Language Diversity in the USA

What are the most widely spoken non-English languages in the USA? How did they reach the USA? Who speaks them, to whom, and for what purposes? What changes do these languages undergo as they come into contact with English? This book investigates the linguistic diversity of the USA by profiling the twelve most commonly used languages other than English. Each chapter paints a portrait of the history, current demographics, community characteristics, economic status, and language maintenance of each language group, and looks ahead to the future of each language. The book challenges myths about the "official" language of the USA, explores the degree to which today's immigrants are learning English and assimilating into the mainstream, and discusses the relationship between linguistic diversity and national unity. Written in a coherent and structured style, *Language Diversity in the USA* is essential reading for students and researchers in sociolinguistics, bilingualism, and education.

KIM POTOWSKI is Associate Professor of Hispanic Linguistics at the University of Illinois at Chicago. Her previous publications include *Language and Identity in a Dual Immersion School* (2007).

Language Diversity in the USA

Edited by

Kim Potowski

University of Illinois at Chicago

CAMBRIDGE
UNIVERSITY PRESS

CAMBRIDGE UNIVERSITY PRESS
Cambridge, New York, Melbourne, Madrid, Cape Town, Singapore,
São Paulo, Delhi, Dubai, Tokyo

Cambridge University Press
The Edinburgh Building, Cambridge CB2 8RU, UK

Published in the United States of America by Cambridge University Press, New York

www.cambridge.org
Information on this title: www.cambridge.org/9780521745338

First published 2010

Printed in the United Kingdom at the University Press, Cambridge

A catalogue record for this publication is available from the British Library

Library of Congress Cataloguing in Publication data
Language diversity in the USA / edited by Kim Potowski.
p. cm.
Includes bibliographical references.
ISBN 978-0-521-76852-8 (hardback)
1. Language and culture – United States. 2. Multilingualism – United States.
3. Sociolinguistics – United States. I. Potowski, Kim. II. Title.
P35.5.U6L36 2010
306.440973 – dc22 2010018303

ISBN 978-0-521-76852-8 Hardback
ISBN 978-0-521-74533-8 Paperback

Contents

List of figures

List of contributors

CARL L. BANKSTON III is Professor of Sociology, Chair of the Department of Sociology, and Co-Director of the Asian Studies Program at Tulane University. A former teacher of English, Bankston lived and worked in Southeast Asia for eight years. His areas of research and teaching include international migration, Asian American communities, and sociology of education. He is co-author of seven books, including *Growing Up American: How Vietnamese Children Adapt to Life in the United States* (1998). He also edited or co-edited eight other books, and has published over one hundred journal articles and book chapters.

MARIA CARREIRA is Associate Professor of Spanish linguistics at California State University, Long Beach. Her publications focus on Spanish as a world language, Spanish in the USA, and teaching Spanish to bilingual Latinos. She is the co-author of a beginning college-level Spanish textbook (*Nexos*, 2005) and the co-author of a book for teaching Spanish to bilingual Latinos (*Sí se puede*).

ANA MARIA CARVALHO is Associate Professor at the University of Arizona, where she directs the Portuguese Language Program. Her research interests include language variation and change, language contact, language attitudes, and dialect and language acquisition. She has published extensively on the contact between Portuguese and Spanish in bilingual communities in northern Uruguay – her most recent publications include the edited volume *Português em Contato* (2009) – and about the acquisition of Portuguese by Spanish speakers.

VY THUC DAO is completing her PhD in Sociology at Tulane University and received her MA in Sociology at the University of Houston. Her areas of research center upon the study of formal organizations, social networks, and ethnic organizations. Currently, she is planning a comparative study of the economic, social, and organizational patterns of recovery and rebuilding by the Vietnamese communities in post-Katrina New Orleans and the Gulf Coast of Mississippi.

ANNA DE FINA is Assistant Professor and Co-ordinator of the Language Program in the Italian Department at Georgetown University. Her research focuses on narrative, language and identity, and language contact. Her most recent publications include *Identity in Narrative* (2003) and the co-edited volumes *Italiano e italiani fuori d'Italia* (with F. Bizzoni, 2003), *Dislocations, Relocations, Narratives of Displacement* (with Mike Baynham, 2005), and *Discourse and Identity* (with D. Schiffrin and M. Bamberg, Cambridge University Press, 2006).

KATHLEEN DILLON is Associate Director of the National Heritage Language Resource Center and Associate Director of the University of California Consortium for Language Learning and Teaching. She has published articles on teaching Russian as a heritage language, and in the literature field she has published on Russian poets of the nineteenth and twentieth centuries. She is a recipient of the excellence in teaching award from the American Association of Teachers of Russian and Eastern European Languages. She is also co-editor of the *Heritage Language Journal.*

KATARZYNA DZIWIREK is an Associate Professor in the Department of Slavic Languages and Literatures at the University of Washington in Seattle. Her publications focus on Polish syntax and semantics, with particular emphasis on cross-cultural differences in expression of emotion. Her most recent project (with Barbara Lewandowska-Tomaszczyk) is *Complex Emotions and Grammatical Mismatches*.

LUCIANA FELLIN directs the Italian Language Program at Duke University. Her work focuses on language ideologies as linked to language obsolescence, maintenance, and revival. She has co-authored textbooks for Italian as a second language, published book chapters and articles on second language acquisition and maintenance and, most recently, on language vitality among Italian immigrant communities in Australia. Presently, she is working on an ethnographic project investigating language and identity in Italian-American communities.

ELVIRA C. FONACIER is the Project Team Leader at the Centre for Continuing Education, University of Sydney, Australia, where she manages the development and delivery of education programs for adult learners. Her research focuses on the teaching and learning of language and literature with special attention to assessment and program evaluation. She also teaches linguistics courses at the University of Western Sydney.

OLGA E. KAGAN is Director of the National Heritage Language Resource Center and Co-ordinator of the Russian Language Program at UCLA. She is also Director of the UCLA Russian Language Flagship Program. She has authored seven textbooks, edited two volumes of scholarly articles, and published articles on teaching heritage learners of Russian. She has received two book awards from the American Association of Teachers of Russian and Eastern European Languages (AATSEEL). She co-edits the *Heritage Language Journal*.

HAE-YOUNG KIM is an Associate Professor of Korean at Duke University. Her academic work focuses on heritage language development and maintenance, morphosyntactic development in Korean, content-based language instruction, and curriculum development for college-level Korean. She has published research articles on Korean heritage learners' attitudes and motivations, development of tense and aspect morphology in Korean as a second language, and classroom discourse in a content-based language class.

RENATE LUDANYI is Director of the German Studies Center at Western Connecticut State University. She is President of the German Language School Conference, an umbrella organization for community-supported private German Language Schools in the USA, where students can complete language prerequisite examinations for study at a German university. She was awarded the Cross of Merit from the Federal Republic of Germany for her work in many areas of pedagogy and school administration.

TERESA L. MCCARTY is the Alice Wiley Snell Professor of Education Policy Studies at Arizona State University, and director and co-Principal Investigator of a large-scale study of Native American language shift and retention. Her recent books include *"To Remain an Indian": Lessons in Democracy from a Century of Native American Education* (with K. Tsianina Lomawaima), *Language, Literacy, and Power in Schooling*, and *A Place To Be Navajo – Rough Rock and the Struggle for Self-Determination in Indigenous Schooling*.

SCOTT MCGINNIS is the Academic Advisor for the Defense Language Institute, Washington Office. Between 1999 and 2003, he served as Executive Director of the National Council of Less Commonly Taught Languages. His twenty-two years in the language teaching profession have included a decade as supervisor of the Chinese language programs at the University of Oregon and University of Maryland. He has published extensively on Chinese as a heritage language in the USA.

BOZENA NOWICKA MCLEES is an instructor at Loyola University. She has broad experience developing and teaching Polish at the secondary and postsecondary levels. Her research focuses on connecting the evolving educational systems in Poland with the existing network of Polish-American schools and organizations in Chicago in order to facilitate heritage language maintenance. She assisted in the development of the Polish government's Certification of Proficiency in Polish as a Foreign Language by administering examinations at her campus.

KIM POTOWSKI is Associate Professor of Spanish linguistics and directs the Heritage Language Cooperative at the University of Illinois at Chicago. Her work on Spanish in the USA investigates language use and identity, including the book *Language and Identity in a Dual Immersion School* (2007), publications about "MexiRican" language and identity, Spanish use in US *quinceañera* celebrations, and linguistic structures such as discourse markers and code-switching. She has also published a book and several articles about Spanish heritage language education.

SUZANNE ROMAINE has been Merton Professor of English Language at the University of Oxford since 1984 and is interested in societal multilingualism, linguistic diversity, language change, language acquisition, and language contact. Her book *Vanishing Voices: The Extinction of the World's Languages*, co-authored with Daniel Nettle, won the British Association of Applied Linguistics Book of the Year Prize in 2001, and has been translated into a number of languages. She has received honorary doctorates from the University of Uppsala and the University of Tromsø.

SONIA SHIRI is the Arabic Language Program Co-ordinator at the University of California, Berkeley. Her research focuses on Arabic sociolinguistics and teaching Arabic as a foreign and as a heritage language. She is the designer of the introductory computer-assisted Arabic course "Arabic without Walls," which will offer Arabic at a distance to students at UC campuses without Arabic programs.

ALBERT VALDMAN is Rudy Professor of French/Italian and Linguistics (emeritus) and Director of the Creole Institute at Indiana University. His research and professional interests span a broad range of areas in applied and descriptive linguistics, including second language acquisition research, foreign-language teaching, sociolinguistics, creole studies with focus on French-based creoles, notably those of Haiti and Louisiana, and French linguistics. He is one of the leading specialists of French in the USA, particularly Louisiana Regional French.

TERRENCE G. WILEY is Professor of Language Policy and Applied Linguistics at Arizona State University, where he co-directs the Language Policy Research Unit of the Southwest Center for Educational Equity and Language Diversity. His research focuses on literacy/biliteracy and language policy. His numerous publications include *Literacy and Language Diversity in the United States* (2005). Professor Wiley is co-editor of the *Journal of*

Language Identity and Education and the *International Multilingual Research Journal*.

YUN XIAO is Associate Professor and Chair of the Modern Languages Department at Bryant University. Her research interests are second language acquisition and pedagogy, heritage language learning, and Chinese teacher education. She has published more than twenty articles and book chapters. Her book projects include the *Readings in Chinese Literature* Series (Volume I, 2007; Volume II, forthcoming); *Chinese as a Heritage Language: Fostering Rooted World Citizenry* (2008) (with Weiyun He), and a forthcoming book series on teaching Chinese as a foreign language (with Michael Everson).

Preface

Take a walk down the streets of any large city in the USA – and increasingly many mid-sized cities and small towns – and you can usually hear more than one language spoken by local residents. Some may think that this linguistic diversity is due entirely to recent immigration. However, as this book seeks to demonstrate, the USA has always been linguistically diverse. And while a large part of our diversity is thanks to immigration, some of it is due to other factors such as land purchases and annexations. In addition, a large portion of today's speakers of Languages Other Than English (often referred to as "LOTEs") in the USA were born and raised in the USA. These are the children and grandchildren of immigrants – they themselves are not immigrants.

Yet it is undeniable that immigration is driving and sustaining our nation's proficiency in many LOTEs today. There are several excellent books about immigrants in the USA, most notably Portes and Rumbaut's (2006) fascinating account of immigrant experiences and the significant roles played by social class, residential patterns, and available networks. These authors note that language is a fundamental dimension of the process of acculturation, and that in the minds of many, the "litmus test of Americanization" is learning English and losing the mother tongue.

Our effort in this volume is to focus precisely on languages other than English in the USA: How did they get here? Who speaks them, to whom, and for what purposes? What changes do these languages undergo as they come into overwhelming contact with English? And more broadly: What factors contribute to LOTEs being retained or lost as the generations progress? Is it even possible to retain a heritage language while also regularly speaking English in the USA?

The first chapter seeks to dispel several persistent myths about linguistic diversity in the USA, particularly the rates of English learning among immigrant groups and the fear that linguistic diversity threatens our national unity. The second chapter explores linguistic and social issues related to languages in contact. The following thirteen chapters begin with a special chapter on Native American languages, followed by a chapter on each of the top twelve LOTEs as listed in order by the number of speakers in the 2007 American Community

Survey. The authors trace patterns of language loss and also highlight factors that contribute to maintenance of ethnolinguistic vitality in the USA. The concluding chapter offers an analysis of US language policy – that is, it explores the history of the "litmus test" of English monolingualism, the extent to which it still persists today, and what the nation can do to promote a more additive, linguistically diverse climate.

I hope that this volume will be of use to several audiences. Educators – whether teaching English as a Second Language, teaching LOTEs as heritage or as foreign languages, designing curricular units about the histories and current demographics of these communities, or offering interdisciplinary courses on immigration – can benefit from details about particular ethnolinguistic groups, and also from having these thirteen groups profiled in one place. Linguists seeking to carry out detailed analyses of particular LOTEs in the USA can use these chapters as a starting point. And I truly hope that members of the LOTE-speaking communities themselves will find pleasure and pride in these portraits, which have been painted with much care by the authors, and that new editions might be produced every ten years with the publication of new Census data.

Acknowledgements

A national portrait of language diversity in the USA, consisting of expert-level detail on thirteen different languages/language groups – combined with equally expert chapters on language contact and future directions for the nation's language policy – would have been impossible for one individual to complete. Thus, my first and foremost thanks are to all the contributors to this book, who lent their considerable expertise and time to this project. They shared a vision that this was indeed an important undertaking, and produced and revised multiple drafts over the course of more than a year. I hope they agree that their individual efforts have combined to produce a collection that is more than the sum of its wonderful parts. Scott McGinnis also provided keen insight as I put together the introductory chapter, as well as the initiative to submit a very well-received panel based on a subset of this material to the 2008 meeting of the American Council of Teachers of Foreign Languages in Orlando, Florida, for which I thank him heartily.

Next: Those who regularly complete manuscript reviews typically understand that they are making a significant contribution to the field, often without public recognition. Thus, I very enthusiastically thank the following experts whose feedback was highly valued by the authors and by me. Heaps of glory and rounds of raucous applause to these reviewers:

Jeff Bale, Arizona State University
Dennis Baron, the University of Illinois at Urbana-Champaign
Joshua Brown, Texas Tech University
Nick Clements, the University of Illinois at Chicago
Caitlin Cornell, the University of Illinois at Chicago
Jose del Valle, City University of New York
Erin Haynes, University of California Berkeley
Herman Heller, City University of New York
C. N. Le, University of Massachusetts Amherst
Scott McGinnis, the Defense Language Institute
Leo Paz, City College of San Francisco
Maria Polinsky, Harvard University
Joe Price, Texas Tech University

Ana Roca, Florida International University
Harold Schiffman, University of Pennsylvania
Sarah Shin, University of Maryland Baltimore County

My editorial assistant, Brad Hoot, did excellent readings of chapter drafts, caught discrepancies, asked good questions, conducted solid research on necessary details, deciphered miniscule printed copy with hand-scrawled markings, and helped keep the project organized, bringing it to conclusion without poking out a single eye.

Andrew Winnard at Cambridge University Press enthusiastically supported this project from the start, and I thank him for his belief in its value and his assistance – along with that of Sarah Green – in bringing it to completion.

Finally, the students in my course on Language Policy and Cultural Identity at the University of Illinois at Chicago (Fall 2007 and Fall 2008) read early versions of many of these chapters and asked good questions, some of which now appear as discussion questions.

1 Language diversity in the USA

Dispelling common myths and appreciating advantages

Kim Potowski[1]

> The official language of the US is English. But today's immigrants are not learning English as quickly as those of the past – it seems like they don't want to fit in to the American way of life. Language diversity in this country is a recent problem due to unprecedented levels of immigration, and we are at risk that the different languages spoken here threaten our national unity.

These myths regarding language are fairly prevalent in the USA at the beginning of the twenty-first century. Yet all of them are false, and both their underlying premises and their implications are damaging on several levels. They are damaging to intergroup relations because immigrants are accused of lacking the motivation or desire to integrate into mainstream US society and learn English. This often leads others to resent them or accuse them of being unpatriotic. They are damaging to immigrant families in that children who come to school speaking a Language Other than English (often referred to as "LOTEs") are pressured into erasing that language, which can lead to academic difficulties as well as problems communicating with family members and retaining cultural traditions. They are also damaging to the nation because they squander vast linguistic resources that could benefit the USA economically, diplomatically, and culturally. This introductory chapter will explore each of these topics as it addresses these three common fallacies.

Isn't English the official language of the USA?

As of the year 2009, the USA does not have an official language. While the great majority of Americans today (80 percent) speak English as a native language – and, in fact, as their only language – there is no law or constitutional amendment establishing a national language. As noted by Heath (1977), the founding fathers:

> recognized that decisions on language choice and change would be made at the local and regional levels by citizens responding to communicative needs and goals they themselves identified. Moreover, early political leaders recognized the close connection between

language and religious/cultural freedoms, and they preferred to refrain from proposing legislation which might be construed as a restriction of these freedoms. (Heath 1977: 270)

According to Schiffman, the USA has no explicit language policy, but we do have a "linguistic culture" that "supports the use of English to the exclusion of almost all other languages, so that an explicit policy that would officialize English is not necessary, and probably never will be" (Schiffman 2005: 121). The development of our national "linguistic culture" will be further explored in this chapter.

The top twelve LOTEs spoken in the US by people aged five and older, as reported in the 2007 American Community Survey, are displayed in Table 1.1. What is immediately noticeable in this table is that almost two thirds of all US LOTE speakers (62 percent) are Spanish-speaking, even though Spanish-speakers make up just 12 percent of the nation's population. In addition, while groups such as French, German, Italian, and Polish speakers have undergone a numerical decline, groups like Russian and Vietnamese experienced tremendous growth during the decade between 1990 and 2000, as well as continuing growth from 2000 to 2007. The ramifications for these trends will be discussed throughout this book.

Table 1.1. *Top twelve non-English languages in the USA*

Ranking	Number of speakers	Percentage of the population	Percentage change 1990–2000	Percentage change 2000–7	Percentage of all US LOTE speakers
English-only	225,505,953	80.27	+8	+5	n/a
1. Spanish	34,547,077	12.30	+62	+23	62.31
2. Chinese	2,464,572	0.88	+53	+22	4.45
3. Tagalog*	1,480,429	0.53	+45	+21	2.67
4. French	1,355,805	0.48	−3	−18	2.45
5. Vietnamese	1,207,004	0.43	+99	+20	2.18
6. German	1,104,354	0.39	−11	−20	1.99
7. Korean	1,062,337	0.38	+43	+19	1.92
8. Russian	851,174	0.30	+191	+20	1.54
9. Italian	798,801	0.28	−23	−21	1.44
10. Arabic	767,319	0.27	+73	+25	1.38
11. Portuguese	687,126	0.24	+31	+22	1.24
12. Polish	638,059	0.23	−8	−4	1.15

Note: * Although some prefer the term "Filipino," the term "Tagalog" is used in the USA Census.
Source: USA Census Bureau 2000a, 2007c.

Some of the most significant implications are for the educational field in the USA – both the field concerned with the education of English language

Table 1.2. *Immigrants who speak English "very well" or "well"*

Ranking	Number of speakers	Percentage who speak English "well" or "very well"
1. Spanish	34,547,077	70.9
2. Chinese	2,464,572	73.4
3. Tagalog	1,480,429	93.0
4. French	1,355,805	92.3
5. Vietnamese	1,207,004	68.6
6. German	1,104,354	95.2
7. Korean	1,062,337	71.2
8. Russian	851,174	74.6
9. Italian	798,801	88.9
10. Arabic	767,319	88.5
11. Portuguese	687,126	77.8
12. Polish	638,059	80.4

Source: US Census Bureau 2007c.

learners as well as the field of foreign language education. It is crucial to note that, in 2002, fully 20 percent of all school-aged children spoke a language other than English at home, a figure which has more than doubled since 1979 (National Center for Educational Statistics 2002a). The field concerned with helping children learn English as well as their school subjects – often referred to as "bilingual education" or "English as a Second Language (ESL)," is clearly affected by these changes. They must find instructors capable of helping these children learn, which requires training in ESL methodology and, ideally, proficiency in the children's first languages. Typically, when these students get to high school and college, they come into contact with the field of foreign language education, which refers to them as "heritage speakers" of the non-English language. Heritage speakers are different from traditional foreign language learners in many ways (Valdés 2001; Potowski and Carreira 2004), so foreign language educators must accommodate instructional materials and methodologies for these increasing numbers of heritage-speaking students. Each chapter in this book will examine educational implications of language diversity in the USA.

Why don't they just learn English?

The fact is that US immigrants and their descendants *do* learn English, and they learn it quickly. Table 1.2 shows that, overall, speakers of other languages report speaking English "well" or "very well." This is the pattern for most immigrants to this country in the past as well as today. Plentiful research has shown that immigrant communities shift entirely to English very quickly, typically within three generations. In fact, when examining thirty-five different nations in the world, in no other country was the rate of mother-tongue shift toward monolingualism in the national dominant language as fast as in the USA (Lieberson *et al.* 1975). Even the most recently arrived groups exhibit patterns of language use that suggest that the adoption of English is well underway (McKay and Wong 2000: 81). Veltman (2000), for example, found that after up to five years in the US, 20 percent of immigrants aged 0–14 at the time of arrival had already adopted English as their preferred, usual language. After five additional years, the number rose to 40 percent. In addition, Veltman found that younger people today are more likely to adopt English than their older peers were when they were young. This is the trend all over the USA and is likely due to urbanization, universal education, mass communication, and greater regional integration into the national economy.

The studies just cited show that immigrants shift very quickly to English. We now turn to the maintenance of heritage languages among their US-born descendants. It is very common for the grandchildren of immigrants not to develop strong proficiency in their family's non-English language. In 2006, Rumbaut, Massey, and Bean found that the "life expectancy" of five languages in southern California (Spanish, Tagalog, Chinese, Vietnamese, and Korean) was no more than two generations. That is, Spanish can be expected to begin to die out with the children of immigrants, and not be spoken well or at all by the grandchildren of immigrants – and the Asian languages die out even faster, often not being spoken well by the children of immigrants. These authors tell us that their findings constitute support for the idea of the USA as a "linguistic graveyard" (p. 458). With immigration constituting 65 percent of the total US population growth and virtually 100 percent of its labor force growth in 2000 (Passel 2007), it is in our best interest that these individuals be well educated; this volume argues that this education should include, in addition to English, literacy and communicative skills in the home language.

It is worth mentioning that immigrants abandon their heritage languages for a variety of reasons that will be explored throughout this book, including peer pressure, lack of opportunity to use the language, or fear that it will interfere with their ability to learn English or get ahead in American society. As noted by Tse (2001a: 33), "[w]hereas knowing English may bring prestige and acceptance, speaking another language – especially a low-status language – can do the opposite" by causing shame for being different or attracting xenophobic reactions in others. Even so, loss of the heritage language can sometimes have serious negative consequences. It can create feelings of linguistic insecurity (Krashen 1998) and identity loss (Fought 2006); Zhou and Bankston (2000a) argue that loss of heritage language and identity leads some students to engage in delinquent behavior at school in the quest for a new identity. Particularly devastating is the weakening of the family, as parental authority is often diminished when parents and children cannot communicate with each other, and elders can no longer transmit family and ethnic values (Rodriguez 1981; Wong-Fillmore 1991; Tse 2001a: 52).

In spite of abundant evidence of rapid acquisition of English, it is today's large numbers of new immigrants that may create the impression of a lack of linguistic assimilation. In his 2004 book titled *Who are We?*, Harvard professor Samuel Huntington expresses concern about the collapse of the US national identity due in part to the persistence of Spanish among Mexican immigrants. "There is only the American dream created by an Anglo-Protestant society," writes Huntington, and "Mexican-Americans will share in that dream and in that society only if they dream in English." However, Huntington would need look no further than the second generation of Mexicans in the USA, who are typically English-dominant, and the third generation, who are monolingual in English, to see that these concerns are largely unfounded. One recent development that has disturbed the migration pattern of some Mexican nationals, however, may in fact contribute to Huntington's alarm. Typically, families would make a few trips to the USA lasting several months to a year to earn money, and then return permanently to Mexico. But as border security has tightened, it has become more dangerous and expensive to make these trips, so many have settled in the USA "reluctantly, with little interest in identifying as Americans" (Kotlovitz 2007). Yet given that the majority (60 percent) of US Latinos are born in the USA and grow up to become either English dominant or English monolingual (Rumbaut *et al.* 2006), there is no strong evidence supporting Huntington's argument.

Fears about immigrants not learning English are often accompanied by what we might call the "my grandparent" myth. It goes something like this: "When my grandparents immigrated from [name of country], they did not need bilingual education or special services in their language. They simply worked hard and learned the language. Today's immigrants want everything handed to them." What this sentiment ignores, however, is that life in the 1800s and early 1900s required very little knowledge of English to make a decent wage in the areas of manufacturing where many immigrants worked. High levels of literacy, or even a high school diploma, were not necessary as they are today. It is very likely that this person's grandparents would be at a much greater disadvantage in the twenty-first century as immigrants to the USA without English abilities.

Finally, although this volume does not address English learning in depth, an important factor in the US language equation is the acute lack of accessible and well-taught English as a Second Language (ESL) classes in many communities. In some cases, when ESL classes are available, some individuals cannot take advantage of them due to scheduling problems involved with holding more than one job – which can entail working 16 hours per day – or problems with transportation or childcare. But the biggest problem seems to be lack of availability of affordable ESL classes. A 2006 study found that 60 percent of the free ESL programs in twelve states had waiting lists, ranging from a few months in Colorado and Nevada to as long as two years in New Mexico and Massachusetts (Tucker 2006). In 2005 there were 1.2 million adults enrolled in ESL courses, which is about one in ten of those who reported speaking English "Less than very well" or "Not at all" (US Department of Education 2005). The federal government provides money for such classes, but each state decides how much of these funds to spend on ESL classes. According to Santos (2007a), advocates for more English classes argue that this state–federal financing split leaves a system whose quality varies widely from state to state, and is lacking almost everywhere. Rather than blame the victims of these shortages, Senator Lamar Alexander of Tennessee, where the immigrant population has tripled since 1990, sponsored a bill in 2006 that would have given legal immigrants $500 vouchers to pay for English classes since so many of the free ones were full. He stated that "Most education policy is the prerogative of state and local governments, but I would argue that the prerogative to help people learn our common language is a federal responsibility" and that "If we make it easier for people to learn English, they will learn it. I think that ought to be a priority of our government, and I don't think it has been" (Santos 2007a).

Senator Alexander's position of helping immigrants attend ESL classes stands in contrast to the idea that laws forbidding the use of non-English languages will somehow promote greater English learning. Some monolingual English-speaking Americans are intolerant of languages other than English spoken in the USA and seek to promote its acquisition through legislative means. In 2007, there were three bills proposed to make English the official language of the USA (S133, HR 769, and HR 997).[2] Although all three were referred to subcommittees but never came up for a vote, this clearly demonstrates that numerous lawmakers and their constituents, much like the large lobbying groups English-only and US English, feel a need to officially protect and promote English. As of 2007, twenty-six states had declared English their official language, while only three states had any kind of protected bilingualism (Hawaii, Louisiana, and New Mexico).[3] And although Native American languages are official or co-official on many reservations, language loss among Native American communities has been systematic, as is described in Chapter 3 in this volume.

In fact, such laws do very little to assist immigrants in acquiring English skills. According to the Institute for Language and Education Policy (Crawford 2006), "official English" policies are:

(1) Unnecessary – the overwhelming dominance of English in the USA is not threatened in any way. Newcomers to this country are learning it more rapidly than ever before. Our language does not need "legal protection."

(2) Punitive – restricting government's ability to communicate in other languages would threaten the rights and welfare of millions of people, including many US citizens, who are not fully proficient in English.
(3) Pointless – Official-English legislation offers no practical assistance to anyone trying to learn English. In fact, it is likely to frustrate that goal by outlawing programs designed to bring immigrants into the mainstream of our society.
(4) Divisive – the campaign to declare English the official language often serves as a proxy for hostility toward minority groups, Latinos and Asians in particular. It is exacerbating ethnic tensions in a growing number of communities.
(5) Inconsistent with American values – Official-English laws have been declared unconstitutional in state and federal courts because they violate guarantees of freedom of speech and equal protection of the laws.
(6) Self-defeating – English-only policies are foolish in an era of globalization, when multilingual skills are essential to economic prosperity and national security. Language resources should be conserved and developed, not suppressed.

Far from simply seeking to promote English proficiency, ulterior motives for such laws might lie elsewhere. Urcioli (2001), for example, argues that race has been remapped from biology onto language. In past discourses on race, it was posited that there were inherently superior and inferior races, each with intellectual traits attributed to them. Such arguments have become less acceptable in public discourse, but language is seen as fair game, allowing it in many cases to become a proxy for discrimination. Unlike biological race, however, most people think that individuals can and should control their language; if they do not, it is considered acceptable for them to suffer the economic consequences. Urcioli contends that what drives movements like the English Language Amendment is precisely such mapping of race onto language. Race ideology emphasized the importance of compartmentalization such that the inferior would not contaminate the superior; acknowledging a LOTE with official status would be analogous with such contamination.

A more effective policy than English-only legislation and all the negativity it generates would be to invest in massive national ESL course networks. But even those who agree that official English policies are unnecessary may ask themselves this question: "Why should the USA, where 80 percent of the citizens are monolingual English speakers, provide services like voting, driver's licenses, and those of other agencies in non-English languages? Doesn't this take away all incentive for immigrants to learn English?" Mayor Bloomberg of New York does not think so. In July 2008 he signed Executive Order 120, probably the boldest act of its kind in the nation, requiring every city agency that has direct interaction with customers to provide language assistance in Spanish,

Chinese, Korean, Russian, Italian, and French Creole, with a telephone-based service linked to interpreters who speak Urdu, Hindi, Arabic, and dozens of other languages. According to Mayor Bloomberg (Santos 2008):

> The fundamental basis of government is its interaction with its citizens. If people don't know what we do, don't know what they should do, what the law requires them to do, don't know how to get services, all the money that we're spending providing those services, providing those laws, is meaningless.

That is, language assistance programs for immigrants link them to the services that the host communities have already decided to provide them, services which contribute to the overall wellbeing of the immigrants, their neighbors, and their surrounding communities. Given the contributions of immigrants to the national economy (Orrenius 2003),[4] there is no reason for the mainstream not to assist them in acquiring services they need and in exercising their rights. As for whether language services remove incentives to learn English, if we refer back to Table 1.2 and the figures about the acute lack of ESL classes and the long waiting lists to enroll, we may conclude the following: While there may be some individuals who feel they can live life in the USA perfectly well using their non-English language – particularly the elderly – it is generally the case that immigrants realize all too well the need for English to get ahead economically and secure the futures of their families. We must also keep in mind that the children of immigrants will be English-dominant and have no need for such language programs.

A few more words about economics are warranted. Chiswick and Miller (2007) report on almost twenty years of research carried out on four continents, research that applies economic models to understanding the causes and consequences of immigrants' proficiency in the host country's dominant language. The three fundamental variables they identified, called the "three Es of language proficiency," were *Exposure* to the destination language, *Efficiency* in its acquisition, and *Economic Incentives* to acquire the language. Their findings, which were universal across the countries studied, included the following:

(1) Destination language proficiency increases with duration in the country, educational attainment, living outside of an ethnolinguistic enclave, a younger age at immigration, and parents' proficiency in the host language (particularly the mother's proficiency);

(2) There is a highly significant and large effect of host country language proficiency on earnings and employment;[5]

(3) Greater typological similarity between the immigrant language and the host language is correlated with greater rates of acquisition, while greater typological distance is correlated with lower rates of acquisition.

The field of economics can thus contribute to our understanding of immigrant language-use patterns.

To conclude this section, we refer to the seminal work of Richard Ruíz (1984), who proposed three fundamental orientations toward language diversity: *language-as-a-problem*, *language-as-a-right*, and *language-as-a-resource*. According to the language-as-a-problem paradigm, linguistic diversity is a problem that needs to be solved. Similarly, language-as-a-right advocates commonly view non-English language groups as a problem with regard to school achievement, but this orientation insists that the solutions should not involve discrimination against such students and their communities. For the language-as-a-resource orientation, linguistic diversity is a national resource that should be developed both within the schools and the larger society. It is within this third context of language-as-a-resource that this volume has been conceived.[6] Promoting linguistic diversity and helping immigrants learn English are not contradictory goals. The authors in this book agree that immigrants to the USA should learn English and should learn it well. However, this goal should not require the abandonment of the heritage language; the loss of heritage languages often has not only personal and familial repercussions, but also represents a loss to the nation as a whole. Language learning for the immigrant should not have to be a zero-sum game, substituting English for one's native language.

Aren't our current levels of linguistic diversity a recent problem due to today's high immigration rate?

Arguments about the supposedly unprecedented proportion of immigrants and the recency of linguistic diversity are unsustainable when we examine the historical facts. The geographical area that is today the USA has always been ethnolinguistically diverse. In addition to the English, early settlers included French, German, and Spanish-speaking populations, not to mention the 300-plus Native American languages that were spoken here. In colonial Pennsylvania, German-speaking immigrants made up about one third of the population and printed newspapers in German, conducted their businesses in German, educated their children in German, and drew up legal contracts in German. In fact, the US Articles of Confederation were printed in English and German. Under the Louisiana Purchase of 1803, the USA acquired a territory with a French-speaking majority; Louisiana's governor from 1816–20, Jacques Villeré, spoke no English when he was elected, and Louisiana's Constitution of 1845 established that the state legislature would conduct business in both French and English. Residents of California have been conducting their lives in Spanish since the Spaniards' arrival in 1542 (not to mention the non-Europeans already living there, who had their own languages). The first Anglo settlers arrived some 275 years later, in about 1820 – thus the Southwest is full of descendants of Spanish-speakers who never immigrated here, but rather whose homelands

Table 1.3. *US foreign-born population*

Year	Percentage foreign-born	Number of foreign-born (millions)	Percentage change
1850	10.0	2.2	n/a
1890	14.8	9.2	318
1900	13.7	10.4	13
1910	14.7	13.5	30
1920	13.2	13.9	3
1930	11.6	14.2	2
1940	8.8	11.6	−18
1950	6.9	10.4	−10
1960	5.3	9.7	−7
1970	4.7	9.6	−1
1980	6.2	14.1	47
1990	7.9	19.8	40
2000	11.1	31.1	57
2005	12.4	35.6	15
2006	12.5	37.9	6

Source: US Census Bureau 2000a.

were annexed by the USA. The 1849 constitution of California recognized language rights of Spanish speakers by stating that all laws, decrees, and regulations be published in both English and Spanish. In 1880, press publications in German, Yiddish, Spanish, Czech, Polish, and Italian were very common. Colorado's 1876 constitution was printed in English, Spanish, and French, and German maintained such a strong presence that many schoolchildren of German descent received a large portion of their primary education in German up until World War I (Schiffman 1996).

Technically, all languages besides those spoken by indigenous Native Americans are in fact historically immigrant languages, and immigration figures prominently in today's discussions about language diversity. This is despite the fact that the proportion of immigrants in the nation today is actually smaller than in the past. In 2006, the foreign-born population was estimated at 37.9 million people, or 12.5 percent of the population (Camarota 2007), which is actually a slightly smaller percentage than the almost 15 percent in 1890 and in 1910, as shown in Table 1.3.

However, it is also true that the foreign-born population dropped to between 5 percent and 9 percent during the sixty years between 1940 and 2000. Thus, the jump to 12.4 percent in 2005 is notable. In addition, the overall US population is larger with each Census, so there are larger *numbers* of foreign-born people living today in the USA than ever in its history. For example, the 14.7 percent

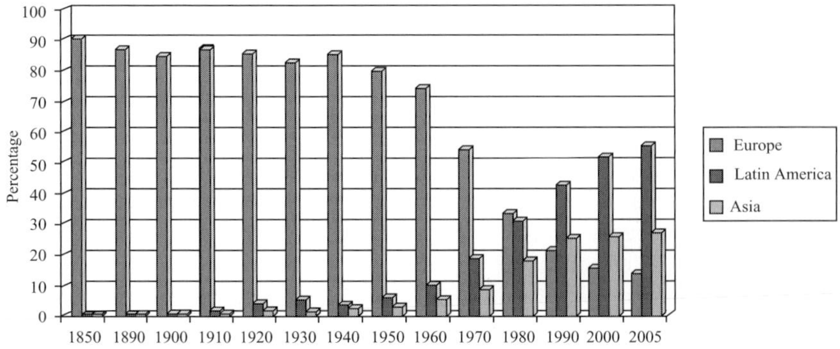

Figure 1.1. Origins of US foreign-born population
Source: US Census Bureau 2000a

foreign-born population in 1910 consisted of 13.5 million people, while the 12.4 percent in 2005 consisted of almost 36 million – almost triple the number of foreign-born people since 1910. These larger numbers and consistent growth also lead to very dense concentration of foreign-born residents in some areas. For example, in 2000 approximately seven in ten people in Miami and Hialeah, Florida, were foreign-born. The largest foreign-born populations in US cities in 2000 were in New York (2.9 million), Los Angeles (1.5 million), Chicago (629,000) and Houston (516,000), and more than half of all non-English speakers lived in three states – California, New York, and Texas – and were Spanish speakers. Yet all regions of the country experienced increases in the foreign-born population, by nearly 90 percent in the South, 65 percent in the Midwest, 50 percent in the West and nearly 40 percent in the Northeast.

The origins of today's immigrants have changed as well. Whereas Europeans formed the bulk of immigrants in the nineteenth and early twentieth centuries, it is now groups from Latin America and Asia that are the most numerous among the US foreign-born (see Figure 1.1). According to the 2000 Census, just 14 percent of today's immigrants to the USA came from Europe, while 26 percent came from Asia and 55 percent from Latin America. Returning to the list in Table 1.1 of the top twelve non-English languages spoken in the USA, many people are surprised at the continuing presence of French, German, and Italian, given that these groups have not seen large waves of new arrivals in the last eighty years. Given current immigration trends, it is likely that Asian languages such as Tagalog, Vietnamese, and Korean will soon displace these three European-origin languages on the list. Particularly notable is that the Census-counted Russian-speaking population grew by 191 percent and the Vietnamese-speaking population grew by almost 100 percent in the years between 1990 and 2000, while Chinese and Korean grew by approximately 50 percent.

An important influence on today's composition of immigrants was the Immigration and Nationality Act of 1965. Influenced by the Civil Rights movement, the USA passed this act abolishing the national-origin quotas that had been in place in the country since 1924. However, some argue that this law has not responded adequately to the ever-changing patterns of immigration. While doing away with racial preferences in immigration by treating all countries equally, regardless of population or immigrant desire to come to the USA, its critics argue that the law ultimately disadvantages many potential immigrants in its preference for skilled workers.

Thus far, we have seen that language diversity has always been present in the USA, and that the foreign-born population is in fact at a proportionally lower concentration than in the past, although numerically larger and from different areas of the world than before. Yet some concerns about immigration that were voiced in the past are repeating themselves today. When immigration peaked during the Industrial Revolution, English-speaking US residents resented what they perceived as a lack of willingness on the part of immigrants to assimilate and learn English. For example, in the late 1800s and early 1900s, nativist Americans criticized Italian immigrants' lack of ability (or willingness, as some accused) to master English. Some even suggested that the Italians, who tended to congregate in their own neighborhoods, were fundamentally different from previous immigrant groups, and racist sentiments emerged in public discourse that Mediterranean groups were morally inferior to the races of northern Europe. But as the Italian immigrants had children and grandchildren, just the opposite was true of their language use: they not only learned English, they largely forgot Italian. As we have seen, the same is true of today's immigrants, yet the same accusations of lack of assimilation are made against them.

Doesn't language diversity threaten our national unity and lead to political strife?

As of 2000, approximately 330 different languages are spoken in US homes (US Census Bureau 2000a).[7] In fact, the 2000 Census itself was printed in six languages: English, Spanish, Korean, Chinese, Vietnamese, and Tagalog. However, as we have already addressed, there is no mistaking the fact that English is being learned by speakers of LOTEs. More importantly, there is evidence to suggest that language diversity does not lead to political problems. Fishman (1991a) conducted an analysis of 238 variables in 170 different nation-states, and found that linguistic heterogeneity could not predict either civil strife or gross national product. Civil strife was related to long- and short-term deprivation and coercive power relationships, while gross national product was connected to issues of modernization and industrialization. Thus, language diversity was not causally related to either civil strife or gross national product; it is not the case that a multilingual society necessarily results in a divided society.

A previous section in this chapter described how quickly immigrants and their descendants are learning English. Yet for some monolingual English-speaking Americans, knowing English is not sufficient to be considered a true American. One must completely abandon the language of their country of origin, as a rite of passage or a cost of entry, as if retaining a heritage language reflected divided loyalties. According to Schiffman (2008), the connection between language and citizenship took more than a century to evolve in the USA, and no idea that any particular language was necessary for being or becoming a citizen existed in the early years of the nation. Kloss (1998) notes that in the 1800s nativism began primarily as an issue of schooling, as mainstream Americans resented paying taxes to support schools run by Catholics or in languages other than English. Public schools began appearing in the 1830s and took upon themselves the goal of "Americanizing" the children of immigrants. In order to become "good citizens," it was reasoned, they needed to know English. Thus, joining of these two issues, citizenship and language, was accomplished (Schiffman 1998).

A letter written by Theodore Roosevelt, published in 1919, clearly demonstrates the national monolingual ideology of the early twentieth century:

> We have room for but one language here and that is the English language, for we intend to see that the crucible turns our people out as Americans, and American nationality, and not as dwellers in a polyglot boarding house; and we have room for but one soul [sic] loyalty, and that is loyalty to the American people.

Roosevelt's provocative term *polyglot boarding house* evokes a sense of transience and poverty; a multilingual nation to him represented a type of Babel-esque slum. He also stated that "[t]here is no such thing as a hyphenated American who is a good American. The only man who is a good American is the man who is an American and nothing else" (1919: 82). Almost a century later, this ideology regarding language is still strongly present in many sectors of the country. As Schmidt (2000) argues, the nation's recent large-scale immigration coupled with persisting ethnolinguistic stratification and inequality has fueled recent US language policy conflicts. Increased immigration has heightened Anglo-American anxieties that English is threatened, along with national unity and identity. A clear example is the growth of lobby groups such as US English, which currently has almost two million members. Shifts in educational terminology reflect this trend as well. As part of 2002's No Child Left Behind, the *Bilingual Education Act* was retitled the *English Language Acquisition Act*, and the Federal *Office of Bilingual Education and Minority Language Affairs* (OBEMLA) was renamed the *Office of English Language Acquisition*.

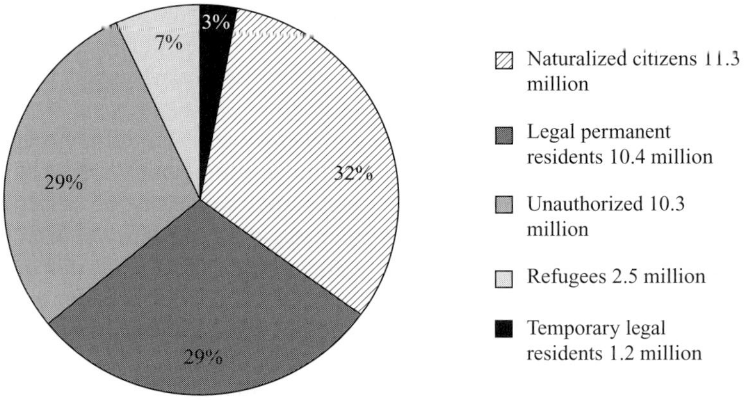

Figure 1.2. Legal status of the 35.7 million foreign-born in USA, 2004
Source: Adapted from Passel 2005

"Bilingual" has become almost a dirty word in educational circles, with more and more pressure to shift children to all-English classrooms as soon as possible. California, Arizona, and Massachusetts have eliminated bilingual education in favor of "sheltered English immersion" (see Freeman and Freeman 1998 and Adams 2006 for greater details on sheltered English immersion), although a similar proposition failed in Colorado.

Yet even while the US Department of Education seems to be adopting an increasingly monolingual and monocultural policy, other Cabinet-level entities – including, almost ironically, the Department of Defense – have publicly announced and promoted the "Defense Language Transformation Roadmap" (US Department of Defense 2005), calling for a policy to "identify and recognize the value of personnel achieving and maintaining the highest levels of proficiency in critical languages by paying a substantially enhanced Foreign Language Proficiency Pay (FLPP)." Clearly at least some elements within the federal government view language diversity as essential to national interests.

We should also note that the overall percentage of foreign-born residents in 2007 who had become naturalized US citizens was the highest level in a quarter of a century and 14 percentage points higher than in 1990 (Passel 2007).[8] This suggests that many immigrants are interested in becoming part of the political process and in being productive members of their community. The legal status of the nation's foreign-born population (Figure 1.2) remains fairly evenly divided between naturalized citizens (11.3 million), legal permanent residents (10.4 million) and unauthorized immigrants (10.3 million). It is often negative attitudes about the unauthorized immigrants that fuels linguistic intolerance towards the other two thirds of foreign-born individuals who are here legally.

A previous section described the undeniable linguistic assimilation of immigrants, but what about the ethnic identity of immigrants and their descendants? Do they think of themselves as "just Americans," or do they hold on to national origin self-identifying terms such as "Pakistani," "Filipino" or "Mexican"? Zhou (2004) claims that today, unlike in the past as embodied in the Roosevelt quote above, "there is no contradiction between an ethnic identity and an American identity." That is, the "hyphenated American" (such as "Pakistani-American") is more common now than in the past. Portes and Rumbaut (1996, 2001) proposed three typologies of the assimilation of the children of immigrants (who are typically referred to as the second generation) which may be helpful in understanding this change. The first model is very much like the traditional concept of the "melting pot" in which the second generation is expected to blend in completely and become mainstream "Americans" who are monolingual in English. In the second typology, the children of immigrants acculturate not to the white Anglophone mainstream, but to inner-city subcultures. However, they too become monolingual in English. The third typology is called "selective acculturation." In the process of selective acculturation, ethnic networks and strong communities support the children of immigrants as they learn to deal with prejudice, navigate the education system, and find a place in the labor market. The outcome is upward assimilation, but combined with bilingualism and biculturalism; it allows a fully legitimate place for the heritage language. Portes and Rumbaut (2001: 309) argue that selective acculturation often leads to better psychosocial adjustment and overall achievement among the children of immigrants because it preserves bonds across generations and gives children a firm foundation to support and guide them. Thus, use of hyphenated identity labels may be a positive sign of increasing reliance on selective acculturation strategies by immigrant communities.

The subtitle of this section asked whether linguistic diversity creates conflict and threatens national unity, and the answer provided by the evidence is "no." What undoubtedly poses a greater threat to national unity and leads to greater conflict among communities is the bullying of immigrants[9] and minority language groups. Following World War I, the US entered a period of isolationism characterized by "a period of witch-hunting and red-baiting" (Schiffman 2008). The Ku Klux Klan re-emerged, not only to terrorize African Americans in the south, but also to intimidate French-speaking Quebecois immigrants in Maine (Vermette 2006). Today we have cases of linguistic repression such as the high school student in Kansas City suspended for speaking Spanish in the hallways (Reid 2005); a teacher in Phoenix who hit children for speaking Spanish in class (Ryman and Madrid 2004); two Vietnamese-Americans chastized for speaking Vietnamese at a graduation ceremony (Pleasant 2008), and employees in New

York fired for speaking Spanish on the job or during breaks (Valenti 2003) even though the US Equal Employment Opportunity Commission (EEOC) states that mandating that employees speak English on the job constitutes national-origin discrimination.[10] A model such as selective acculturation would provide a healthier framework for integrating immigrant groups into mainstream activities while simultaneously encouraging ethnolinguistic diversity.

Appreciating advantages: Proponents of linguistic diversity

In spite of having a national linguistic culture that is decidedly monolingual, counterforces have begun to appear in the USA that challenge a monolingual ideology.[11] Some national groups, such as the Alliance for the Advancement of Heritage Languages (National Heritage Language Resource Center 2007), as well as city-based efforts like those in San Bernadino, California (Sauerwein 2003) and in Chicago (Multilingual Chicago n.d.), have declared appreciation of the multilingual character of these cities and seek to promote the learning of English *in addition to* the maintenance of heritage languages by immigrant children. This goal of English acquisition with heritage language maintenance has been referred to as *English Plus*. Crawford (2006: 7) describes English Plus in the following way:

> This approach begins with the recognition that, of course, we should pursue the goal of English proficiency for all Americans. But while English is necessary, it is not sufficient in today's world. To prosper economically and to provide security for our people, we need well-developed skills in English, plus other languages. Step one is to conserve and develop, not destroy, the language resources we already have. Rather than treating bilingualism as a nuisance or a threat, we should exploit our diversity to enrich the lives of individuals and foster the nation's interests, while encouraging ethnic tolerance and safeguarding civil rights.

As noted by Valdés (forthcoming), "if a society views dual cultural and ethnic membership as positive, and if children are made to feel that there are no insurmountable contradictions in belonging to two groups," it is more likely that they will develop into bilingual and bicultural individuals.

While these groups are primarily concerned with English acquisition and heritage language maintenance among immigrant families, other groups work to have mainstream English-speaking children study other languages. US high schools, for example, have long offered foreign language classes. According to Rhodes and Branaman (1999), almost 90 percent of US high schools offer foreign languages, although the National Center for Education Statistics (2002a) reports that slightly less than 50 percent of all students in grades nine through twelve were enrolled in foreign languages in 2000 (yet this did represent an increase of almost 40 percent from 1990). Spanish had the highest

Table 1.4. *US college foreign language enrollments*

Language	2002	Percentage of total language enrollment 2002	2006	Percentage of total language enrollment 2006	Percentage change, 2002–06
1. Spanish	746,267	53.4	822,985	52.2	10
2. Chinese	34,153	2.4	51,582	3.3	51
3. Tagalog	1142	0.1	1569	0.1	37
4. French	201,979	14.5	206,426	13.1	2
5. Vietnamese	2236	0.2	2,485	0.2	11
6. German	91,100	6.5	94,264	6.0	3
7. Korean	5,211	0.4	7,145	0.5	37
8. Russian	23,921	1.7	24,845	1.6	4
9. Italian	63,899	4.6	78,368	5.0	23
10. Arabic	10,584	0.8	23,974	1.5	127
11. Portuguese	8,385	0.6	10,267	0.7	22
12. Polish	1053	0.1	1,379	0.1	31
TOTAL	1,183,547	85.3	1,317,028	84.3	133,481

Source: Modern Language Association 2007.

enrollment (4,058,000 students) followed by French (1,075,000), German (283,000), Italian (64,000), Japanese (51,000), and Russian (11,000). The greatest increase in student enrollment was in Japanese, which jumped 102.5 percent during this ten-year period.

As for US colleges and universities, Table 1.4 displays the top twelve non-English languages spoken in the USA (repeated from Table 1.1) and the number of students studying these languages at US colleges and universities in 2002 and in 2006. Students of these twelve languages accounted for 84 percent of all college foreign language enrollments in 2006. As in the high schools, Spanish is the most widely studied foreign language in US postsecondary institutions, accounting for 52 percent of all enrollments. The next most numerous are French (13% of enrollments), German (6%), and Italian (5%). However, the greatest growth in the number of students was in Arabic, which grew by an astounding 127%, followed by Chinese (51% growth), Tagalog (37%), and Korean (37%). It is likely that the increase in enrollments in these four languages is due in large part to an increase in the population of heritage speakers of these languages. As mentioned earlier, the field of foreign language education must continue to develop appropriate materials and methodologies for heritage-speaking students.

Although the languages being studied in US postsecondary institutions reflect certain broad population growth patterns in the nation, foreign language study in the USA is still quite low. The 2006 rate of postsecondary language study was 8.6 language course enrollments per 100 total student enrollments, which is almost half of the 1965 rate (16.5 per 100). It is even less common to find foreign language programs where they potentially could do the most good: elementary schools. Schiffman (2008), in a fascinating account of language history in the USA, notes that, at the close of World War I in 1918, foreign languages were "chased from the elementary schools in state after state, and relegated to high-school instruction only." Since at that time only 5 percent of the US population attended high school, foreign language instruction was essentially abolished for 95 percent of the population, under "the covert assumption . . . that 'foreign' language was not a necessary part of any child's education, but useful only for adults, especially for those college-bound."

Eighty years later, in 1997, the Center for Applied Linguistics found that 31 percent of elementary schools[12] surveyed offered foreign language programs, which was up from 22 percent in 1987. However, preliminary findings from their 2007–08 survey reveal a drop from 31 percent to 25 percent of elementary schools teaching foreign languages. Some schools cited reasons for the decline, including budget cuts, a shortage of teachers, and constraints from No Child Left Behind's emphasis on math and reading (Center for Applied Linguistics 2008). Although at least eight states (including Arizona, Arkansas, Louisiana, Montana, New Jersey, North Carolina, Oklahoma, and Wyoming) have enacted mandates for teaching non-English languages at the elementary school level, these mandates are unfunded everywhere except Louisiana and Wyoming. That is, even states with laws requiring that foreign languages be taught in elementary schools often lack the funds to comply with these laws. In other areas, educators have worked without a state mandate to try to promote elementary school foreign language offerings.

These findings are particularly disheartening because an earlier start in language study usually leads to higher levels of proficiency. The advantages of high levels of multilingualism are multiple, both for individuals and societies. At the individual level, in addition to the obvious practical benefit of speaking two or more languages, multilingualism may provide cognitive advantages. In a Tel Aviv University study, Kavé *et al.* (2008) found that multilingual elders performed significantly better on cognitive-screening measures than comparable monolingual elders, indicating that multilingualism may slow the mental aging process. Similarly, Bialystok, Craik, and Freedman (2007) found that, among patients with dementia, bilinguals showed symptoms an average of four years later than monolinguals, suggesting that knowing more than one language delays the onset of dementia. Bilingualism may have positive effects on children's development as well (see Hakuta 1989 for an overview), especially in the case of nonverbal assessments of intelligence (Hakuta 1987), and there is evidence that the literacy skills developed in the heritage language can transfer to the second language, aiding the development of literacy in English (Roberts 1994; Bialystok, Luk, and Kwan 2005), though the extent of literacy transfer depends on the researcher's definition of literacy and the similarity between the languages and writing systems involved. In addition to the cognitive and practical advantages to individuals, multilingualism benefits society as a whole. Beyond the economic and national security benefits of a multilingual population explored above, Tse (2001a) makes clear three main advantages: "the nation benefits by having citizens who are linguistically and culturally savvy to advance international business, the nation benefits politically by possessing a rich diplomatic and national security corps, and the country gains educationally by stemming the shortage of foreign-language teachers, especially in the less commonly taught languages" (Tse 2001a: 49–51).

Aims and organization of this book

This book is aligned with the counterforce to US monolingual hegemony. With a foregrounding in immigration trends (this introductory chapter) and language contact phenomena (Chapter 2), it seeks to contribute to the appreciation and promotion of linguistic diversity in the USA by profiling the twelve most commonly spoken non-English languages in the USA. A complete survey of US languages also requires a discussion of indigenous languages that were here before the arrival of Europeans, even though they do not form one language group and are not on the top twelve list. One of the long-standing issues in an analysis of heritage languages in America is, in fact, the distinction between immigrant heritage languages – to which we have devoted twelve individual chapters – and the indigenous heritage languages – at least 175 in number by our contributor Terri McCarty's calculations, but to which we have devoted a single chapter. This is not to minimize the value in analyzing Native American languages on a case-by-case basis, but merely reflective of the limitations of this volume. There is an unfortunate commonality among the vast majority of Native American languages that provides additional justification in treating them in the aggregate; namely, that for the vast majority of them, the more pressing question is not how can these languages be better preserved but, rather, whether these language can be kept from dying out altogether. It remains in our view the most practical approach, and we have entrusted this chapter to someone who is eminently well qualified to write it.

Therefore, a total of thirteen languages or language groups are profiled in this collection. This introductory chapter has outlined general issues related to LOTEs in the history of the USA. Chapter 2, contributed by one of the world's leading experts on bilingualism, Suzanne Romaine, explores issues of languages in contact that are prevalent not only in the USA, but wherever there are multiple languages spoken by a cohesive population. The following thirteen chapters begin with the special chapter on Native American languages, followed by each of the top twelve languages displayed in Table 1.1, in an attempt to discover patterns of language loss as well as factors that contribute to maintenance of ethnolinguistic diversity. The book's concluding chapter, contributed by language policy expert Terry Wiley, offers an overview of US policies toward language and suggested directions for the future.

According to Veltman (2000), no immigrant group, with the possible exceptions of the very isolated communities of the Amish or Hassidic Jews, has been able to preserve its minority language longer than two or three generations. That is, contrary to the fears of Huntington (2004) or groups such as US English, there is no evidence that any minority language group is resisting English. In spite of the undeniable existence of linguistic assimilation in the USA, we might view such assimilation as existing on a continuum, with absolute heritage language loss and English monolingualism on one end, and fluent bilingualism on the other. The objective of this book is to challenge the need for absolute ethnolinguistic assimilation and argue for a degree of bilingualism, by presenting case studies of the nation's most commonly spoken non-English languages with an eye to assessing the factors that both support and challenge their vitality and longevity. According to Portes and Schauffler (1996: 25), it is "the character of the immigrant community – its internal diversity, history, and cohesiveness – that seems to hold the key to whether second generation children successfully combine two languages." Each of these chapters, then, seeks to explore the internal diversity, history, cohesiveness, and other factors that contribute to the intergenerational transmission of non-English languages in the USA.

In putting together their chapters, the authors evidence what Romaine (1996: 283) terms "certain social and political assumptions about the value of cultural pluralism and the negative aspects of forced assimilation." But heeding the warning of Veltman (2000: 65), our intent is not to compare rates of language shift across language groups, which may lead to the erroneous conclusion that some groups maintain their mother tongue more than others. It is more appropriate and objective to examine each language group in its own unique sociolinguistic and cultural context with its own distinctive features.

Thus, this book examines the ways in which groups have assimilated linguistically and the ways in which they have been able to maintain their ethnic languages, using as a starting point the model of variables presented by Giles, Bourhis, and Taylor (1977), shown in Figure 1.3. Other factors not contained in this model can also affect the maintenance of a minority language, including the number of speakers in a person's social network (Wei *et al.* 1992), the degree of contact that takes place between second and third generation heritage language speakers and new monolingual immigrants from the country of

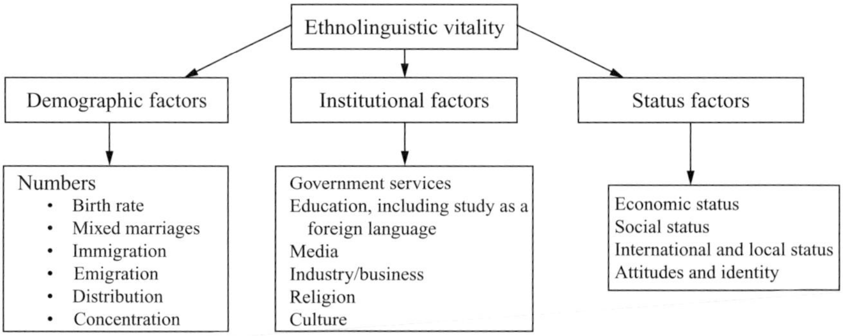

Figure 1.3. Variables that affect ethnolinguistic vitality
Source: After Giles, Bourhis, and Taylor 1977

origin, and periods of time spent in the country of origin. All chapters present historical and demographic details about each language group, followed by an exploration of the presence of the language in the USA through arenas such as the media, government, business, and education. Education is considered a particularly important realm for the possible maintenance of languages other than English, so this section is often longer than the others. Each chapter concludes by arguing what the current constellation of variables suggests for the longevity of the language. However, we must recall that the current state of knowledge does not permit definitive conclusions regarding the relative importance of each factor or any combination of factors contributing to language maintenance or shift.

To conclude this introduction, there are two basic assumptions driving this collection. The first assumption is that linguistic diversity is a resource, not a problem. As discussed by Brecht and Ingold (2002), the USA has "an unprecedented need for individuals with highly developed language competencies not only in English, our societal language, but also in many other languages." Since this assessment was made, a wide range of initiatives and proposals have reflected the heightened recognition by leadership within the federal government to identify and strengthen those resources – to name but two, the Defense Language Transformation Roadmap (US Department of Defense 2005) and the National Security Language Initiative (US State Department 2006). More importantly, this recognition has moved beyond defense and security motivations, and has also expanded below the federal level of support. For example, late in 2007, three states – Ohio, Oregon, and Texas – were selected for significant financial support by the US Departments of Defense, Commerce, and Labor to help refine the nation's policy on foreign language proficiency.

Before presenting the second assumption of this volume, it is appropriate to make an important point about education. It is ironic that we invest such time and resources in foreign language instruction – over 1.5 million enrollments in colleges and universities alone according to 2006 survey data by the Modern Language Association (MLA 2007) – yet we squander the heritage language resources we have right here. Heritage language learners, as defined earlier, are raised in a home where a non-English language is spoken and they understand the minority language to some degree. By way of comparison, consider the amount of time it takes for the true foreign or second language learner to reach high levels of proficiency. Data compiled over decades by the Foreign Service Institute reveal that the average learner needs between 2,400 and 2,760 hours to reach a level of working professional proficiency in Chinese. Translated into classroom seat time, this is between 80 and 92 weeks of 30 contact hours per week (McGinnis 1994). Taken together with the sociocultural knowledge that only a heritage speaker will have, it seems highly economical to tap into our national heritage language pipeline.

In fact, sections of the US government have increasingly come to recognize the importance of identifying and encouraging the maintenance and enhancement of these national linguistic resources. In May 2007, General Dynamics Information Technology was awarded a contract by the US Department of Defense National Security Education Program to develop a national volunteer civilian National Language Service Corps. Members of that corps would be available for federal activation during times of international crisis, national emergency, or to fulfill other national needs. The presumption is that for such a program to be worth the money invested in it, a significant number of diverse heritage language speakers need to be not only identified, but also encouraged to retain their heritage languages. In this vein, several states including California, Connecticut, Michigan, New Jersey, New York, and Virginia have begun offering students foreign language or general credit for their studies at a heritage language school (ACTFL 2008).

Finally, the second assumption of the present volume is that people have a right to maintain their ethnic language and not compromise their US citizenship or their perceived "Americanness." The outright mandate to abandon a heritage language is in violation of what the United Nations considers a basic human right (Office of the High Commissioner for Human Rights 1992),[13] and although the USA does not outlaw heritage languages, pressure to refrain from using non-English languages can be strong. The news events cited earlier – the students hit or expelled, and the employees fired – provide examples of linguistic intolerance. Clearly the sentiments expressed by the US government in the 1990 Native American Languages Act (Table 1.5) have not trickled down to many educators, employers, and the population at large.

Table 1.5. *Excerpts from the 1990 Native American Languages Act*

- There is convincing evidence that student achievement and performance, community and school pride, and educational opportunity is clearly and directly tied to respect for, and support of, the first language of the child or student;
- It is clearly in the interests of the United States, individual States, and territories to encourage the full academic and human potential achievements of all students and citizens and to take steps to realize these ends;
- Languages are the means of communication for the full range of human experiences and are critical to the survival of cultural and political integrity of any people; and
- Language provides a direct and powerful means of promoting international communication by people who share languages.

Source: Demmert and Arnold 1996.

Conflicts over language may in fact be mostly symbolic, hiding other fundamental cleavages that are developing in the USA. McKay and Wong (2000: 45) argue that the debate over bilingual education is in part a battle over the demographic composition of the nation: One side wants to control borders and assimilate immigrant children, while the other accepts that diversity is here to stay, showing a reflection of the rest of the world, and should be a hallmark of the nation's policy and planning. As mentioned earlier, Fishman (1991a) noted that majority–minority relations of exploitation and competition, not language differences, are the source of ethnic tensions. This was echoed by López (1991: 133), who posits that much of the controversy over language in the USA has obscured (or perhaps served as a proxy for) racial hostility and conflict. Those involved in language education see an opportunity to promote linguistic pluralism, particularly when faced with an ever-growing population of heritage language learners.

It is our hope that this collection promotes critical thought and discussion among language educators, demographers, sociologists, economists, and others interested in the language diversity we currently enjoy in this nation, and the ways in which we can preserve and increase this diversity while at the same time promoting English proficiency and positive intergroup relationships. Given that language is often closely aligned with differences in socioeconomic level, legal status, ethnicity, and other factors,[14] it is naïve to assume that a linguistic utopia is possible. However, the authors in this volume seek to foster appreciation of linguistic and cultural difference as part of the national concept of what it means to be American – that is, language diversity as both a right and a resource.

DISCUSSION QUESTIONS

1. Make a list of the myths regarding LOTEs debunked in this chapter. Can you think of other common beliefs about non-English languages in the USA? Which do you think are true and which are false? Next, consider Ruíz's (1984) typology of orientations toward language diversity (language-as-a-problem, language-as-a-right, and language-as-a-resource). Do these myths share a common orientation? What else do they have in common?
2. Choose a country other than the USA, and compare its language policy and linguistic diversity with those of the USA. How are they similar or different?

2 Language contact in the USA

Suzanne Romaine

Introduction

The USA presents rich terrain for studying processes and outcomes of language contact. Home to approximately 311 languages, it is not only the fifth most linguistically diverse country in the world (Gordon 2005), but also currently the fifth largest Spanish-speaking nation (CIA 2008). This multilingual reality is often overshadowed by the predominance of English, spoken by just over 80 percent of the largely monolingual population (US Census Bureau 2000a). Multilingual since time immemorial, the territory currently occupied by the USA has hosted a full gamut of contact phenomena, from instances where only a few words are borrowed from one language into another, to others in which new languages of various kinds are created. Long before Europeans arrived, many Native American groups solved the problem of communication across tribal boundaries through lingua francas (i.e. common languages) such as Mobilian Jargon (a pidginized form of Choctaw-Chickasaw in widespread use across the Mississippian complex), and Chinook Jargon (an interethnic pidgin spoken along the Pacific northwest coast from Oregon to the Alaska panhandle and inland along major rivers).

Three great waves of European colonization introduced English along with at least seven major languages (Danish, Dutch, French, German, Russian, Spanish, and Swedish), three of which (Spanish, French, and German) became prominent languages of immigration. Each of these provided sources for common American words (e.g. Swedish *smorgasbord*, Dutch *scout*, French *prairie*, German *kindergarten*, Spanish *ranch*). Contact between these European languages and already present languages resulted in more cross-linguistic influence, including the creation of mixed languages such as Michif, spoken in parts of North Dakota and a few other places in the western USA and Canada by the descendants of male French speakers and female Cree speakers, who merged into a new ethnic group, the Métis (see Romaine 2001 for discussion of the influence of indigenous and immigrant languages on English). Various contributors to this volume note the emergence and use of a number of newer mixed varieties resulting from contact between English and minority languages such as Spanish (Spanglish), German (Denglish-Deutsch-Englisch), Tagalog (Taglish or Enggalog), Russian (Russlish) and Polish (Polglish).

Although the USA is now the main center of gravity for global English due to its dominant position as an industrial, technological, and political superpower, English speakers were relatively late participants in the expansion of European colonialism; long before English was much used outside the British Isles, Portuguese, Spanish, and Dutch had spread around the world. Some indigenous peoples and their languages weathered varying cycles of conquest. For example, Tewa was subject to American colonization and experienced varying degrees of contact with and influence from Spanish as well as from their Hopi neighbors. Likewise, many native communities in Canada and the northeastern USA such as the Mohawk experienced a century of contact with French missionaries and traders followed by intensive contact with English. After 500 years of survival and maintenance of all these once-numerous and diverse languages and cultures in the face of aggressive assimilative influences, including forced removal from their lands to reservations and boarding schools, the balance is now seemingly tipped in favor of a shift towards exclusive use of English (see Chapter 3).

This chapter is devoted to defining and clarifying some key concepts essential to understanding the linguistic effects of contact on minority languages in the USA. Unfortunately, not all researchers use key terms referring to both the processes and outcomes, such as *borrowing*, *interference*, *transfer*, *convergence*, *shift*, *code-switching*, *mixing*, in the same way, which makes comparison across studies difficult. Although the contact phenomena illustrated in this and other chapters in this volume derive specifically from contact between English and other languages in the USA, they reveal mechanisms occurring to some degree in the repertoires of most bilingual persons and in most bilingual communities the world over. Despite the spread of global languages, multilingualism remains a reality for most of the world; around two thirds of the world's population is bilingual (Baker and Prys Jones 1998: vii). With roughly 6,900 languages, but only about 200 nation-states, bilingualism or multilingualism is present in practically every nation in the world, whether officially recognized or not.

This means that languages are in contact nearly everywhere and few languages develop without contact. Unprecedented mobility is creating new hybridized language varieties. More than half of the nearly 400 million people around the world who speak Spanish, for example, do so in situations of intensive contact with other languages. This has had consequences for the varieties of Spanish developing in these contexts (Silva Corvalán 1995). Indeed, a number of unique varieties of Spanish developed and are continuing to evolve in the USA, where Spanish is the immigrant language with the greatest time depth. Spoken since the sixteenth century in what is now the USA, varieties of US Spanish span a spectrum of vitality ranging from now moribund Isleño Spanish (spoken by a few remaining elderly descendants of late eighteenth-century immigrants from the Canary Islands, now living in Louisiana's St. Bernard Parish, and largely isolated from other Spanish-speaking populations) to fully developed native varieties brought by each new immigrant individual/group who was born to Spanish-speaking parents and had sufficient exposure to acquire it natively.

Studying language contact: Terminology and ideology

The study of language contact raises numerous questions that are both descriptive and theoretical. Consider, for instance, how to describe what goes on when bilinguals like Blanca (a 9-year-old bilingual girl of Puerto Rican descent living in Spanish Harlem in New York City) produce utterances such as (1) (Zentella 1997: 117).

(1) Hey Lolita, but the Skylab, the Skylab *no se cayó pa(-ra) que se acabe el mundo*. It falls in pieces. *Si se cae completo*, yeah. The Skylab *es una cosa que (e-)stá rodeando el* moon taking pictures of it. *Tiene tubos en el medio. Tiene tubos en el medio*. It's like a rocket. It's like a rocket. [Spanish in italics]

"Hey Lolita, but the Skylab, the Skylab ('didn't fall for the world to end'). It falls in pieces. ('If it falls whole'), yeah. The Skylab ('is something that's going around the') moon taking pictures of it. ('It has tubes in the middle') [repeated]. It's like a rocket [repeated]."

Describing what Blanca does is perhaps somewhat easier than formulating theories about bilingual competence capable of explaining the processing and production of such utterances (MacSwan 2000, Muysken 2000, Myers-Scotton 2003). Linguists use terms such as "code-switching" and "code-mixing" to characterize speech drawing on more than one language. Most linguists accept that mixing is not a random jumble or free-for-all, but rather a complex system composed of a variety of rule-governed patterns and constraints. Nevertheless, both within and outside the communities surveyed in this volume, the sort of mixing and switching that Blanca and her friends find normal and at times even necessary in their everyday lives has been regarded as a sign of imperfect competence, if not downright ignorance and laziness, rather than as a legitimate mode of communication in its own right. Negative names for these mixed varieties such as Spanglish, Tex-Mex, *español tuerco* ("twisted") or *mocho* ("broken") reveal the stigma attached to their use. Polish-Americans traveling in Poland were commonly regarded negatively for mixing Polish and English (see Chapter 15). Despite negative attitudes, these mixed modes of speaking serve important functions in communities, where they embody the linguistic and cultural hybridity of their speakers. A 14-year-old boy of Mexican descent living in California described this as the normal way of speaking to bilinguals (Pease-Alvarez 2002: 126):

> If there's a bilingual person, that's how you talk. It runs through everybody, all the bilingual people. It's like if you're addicted to drinking or you're a caffeine junky. When you are talking to a bilingual person, you gotta always speak English and Spanish, always. It just comes out of your mouth, you know. It's just how it is.

Despite the common occurrence of language mixing and switching among both children and adults, professionals such as speech therapists (often monolinguals) have viewed it as harmful and have given advice to parents that is not in line with the realities of normal bilingual development in bilingual communities. Beliefs about bilingualism causing stuttering and delayed onset of language are also widespread, despite lack of evidence for them. Some researchers have even treated mixing as a stage in children's development that must be overcome if children are to be "true" bilinguals.

Even before the concentration of mainstream linguistic theory on Chomsky's (1965: 3) abstraction of an imagined "ideal speaker–listener, in a completely homogeneous speech-community, who knows its language perfectly," the study of bilingualism was plagued with a tendency to elevate a similarly hypothetical "ideal bilingual" to special theoretical status as someone with "native-like control of two languages" (Bloomfield 1933: 56). Weinreich's (1968: 73) view of the ideal bilingual who "switches from one language to another according to appropriate changes in the speech situation (interlocutors, topics, etc.), but not in an unchanged speech situation," for instance, does not readily accommodate the norms of many bilinguals like Blanca, who not only switches between Spanish and English, but also mixes words from both languages within the same utterance.

This example shows how the predominantly monolingual orientation of linguistic theory has left its mark on both researchers' terminology and their theoretical concerns. Despite the normality of multilingualism and the centrality of language contact to the evolution of language, research on multilingualism has played a relatively marginal role within linguistics until the last few decades. As Romaine (1995: 1) remarks, "It would certainly be odd to encounter a book with the title, *Monolingualism.*" Baetens-Beardsmore (2003: 10) reflects similarly on how monolingual thinking in a *de facto* multilingual world has rendered linguistic diversity problematic:

> There is a deep-seated and widespread fear of bilingualism. Moreover, there is an all-pervading tendency to couple the notion of "problems" to that of bilingualism, a connotation that never comes to mind in discussions on unilingualism.

In her discussion of some of the myths concerning linguistic diversity prevalent in the USA, Potowski (Chapter 1, this volume) examines some of the historical sources and the continuing hegemony of rhetoric constructing multilingualism as problematic and divisive to American national unity. Ultimately, this ideology is a legacy of a culturally particular construal of the relationship between nations and languages that emerged during the late eighteenth and early nineteenth centuries when new national identities along with the languages and cultures linked to them were created out of the politics of European nation-building. The newly emergent national languages were in effect those of dominant ethnic groups. Then, as now, it is policies pursued within national boundaries that give some languages (and their speakers) the status of majority and others that of minority. The hegemony of monolingual ideologies has also meant that multilingualism is understood at best as multiple monolingualisms in distinct languages to be mastered separately in standard form and kept pure of outside influence. Against this yardstick, mixed-speech varieties such as Spanglish have been regarded both by linguists and ordinary people as somehow deviant, the result of imperfect competence.

Thus, the very notion of Spanglish clashes with US monolingual ideology no less than it does with what del Valle (2006) calls the ideology of hispanofonía (i.e. the unity of the Spanish-speaking world). Víctor García de la Concha, President of La Real Academia de la Lengua Española (Royal Academy of the Spanish Language) founded in 1713, condemned Spanglish as neither a language nor a dialect, not even a jargon, but the artificial fabrication of eccentric intellectuals with a political agenda. In his view it was a sign of marginality and mental deprivation. A visitor from Norway similarly dismissed the Norwegian spoken by immigrants in the USA as "no language whatever, but a gruesome mixture of Norwegian and English" (Haugen 1977: 94).

Accepting such prescriptive views would lead to the unfounded conclusion that the majority of bilingual speakers are not ideal bilinguals because they appear to have less than native-like control of both languages. Related concepts such as "balanced bilingualism" have also been premised on the false assumption that bilinguals consist of two monolinguals. Yet real-world bilinguals are rarely equally fluent in both languages on all possible topics because they have typically not had the same experiences in both languages. Therefore, it does not make much sense to assess bilinguals as if they were two monolinguals. Cooper (1971), for instance, found that Spanish/English bilinguals had different scores on word-naming tasks depending on whether the domain of use was family, neighborhood, school, etc. In some domains they would have been rated as balanced bilinguals, while in others they would not. Any society producing functionally balanced bilinguals who used both languages equally well in all contexts would soon cease to be bilingual because no society needs two languages for the same set of functions (Fishman 1971: 560).

Despite the fact that the search for the ideal balanced bilingual with native-like fluency is elusive and largely an artifact of a narrow theoretical perspective founded on the monolingual as its point of reference, much of the research concerning the advantages and disadvantages of bilingualism and bilingual education has tried to ignore the social context in which bilingualism develops and changes over time. Due to the inherent connection between proficiency and function, bilingualism *per se* cannot be meaningfully measured apart from the situation in which it functions for particular individuals or groups. Related concepts such as dominance also have to be seen in context. Differing levels of use and choices made in different domains determine the course of evolution of bilingualism. In other words, the degree of bilingualism depends on the answer to Fishman's (1965) basic question of who speaks what to whom and when. In multilingual settings, speakers are not always able to *choose* the language they prefer. Their choice is constrained by the knowledge they have of various languages and the ability they have to use them, as well as by the extent to which their interlocutors will understand them.

For most US immigrant minorities, bilingualism is largely a temporary and transitional stage in intergenerational language shift, propelling a community from total monolingual competence in the native language to virtual monolingual competence in English. The older generation may be largely monolingual, not ever acquiring English well, and the youngest generation may likewise be monolingual, but in English rather than the parents' native language. Even where monolingual first generation parents speak their language at home, their children are exposed to English through older siblings and playmates. Once they go to school, exposure to the home language often becomes minimal and productive skills in the language are severely limited. Thus, by the third (and sometimes even second) generation, immigrants are generally dominant in English; the immigrant language, if they can speak it at all, reveals signs of incomplete acquisition, attrition, and influence from English. There may be a continuum of types of acquisition, attrition and proficiency occurring even within the same family (Gonzo and Saltarelli 1983, Finocchiaro 2004). The proficiency of older children in the parents' language is often greater than that of the younger children, but many do not reach native-like proficiency.

The issue of competence cannot be separated from the issue of decreasing usage. When the frequency of irregular and marked forms falls below a critical threshold, it is less likely that younger speakers will acquire them as they increasingly use English. Because immigrant languages are used and acquired primarily in the home and informal in-group settings among networks of family and friends, the younger generation may not acquire forms appropriate for more formal contexts. A case in point is the Vietnamese younger generation in the USA, who use English in most domains and therefore do not know how to use the multiplicity of status pronouns and complex titles (see Chapter 8). Likewise, second generation speakers of languages such as German, French, Italian, and Spanish with so-called T/V systems of address that index familiarity and intimacy (e.g. *tu* in French, Italian, Spanish) v. formality and distance (e.g. French *vous*, Italian *Lei*, Spanish *usted*) tend to overuse the familiar forms. The fact that this distinction is not matched in English (which has only socially unmarked *you*), may be a contributing factor in the overgeneralization of familiar forms. The restriction of languages to the domestic sphere may also entail lack of literacy and other skills that would normally be acquired at school. Kagan and Dillon (Chapter 11, this volume) discuss the links between the Russian competence of children in the third and fourth waves of immigration and the amount of education received prior to immigration.

Traditional community and family structures and practices that once supported the transmission of language and culture have also weakened in indigenous communities. Major changes in socialization patterns have made the formerly normal process of acquiring languages such as Navajo at home the exception rather than the rule. Spolsky (2002a) compared the change between 1970, when 90 percent of children entered school as Navajo monolinguals, and today, where the situation is reversed; most children entering school are English monolinguals. As the numerically strongest Native American language, Navajo serves as a bellwether for what is happening to indigenous languages in North America. In Pueblo communities of New Mexico, for instance, people once added Spanish and then English to their repertoires, but now English is replacing greeting and address forms in traditional Navajo, varying by age, status, gender, context, and kinship relations (Field 1998).

The precise trajectory of shift and its linguistic consequences differs somewhat among and within different groups, depending on a number of factors. Spanish and English have been in contact since the sixteenth century, but Navajo and English have been in contact for only about 150 years. The specific historical origins of each immigrant group and the ways in which different contexts of reception have affected the socioeconomic adaptation of first generation immigrants have had consequences for the linguistic repertoires of their children. Narrow definitions of bilingualism have not only had ramifications for bilingual education policies but have dictated a number of important research questions relating to children's bilingual development. Erroneous beliefs have overshadowed the generally positive influence of fluent bilingualism on school achievement (Portes and Hao 2004: 11,920–1). Instead of being provided with better opportunities for language maintenance, children of immigrants have often been blamed for not learning "their own" language. Yet, without access to a formal variety through overt instruction, the development of speaking and literacy skills in the immigrant language has usually been extremely limited and even curtailed entirely.

Where a proficiency continuum develops between two languages in contact, resulting either from incomplete acquisition and/or attrition of the minority language due to restricted exposure and use, individuals with differing degrees of bilingual competence may be located at various points along the continuum of acquisition and shift. Changes initiated by one individual may spread to others, resulting eventually in patterns of community usage such as we see in Spanglish or Isleño Spanish (Lipski 1993), or vernacular varieties of French (Chapter 7, this volume), which are different from monolingual varieties of Spanish or French spoken elsewhere.

Diglossia and domains

The concepts of diglossia and domain are helpful in understanding the different ways in which linguistic resources are organized in multilingual communities, and the factors influencing speakers' choices. Diglossia is a common form of societal bilingualism in which two varieties or languages are functionally compartmentalized. A classic example among the minority languages in this volume is Arabic (Chapter 13, this volume). In Arabic-speaking countries around the world, such as Egypt and Iraq, the language used at home is typically a local variety of Arabic, while the language recognized publicly is modern standard Arabic, which takes many of its normative rules from the classical Arabic of the Koran. The standard language is used for so-called "high" functions such as giving a lecture, reading, writing, or broadcasting, whereas the home variety is reserved for "low" functions such as interacting with friends at home.

The high (H) and low (L) varieties differ considerably in grammar, phonology, and vocabulary, but also with respect to a number of social characteristics. L is typically acquired at home as a mother tongue and continues to be used throughout life. By contrast, H is learned later through schooling and never at home. The separate domains in which H and L are acquired immediately provide them with separate institutional support systems, which contribute to their stability. A case in point are some of the local varieties of German brought to the USA by Anabaptist immigrants such as the Amish, Hutterites, Mennonites, and others which have survived alongside English for nearly 400 years (Chapter 9, this volume). Degree of religious conservatism corresponds with extent of competence in German. Among the most conservative groups like the Old Order Mennonites, a strict and stable situation of diglossia with bilingualism exists with no mixing of English and German. Among other less conservative groups, shift to English is swift and complete as soon as English intrudes into what were German domains.

Diglossia has a number of other consequences, among them a tendency for speakers to regard H as the "real" language. When Arabic is used in contexts where it is a minority language, the colloquial varieties may be particularly vulnerable to loss and attrition because they are rarely taught as a result of the belief that only H is appropriate for school. In addition, as Shiri (Chapter 13, this volume) points out, where multiple local varieties of Arabic co-exist, Arabic speakers may switch to another language in order to make themselves understood to someone speaking a different L variety of Arabic, or they may try to accommodate to their addressee's variety by adopting some features of it and avoiding distinctive features of their own L. Over the long term, there may be a shift to Eastern (particularly urban Egyptian and Levantine) varieties of Arabic.

In the Chinese diaspora, speakers' linguistic backgrounds display considerable diversity, encompassing major regional languages spoken by at least fifty-six different ethnic groups in China. Although these languages are not mutually intelligible, they are united by a common writing system and linked to standard Mandarin Chinese referred to as *Putonghua* "common language" (Chapter 5, this volume). As in the case of Arabic speakers who speak a home variety considerably different from the one in which they are educated, so too, for example, do those Chinese who speak Hokkien, Cantonese, Min, etc., but study Mandarin at school. In the case of Italian, many immigrants (especially those largely uneducated persons in the first great migration wave of the late nineteenth and early twentieth centuries) spoke only or primarily varieties predominantly from southern Italy that were labeled as "Italian," but were actually regional languages, or distinct local varieties not mutually intelligible with standard Italian (Chapter 12, this volume). In the absence of public use and new input or renewal from continuing immigration, these regional forms tend to decline or in some cases were preserved in an archaic, fossilized form mainly as idiosyncratic personal/family varieties. Meanwhile, in Italy, as standard Italian spread into more common use, especially after World War II, use of regional languages and dialects decreased. Valdman (Chapter 4, this volume) notes a similar diglossic relationship among vernacular and creole varieties of French in the USA vis-à-vis standard French.

Similar processes of convergence, dialect leveling, or what some have called *koineization* are affecting other minority languages in the USA. The term *koiné* refers to a variety of a language serving as a means of communication among speakers of related varieties or dialects. Spanish immigrants, for example, have brought a rich multiplicity of forms of Spanish from twenty-seven nations, including at least nineteen different Latin American countries (Chapter 4, this volume) so that large US cities such as New York, Los Angeles, and Chicago are beginning to see individuals of mixed Hispanic ethnicity, such as so-called "MexiRicans" (Potowski 2008). Although these regional varieties of Spanish are generally mutually intelligible, Mexican Spanish predominates because people of Mexican origin overwhelmingly outnumber other Latino populations. Mexicans are not only the largest but also the fastest growing Hispanic group. In Los Angeles County, which has by far the largest number of Latinos in the USA (4.6 million according to the American Community Survey, US Census Bureau 2008), certain neighborhoods contain high densities of Spanish speakers, making them epicenters for dialect contact. For instance, 81.7 percent of the population is Hispanic in the Pico-Union District of Los Angeles, making it a prime locus for the emergence of a new highly localized Los Angeles variety of Spanish (see also Morales 2002). Here a unique American Spanish *koiné* is being created through the loss of certain features of non-Mexican varieties and convergence toward Mexican norms. Salvadorian second generation speakers of Los Angeles have given up phonological features of lowland Spanish, replacing aspirated [h] and velarized [ŋ] with a highland, Mexicanized pronunciation (e.g. /basta/ and /pan/ instead of /bahta/ "enough" and /paŋ/ "bread", Parodi 2003: 26–7).

Linguistic processes and outcomes of language contact

Contact travels along a potentially two-way street. Hence, the phenomena described in this chapter may apply equally well to English as they do to indigenous and immigrant languages in the USA. Nevertheless, where more than one language exists in a community, they are rarely equal in status. Languages and language varieties are always in competition, and at times in conflict. Knowledge of the varied sociolinguistic histories of relationships between speakers and groups within a contact situation is key to understanding the direction and extent of influence of one language on another. Where one group aggressively imposes its language on another, contact may result not only in language shift, but in the disappearance of the dominated language. Borrowing typically follows a path from a prestige language to a nonprestige language. Thus, in the USA, the incorporation of English features into Spanish is a linguistic reflex of the dominant position of English, while in Mexico and other parts of Latin America the intrusion of Spanish elements into indigenous languages like Náhuatl and Quechua indexes the role of Spanish as the language of social mobility and political power. Likewise, some varieties of Pennsylvania German in the USA show strong impact from English, while the English spoken by the same communities remains fairly intact from German influence (Burridge 2006). The fact that Navajos are shifting to English rather than Anglos to Navajo is because virtually all Navajos are exposed to English, but few Anglos (and not even all Navajos) are exposed to Navajo. This is reflected in the minimal effect of Navajo borrowing in English. The most commonly heard Navajo word in English is probably *chitty* (Navajo *chidí* "car"). In Farmington, New Mexico, some businesses have names such as *Chitty Lube* and *Cheap Chitty* (Schaengold 2004: 73). Beyond New Mexico, however, the influence of Navajo on standard English has been even more negligible (*cf. hogan*, a Navajo term for a dwelling built from earth and supported by upright or slanting timbers). We must not lose sight of the fact that contact initially takes place between local varieties of English and other languages. Yiddish, for instance, can be expected to have had little impact on varieties of English spoken, say, in South Dakota, while it has had a big influence on those spoken in the Greater New York and Los Angeles areas, where there are large concentrations of Yiddish speakers.

In one of the fullest treatments of what he called "interference" in bilingual speech, Weinreich (1968: 1) used the term to refer to any difference existing between the speech of monolinguals and bilinguals. Others have preferred the more neutral term "transfer" or "cross-linguistic influence" (terms associated with the field of second language acquisition) to refer to the adoption of any elements or features from one language into another. Either language can act as source or recipient so that Spanish speakers may impose Spanish features on English in the course of acquiring it as a second language, or they may adopt English features in their Spanish as English comes to be their more dominant language. It can sometimes be difficult to disentangle the effects of these two types of transfer. Transfer patterns differ depending on whether or not the speakers were born in the USA, and on the age at which they became bilingual. Chinese immigrant children who arrived in the USA after age 10, for example, tended to transfer features from Chinese into their English, while American-born childhood bilinguals tended to transfer English features into their Chinese (Liu *et al.* 1992).

What is referred to as a foreign accent is an obvious reflection of cross-linguistic influence in pronunciation. This results from speakers' use of the sounds of their native language in producing words in the target language. Thus, the variety of English used by some Pennsylvania German speakers shows devoicing in word-final obstruents (e.g. *had* is pronounced with final /t/ so that it rhymes with *hat*) and intonation patterns more characteristic of German (Burridge 2006). So-called discourse markers such as *well*, *you know*, *oh*, *so*, are also often transferred into Pennsylvania German and into Spanish (Torres and Potowski 2008). Borrowed words (sometimes also called loanwords and loan blends) are particularly common in cases of so-called "immigrant bilingualism" for obvious reasons. When moving to a new setting, speakers will encounter many things specific to the new environment or culture and will adopt readily available words from the local language to describe them. Indeed, the first Americanisms probably were borrowed from the Indian languages spoken by the indigenous tribes with whom the first English settlers had their earliest contacts. Most of these words indicate natural and cultural objects with no counterparts in England. In 1608 Captain John Smith, for instance, mentioned a strange animal referred to variously as a *rahaugcum* or *raugroughcum* (Algonquian "scratcher"). Not until 1672 did the word became conventionalized in the form we know it today as *racoon*. Similarly, *squash* emerged from *isquontersquashes* "vegetables eaten green." In addition to names for flora and fauna, there were also place names such as *Massachusetts* (Algonquian "place of the great hills") and names for objects of Indian culture such as *tomahawk*, *moccasin*, and *tepee*. By the same token, speakers of indigenous languages adopted English words for some newly introduced European cultural objects. Navajo borrowed *chair* probably because speakers found it easier to use the English term rather than describe it in Navajo (Schaengold 2004: 3). Navajo words tend to be long and descriptive, so that a word like "chair" would be represented as *bik'i'dah'asdáhí* "the thing upon which one sits."

Although the term "borrowing" has often been used to refer specifically to the importation of words from one language to another, it is sometimes used in a broad sense to encompass the transfer of linguistic features of any kind or size from one language to another as a result of contact. In this broad sense then it may overlap with what Weinreich and others have called interference. In any case, it is not possible to talk about the borrowing of words without also taking into account the fact that words do not exist in isolation; in order to be used, they must interact with phonology, syntax, morphology, and semantics of the host (i.e. borrowing) language, whose structure will typically differ from that of the donor language. Degree and type of integration depend at least partly on the structure of the borrowing language, as is already evident from the examples of *raccoon* and *squash* borrowed into American English from Native American languages, where they would have been pronounced quite differently.

When English nouns are phonetically and morphologically integrated into languages like German, French, Spanish, and Italian that categorize nouns into gender classes, they also acquire gender. English nouns such as *fence* (*cf.* Italian *il recinto*) and *yard* (*cf.* Italian *il giardino*) become feminine in Italian, as indicated by the form of the definite article and the *-a* ending (*la fenza*, *la yarda*), while others such as *car* become masculine in Italian *il carro* (*cf.* Italian *la macchina* "car" and *il carro* "cart"). In some cases gender assignment is variable, while in others it may follow the classification of the equivalent word in the donor language. Thus, *fridge* (*cf.* German *der Kühlschrank*) and *shop* (*cf.* German *der Laden*) become masculine in German. Similarly, Poles in the USA adapted English "street" (*cf.* Polish *ulica* "street") as *sztreta* (Chapter 15, this volume). Instead of borrowing English *bossy* wholesale, Pennsylvania German speakers created a loan blend by combining English *boss* with the German suffix *-ig* to create *bassig*.

Generally speaking, nouns are more frequently borrowed than verbs because it is easier to borrow free rather than bound morphemes (i.e. forms with grammatical functions that cannot occur on their own, such as the German suffix *-ig*). In many languages verbs carry various inflections comprised of bound morphemes. Chinese and Vietnamese do not regularly mark plurals, so when English nouns are borrowed into these languages they do not require grammatical integration, but words from those languages borrowed into English do. Nevertheless, English transfers may require integration into the system of tonal contrasts, so that in Vietnamese, for instance, they may adopt mid or high tone (Clyne 2003: 143). Depending on language type, borrowed verbs may require morphological integration into verbal paradigms. While verbs can be borrowed into Vietnamese with no morphological adaptation, Italian and Spanish adopt verbs into particular classes comprised of different roots and infinitival endings. In Italian the only class permitting new members has infinitives ending in *-are*; thus, English *shift*, *paint*, and *deliver* are incorporated as *shiftare*, *paintare*, and *deliverare*, respectively. In Spanish the majority of new verbs share a special ending *-ear*, e.g. *telefonear* "to call," *lunchear* (*cf. almorzar*) "to eat lunch," *parquear* (*cf. estacionar*) "to park." Valdman (Chapter 7, this volume) gives examples from Louisiana French such as *Ils voulaient check sur la situation* "They wanted to check out the situation" and *J'ai drive en ville* "I drove into town," where the verbs *check* and *drive* are not assimilated to the equivalent forms they would have in standard French (i.e. *ils voulaient checker, J'ai drivé en ville*), nor do they preserve the correct English infinitival form (i.e. *ils voulaient to check, J'ai drove en ville*).

As many of these examples show, borrowing does not always occur in response to the need to fill a gap; that is, Spanish, French, German, and Italian already have their own native equivalents for words such as *car*, *refrigerator*, *park*, *drive*, etc. The degree of acceptance of foreign items has been frequently associated with language type, as suggested by Weinreich's (1968: 61) observation that "a language with many restrictions on the form of words may be proportionately more resistant to outright transfer and favor semantic extension and loan translation instead." Mohawk, for example, has tended to create new native words for new objects rather than to borrow foreign words. The fact that verbs have never been borrowed has been attributed to the complex inflectional and derivational affixes necessary to both nouns and verbs that make the borrowing of foreign words cumbersome. The obligatory affixes on verbs are especially complex, which may partly explain why all of the words borrowed into Mohawk are nouns (Bonvillain 1978: 32). Field (1998: 67) makes similar remarks about Navajo verbs remaining impervious to any English interference, despite increased tolerance towards mixing and code-switching.

For over a hundred years, scholars of language contact have debated the question of what can and cannot be borrowed. Although some contact phenomena and types of change are more common and probable than others in certain situations, there are no absolute linguistic constraints on either borrowing or interference (Thomason 2001: 131). Various proposed hierarchies of and constraints on borrowing all have exceptions. There are cases, for example, where bound morphemes are borrowed and speakers often find solutions to apparent structural difficulties and typological incongruencies hindering the smooth integration of loans. In Navajo the most typical and only productive strategy for incorporating an English verb involves a frame consisting of a conjugated Navajo auxiliary verb *áshłééh* "make or prepare something" (Schaengold 2004: 44).

These considerations are reflected in (2a), where using the English word *bookshelf* is a simpler and more precise way of naming the object than translating it into Navajo as "the [thing] into which multiple objects are placed." Using the *áshłééh* construction to incorporate *save* avoids the requirement for Navajo verbs to include morphology describing the shape of any handled object (Schaengold 2004: 53–4). The Navajo auxiliary verb *áshłééh* "make or prepare something" carries the inflections for person, number, and tense. Compare the monolingual equivalent in (2b).

(2a)	**Bookshelf** ła' shá	**save** ání-lééh.	"Save me (one) bookshelf"
	bookshelf one for me	save 2nd.sing.-make	
(2b)	Naaltsoos biih ná'niłí	ła' shá	hasht'e'
	bookshelf 3rd.into it.place.multiple.obj.nom.one.1st.for		in storage (adv)
	niní'ah		
	2nd.sing move object		

Borrowed forms are easier to detect than borrowed patterns, as can be seen in the case of so-called loan shifts, semantic shifts, semantic extensions, and calques (also called loan translations). The chapters in this volume provide examples where the meaning of a word in a minority language is extended so that it corresponds to that of a related English word. Russians in the USA often use the Russian word *shkola* to refer to college and even graduate school, whereas in Russian *shkola* refers only to K-12 (Chapter 11, this volume). Similarly, Russian *klass* has a much more limited meaning than its apparent English equivalent "class," but Russian-speaking students tend to translate every instance of English *class* with Russian *klass*. In other cases semantic shift may occur in the absence of semantic similarity. Italian *fattoria* means "small farm," but in the Italian-American community it came to mean "factory" (*cf.* Italian *fabbrica*), due to its phonetic similarity with the English word.

The words in the two languages do not have to resemble each other phonetically for a loan shift to take place. Portuguese/English bilinguals extended Portuguese *frio* "cold spell" to mean "infection" by analogy with English "cold."

Such extensions are motivated by analogies made at different levels. The greater the similarity between two languages semantically and phonetically, the greater the potential for loan shifting to occur. In the first type of semantic extension, the motivation to make an analogy between two words is phonetic, even though the comparison may be semantically empty. In other words, it is more or less accidental that Italian *fattoria* and English *factory* are phonetically similar; semantically, they have nothing in common. In the case of Portuguese *frio* and English *cold*, however, the two are cognate at the semantic level, but do not share all of the same extensions. In this case it is partial equivalence at the semantic rather than phonetic level that allows the analogy to take place. Still another kind of loan shift of this general type may be motivated by partial phonetic and semantic identity. French/English bilinguals use English *library* to refer to a "bookshop" by analogy with French *librairie* "bookshop" (*cf.* French *bibliothèque* "library"). Here the apparent semantic similarity between a library as a building for books, and the bookshop as a place where books are sold is supported by the phonetic similarity of the terms in both languages.

Another type of borrowing called calquing or loan translation often passes unnoticed because it incorporates no foreign material. US Spanish *tener un buen tiempo* (*cf. pasarla bien* or *pasarlo bien*) is a word-for-word translation from the English expression "to have a good time" (Rothman and Rell 2005: 522). In his discussion of French in the USA, Valdman (Chapter 7, this volume) cites the use of expressions such as *il[s] ont couru ennehors de sel* "they ran out of salt" (*cf.* monolingual French *ils ont manqué de sel* "they lacked salt") calqued on an English model. These kinds of borrowings are not always intelligible to monolinguals because they are modeled on the structure of another language. Acadian French has incorporated English prepositions and phrasal verbs so that the English loan *back* replaces the role of the French prefix *re-* to produce loan blended verbs such as *venir back* (*cf.* French *revenir* "to come back") *mettre back* (*cf.* French *remettre* "to put back") (King 2000: 116–25). In US varieties of Spanish the English phrasal verb pattern is borrowed but expressed in Spanish, e.g. *te llamo pa'trás* "I'll call you back" (Otheguy 1993). Here Spanish *para atrás* "behind" is used to translate the English meaning of "back" and is also used in calqued expressions such as *dar atrás* "to give back" (*cf.* Spanish *devolver*). This example also involves an element of semantic extension because Spanish *atrás* and English *back* are only partially equivalent in meaning; *atrás* is restricted to location and does not include the concept of repetition or return (e.g. *come back*, *call back*).

Other cases may be difficult to classify unambiguously as loan shifts or loan translations. Consider an 83-year-old Dutch man, who has lived in the USA for over sixty years, who used *oproepen* instead of *opbellen* (the correct monolingual word meaning "call up someone on the telephone"). One can consider *oproepen* either as a literal translation of English "call up" or as the correct Dutch word *oproepen* which has received an extended meaning under the influence of English "call up" (Jaspaert and Kroon 1992: 143). In similar fashion it may not always be possible to distinguish influence from a speaker's first language from phonological integration, as in this example where an Italian-born grandmother addressed her Australian-born granddaughter (Finocchiaro 2004: 281): "Cheeky girla! *Vai a giocare nella* yarda" ("Cheeky girl. Go and play in the yard."). Here *cheeky*, *girla* and *yarda* are all English borrowings, but the final *-a* on *girla* (*cf.* Italian *la ragazza*) and *yarda* may reflect the influence on the grandmother's English of Italian syllable structure, which does not allow final consonants. Likewise, speakers of Spanish in diverse US locations such as LA and NY use many direct borrowings such as *la carpeta* instead of *tapete* for "carpet" and *la marqueta* instead of *el mercado* for "market" in utterances otherwise entirely in Spanish (Silva-Corvalán 1994; Zentella 1997).

The existence of calques and semantic shifts shows that contact does not manifest itself solely in terms of outright borrowing of elements from one language to another; it may also involve transfer of patterns. Still other even more subtle effects of contact may include simplification or regularization of irregularity in paradigms, reduction of variants or options, overgeneralization, or acceleration of changes already underway in the minority language. Chapters 4 and 7 on Spanish and French (in this volume) provide examples of such changes; other cases are documented elsewhere. Clyne (2003: 141) observed overgeneralization of the *-s* plural among younger generations of German speakers in Australia. This represents a simplification because German has five different plural markers, leading Clyne and others to conclude that contact facilitates the spread of more common, unmarked, and frequent variants. The *-s* plural of course is also directly matched in English *-s* plurals. Similarly, both Pennsylvania German and Los Angeles Spanish show an increased frequency of structures like the progressive (e.g. "she is working in the garden") with parallels in English (Burridge 2006), and subject pronouns are more frequently expressed overtly in environments that would be pragmatically odd for Spanish monolinguals (*cf. yo tengo* v. *tengo*) "I have" (Silva Corvalán 1994 in Los Angeles; Otheguy and Zentella 2007 in New York). Although subject pronouns are optional in Spanish, English is a strict SVO (subject-verb-object) language with obligatory expression of a grammatical subject. The varieties of German spoken by second generation immigrants in English-speaking countries like the USA and Australia reveal convergence toward English syntax. In (3a) the speaker forms the present perfect tense with the auxiliary verb *haben* "to have" (rather than with *sein* "to be"), and uses English rather than German word order, as in (3b) (Clyne 2003: 80).

(3a) Wir *haben gegangen* zu Schule in Tarrington
we have gone to school in Tarrington
"We went to school in Tarrington."

(3b) Wir sind in Tarrington zur Schule gegangen.
we are in Tarrington to school gone

Mixed languages

Generally speaking, the more structural overlap there is between languages in contact, the greater the potential for extensive grammatical borrowing, code-switching, and convergence, especially where there is stable, well-established multilingualism. Although the bilingual individual is, as Weinreich (1968: 6) so aptly put it, the ultimate locus of contact, the effects of contact are also manifest at the community level. The possible conventionalization of code-switching into a bilingual mixed language makes a neat separation between bilingualism as a societal and individual phenomenon impossible. Borrowings that start off as code-switches may recur over time in the speech of more and more individuals so that switched components become fossilized to the point where eventually speakers no longer recognize as distinct what once were two separate codes, and the mixed language may be transmitted to the next generation independently of its component languages. In this way the use of various linguistic phenomena identifiable historically as belonging to two or more different languages is no longer dependent on bilingualism. Most modern Michif speakers, for example, know neither Cree nor French.

The variety that Schaengold (2004: 67) refers to as Bilingual Navajo may be gradually shifting from being simply a product of code-switching by fluent bilinguals to becoming a new mixed language. It is spoken not only by fluent bilinguals, who borrow elements of English into Navajo, but also by those whose command of Navajo is not good enough to continue to switch between both Navajo and English. Schaengold regards Bilingual Navajo as a variety of Navajo rather than English because it comprises English words embedded into a Navajo grammatical frame. Navajo syntax and phonology are maintained; English elements are all content morphemes and no English prefixes and suffixes are used in this mixed code. Both Navajo and Spanglish thus show some key features of mixed languages in that both have their own rules and constraints, as well as their own sociolinguistic role in the community repertoire. Spanish monolinguals find it difficult to understand Spanglish due to the extent of English borrowing, phonological adaptation, and calquing.

Like Spanglish, Bilingual Navajo functions as an in-group language of solidarity not understood by outsiders. Neither English monolinguals nor Navajo monolinguals can understand Bilingual Navajo and fluent bilinguals cannot automatically speak it. This intelligibility gap reflects the fact that English components of Bilingual Navajo are often so thoroughly nativized, they would not be recognized by English monolinguals.

Given the intensity of contact with English, especially among younger generations in the USA, many minorities fear the loss of their language, an anxiety widely shared by members of many other minority communities the world over. Some, like O'Rahilly (1932: 121), see bilingualism itself as a step along the road to linguistic extinction, as suggested in his remarks on Manx (a Celtic language related to Irish and Scottish Gaelic, once widely spoken on the Isle of Man):

> From the beginning of its career English influence played havoc with its syntax, and it could be said without some exaggeration that Manx is merely English disguised in a Manx vocabulary. Manx hardly deserved to live. When a language surrenders itself to foreign idiom and when all its speakers become bilingual, the penalty is death.

While O'Rahilly seems to be describing a kind of convergence between Manx and English consisting of Manx words inserted into an English syntactic frame (similar to (3a) above), some varieties of Pennsylvania German appear to be heading in the other direction towards something akin to an English lexicon embedded within a structure still distinctively German (Burridge 2006). Spanglish, however, displays a somewhat different pattern of mixing involving words of English or Spanish origin pronounced with the phonological rules of the other combined into one grammar (Rothman and Rell 2005: 521). Unlike Michif (with Cree verbs and French nouns inserted into Cree syntactic structures, and a phonology combining sounds from both languages), the vocabulary mix in Spanglish is not compartmentalized into different subsystems. As yet, linguists have not reached consensus concerning how so-called mixed languages displaying these various kinds and degrees of mixing should be defined, how they are created, which varieties might qualify, or the extent to which they are distinct from code-switching (Bakker and Mous 2003, Matras and Bakker 2003).

Thomason (2001: 61) rightly regards attitudes as the "wild card" in understanding processes and outcomes of language contact, making contact-induced change essentially unpredictable. Attempts to formulate linguistic constraints on contact phenomena have failed because both the direction and extent of linguistic interference is ultimately socially determined. The loosely knit community of Yaqui Indians, for example, has been receptive to cultural, as well as lexical and grammatical, influence from Spanish, while the more tightly knit Arizona Tewa community has been far less open to Spanish influence of any kind. This difference is manifested in the number of Spanish loans and calques. Although nearly all adult Tewa also speak Hopi as a result of generations of intermarriage between the two groups, there are almost no Hopi loanwords in Arizona Tewa. Indeed, after contacts with Apacheans, Spanish, and Hopi lasting over 100, 150, and 190 years respectively, Arizona Tewa shows evidence of having adopted only two Apachean, seventeen Spanish, and only one Hopi loanword (Kroskrity 1993).

Although some have viewed code-switching and mixing as part of the process of shift ultimately culminating in language death, others see it as a strategy promoting maintenance. Despite the fact that the formation of Bilingual Navajo is a symptom of shift, it may indicate that shift is not progressing as rapidly as it otherwise might. In the long term it may even help maintain Navajo, albeit not in its traditional monolingual form (Schaengold 2004: 16). While O'Rahilly, whose prognosis for the future of Manx seems more like an indictment prompted by monolingual ideology, would probably not have welcomed the survival of a form of Manx mixed with English, his dismissal of such a possibility flies in the face of the pragmatic realities of language contact. Haugen (1953 [1969]: 71) described well the accommodations made by Norwegian immigrants who "in becoming bilingual within the American cultural environment . . . were forced to modify their Norwegian if they wished to continue using it." The modifications reflected a compromise between their desire to adopt English loanwords as prestige markers and their condemnation as foreign elements destroying the purity of Norwegian. As Haugen explained (1977: 332):

> Even though they admired the book norms exhibited by clergymen, they did not approve of people from their own group who tried to speak a "pure" Norwegian like that of the ministers. On the other hand, they poked fun at those who adopted excessive numbers of English words, calling them "yankeefied" and holding them to be "proud", "trying to be big shots" and the like. Most people steered a middle course between these extremes, and while professing a low opinion of their own dialects, an attitude reflecting their low status in the homeland, they went right on using them into the second and third generation. In doing so they created quite unconsciously a communicative norm which anyone who has known their society will immediately recognize as genuine.

Attitudes are also key when considering the direction of future trends for Spanglish. With continuing immigration replenishing the Spanish-speaking population, it is doubtful whether Spanglish will replace Spanish in the USA. Nor, however, is it likely to disappear. Those who too readily dismiss Spanglish as a transient phenomenon overlook the fact that mixed languages persist over long periods of time, despite the negative prestige attached to them, partly because they serve important functions as markers of in-group identity. For some Latinos, Spanglish is more than just a habitual strategy of speaking to other bilinguals; it has become an important sign of group membership, as suggested by Anzaldúa (1999: 77):

> For a people who are neither Spanish nor live in a country in which Spanish is the first language; for a people who live in a country in which English is the reigning tongue but who are not Anglo; for a people who cannot entirely identify with either standard (formal, Castilian) Spanish nor standard English, what recourse is left to them but to create their own language? A language which they can connect their identity to, one capable of communicating the realities and values true to themselves – a language with terms that are neither español ni inglés, but both. We speak a patois, a forked tongue, a variation of two languages.

Finding herself at odds with the community of both English and Spanish speakers who regarded her language as wrong, Anzaldúa contended that until she could accept the legitimacy of Tex-Mex (the Texas form of Chicano Spanish), she could not accept her own legitimacy.

Failure both within and outside the communities concerned to recognize mixed speech as a legitimate mode of communication in its own right has had a number of consequences. One practical consequence of the fact that standard, monolingual Spanish is not generally spoken in Miami is the need for court interpreters to have a command of Spanglish (Jongh 1990: 277). Another concerns the assessment of bilingual competence. If ability is evaluated in situations where bilinguals are forced to use a single code (e.g. in contacts with members of a monolingual community), communicative competence may seem less rich than it actually is. This results from the fact that the structure of each code taken separately is usually reduced in some dimension. Bilingual speakers' repertoires are fully exploited in those multilingual settings where they can call on resources from each of the available codes and on strategies for switching between them. In principle, the whole lexicon of the two languages is at the disposal of proficient bilinguals. Thus, code-switching is a mode of bilingual performance allowing bilinguals to display their full communicative competence (Lavandera 1978).

Although there is little doubt that mixed languages may serve important functions as markers of identity, as Anzaldúa (1999) and others such as Morales (2002) and Stavans (2003) suggest, not all would agree with her (or Thomason 2001 for that matter) that mixed languages are the products of conscious creation or deliberate invention on the part of bilingual communities rather than unintended outcomes of intensive language contact. It is important, nevertheless, to distinguish Spanglish from what Hill (1995) has called "Mock Spanish," used almost entirely by middle- and upper-middle-income college-educated Anglo speakers of English addressed to other Anglos of similar status. Mock Spanish is pronounced in an entirely English phonology and follows English grammatical rules. Moreover, the use of hyperanglicisms and deliberately bold and ludicrous mispronunciations such as /græsiæs/ (*gracias* "thank you") serve to mark this register as an elitist racist discourse. Mock Spanish consists of fragments such as *el cheapo* (referring to anything cheap), or *no problemo* "no problem," which is not grammatical Spanish because it is calqued on English (*cf.* Spanish *no hay problema*). These Mock Spanish creations imply that Spanish is a simple language; by adding an *-a* or an *-o* to an English word, anyone can master it with little effort, even the Hollywood alien terminator portrayed by Arnold Schwarzenegger, who made famous phrases such as *hasta la vista, baby*. This expression became an immensely popular slogan continuing to circulate in American usage. Schwarzenegger himself capitalized on it in his bid to become Governor of California, where he used it as a threat to his opponents. Semantically and pragmatically however, the meaning of *hasta la vista* is, if anything, exactly the opposite of what it means in Spanish, where it is a leave-taking formula and not a threat to kill someone. The explosion of Mock Spanish in films, television shows, greeting cards, video games, coffee-cup slogans, bumper stickers, refrigerator magnets, etc., reveals how the linguistic resources of other groups are expropriated and incorporated into mainstream primarily monolingual discourse, but often with opposite meanings from those intended in the source language.

Conclusion

The examples discussed in this chapter have shown that it is impossible to predict exactly what will happen in any particular case of language contact. Although the domains of theory and description are obviously intertwined in that theories ultimately must be tested against data, the primary focus of this chapter has been descriptive rather than theoretical. As Clyne (2003: 192) notes, none of the existing theoretical frameworks satisfactorily accommodates all contact phenomena under a single umbrella. Despite the fact that some researchers have argued that borrowing and code-switching are separate phenomena, there is often ambiguity in the language-mixing patterns of bilinguals. There is much to be said for a continuum model of types and degrees of contact reflecting both linguistic and social factors (such as proficiency and attitudes) and for referring to tendencies rather than universals. Borrowing may range from a few words to entire grammatical structures, and borrowed items may show various degrees of integration at various levels. Borrowing can occur in the speech of those with only monolingual competence, while code-switching and mixing imply some degree of competence in the two languages.

The chapters in this volume also reveal how English is displacing most of the languages it came into contact with as its speakers expanded and consolidated their influence. Later waves of immigrants found the English language already in place for the most part and adapted to it. The American bilingual experience for many indigenous and immigrant groups has been largely subtractive rather than additive; that is, rather than adding a second language to their first, the final outcome of acquiring English has resulted in the loss of their native tongues through a process of shift over several and sometimes even one generation. Despite rapid processes of language change affecting language maintenance among the adult population, and disrupting transmission to the younger generation, the chapters in this volume also point to a number of developments providing increased prospects for maintaining and renewing minority languages. For immigrant populations, for instance, opportunities for travel and cultural exchange with their countries of origin, access to new media such as satellite broadcasts, films and an ever-increasing variety of forms of computer-mediated communication (chat rooms, email, instant messaging), and in some cases, continuing immigration, offer possibilities not available to earlier immigrants for maintaining language and culture. Some languages such as Chinese, Arabic and Korean, designated critical to US national security, are benefiting from money targeted at increasing the number of Americans beyond the immigrant communities learning these languages, but it is unclear to what extent this support may aid heritage language learners who generally have cultural motivations for acquisition. Meanwhile, heritage language programs enable languages to be used beyond the domestic domain. Revitalization programs underway among indigenous populations are likewise providing opportunities for learning and relearning ancestral languages.

DISCUSSION QUESTIONS

1. The author states that, in the USA, "multilingualism is understood at best as multiple monolingualisms in distinct languages to be mastered separately in standard form and kept pure of outside influence." Explain what she means by this and why it is an erroneous position.

2. Why are attitudes considered the "wild card" in understanding the processes and outcomes of language contact?

---

3 Native American languages in the USA

Teresa L. McCarty

Introduction

Of 300 languages indigenous to what is now the USA, 175 are still spoken (Krauss 1998). The language with the most speakers – 178,000 in the 2000 Census – is Navajo but, as Table 3.1 shows, most Native American languages have many fewer speakers. More than a third have just a handful of elderly speakers. For example, Eyak, a language once spoken by people indigenous to what is now southern Alaska, lost its last speaker, Marie Smith Jones, in 2008. All Native American languages are endangered, as Native children are increasingly socialized in English. The causes of this are complex – a topic we will discuss later in this chapter. The consequences are grave, for, unlike speakers of languages spoken elsewhere in the world, Indigenous communities have no external pool of speakers from which to replenish their numbers. "The loss of the indigenous language is terminal: language death" (Warner 1999: 72). Given this situation, language revitalization is a significant goal in Native American communities throughout the USA.

Tribal sovereignty

Understanding Native American language issues requires understanding the unique legal and political status of Native peoples in the USA. The term "Native American" encompasses diverse American Indian tribes, Alaska Natives, and Native Hawaiians who share a status as first peoples, with the right to exercise tribal sovereignty, which is the "right of a people to government, self-determination, and self-education," including the right to linguistic and cultural expression according to local languages and norms (Lomawaima and McCarty 2006: 10).

From their first encounters, American Indians and Europeans interacted on a government-to-government basis. American Indians "were not considered a part of the nation," and the federal government dealt with them "much as it would with foreign nations, using a mixture of diplomacy, treaties, and warfare" (Snipp 2002: 2). The federal–tribal relationship was subsequently codified in the US Constitution and in treaties (which the federal government

Table 3.1. *Top ten Indigenous languages spoken in the USA*

Language	Number of speakers	Primary location of speakers
Navajo	178,000	Arizona, New Mexico, Utah
Western Ojibwe	35,000	Lake Superior region, Montana, North Dakota
Dakota	20,355	Minnesota, Montana, Nebraska, North Dakota
Choctaw	17,890	Mississippi, Oklahoma
Western Apache	12,693	Arizona, New Mexico
Cherokee	11,905	Oklahoma, North Carolina
Tohono O'odham	11,819	Arizona
Central Yup'ik	10,000	Alaska
Eastern Ojibwe	8,000	Michigan
Zuni	6,413	New Mexico

Sources: Benally and Viri 2005; Grimes 1996; NCELA 2002.

has frequently violated), judicial rulings, and federal law. In exchange for land, Native peoples entered into a trust relationship with the federal government in which it recognizes a binding responsibility to honor certain guarantees in education, health, and other areas, and "to represent the best interests of the tribes and their members" (American Indian Policy Center 2002: 1). This legal–political relationship is unlike that of any other ethnolinguistic group in the USA. As we will see, the tribal–federal relationship has profoundly influenced the present status of Native American languages, and it continues to shape the possibilities for Native language revitalization today.[1]

History

In the swirl of interests that engulfed the North American continent following the European invasion, multilingualism was common, a tool of trade and inter-tribal communication and the diffusion of Christianity and European ideals. Beginning with Christopher Columbus' fifteenth century invasion, the Spanish Catholic Church instituted a program to "civilize" Native peoples through forced settlement in villages and the indoctrination of children in Spanish literacy and numeracy. Instruction in Indigenous languages was also part of the Spanish program, and, as a consequence, nearly all Indigenous languages in what is now the southwestern and southeastern USA were committed to writing by Spanish missionaries (Spicer 1962; Goddard 1996). The policy of using Native languages as media of instruction and religious conversion continued with English, French, German, Russian, Dutch, and Roman Catholic missionaries. Native Americans also developed their own writing systems. Cherokee, for example, has been written since Sequoyah completed his famous syllabary or "talking leaves" in 1821.

Western European policies of expedient tolerance toward Native languages (McCarty 2004) changed after the American Revolution, as the new federal government turned its attention to "pacifying" Native peoples in the quest for their lands. Toward that end, Congress passed the 1819 Civilization Fund Act to support missionary schooling. As the law's title suggests, European colonizers equated education with "civilization," the goal being forced assimilation designed to literally clear the path for Anglo-European settlement. By the late nineteenth century, the primary tools for this were federal boarding schools, "a controlled environment where behavior and belief would be shaped by example and instruction" (Lomawaima 1994: 112). Whereas earlier mission schools, with their overriding aim of Christianization by whatever means possible, often taught in the Native language, prohibitions against speaking Indigenous languages in federal schools were strictly enforced. Accounts abound of children being ridiculed, beaten, and having their mouths "washed" with soap for speaking their mother tongue (McCarty 2002; Reyhner and Eder 2002).

Over the next few decades, the Bureau of Indian Affairs (BIA) came under intense criticism for these practices, leading federal officials to loosen prohibitions against Native American languages and to authorize the development of Native language readers. Although they had a clear assimilationist agenda, these texts were often appropriated for Indigenous ends. The late Lakota anthropologist, Beatrice Medicine, observed that the BIA's Lakota readers were "welcome additions to Christian hymnals and bibles" and reflected "the initial impact of bilingual and bicultural education for . . . the Native population" (Medicine 2001: 50).

One unintended consequence of the boarding school system was the forging of an alliance of Native peoples from diverse tribes who grew up together in the schools, and who, in the context of the 1960s American Indian and civil rights movements, pushed for tribal sovereignty and education reform. The upshot was a new federal policy of tribal self-determination, supported by legislative victories such as the 1972 Indian Education Act and the 1975 Indian Self-Determination and Educational Assistance Act. Together with the 1968 Bilingual Education Act, this legislation laid the legal and financial framework for teaching Native American languages and cultural content in schools serving Native students.

Demographics

No one knows precisely the number of Native peoples present in the Western hemisphere when Christopher Columbus reached what came to be called the Americas on October 12, 1492. Population estimates for the coterminous USA

Table 3.2. *Top ten most populous American Indian/Alaska Native groupings: 2000*

Tribe/tribal grouping	Number reporting "American Indian tribal grouping alone or in any combination"	Number reporting "American Indian tribal grouping alone"
Cherokee	729,533	281,069
Navajo	298,197	269,202
Latin American Indian	180,940	104,354
Choctaw	158,774	87,349
Sioux (Lakota, Dakota)	153,360	108,272
Chippewa	149,669	105,907
Apache	96,833	57,060
Blackfeet	85,750	27,104
Iroquois	80,822	45,212
Pueblo (includes multiple Pueblos in Arizona and New Mexico)	74,085	59,533

Source: US Census Bureau 2002: 10.

and Canada range from 900,000 to 12.3 million (Thornton 1987: 26). Although these numbers are contested, what we do know is that following the European invasion, European-introduced diseases and genocidal campaigns to usurp Native lands plunged Native populations and languages into drastic decline.

At the turn of the twenty-first century, 4.1 million people in the USA (1.4 percent of the total population) identified as American Indian and Alaska Native (AI/AN), including 2.5 million people who reported only American Indian and Alaska Native heritage (US Census Bureau 2002). An additional 874,000 people identified as Native Hawaiian and "other Pacific Islander" (NHOPI) (US Census Bureau 2001b: 1, 8). These numbers represent a more than 100 percent increase over the 1990 Census (US Census Bureau 2002: 3), which is due both to natural population growth and changes in Census categories enabling individuals to claim more than one "race."

Approximately one third of the AI/AN population are children under the age of 18, compared with 22 percent of individuals classified as "non-Hispanic Whites" (Snipp 2002; US Census Bureau 2007a: 7). More than a quarter of the AI/AN population – double the proportion of the population as a whole – lives below the poverty line (US Census Bureau 2006a: 12). Native Americans reside in every state and US territory, representing more than 560 federally recognized tribes, 619 reservations and Alaska Native villages, and 62 Native Hawaiian homelands (see Figure 3.1) (US Census Bureau 2001a: 9; Snipp 2002: 12). As Table 3.2 shows, numerically, the largest American Indian tribe is Cherokee, with a population of 729,533, of whom 281,069 reported "Cherokee alone" in

Table 3.3. *US urban areas with the largest American Indian/Alaska Native (AI/AN) population: 2000*

City and state	Rank by AI/AN population alone or in combination	Rank by total population	Number of AI/AN population alone or in combination	Percent AI/AN of total population
New York, NY	1	1	87,241	1.1
Los Angeles, CA	2	2	52,092	1.4
Phoenix, AZ	3	6	35,093	2.7
Tulsa, OK	4	43	30,227	7.7
Oklahoma City, OK	5	29	29,001	5.7
Anchorage, AK	6	65	26,995	10.4
Albuquerque, NM	7	35	22.047	4.9
Chicago, IL	8	3	20,898	0.7
San Diego, CA	9	7	16,198	1.3
Houston, TX	10	4	15,743	0.8

Source: US Census Bureau 2002: 8.

Table 3.4. *US urban areas with the largest Native Hawaiian and Other Pacific Islander (NHOPI) populations: 2000*

City and state	Rank by NHOPI population alone or in combination	Rank by total population	Number of NHOPI population alone or in combination	Percent NHOPI of total population
Honolulu, HI	1	46	58,130	15.6
Chicago, IL	2	1	19,203	0.4
Los Angeles, CA	3	2	13,144	0.4
San Diego, CA	4	7	10,613	0.9
Long Beach, CA	5	34	7,863	1.7
San Jose, CA	6	11	7,091	0.8
Sacramento, CA	8	40	6,833	1.7
San Francisco, CA	8	13	6,273	0.8
Seattle, WA	9	24	4,977	0.9
Hayward, CA	10	154	4,709	3.4

Source: US Census Bureau 2001a: 7.

the 2000 US Census. Navajo, with a population of more than 298,000, is the second most populous tribe and has the largest land base, with a reservation the size of Ireland, spread across three southwestern states (US Census Bureau 2002).

Many Native Americans, including 29 percent of all AI/AN children, reside within reservation lands or Alaska Native villages (Snipp 2002: 12) (see Figure 3.1). Just under 23,000 Native Hawaiians reside within Hawaiian homelands.[2] As Tables 3.3 and 3.4 illustrate, many Native people also live in urban areas,

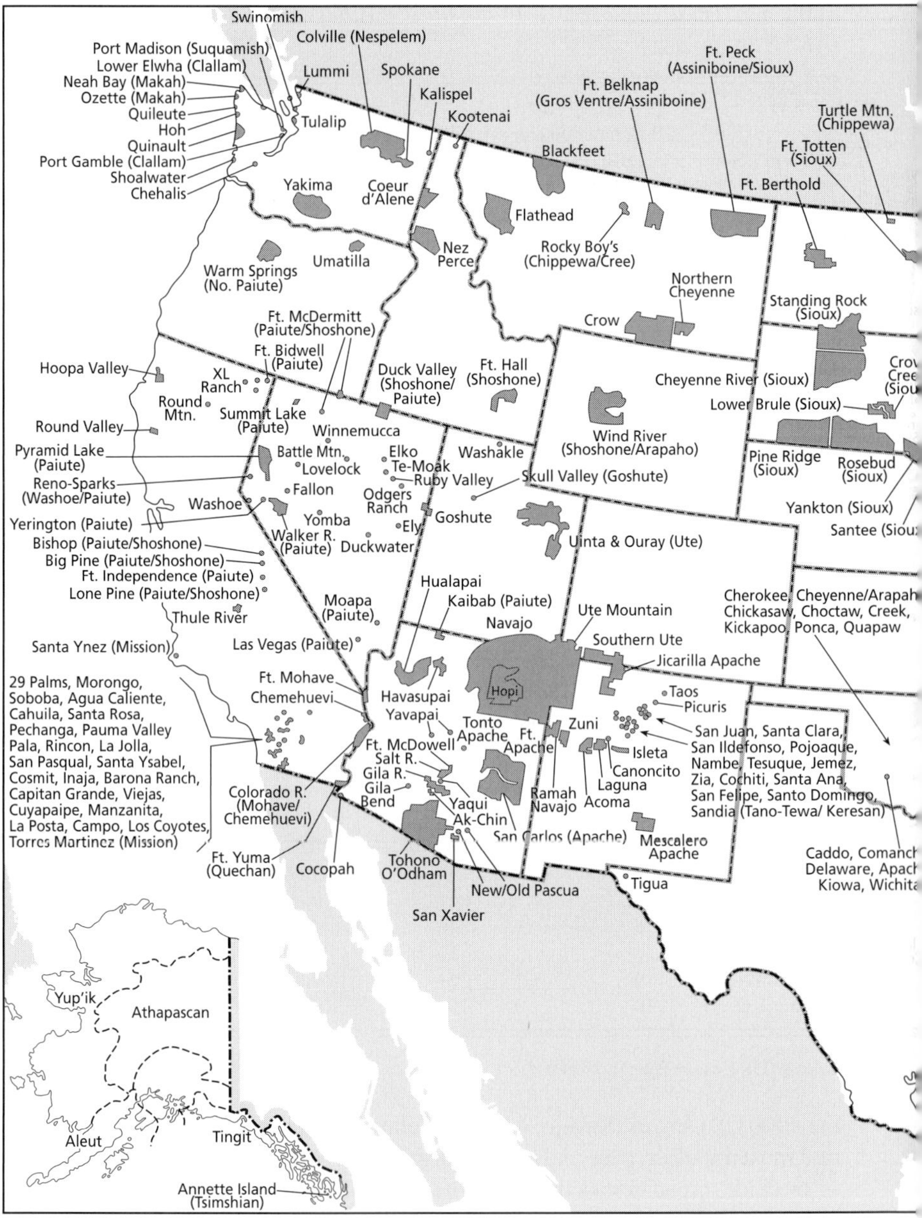

Figure 3.1. American Indian and Alaska Native reservations and tribal lands
Source: McCarty and Watahomigie 2004: 80

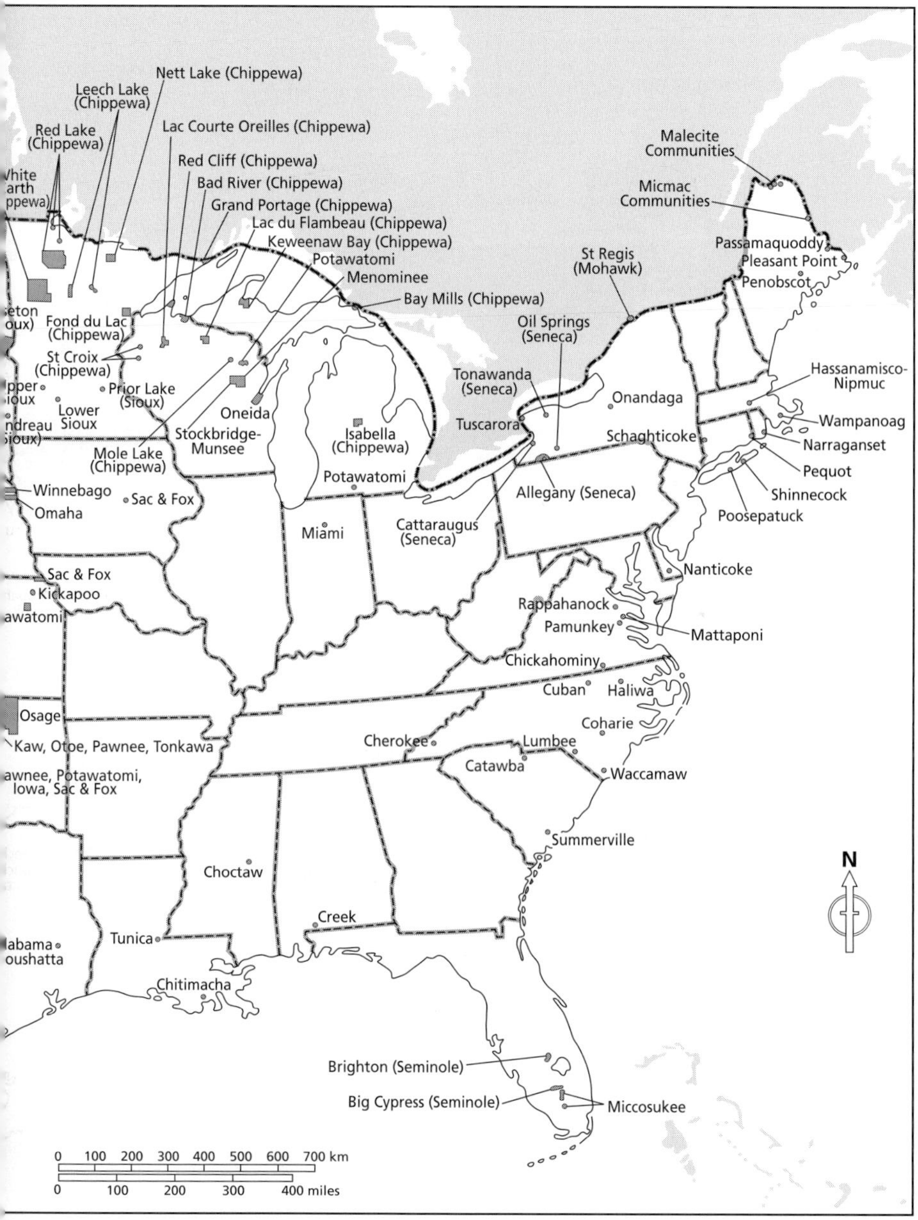

Figure 3.1. (*cont.*)

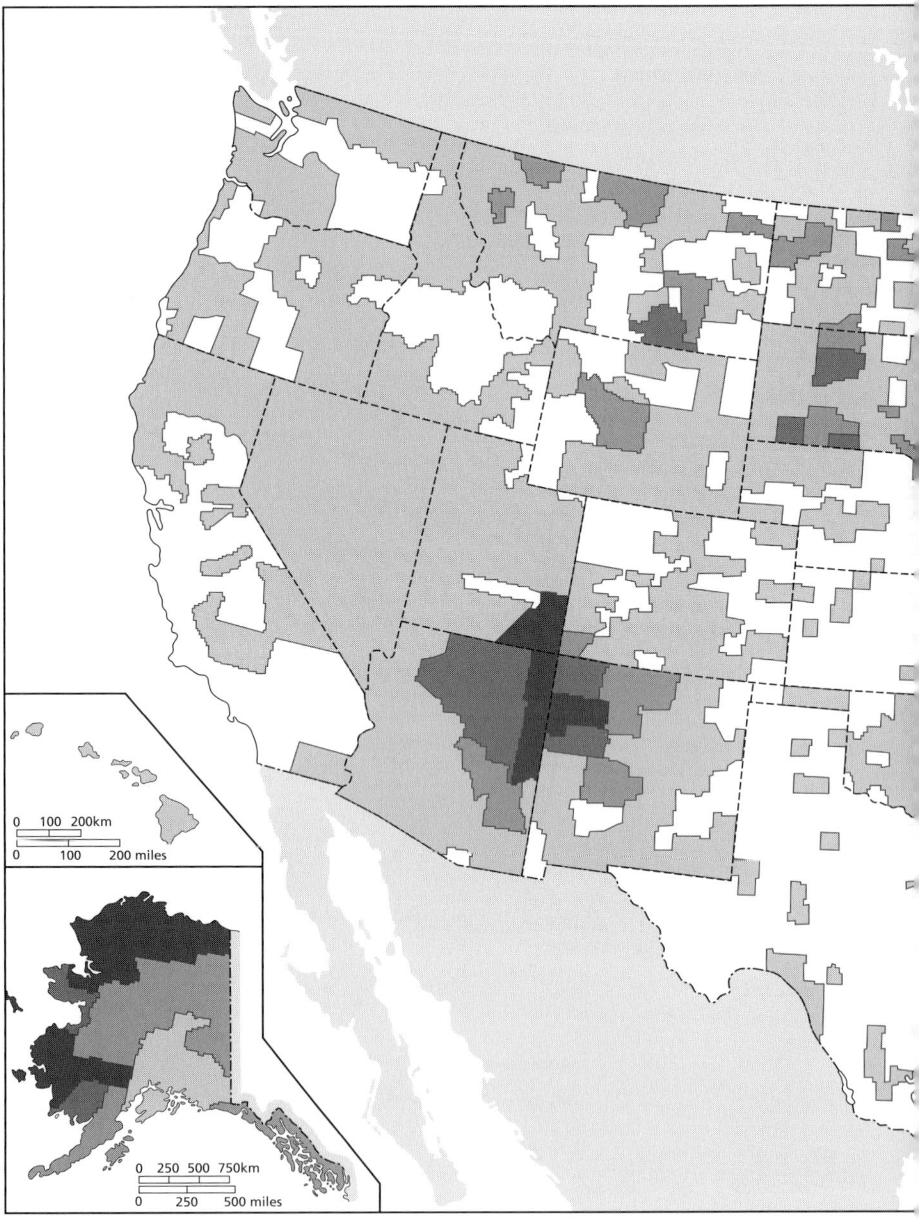

Figure 3.2. Native American speakers, population distribution: 2000
Source: US Census Bureau 2000b

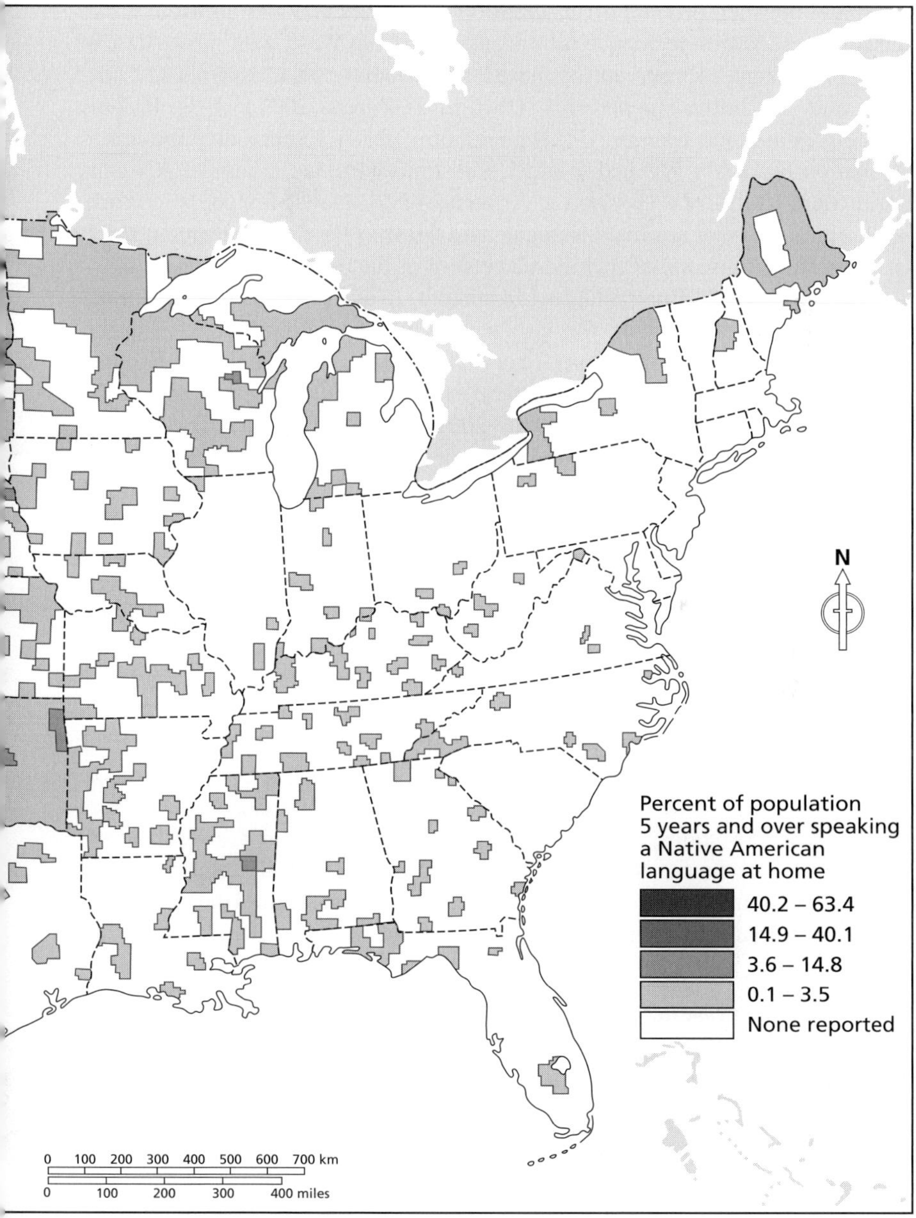

Figure 3.2. (*cont.*)

and travel between on- and off-reservation residences is common. Both urban and rural/reservation residence is concentrated in the West, with most AI/ANs living in Arizona (13 percent of the AI/AN population), California (12 percent), and Oklahoma (12 percent) (US Census Bureau 2007a: 3, 5). Proportionately, Alaska has a larger AI/AN population; nearly 13 percent of the state's population is AI/AN. Ranked in order, the states with the largest AI/AN populations are California, Oklahoma, Arizona, Texas, New Mexico, New York, Washington, North Carolina, Michigan, and Alaska (US Census Bureau, 2002: 4). Altogether, these states include 62 percent of the total AI/AN population.

Over half the NHOPI population (58 percent) lives in Hawaii and California. In 2000, the ten states with the largest NHOPI populations were, in order: Hawaii, California, Washington, Texas, New York, Florida, Utah, Nevada, Oregon, and Arizona. Combined, these states represent 80 percent of the NHOPI population (US Census Bureau 2001a: 4–6).

In 2006, 72 percent of AI/ANs 5 years or older were reported as speaking only English at home (US Census Bureau 2006a: 7). Of those reporting a non-English language spoken at home, more than 63 percent said they spoke English "very well" (US Census Bureau 2006a: 7). The Summer Institute of Linguistics' *Ethnologue* reports a total of 361,978 speakers of Indigenous American languages (Grimes 1996). All of these numbers should be used with caution, as Census categories can be confusing and speakers may overestimate their language ability or deny it due to linguistic discrimination (Krauss 1998; NCELA 2002). Figure 3.2 shows the distribution of Native American language speakers in 2000. The largest numbers of speakers reside in Alaska and the Four Corners region of the Southwest (Arizona, New Mexico, Utah, and Colorado), followed by the northern Plains. There are significant numbers of speakers in other Western states, around the Great Lakes region, and in Oklahoma, Mississippi, and the far Northeast. This distribution generally corresponds to the main locations of the "top ten" groups shown in Table 3.1, and the population size and distribution shown in Tables 3.2 and 3.3 and Figure 3.1.

Public presence

Historically, Native American languages had a strong public presence in all arenas of social life. During the Hawaiian monarchy, for example, Hawaiian was the language of government, religion, business, the media, education, and interethnic communication; even "the children of immigrants . . . spoke Hawaiian with native-speaker fluency" (Wilson 1998: 127). Like other Native American languages, Hawaiian fell into disuse in both public and private domains as a direct result of US military aggression, genocide, and compulsory English-only schooling. As a consequence, most Native American languages now have their primary public presence within circumscribed local domains. There *are* some exceptional instances of Native languages in the wider public sphere, however. During World War II, the Navajo, Choctaw, Comanche, and Lakota Code Talkers in six US Marine divisions were responsible for transmitting military information in their mother tongue via telegraphs and radios. Their contributions are widely credited with hastening the end of the war (Gease 2002).

This section explores contemporary Native American language use in the key public domains of government, religion, the media, and education. While it is impossible to do justice to all Native American languages and language use domains, the examples provide a sense of the continuing vitality of these languages and their role in Native cultural life and self-determination.

Government

In 1987, Navajo sociolinguist Alyce Neundorf documented the significance of bilingualism within the Navajo Tribal Council, where, she argues, interpreting from Navajo into English serves as a stepping-stone to power (Neundorf 1987: vii; Spolsky 2002a: 152). Interestingly (and indicative of language hierarchies), Neundorf found that interpreting from English to Navajo has much less social currency. Today, proficiency among high-ranking tribal officials (e.g. the Navajo Nation president and vice president) is expected, and Navajo predominates at local chapter meetings (similar to a town hall). Code-switching for lexicon associated with Anglo-American institutions and personnel is common, meeting minutes are recorded in English, and council delegates often use English to report to home communities (Benally and Viri 2005). As Spolsky (2002a) reports,

> Formal parliamentary statements [are] made in English ("Referring to section 5B of the bill tabled yesterday"), but many speeches . . . then switch into culturally sensitive and rhetorically Navajo presentations, with full and appropriate kinship references. . . . [T]hose who do not speak Navajo . . . must depend on the simultaneous interpretation into English now provided through headphones. (p. 154)

Native languages remain important resources in the theocratic Pueblos of New Mexico as well. Benjamin, Pecos, and Romero, writing of the Keres-speaking Pueblo of Cochiti, note that, "Critical to this form of government is the underlying commitment [leaders] have . . . to the traditional lifestyle . . . the more a person engages in [government-related] events, the more . . . competent he or she becomes" in Keres (1996: 119–20). The interpenetration of tribal governance with Native religious systems in Pueblo societies creates unique opportunities for Native language use. Describing the Keres-speaking Pueblo of Acoma, Sims states that "oral Acoma . . . continues to be an important part of council deliberations and public meetings . . . as well as in conducting the internal affairs of the pueblo's socioreligious life," although "younger adults rely on a mix of English and Acoma or on English only" (2001: 64).

Religion

As the previous subsection suggests, the religious sphere remains a bastion of Native language use in many Native communities. Traditional Navajo religion, for example, involves complex and "carefully prescribed rituals conducted by highly trained singers or medicine men" who apprentice for years to learn the long poetic prayers and songs that constitute a vital core of Navajo life (Spolsky 2002a: 147). Among the Arizona Tewa, ceremonial leaders "require and enforce an explicit proscription against the use of foreign words" during ritual performances, and talk in the kiva (a ritual chamber of great symbolic importance in Pueblo societies) "would lose its integrity if it admitted expressions from other languages" (Kroskrity 2000: 338). Benjamin *et al.* (1996), Romero (2003), and Sims (2001) note similar linguistic practices at Cochiti and Acoma Pueblos. Hopi scholar Sheilah Nicholas (2008) explains that these practices promote the ideals of respect, obligation, reciprocity, and humility, enabling young people to develop a sense of aesthetics for Hopi culture and confirming the kiva as a stronghold for the Native language.

As discussed earlier, Christian sects also have promoted Native language literacy, although often in opposition to Indigenous values and beliefs. Literacy in Anglo-American churches, however, has frequently been co-opted for Indigenous ends. In a case study of Navajo literacy, McLaughlin (1992) reports that, "one important way for . . . churchgoers to act is to read and write Navajo for indigenous purposes in home settings unconnected to church . . . and identified as . . . crucial to the survival of Navajo language and culture" (p. 152).

Perhaps the most widespread religious context in which Native American languages are prominent is the Native American Church (NAC), a multitribal religion that emerged as a resistance movement during the late nineteenth century. Founded by Comanche leader Quanah Parker, the NAC has spread throughout the USA, and ceremonial songs and prayers are given in Native languages appropriate to particular tribal contexts.

Media

Print and audio-visual media are contentious domains for Native language use, as mainstream media are rife with racist stereotypes and misrepresentations. Images of "Tonto and the Lone Ranger" still appear on television and in film, and more subtle but equally dehumanizing portrayals populate multiple literary genres (McCarty 2008). Yet many authentic Native language media exist. Historically, one example is the *Cherokee Phoenix*, which rolled off the presses on February 28, 1828 – eight years after Sequoyah published his syllabary – and is still published today (Worthy n.d.). The paper garnered international attention but had as its primary audience the diasporic Cherokee community in present-day Georgia, Alabama, Tennessee, North Carolina, Arkansas, Oklahoma, and Texas. In 1834, the first Hawaiian-language newspaper was published (*Ka Lama Hawai'i*) and by 1900, over 100 Hawaiian-language newspapers were in circulation (Wilson 1998). The first newspaper in Navajo was *Ádahooníłígíí (Events)*, published by the BIA during World War II to inform tribal members of wartime events.

Today, numerous Native American dailies, weeklies, and monthlies are published. Most are in English, but many include Native language columns and sections. In addition, at least one scholarly journal, the *Journal of Navajo Education*, included scholarly articles and poetry in a Native American language (Navajo); unfortunately, the journal was discontinued in the 1990s due to lack of resources for its publication and distribution.

There is a growing Native language literature for readers of all ages, much of it stemming from federally funded bilingual–bicultural education programs. Writers such as Tohono O'odham linguist and poet, Ofelia Zepeda, and Navajo poet and playwright, Rex Lee Jim, publish in their mother tongue, contributing to a corpus of Native American poetry, song texts, and other literature (e.g. Evers *et al.* 1983; Hinton and Watahomigie 1984; Zepeda 1995; Jim 1998). Some of these texts have been recorded in CD-ROM format, as with Zepeda's (1997) *Jewed 'I-Hoi: Earth Movements*.

Audio-visual media are increasingly being used for Native language documentation and revitalization. Among the Ojibwe in Minnesota, a project is under way to videotape elders conversing in semiscripted settings, many full of humor, to preserve and teach natural speech (Hermes and Roach 2007). Talking storybooks incorporating videos of community members and animated children's songs are part of the Arapaho Tribe's language revitalization efforts in Wyoming. Part of this work involved adapting Walt Disney's animated movie, *Bambi*, with voicing by Arapaho children and adults (Greymorning 2001). Computer technology has also been used to produce online dictionaries and other language documentation and teaching materials.

An even larger media outlet is Canyon Records, headquartered in Phoenix, Arizona, which has produced traditional and contemporary Native American music for more than fifty years. At the time of writing, the company had produced twenty-two Grammy-nominated records (Canyon Records 2008). Other mass media include radio stations with Native American programs in states throughout the USA, many of them operated by Native nations.

Education

The foregoing discussion highlights the fact that much of the media utilizing Native American languages serves local education needs. Education represents the most extensive – if challenging – public domain for contemporary

Native American language use. Approximately one third of the Native American population are school-age children who attend federal Bureau of Indian Education (BIE) schools, tribal- or community-controlled schools under BIE purview but operated by Native American school boards, state-supervised public schools, public charter schools, private schools, and mission or parochial schools. Students often rotate through several of these school systems over their academic career, sometimes even within a single academic year. Although many schools are located within reservations or Alaska Native villages (and thus have a majority AI/AN enrollment), (half of all Native American students attend public schools with less than 25 percent Native American enrollment (National Center for Education Statistics 2008). Further, less than 5 percent of teachers serving Native students are Native American (National Center for Education Statistics 2008). Obviously, this limits opportunities for Native language instruction.

Understanding the possibilities for Native language teaching in this education environment requires some sense of how it came about. Well into the twentieth century, Native American languages were outlawed in federal Indian schools. It was not until the mid-1950s, with the passage of federal legislation to fund school construction on federal lands, that public schools became locally available to American Indian students. Although Native languages were not necessarily prohibited in public schools, neither have they been well supported.

The first school to provide systematic instruction in a Native American language was established in 1966 at Rough Rock, Arizona, within the Navajo Nation. The school opened the first Native American publishing center, taught initial literacy in Navajo, and created innovative programs to certify Native teachers. It also galvanized federal policy changes that enabled other Native American communities to operate bilingual–bicultural schools (McCarty 2002). Today there are 122 tribal/community-controlled schools; all offer some form of Native language and culture instruction.

Although they are locally controlled, these schools are subject to federal mandates under the Department of Interior's BIE, the office charged with overseeing BIA-funded schools. In addition to tribal/community schools, the BIE oversees 184 elementary and secondary schools on 63 reservations in 23 states with a total enrollment of 46,000 students (US Department of the Interior 2004). These schools tend to place much less emphasis, if any, on Native language and culture instruction.

Charter schools are an increasingly popular, if controversial, option for bringing Native linguistic and cultural content into the school. The controversial nature of these schools stems not from the fact that some are Indigenous-serving institutions, but from more general concerns about the privatization of public education and the diversion of resources from struggling and underfunded public schools. For Indigenous communities that have experienced centuries of inferior and assimilative schooling, Native-operated charter schools are one option for asserting local education control. Today, thousands of Native American students are enrolled in charter schools, which "offer the opportunity to create and offer curriculum geared toward local cultures" (Tirado 2001: 14).

Native language programs also exist at the postsecondary level. In 1968, the Navajo Nation opened Navajo Community College (now called Diné College), the first college established by Native Americans for Native Americans. Diné College offers thirteen Navajo language courses, including Navajo as a second language, Navajo literacy and composition, Navajo linguistics, Navajo grammar, and courses designed to endorse Navajo language teachers (Slate 2001). There are currently thirty-three such colleges, including one, Haskell Indian Nations University, which is an intertribal university enrolling approximately 1,000 students representing 150 tribes.

Although schooling for Native Americans is complicated and compromised by federal mandates and purse strings, it remains a crucial arena for the exercise of tribal sovereignty and self-determination. As this section suggests, much of this revolves around the right (and the fight) to teach and maintain tribal languages – a topic we turn to next.

Evidence of language shift to English and maintenance[3]

Language shift to English is occurring at an escalating pace in Native American communities. Krauss (1998) classifies the 175 Native American languages still spoken as follows:

- *Class A*, the twenty languages still spoken by all generations;
- *Class B*, the thirty languages spoken by the parent generation and older;
- *Class C*, the seventy languages spoken by the grandparent generation and older; and
- *Class D*, the fifty-five languages spoken only by the very elderly, often less than ten people.

A fifth category is *Class E*, the innumerable languages no longer spoken and now described as "extinct." Some linguists have proposed that this category be further delineated into "dormant" or "sleeping languages" to refer to those for which there is written documentation and a living heritage community, providing a foundation for the language to be used again (Leonard 2008: 23; see also Hinton, 2001a).

Like all classifications, this one simplifies the complexity of language use and change. For example, Tohono O'odham – a Uto-Aztecan language spoken by people indigenous to what is now southern Arizona and northern Sonora, Mexico – is placed in class A, although it is more accurately represented across a spectrum of classes A–C, depending on a particular speech community's history and locale. Krauss' classification nevertheless alerts us to the fact that "unless there is radical change and success at reversal of language shift, by 2060 . . . all but 20 [Native American languages] would be extinct . . . Every one of . . . these languages is severely endangered" (p. 11).

How did the present situation come about? Although no single factor is determinative, Native American language attrition can be traced to federal policies of containment, dislocation, and genocide, and to contemporary pressures associated with English media, technology, and schooling. The loss of Eyak, for example – the Alaska Native language mentioned in the chapter introduction – is directly attributable to the fact that for more than a century, Alaska Native children suffered physical abuse for speaking their mother tongue in school. As a consequence, many graduates came to see their bilingualism as a hindrance rather than an asset, and chose to socialize their children in English only. Even where Native American languages are still acquired as first languages, children learn early that English is the language of power and that they can accomplish most of life's necessities without their mother tongue.

The remainder of this section provides brief descriptive portraits of four Native American language revitalization projects that span all five categories in Krauss' (1998) classification and exemplify a range of language regeneration efforts. A key strategy in all four cases is Native language immersion, instruction providing all or most content in the Native language.

Wôpanâak language revival

Wôpanâak (also called Wampanoag, Natick, and Massachusett) is an Algonquian language once spoken by peoples Indigenous to what is now southeastern New England. These speech communities were hit hard and early by the European invasion, and in 1908, the last native speaker passed away, making Wôpanâak a class E ("sleeping") language. The 3,000 Wôpanâak on Cape Cod and Martha's Vineyard are nonetheless implementing bold efforts to resurrect their heritage language, using the 1663 Eliot Bible, "the undisputed treasure of Massachusett linguistics" (Hale 1997: 9), and nineteenth-century lexicons, letters, diaries, and legal documents written by native speakers.

The Wôpanâak Language Reclamation Project began in 1993 as a collaborative effort between three tribal councils. The effort was spearheaded by tribal member Jessie Little Doe Fermino Baird. Working with linguist Kenneth Hale, she mastered the language, earned a master's degree in linguistics, and began formulating a Wampanoag dictionary and language curriculum and teaching Wôpanâak classes (Feldman 2001). Although challenged by the fact that there are no first language speakers ("no one alive knows what [the Native language] sounded like," a tribal leader points out [Daly 2002: 4]), the goal is for tribal members to relearn the heritage language and use it with their children (Hale 1997: 10; see also Ash *et al.* 2001: 28–32).

The California Master–Apprentice Language Learning Program

Prior to European contact, present-day California was one of the most linguistically and culturally diverse regions of the world, with 300,000 to 400,000 Native people who spoke 100 languages (Hinton 1998: 85; 2001b: 217). Successive waves of colonization by Spanish missionaries, Mexican ranchers, and Anglo-American gold seekers brought devastating disease, slaughter, and enslavement (Sims 1998; Hinton 2001b). Today, fifty California Native languages are still spoken, but none as a first language by children. Most can be placed in Krauss' class D.

In this context, a unique language revitalization effort has begun called the Master–Apprentice Language Learning Program (MALLP) (Hinton 1998: 87–8). The MALLP pairs master speakers/teachers with younger language learners who work together for months and years at a time, engaging in everyday activities in the heritage language. The teams' work is complemented by immersion camps that bring together older speakers and younger language learners (Sims 1998; Supahan and Supahan 2001). Many apprentices have become conversationally proficient and the MALLP movement continues to grow. "The passion and dedication of those who are working with their languages is obvious and inspiring to others," Hinton states; "[i]t is a healthy movement . . . toward recovery from the devastating social and cultural wounds inflicted by the European incursion into California" (1998: 92).

Hawaiian-medium education

A Polynesian language, Hawaiian is closely related to Māori and Samoan, and more distantly to Fijian and Malay. Although Native Hawaiians were only incorporated into the federal system in the last fifty years, their experiences bear the imprint of those of other Native Americans. Following the illegal US takeover of the Hawaiian Kingdom in 1893, bans ensued on Hawaiian-medium instruction along with mandates that all business be conducted in English. By the mid-twentieth century, just a few hundred Hawaiian speakers remained, placing Hawaiian at the time in class D (Wilson and Kamanā 2001).

In the 1960s and 1970s, a "Hawaiian renaissance" took root, and in 1978, a new state constitution designated Hawaiian and English as co-official (Warner 2001). In 1983, a group of parents established *'Aha Pūnana Leo* – Hawaiian "language nest" preschools that enable children to interact with fluent speakers entirely in Hawaiian and to cultivate fluency in Hawaiian language and culture. Today, Hawaiian-medium education serves 2,000 students of Hawaiian and non-Hawaiian ancestry in a co-ordinated set of schools, from preschool to public high schools and university programs. According to two of the program's co-founders, William Wilson and Kauanoe Kamanā (2001), Hawaiian-medium education has produced a new generation of speakers, demonstrated superior academic results, and created a more general climate of Hawaiian-language support.

Navajo immersion at Tséhootsooí Diné Bi'ólta'

Despite a relatively large number of speakers, the Navajo language faces an uncertain future. In 1970, Spolsky surveyed 3,500 Navajo 6 year olds, which revealed 90 percent to be fluent Navajo speakers (Spolsky 2002a). Twenty years later, a survey of 682 Navajo preschoolers found that over half were considered by their teachers to be English monolinguals (Platero 2001). "The Navajo language is at a crossroads," Benally and Viri (2005) state: "It is at a stage where it can . . . be strengthened in daily use, or it can continue to decline" (p. 106).

The status of Navajo spans classes A–C, depending on the community. Given this situation, the Navajo Nation has mandated Navajo-medium instruction in all its Head Start (federally funded) preschools. Some K-12 schools also have Navajo immersion programs. One of the better documented programs is at Tséhootsooí Diné Bi'ólta' (TDB, The Navajo School at the Meadow Between the Rocks), on the reservation's eastern border. When the program began in 1986, less than a tenth of the program's 5 year olds were considered "reasonably competent" Navajo speakers, but at the same time, they were identified as "limited English proficient" (Holm and Holm 1995; Arviso and Holm 2001: 204–5). The district opted for a voluntary immersion program that has blossomed into a full-immersion K-8 school with plans for expansion through grade twelve. Longitudinal program data show that Navajo immersion students consistently outperform their peers in English-only classrooms in English reading, writing, and mathematics while developing strong oral and written Navajo skills (Holm and Holm 1995; Johnson and Legatz 2006). Moreover, program co-founder Wayne Holm states, "What the children and their parents taught us was that Navajo immersion gave students Navajo pride" (2006: 33).

Summary: Language revitalization "from the bottom up"

The foregoing examples illustrate grass roots or "bottom up" language planning (Hornberger 1996). Wopanaak (class E in Krauss' (1998) framework) is being repositioned from the pages of history to a living language of new speakers. The MALLP is successfully revitalizing Native California languages (class D) and has been adapted by other tribes. Hawaiian language revitalization (class C–D) began with a few parents whose efforts made Hawaiian-medium education available from preschool to graduate school. Tséhootsooí Diné Bi'ólta' is marshalling community resources to strengthen Navajo (class A–C) and enhance student achievement.

These programs exemplify the variety of Native American language revitalization projects under way throughout the USA (for additional examples, see Hinton and Hale 2001; McCarty and Zepeda 2006). All are part of a national language revitalization movement that has brought about significant policy change at the federal level, including the 1990/92 Native American Languages Act and the 2006 Esther Martinez Native American Languages Preservation Act, which support the teaching and restoration of Native American languages.

Conclusions

Native American languages are characterized by both their diversity and the increasing threats to that diversity. The vitality of these languages has been profoundly shaped by a history of colonization, missionization, and linguistic and cultural oppression, which have precipitated language loss. The fact that so many Native American languages are still spoken is testimony to the tenacity of Native American communities and tribal self-determination. Today, the primary public presence of the 175 Native-American languages still spoken is in local domains. However, media, technology, and schooling are increasingly prominent outlets for promoting Native languages and the cultural knowledge they embody.

This chapter has briefly explored some of the promising language restoration initiatives under way. All are examples of language planning from the bottom up that has mobilized important "top-down" policy changes. Ultimately, each Native American community must decide on language planning options in accord with the local context, needs, and vision for present and future generations. The examples here suggest that when communities, families, and schools work in concert, much can be accomplished to ensure that Native American languages continue as vital learning resources for children and as living carriers of diverse Native American cultural identities.

DISCUSSION QUESTIONS

1. What are some of the unique characteristics of Native American languages and language communities, and what are the implications for language shift, revitalization, and maintenance?

2. How have schools been a force both for loss and for revitalization of Native American languages? How might schools be more effective resources for Native American language revitalization and maintenance?

---

4 Spanish in the USA

Kim Potowski and Maria Carreira

Introduction

Spanish is the most commonly spoken non-English language in the US, with the 2007 Census update citing 34.5 million speakers on the mainland (that is, excluding Puerto Rico, where it is spoken by nearly everyone). As noted in Table 1.1, there was a 62 percent growth in the Spanish-speaking population between 1990 and 2000 and a further 23 percent growth between 2000 and 2007. In fact, it is predicted that Latinos – a term we will be using interchangeably with "Hispanics" – may contribute more net growth to the US population than all other groups combined after 2020 (US Census Bureau 2000). What surprises many people is that the USA has currently the fifth largest Spanish-speaking population in the world, with more Spanish-speakers than any other nation except Mexico, Colombia, Spain and Argentina (CIA 2008).

Spanish is also the non-English language that hails from the greatest number of different countries. In total, Spanish-speakers from nineteen different Latin American countries were present in the "Hispanic" category of the 2000 Census. The Spanish spoken in these countries is mutually intelligible for the most part, yet different linguistic and cultural backgrounds create an interesting Spanish-speaking mosaic in the USA. As we will see in this chapter, there are many factors that appear to favor the maintenance of the Spanish language in the USA, yet despite its strong presence in the media and many educational efforts, shift to English is clearly happening by the third generation.

History

Spanish, like all Romance languages, originally derived from Latin. This particular dialect of Latin was spoken in northern Spain. It rose to prominence during the "Reconquest," when Christian kingdoms in northern Spain fought to take control of southern Spain from the Moors, an Arabic-speaking group who had invaded the Iberian Peninsula in 711. In 1492, when the last Moor stronghold fell to the northern military, Queen Isabel of Castile and King Ferdinand of Aragon declared that the dialect of Castile, called Castilian, would be the official language of the kingdom. In common usage today, "Castilian" is synonymous with "Spanish." Over the next centuries, waves of Spanish explorers and colonists transported the Spanish language to Latin America and other parts of the world (Penny 2002). As is common with most languages, Spanish underwent many changes in its new homelands, and today there are marked differences in how Spanish is spoken around the world. Yet for the most part, people can understand each other, in much the same way that English speakers from the USA, the UK, Australia, and India can understand each other despite dialect differences.

In what is currently US territory, Spanish has been spoken since the sixteenth century, when Spanish explorer Ponce de León arrived in Florida in 1513. The Spaniards founded St. Augustine soon thereafter, in 1565, which is now the oldest continuously occupied European settlement in the modern territory of the USA. As the size of the USA expanded due to wars and land purchases, its Spanish-speaking population increased. For example, when the USA made the Louisiana Purchase from the French in 1803, there were many Spanish speakers who had moved to that area when it briefly belonged to Spain from 1763–1800. However, the largest increase of Spanish speakers came with the end of the Mexican–American war in 1848, when Mexico lost nearly half of its territory, including all of modern-day California, Nevada, and Utah, and parts of modern-day Arizona, Colorado, New Mexico, Texas, and Wyoming. This annexation resulted in all of the territory's Spanish-speaking Mexican residents becoming American citizens overnight. Finally, the Spanish–American War of 1898 saw the annexation of Cuba and Puerto Rico. Cuba gained its independence in 1902, but Puerto Rico remained a territory of the USA, where Spanish is the first language and the citizens hold US citizenship.

More recent influxes of Spanish speakers include Mexican workers brought in under the "bracero" programs during World War I, Cuban "Marielitos" in the 1980s and the "Balseros" in the 1990s, many economically motivated groups from Puerto Rico and the Dominican Republic, and Central Americans fleeing civil unrest in the latter part of the twentieth century. The Center for Immigration Studies (2003) estimates that an average of 1.5 million legal and undocumented immigrants arrive in the US each year, 46 percent of whom come from Spanish-speaking Latin American countries. Mexico is the country of origin of most of these immigrants (64 percent). Other countries that contribute large numbers of immigrants are El Salvador, Cuba, the Dominican Republic, Guatemala, and Colombia (US Census Bureau 2003a).[1]

Demographics

In 2000, Census-counted Hispanics constituted 14 percent of the US population.[2] However, their demographic presence varies widely from one

Table 4.1. *States with the largest Spanish-speaking populations*

	Ages 5 +	Percentage of all US Spanish speakers
California	9,212,392	28.56
Texas	5,932,609	18.39
Florida	3,031,002	9.39
New York	2,454,592	7.61
Illinois	1,450,811	4.49
Arizona	1,155,803	3.58
New Jersey	1,078,532	3.34
Georgia	547,778	1.69
Colorado	515,762	1.59
New Mexico	485,757	1.50
Total in USA	34,547,077	

Source: Modern Language Association 2009, US Census Bureau 2007c.

state to another. For example, the nation's highest concentrations of Hispanics are found in New Mexico (which is 44% Latino), California (36%), Texas (35%), Arizona (29%), Nevada (24%), and Florida (20%). By contrast, Latinos make up just 1% of the population of Vermont. Table 4.1 displays the ten states with the largest Spanish-speaking populations. It is worth noting, though, that while some areas are relatively sparsely populated – particularly in New Mexico and western Texas – they have very high concentrations of Latinos. Some cities, such as New York, Los Angeles, Chicago, and Houston, have both large raw numbers and high concentrations of Hispanics. We will see later how geographic concentration has a positive effect on minority language maintenance.

In addition, as is evident from Table 4.2, Latinos are largely urban dwellers. 92 percent reside in a metropolitan area or in close proximity to one. Accordingly, in all but two of the ten largest American cities (Philadelphia and Detroit), the Latino presence amply exceeds the national average of 14 percent.

Approximately 70 percent of US Latinos – that is, 28 million out of the 42 million Hispanics in the USA – speak Spanish at home. This means that one out of ten American households is Spanish speaking (Pew Hispanic Center 2007), although it is important to remember that of all US Spanish speakers, 71 percent claim to speak English "very well" or "well" (US Census Bureau 2007c). The ratio of Spanish speakers is significantly higher in areas of high Latino concentration such as those represented in Table 4.2 – for example, 92 percent of households in Hialeah, Florida, near Miami, are Spanish speaking.

Table 4.2. *Ten largest urban areas in total population and in Latino population*

City and state	Rank by total population	Rank by Hispanic population	Percent Latino of total population
New York, NY	1	1	27.0
Los Angeles, CA	2	2	46.5
Chicago, IL	3	3	26.0
Houston, TX	4	4	37.4
Philadelphia, PA	5	24	8.5
Phoenix, AZ	6	6	34.1
San Diego, CA	7	9	25.4
Dallas, TX	8	8	35.6
San Antonio, TX	9	5	58.7
Detroit, MI	10	72	5.0

Source: US Census Bureau 2000a.

Thus, in terms of demographics, the US Latino population and its Spanish-speaking contingent are both numerically large and geographically concentrated. Geographic concentration has been shown to play a major role in the preservation of minority languages (Portes and Rumbaut 1996, 229). In particular, regarding Spanish, Alba *et al.* (2002) found that a third generation Cuban child living in Miami, where 50 percent of the population is Spanish-speaking, is twenty times more likely to be bilingual than a child living in an area where just 5 percent of the population speaks this language. A similar, though smaller, effect was found to hold for Mexicans as well. The other primary factor correlated with Spanish maintenance was whether or not the parents had married a Spanish speaker.

According to the 2000 Census, the three largest Hispanic groups in the USA are Mexican (59%), Puerto Rican (10%), and Cuban (4%). Typically there have been large concentrations of Mexicans in the Southwest, Puerto Ricans in the Northeast, and Cubans in Miami. However, more diverse communities are beginning to emerge. Table 4.2 displays the ten largest groups and the cities they most commonly live in. Larger US cities such as New York, Los Angeles and Chicago are also beginning to see individuals of mixed Hispanic ethnicity, such as "MexiRicans" (Rúa 2001; Potowski 2008).

Of the US Latino population, it is estimated that 40 percent are foreign-born (see Table 4.3) and 60 percent are born in the USA. This distinction can be important for language use and retention. Those Hispanics born abroad have usually experienced sustained and often monolingual development in Spanish. Research has indicated that the later the age at which home Spanish speakers begin to acquire English, the stronger their Spanish grammatical systems will be

Table 4.3. *Ten largest Hispanic groups by country of ethnic origin*

National origin	Total number	Percentage of US Latino population
Mexico	20,640,711	58.5
Puerto Rico	3,406,178	9.6
Cuba	1,241,685	3.5
Dominican Republic	764,945	2.2
El Salvador	655,165	1.9
Colombia	470,684	1.3
Guatemala	372,487	1.1
Ecuador	260,559	0.7
Peru	233,926	0.7
Honduras	217,569	0.6

Source: US Census Bureau 2000a.

(Montrul 2002). US Hispanics have the highest birth rate in the nation, thus the proportion of US-born Latinos may soon become even larger than it already is. As we will see in a later section, there is a strong tendency for Spanish speakers to shift to English by the third generation in the USA. Therefore, these demographic trends indicate that the presence of Spanish in the USA is being bolstered by the new arrival of monolingual immigrants, but not by those who are the grandchildren of these immigrants.[3]

Public presence of Spanish

The previous section showed that Spanish speakers are numerous and concentrated. This section will present a brief description of the presence of Spanish in public life in the USA, which is quite large given the numbers of Spanish speakers in the nation. One can be attended to in Spanish over the telephone and in person for many basic services including the Department of Motor Vehicles, police, hospitals, utility companies, banks, fast-food restaurants, supermarkets, many libraries, and airports, either because Spanish service is officially offered by the organization or because it employs individuals who are Spanish speakers. In this section we will focus on the presence of Spanish in government, the media, business, and education.

Government

In the realm of government, public policy, and politics, Spanish presents a mixed profile. On the one hand, many Americans see it as a threat to their country's identity and linguistic integrity. On the other, elected officials see it as a critical tool for communicating effectively with the Latino population and gaining its support. Chapter 1 presented information on the status of official language statutes in the USA. As of 2007, twenty-one states have laws declaring English an official language. In many cases, it was the presence of Spanish speakers that prompted such legislation in the first place. For example, Spanish is commonly thought to be a co-official language in New Mexico, yet in reality that state was declared "English Plus" in 1989. Despite the existence of official English laws in Arizona and California, Spanish is still spoken widely throughout these states, and many government documents and services are available in both English and Spanish. In fact, government agencies in most states and at the federal level can commonly communicate in Spanish.

Beginning with Bill Clinton's administration, the State of the Union address and other Presidential speeches have been translated into Spanish (available at www.whitehouse.gov). Even some non-Hispanic politicians have delivered speeches in Spanish to Hispanic majority constituencies. This speaks to the strong and growing political presence of Latinos in the USA.

The 2007–08 presidential primaries offer a particularly revealing example of the dual status of US Spanish. Wooing the Latino electorate, the democratic candidates took part in the first-ever Presidential debate on a Spanish-language network on September 9, 2007. Throughout the evening, the candidates explained their positions on the most important issues impacting the Latino community, notably immigration, the economy, education, and the war. However, when the debate veered toward the issue of language, they found themselves in an uncomfortable spot. Asked if they would be willing to promote Spanish as the second official language in the USA, only one candidate, Dennis Kucinich, answered in the affirmative. Chris Dodd, on the other hand, opined that we should teach more Spanish, but not as an official second language. The rest of the candidates avoided a straight answer (Lovato 2007).

Media

Multiple types of media are widely available in Spanish, either created in the USA or imported from Latin America or Spain. In 2007, there were 730 radio stations and 200 television stations broadcasting in Spanish in the USA (Arbitron 2007). While the foreign-born make up the largest share of this market, US Latinos also rely on this media. Traditionally, it was believed that as soon as US Hispanics learned enough English, they preferred their advertising, public service announcements, and news in English. But media consumption trends show that even Latinos who are very fluent in English prefer receiving certain information in Spanish, including information about US Latinos and about Latin America, sports, music, and some advertising. In fact, in Los Angeles and Miami, Spanish-language television and radio have a larger audience than their English-language counterparts. Likewise, in New York City – the nation's largest radio market – Spanish-language stations La Mega 97.9 and AMOR 93.1 occupy the second and third spots in terms of market share (Arbitron). Spanish is also widely present in newspapers and other print forms. In 2006, Western Publication Research documented nearly 1,851 print publications in the USA written wholly or partially in Spanish. These include 38 dailies, 384 weekly newspapers, and 513 magazines (Whistler 2007).

Illustrating the financial success of this market, Whistler (2007: 1) states:

> This year we can note that Hispanic Print, at $1.54 billion, has surpassed the ad revenues for the UK's magazine revenues and Internet revenues, which are about $1.3 billion each.

As for the Spanish book market in the USA, industry consultants Kiser and Associates put its size at $350 million and document more than one hundred wholesalers and retailers in this country that specialize in Spanish-language material (Kiser and Associates n.d.). Notwithstanding these impressive figures, the Spanish-language book market faces significant challenges. These include the limited availability of Spanish-language titles in mainstream bookstores and libraries, the preference for English-language books among acculturated Latinos, and the inherent difficulty of selling books to a market as linguistically and culturally diverse as the US Latino market (Rodríguez-Martín 2006).

Business

Commercially speaking, the size and concentration of the Latino population translates into a market that is lucrative both locally and nationally. Countless public and private enterprises serve this market, particularly in Miami, which *Time* magazine described as "the frontier city between 'America' and Latin America," where the Latin American headquarters of AT and T, General Motors, Disney, and Iberia Airlines among many others have been established, and where "[the city's] success has been its ability to use its immigrant population to offer American products and business savvy in a Latin environment" (Booth 2001). The linguistic impact of these and other enterprises is threefold: (1) They fuel the need for a bilingual Spanish–English workforce, (2) They elevate the economic and social profile of Spanish in this country (Carreira 2002), and (3) They are a source of rich linguistic input for US Latinos, providing opportunities for them to use Spanish in their everyday lives (however, see the findings of Gorman and Potowski (2009), cited earlier, suggesting that there may not be much contact between these groups).

Given the tremendous buying power of the US Latino market – the largest Spanish-speaking market and the ninth largest overall market in the world – this group's language preferences are increasingly studied and heeded by marketers (Business Editors 2002).

Education

This section will explore the teaching of Spanish both as a foreign language and as a heritage language in the USA. Spanish is the most widely taught non-English language in US high schools and postsecondary institutions. Of the 1.4 million US college students enrolled in language courses in fall 2002, Spanish was studied by 53 percent of them (Welles 2004). At the secondary level, the numbers are even more impressive. In 2000, 69 percent of high school foreign language students were studying Spanish, for a total of 6 million students (National Center for Education Statistics 2002b). Professionals from all walks of life – including this nation's most powerful politicians – are also learning Spanish. For members of Congress there's even a ten-week program called "Spanish on the Hill" (Jordan 1999).

In the larger US cities, the concentration of Latino students is remarkable. According to Stearns and Watanabe (2002), there are approximately 7,000 public schools in the USA with a Latino population between 50 percent and 100 percent, most notably Los Angeles, California (where 71% of public schools are over one half Latino), Miami-Dade County, Florida (58% of public schools), New York City (34%), and Chicago, Illinois (33%). Given the huge and growing presence of students who have some background in Spanish, there are also school-based Spanish programs created especially for US Spanish speakers who grew up speaking the language, but who typically have not been able to develop reading and writing skills in the language. These students are often called heritage speakers, a term which was defined in Chapter 1 of this book as referring to individuals who grow up in households where a minority language is spoken, yet they are schooled in the country's majority language. Such individuals usually end up functionally bilingual, but dominant in the majority language in which they were schooled. In our case, although children of Spanish-speaking immigrants usually maintain communicative competence in their family's heritage language, they often do not develop age-appropriate levels of literacy, vocabulary, and grammatical systems in it. This is why special curricula have been developed for heritage speakers that address their specific communicative strengths and needs.

Despite the strong need for Spanish for heritage speaker programs, a survey conducted by the National Foreign Language Center and the American Association of Teachers of Spanish and Portuguese found that only 18 percent of US colleges and universities offered such courses (Ingold *et al.* 2002). At the high school level, the lack of heritage courses is even more pronounced, with only 9 percent of schools in 1997 offering such courses (Rhodes and Branaman

1999). This means that the majority of Spanish heritage speakers in the USA receive instruction in Spanish as a foreign language. In a later section, we will explore how heritage programs may better contribute to heritage language maintenance.

There are also some forms of education at the elementary level that promote foreign and heritage language learning. One-way immersion teaches foreign languages to English-speaking children during a significant portion of the school day (Center for Applied Linguistics 2006a). Two-way immersion also teaches a minority language during a large percentage of the day, but the classrooms contain a mixture of both English-speaking and heritage speaker children. By one estimate, 93 percent of US two-way immersion programs teach in Spanish (Center for Applied Linguistics 2006b). Finally, a program type called Foreign Languages in the Elementary Schools (FLES) teaches minority languages for just thirty to fifty minutes per day, three to four times per week. Currently, 25 percent of US elementary schools in the US offer FLES programs (Center for Applied Linguistics 2008), and the majority of them teach Spanish.

An interesting thing happens at elementary schools with FLES programs that also have large Latino populations: the FLES Spanish courses are filled with heritage Spanish-speaking children. Since these children already possess communicative competence in Spanish – even if they are actually dominant in English – such students typically do not get much out of a traditional FLES curriculum, which is designed for children learning Spanish as a foreign language. The same problem would occur if native speakers of English were to take courses in English as a Second Language. Some work has begun to address the needs of heritage speakers in K-8 contexts (New York State Education Department 2004; Carreira 2007; Potowski *et al.* 2008).

What seem to be missing from the US Spanish language landscape, however, are Saturday schools for Spanish-speaking schoolchildren. Rodriguez (2007) documents the efforts of several parent groups in Los Angeles to create such language and culture groups, noting that the Chinese- and Japanese-speaking communities in the area have had successful Saturday programs for years. While our co-contributors in this book document Saturday school efforts of several language groups around the nation, Spanish is noticeably absent in this regard. This may be due to family beliefs that children will acquire sufficient Spanish, constraints on family time and budget, and perhaps concern about children's English development, either real or based on public perception.

Evidence of language shift to English and of Spanish maintenance

In all, it is primarily demographic factors and market forces that are creating highly favorable conditions for the maintenance and growth of Spanish in the USA. However, linguistic research suggests that these forces alone cannot sustain it indefinitely. To live on, minority languages must reproduce themselves among successive generations in the US. In the case of Spanish, given that 60 percent of US Spanish speakers are born here, intergenerational transmission of Spanish will be crucial for its survival. Yet even in the immigrant generation, some Hispanics abandon the use of Spanish in favor of English (Veltman 2000: 81).

Before we discuss evidence of shift to English and of maintenance of Spanish in the USA, we will first offer a few general details about the Spanish language as it is spoken in various communities of the USA.[4] Given the large number of countries of origin of US Spanish speakers, there is no single US Spanish variety, but rather a rich multiplicity of types of Spanish spoken in the nation. In the Southwest, for example, one predominately hears Mexican varieties of Spanish, while in the Northeast and Southeast one predominately hears Caribbean Spanish.

Perhaps the most noticeable trait of US Spanish, used by Spanish speakers of all national backgrounds, is the mixture of Spanish and English in the same conversation. This common practice in many bilingual communities, described in Chapter 2 of this volume, is referred to as *code-switching*. Speakers can code-switch within a single sentence, such as "I got there at two o'clock *pero ya no estaban* [but they weren't there anymore]," or between separate sentences, such as "*Dijo que no quería jugar* [He said he didn't want to play]. He had too much homework." Sometimes a code-switch within a sentence consists of just one word, such as "*Se quedó allí leyendo un* [He/she stayed there reading a] magazine." It is important to realize that not all code-switches into English happen because the speaker does not know how to say certain things in Spanish – in fact, one study showed that fully 75 percent of code-switches were words that the speakers knew in both languages (Zentella 1997). So why do people switch into English or into Spanish instead of just sticking to one language, especially if they know all the words they need? It is a very common phenomenon in bilingual communities to code-switch in order to signal ethnic identity, quote someone directly, emphasize, clarify or elaborate what is said, or to shift topics, among other functions.

Other common features of US Spanish include the use of word *borrowings*, such as *nicle* for "nickel" and *wachar* for "to watch." It is often the case that today's criticized borrowings enter tomorrow's formal dictionaries, as was the case with *checar* for "to check." Another feature is called a *semantic extension*, in which words that mean one thing in monolingual Spanish-speaking countries take on a new meaning in the USA. For example, the word *librería* in monolingual contexts refers to a bookstore, but in the USA it has taken on the meaning of "library." Finally, entire phrases can be borrowed (or *calqued*) into Spanish, such as *correr para presidente* for "run for president."

Table 4.4. *Language dominance, by generation*

Language preference	Total Latinos (%)	First (foreign-born) (%)	Second (%)	Third (%)
English dominant	25	4	46	78
Bilingual (equal)	28	24	47	22
Spanish dominant	47	72	7	–

Source: Suro 2002: 13.

Some people refer to these phenomena as "Spanglish," while others reject this term as pejorative and not useful in distinguishing very different processes from each other. It is important to remember that whenever there are languages in contact, it is very likely that these phenomena will take place.

Signs of shift

Currently, a large majority of US Latinos (75 percent) speaks Spanish to some degree, while another 25 percent are for the most part restricted to English for communication. However, the number of Spanish-proficient Latinos is projected to decline over the course of this century as a result of intergenerational linguistic shift. As a general rule, the foreign-born strongly prefer their native language over English. But with each successive generation in the USA, mastery of this language declines sharply. By the third generation, few remain proficient in the language of their grandparents. This pattern has been amply attested among US Latinos (Table 4.4).

So far, the generational loss of Spanish speakers as shown in Table 4.4 has been offset by a steady flow of new immigrants from Latin America. However, with Latino birthrates rapidly outpacing immigration rates, the number of Spanish speakers will undoubtedly decline over the course of the century. The question is, by how much?

The weight of the evidence suggests that the ongoing generational loss of Spanish is both swift and pervasive. For example Veltman (2000) provides evidence that Spanish speakers are more likely to adopt English today than their older peers did when they were young, concluding that the ability of Latinos to maintain dominant use of Spanish has receded significantly since 1976 (see also Rivera-Mills 2001).[5] In a recent study of Southern California, Rumbaut, Massey, and Bean (2006) found that "the ability to speak Spanish very well can be expected to disappear sometime between the second and third generation for all Latin American groups" (p. 458). Many scholars, including Hudson-Edwards, Hernández Chávez, and Bills (1995) believe that American-born Latinos alone cannot sustain Spanish in this country:

> maintenance of Spanish in the Southwest, in terms of raw numbers of speakers only, is heavily dependent upon a steady transfusion of speakers from Mexico to communities in the United States, and offer no warrant for the survival of Spanish beyond a point when such speakers are no longer available to replace speakers north of the border lost through mortality or linguistic assimilation. (p. 182)

Closer examination of the grammatical systems of individual US Latinos also reveals signs of language shift. Silva-Corvalán (1994) showed that many verbal constructions, such as the subjunctive, the conditional, and compound verb tenses, are far less frequent in the Spanish of third generation speakers than second and first generation speakers. Lipski (1993) also outlines some of the characteristics of Spanish speakers with very low proficiency, while Montrul (2002, 2005, 2007) has shown that several underlying grammatical representations are not acquired by Latinos raised bilingually in the USA. Thus, by the third generation, US Hispanics are dominant in English, and their Spanish – when they can speak it at all – shows signs of incomplete acquisition, attrition, and many contact features.

Signs of maintenance

The previous section outlined evidence of shift to English. However, some recent research suggests that the generational loss of Spanish may not be as radical as previously believed. For example, contradicting Veltman (2000), a survey from the Pew Hispanic Center/Kaiser Family Foundation (2004: 5) indicates that more than one half of third generation Latino adults are relatively proficient in Spanish, suggesting that "the loss of speaking competence in Spanish in favor of English may not happen as comprehensively, rapidly and readily as some scholars suggest." That said, it bears noting that this last study also found telling signs of language shift. In particular, Latino parents indicated that English is the primary language used by their children when speaking to their friends. Also, bilingual Latinos reported making more extensive use of English than Spanish outside of the home environment.

Comparing data from the 1980, 1990, and 2000 US Census reports, Mora, Villa, and Dávila (2006) argue that there is actually a high degree of transmission of Spanish between first and second generation Latinos. Similarly, in their study of third generation Cuban and Mexican children that we cited earlier, Alba *et al.* (2002) found lower rates of English-only speakers – that is, higher rates of bilinguals – than was observed for Europeans in the early twentieth century and among current third generation immigrants from Asia. This study also found that family and community contexts are better predictors of linguistic proficiency among third generation Cubans and Mexicans than is generational standing; Torres and Potowski (2008) also found that generation was not as tightly bound to Spanish proficiency as is often believed. All things

Table 4.5. *The Latino market by generational distance*

	Generational distance	Percentage of the Latino population	Percentage of life in the USA	Language
Foreign-born	Newcomers	18	Less than 1/3	Spanish only
	Transitionals	21	1/3 to 2/3	Spanish mostly
	Transplants	22	Greater than 1/3	Equally bilingual
US-born	Maintainers	25	100%	Mostly bilingual*
	Adapters	14	100%	English only

Note: * Although these terms are not defined in the original publication, we take this term to mean that the person speaks mostly English but has fairly strong communicative ability in Spanish.
Source: Allen and Friedman 2005: 85.

being equal, children from families that are supportive of Spanish and who live in high-density ethnic neighborhoods in regions with a biethnic identity have the highest chance of becoming bilingual, underscoring the role of geographic concentration in the preservation of US Spanish.

Coming from a different perspective, market research indicates that length of residency in the USA and affective factors play a decisive role in shaping the linguistic profile of US Latinos. Using the concept of "generational distance," this line of research identifies five subpopulations of US Latinos, as shown in Table 4.5. With the exception of *Adapters*, who can only be reached in English, many Latinos are more emotionally receptive to advertising done in Spanish. Interestingly, the distinguishing feature between Adapters and *Maintainers*, both of whom are American-born and English dominant, appears to be the home culture. Maintainers come from homes where the cultural values and customs of the parents' home country predominate over those of the mainstream Anglo US culture – hence their emotional attachment to things Hispanic, including the language. By contrast, adapters come from largely Americanized homes (Allen and Friedman 2005).

An important question to explore is whether US Latinos consider it important for themselves to know Spanish. Some research indicates that they do in fact consider Spanish an important component of their identity, yet most studies point to the belief that one can be equally Latino whether one knows Spanish or not (for example Zentella 1997).

Spanish does have a good deal of international status, which may contribute in some degree to its maintenance in the USA. In all, there are over 400 million people in the world that speak it, making it the fourth most spoken language in the world after Chinese, Hindi, and English (Graddol 2000). And in almost all of the countries where Spanish is spoken, it is the official national language, dominant over local or indigenous languages (often in much the same way that

English is dominant over Spanish in the USA). The Royal Spanish Academy (*Real Academia Española*), a widely respected institution founded in Spain in 1713, serves to regulate formal matters of the language through the publication of dictionaries and grammars. A number of academies were also founded in Latin American and North America throughout the nineteenth and twentieth centuries, and in 1951 they joined to form the Association of Spanish Language Academies (*Asociación de Academias de la Lengua Española*), with a total of twenty-two members. The USA is also home to three of the more than seventy centers of the Cervantes Institute, an organization created by the government of Spain to promote Spanish language and culture, which now has centers in thirty nations around the world.

However, the domestic status of the language in the USA is clearly not as high as in Latin America or Spain. In addition to the negative comments one may hear in public when speaking Spanish (or any other non-English language, in fact), there have also been widely publicized cases of discrimination against speaking Spanish. For example, in 1995 a Texas judge ruled that a mother who spoke Spanish to her daughter was committing a type of child abuse and threatened to take away custody (Verhovek 1995); in 2004, an Arizona teacher made the news for hitting children who spoke Spanish in class (Ryman and Madrid, 2004); in New York, three women were fired from a Sephora beauty store for speaking Spanish during their breaks (Valenti 2003); and in Kansas City, a high school student was suspended for speaking Spanish in the hallway (Reid 2005). The sad irony that the most studied foreign language in the nation is criticized when spoken by those who actually speak it natively is an example of mainstream US attitudes toward non-English languages: it seems that many people feel these languages should be spoken only abroad, not on US territory.

Conclusions

Spanish is the most publicly present and vibrant non-English language spoken in the USA, the language most studied in high schools and universities, the language most people will tell you that they wish they could speak. Ironically, US public school policies do not typically allow heritage Spanish-speaking children the opportunity to continue developing age-appropriate communication and literacy skills in Spanish, nor is public use of Spanish always welcomed by the general populace.

In spite of strong public presence stemming from large numbers and demographic concentration, there are clear indications that the future vitality of Spanish in the USA rests on continued immigration from Latin America. Intergenerational transmission of the language rarely extends beyond the grandchildren of immigrants. An increase in truly bilingual programs, such as dual immersion, may contribute to the longevity of Spanish through the generations,

Table 4.6. *Discussion question #2*

City = Group 1 = Group 2 =		1990 Census	2000 Census
Percentage of local Latino population	Group 1		
	Group 2		
Percentage of total local population	Group 1		
	Group 2		

but it seems more likely that, as the Latino population shifts entirely to English, the Spanish language will continue to thrive only through the arrival of new monolingual speakers.

DISCUSSION QUESTIONS

1. The authors cite a study (Alba *et al.* 2002) in which a third generation Cuban child living in Miami is twenty times more likely to be bilingual than a child living in another town where just 5 percent of the population speaks Spanish. Describe some of the experiences that you think the child would encounter in Miami (and not in the other town) that would lead to stronger proficiency in Spanish.

2. Choose one of the cities from Table 4.2 in this chapter. Using the US Census website, complete Table 4.6 with as many details as you can, including the area's two largest national origin groups (Group 1 and Group 2). Then, make predictions about the proliferation and maintenance of Spanish in the area.

5 Chinese in the USA

Yun Xiao

Introduction

According to the 2007 American Community Survey conducted by the US Census Bureau, Chinese is the second most common non-English language in the USA (Table 1.1). Chinese is also the most commonly spoken language in the world, spoken by approximately one fifth of the world's population, including the 1.3 billion people living in China. Also indicated in the Census was a 75 percent increase in the US Chinese-origin population, from 1,645,472 in 1990 to 2,879,636 in 2000 (forming 1.02 percent of the US population). The data also suggest that, rather than forming a totally assimilated group, the Chinese population is a relatively new immigrant group, in that 70.8 percent of them were foreign-born, with or without a naturalized citizenship, as compared with 10.1 percent of the overall total foreign-born population in the USA. Moreover, out of the Chinese foreign-born, 75.6 percent arrived after 1980, which indicates that the majority of the Chinese population in the USA is comprised of individuals who arrived as adults or between the ages of 6 and 18 who have fully or partially acquired Chinese as a first language.

Studies on East Asian languages show that, like the other minority languages in the USA, there is a fast and prevalent generational language shift among recent Asian immigrants and their descendants in the USA (Kondo-Brown 2006). Research on Chinese as a heritage language also reveals increasing attrition (Xiao 2008a). This chapter will explore issues of Chinese-language maintenance and shift in the USA.

History

Chinese belongs to the Sino-Tibetan language family and is the oldest written language in the world, with a history of almost four thousand years. It is also one of the few written languages with a pictographic origin, which grew and developed over time into characters. The history of the Chinese language can be traced back to the period known as the Shang Dynasty (1600–1100 BCE), during which texts were inscribed on bones and shells. Due to the intensive

	horse	doctor	listen	buy	sell	country
Traditional character form:	馬	醫	聽	買	賣	國
Simplified character form:	马	医	听	买	卖	国

Figure 5.1. Comparison of traditional and simplified Chinese character forms

labor of production in which many people were engaged, the Shang texts tended to be short and formulaic. This tradition was extended to the succeeding Zhou dynasty (1100–300 BCE), the time period when Confucius' and Mencius' works were most influential. Terse and monosyllabic, early written Chinese was not for mass communication but for official use or scholarly works, and was drastically different from the spoken form.

The dialect spoken by the people in the Han Dynasty (206 BCE–220 CE) was eventually recognized as "the" Chinese language, known as *Hanyu* (the language of the *Han* nationality); and its writing symbols were known as *Hanzi*, the script of the *Han* Chinese (*Xinhua Cidan* 2001: 378). Today, the position of the Chinese government is that the Chinese language encompasses seven major regional dialects, including Mandarin, *Wu*, *Xiang*, *Yue* (Cantonese), *Gan*, *Min*, and *Hakka* – although most of these are not dialects of a single language but actually mutually unintelligible languages – which are spoken by fifty-six different ethnic groups in China and united by the *Hanzi* script.

In 1949, when the People's Republic of China was founded, Mandarin Chinese was declared the nation's official language, and both the pronunciation and the script underwent reforms. The multidialect pronunciation was standardized on the basis of the *Beijing* dialect and represented by a new romanization system called *pinyin* (which means "the combination of sounds"). This standardized Mandarin Chinese is called *Putonghua*, the national "common language," and is mandated to be used as the instructional medium in mainstream schools. At the same time, the written form was simplified, with the strokes of the 2,000 most frequently used characters reduced on average from 11.2 to 7 each (Wu 1978) (see Figure 5.1). With the Chinese government's continuous effort in standardizing written Chinese and promoting *Putonghua*, the most recent official Survey on Chinese Language Use from 1998–2001 (中国语言文字使用情况调查报告) revealed that 95.25 percent of the total Chinese population use the standard *Putonghua* written form for written communication, while 53.06 percent can communicate with *Putonghua*, and 86.38 percent can do so with regional Mandarin dialects. Moreover, the younger and more educated the speakers are, the more likely they are to use *Putonghua*.

Specifically, 70.12 percent of the people of age 15–29 speak *Putonghua*, as do 86.77 percent of those with a college education and beyond. Meanwhile, other regional dialects and languages are still being used at the local level. For instance, Cantonese is popular in Hong Kong, *Min* in *Fijian* Province, and *Gan* in *Jiangxi* Province. Due to the remarkable diversity of speakers' linguistic backgrounds, "Chinese" has a number of synonyms. It is named *Putonghua* or *Hanyu* in China, *Guoyu* (national language) in Taiwan, and Mandarin or Chinese in the rest of the world.

By and large, Chinese was not heard in the USA until the 1840-era California Gold Rush, when the first wave of Chinese immigrants arrived. Following these pioneers, Chinese immigration into the USA went through ups and downs, following the pulse of US–China relations and US immigration policies. The first-wave arrivals were mostly Cantonese-speaking peasants or fishermen by origin. Poorly educated and culturally ill prepared, they started the journey with a dream of finding fortune in the "Gold Mountain" but ended up struggling in an environment dogged by inequality and racial discrimination, as manifested in the Chinese Exclusion Act in 1882. This Act suspended the immigration of skilled and unskilled Chinese laborers for ten years and prohibited the naturalization of any Chinese citizens. It greatly slowed Chinese immigration and limited opportunities for the Chinese population already in the USA. Excluded and marginalized, most of the Chinese immigrants were congregated in Chinatowns in the western states and territories. By the time of the 1870 Census, there were 63,199 Chinese living in the USA, of whom 78 percent resided in California (Chang 2003: 93). Seeing no opportunities in the new land, they saw renewed hope in their homeland and hence prepared their children for return to China with Chinese language and cultural training (Koehn and Yin 2002).

Subsequently, there were two more major waves of Chinese immigration: one was spurred by the 1949 Communist revolution and the other by the dramatic changes in the late 1970s. Compared with their first-wave counterparts, the second- and third-wave arrivals were not only more educated and financially better off but also happened to arrive in better times and better environments, improved first by the enactment of new immigration policies in 1965 and then by the normalization of US–China relations, as well as China's historic open-door and economic reforms in the late 1970s. Instead of using the receiving country as a springboard for a better life in their homeland, the later arrivals view the USA as a land of opportunities and have the desire to assimilate into the host culture, and hence they prepare their children for mainstream language and job skills.

The second-wave arrivals (1949–79) were mostly from Chinese-speaking regions other than mainland China, such as Taiwan or Hong Kong, due to the fact that US–China relations were not normalized during that period. By 1980, there were 812,178 persons of Chinese origin (0.36 percent of the US population)

Table 5.1. *States with the largest Chinese-speaking populations*

	Ages 5 +	Percentage of all US Chinese speakers
California	519,940	33.53
New York	290,454	18.73
Texas	83,641	5.39
New Jersey	74,593	4.81
Massachusetts	63,490	4.09
Illinois	54,773	3.53
Pennsylvania	42,193	2.72
Maryland	39,898	2.57
Washington	36,590	2.35
Virginia	29,667	1.91
Total in USA	2,464,572	

Source: Modern Language Association 2009, US Census Bureau 2007c.

living in the USA. Compared with the second wave, the third wave of Chinese immigration was characterized by (1) a rapid influx of arrivals (which more than tripled from 1980 to 2000) and (2) the largest number of Chinese scholars and students in American history, who spoke Mandarin Chinese and tended to affiliate themselves with American universities or research institutions (Chang 2003). The number of Chinese students, scholars, and their families who entered the USA increased from just 1,000 in 1979 to over 50,000 in 1999 (Li 2002). By 2006, there were 98,307 Chinese-speaking students in the USA, forming 17.38 percent of international students. Moreover, with the speedy development of US–China commerce and trade, the influx of Chinese speakers includes not only scholars and students but also business professionals, convention attendees, and tourists, with a total of 320,000 from China alone in 2006, up 19 percent from 2005 (Office of Travel and Tourism Industries 2007).

Demographics

Since the pioneer Chinese immigrants landed in the West in the mid-nineteenth century, California has been the hub of Chinese immigrants in the USA, with later arrivals gradually spreading to the Northeast and other regions. Table 5.1 shows the ten states with the largest Chinese-speaking populations. The list is topped by California and New York, where one finds the largest Chinatowns – both longstanding communities and new ones that have sprung out of old ones,

Table 5.2. *Cities with Chinese American populations greater than 30,000 people*

City and state	Rank by Chinese population	Number of Chinese speakers	Percent Chinese of total population
San Francisco, CA	1	160,947	20.7
Queens, NY	2	147,037	6.6
Brooklyn, NY	3	125,358	5.1
Manhattan, NY	4	91,588	6.0
Los Angeles, CA	5	73,868	2.0
Honolulu, HI	6	68,849	18.5
San Jose, CA	7	57,974	6.5
Chicago, IL	8	34,370	1.2
Oakland, CA	9	34,253	8.6
Fremont, CA	10	31,517	15.5
Alhambra, CA	11	31,099	36.2

Source: Chinese American Data Center n.d.

such as Monterey Park and Cupertino in California, and Flushing and Sunset Park in New York.

Table 5.2 shows the eleven US cities with Chinese populations over 30,000. Six of these are in California, with Alhambra being over 36 percent Chinese and San Francisco over 20 percent. Although there are only three cities in the state of New York in this category, the aggregated number is an eye-opening total of 363,983 people.

Despite such a long history of ethnic congregation, there has been rapid acquisition of English among Chinese-speaking communities. Data from the 2000 US Census show that, out of the two million Chinese speakers 5 years and older in the USA, the majority (70 percent) speak English "very well" or "well." More revealingly, there is a notable generational difference in language use. Bayley (2004: 274) reports that those above 18 years old used "mainly or only" English 47 percent of the time, while those under 18 used it 81 percent of the time. This is a clear indication that most of the younger generation have shifted from Chinese to English. Such data are at odds with the age-old assumption that Chinese immigrants were least likely among immigrant groups to adopt English as their usual language (Crawford 1992: 127). What factors contribute to the highly congregated and heritage-loyal Chinese immigrants and their descendants losing the battle to maintain their heritage language, just like other immigrant groups in this country? To raise the awareness of this issue, this chapter will, from various angles, provide data and evidence concerning Chinese as a heritage language in the USA.

Public presence of Chinese

The Chinese were one of the pioneer immigrant groups in the American west, but the influx did not build momentum until 1979, when US–China relations were normalized and China opened its doors to the international community with drastic economic reforms. Before long, China emerged as a global economic leader and the second-largest trade partner with the USA. This brought unprecedented attention to the Chinese language and Chinese speakers. They have – for the first time in history – entered the American mainstream in all spheres, such as government, business, media, and education. Chinese-language development has been recognized as being critical to US security and prosperity, and learning Chinese is no longer solely in the interest of immigrant families but a key issue for many mainstream Americans for international competition and success. The field of Chinese language learning has seen a number of significant initiatives at both local and federal levels, such as the newly established Chinese immersion programs at the K-12 level, called Chinese Flagship models, Advanced Placement programs, and STARTALK, a federally funded summer Chinese immersion program with options in the USA and abroad. These programs are discussed in more detail later in this chapter.

China's recent economic boom has rapidly increased its visibility and public presence in the USA and around the world. A survey of US public perception of the influence of different world nations shows that 60 percent of Americans believe that China is one of the countries with the most influence on the USA, and that China's economy will grow to overtake both Britain and Japan within ten years, becoming as large as the US economy within two decades (Chicago Council on Global Affairs 2006). The influence of China as an economic force has ushered in the "explosion of Chinese," in the words of an American parent whose daughter participated in the Portland Kindergarten Immersion Program:

> Mandarin has become a red hot language, surpassing more traditional European languages in interest, and Portland's Mandarin Immersion Program has emerged as a national model for K-12 Mandarin language instruction. Two years ago, Portland Public Schools joined forces with the University of Oregon and received a major federal grant to create a kindergarten-through-college instructional model for Mandarin. Now, educators and reporters from throughout the nation and the world come to Portland to see what we're doing and learn from our trials and errors. Our kids have been photographed, filmed, tested, taped, assessed and observed. Visiting dignitaries are a frequent sight in their classroom. (Brickson 2007: 1)

This echoes the increasingly common presence of Chinese in seemingly all domains, from business, trade, media, to education and international affairs, not to mention that many things we buy from the store are made in China.

Government

Like the major European languages such as French and Spanish, Chinese is a working language in the United Nations and one of the six languages used for the *United Nations Juridical Yearbook 2000*. In some US states such as California, Chinese is one of the non-English languages used for the publication of official state documents. In 1997, the US Library of Congress adopted the Chinese Romanization system – *pinyin* – for cataloging practices, bibliographic records, and online retrieval. Meanwhile, Chinese has had a significant presence on the US government's agenda. In 2006, US President George W. Bush launched the National Security Language Initiative to dramatically increase the number of Americans learning critically needed foreign languages, one of which was Chinese. In the meantime, fourteen US–China Institutes and twenty-one Confucius Institutes have been established in the past few years by a large number of higher education institutions in collaboration with the Chinese government, and sixty more are being planned for the near future. With a strategic focus on China–US relations, these institutes aim to promote, develop, and facilitate educational, cultural and trade exchanges, Chinese-language learning, and teacher training.

Media

Chinese-Americans have a long history of publishing their own newspapers (Zhao 2002). Since the 1850s, there have been more than 100 Chinese newspapers and journals, most of which were written in Chinese script, either in traditional or simplified character form. The largest daily Chinese-language publication is *World Journal* (世界日報, also known by its English subtitle *Chinese Daily News*), covering news from China, Hong Kong, Taiwan, and North America. It employs more than 1,000 journalists, with 25 reporters and 12 translators in the New York area alone. This paper is published by independent operations in cities including New York, Los Angeles, San Francisco, Chicago, Houston, Vancouver, and Toronto, and it is one of the few US daily newspapers distributed on a national basis, with a US circulation of almost 300,000.

Since China entered the global market in 1979, Chinese media has been opened to the rest of the world and undergone remarkable growth. Today numerous Chinese television channels and programs are either directly imported from China or created in the USA, with the leading ones being CCTV4, Phoenix's North America Chinese Channel (PSTV), KyLin TV (麒麟), New Chinese (新唐人), and South East TV (SETV). CCTV4 is China's central TV network, which has a daily share of time on the US International Channel. Phoenix's North America Chinese Channel is known as the "Chinese CNN,"

Table 5.3. *China's trade with the USA ($ billion)*

Year	2002	2003	2004	2005	2006	Quarter 1, 2007
US exports	22.1	28.4	34.7	41.8	55.2	14.5
Percentage change	15.1	28.5	22.2	20.5	32.1	15.5
US imports	125.2	152.4	196.7	243.5	287.8	71.4
Percentage change	22.4	21.7	29.1	23.8	18.2	19.3
Total	147.3	180.8	231.4	285.3	343.0	85.9
Percentage change	21.2	22.7	28.0	23.3	20.2	18.8
US balance	−103.1	−124.0	−162.0	−201.6	−232.5	−57.8

Source: US–China Business Council 2008.

which provides 24/7 news and locally produced programs with in-depth reports on issues of concern to Chinese communities, and which has the largest cohort of Chinese viewers in the USA. KyLin TV has just been born out of South East TV (SETV), a television station from the *Fujian* province in China, which provides twenty-six live broadcast channels that are watched by more than 700 million Chinese-speaking viewers worldwide. New Chinese (新唐人) is a newly established US-based independent channel, which is widely received by Chinese-speaking households through small household satellite dishes.

Moreover, since the advent of the internet, Chinese has become the second most frequently used language on the internet (after English), with more than 103 million users.

Business

China's international exports are growing at a thunderous rate. Between 1990 and 2004, the volume of Chinese exports increased by 850 percent (US–China Business Council 2008). During the same period, its share of world trade in manufactured goods rose from 2 percent to 11.5 percent. At the end of April 2007, China's global trade surplus hit $63.3 billion, 88 percent higher than in the first four months of 2006. China is now America's second-largest source of imports, as well as its fourth-largest export market, and is second only to Canada in total volume of trade with the USA (US–China Business Council 2008). In fact, US imports from China far exceed US exports to China, and the US bilateral trade deficit reached hundreds of billions of US dollars each year in the past five years, with $57 billion at the end of the first quarter alone in 2007 (see Table 5.3).

As shown in Table 5.3, there has been an enormous imbalance in China–US trade and commerce since 2002. As this imbalance presses ahead, Americans feel, more and more, the increasing pressure of international competition and the urgent need for Chinese language proficiency in the USA.

Education

Chinese-language education has long been neglected in mainstream American schools, with minimum or close to zero enrollments at all levels. A report on 2001–2 Chinese enrollments at the pre-collegiate level by the Secondary School Chinese Language Center indicated that 203 schools in 31 US states offered Chinese-language classes, with a total enrollment of 23,900 (McGinnis 2005a), which accounted for less than 1.3 percent of the total foreign language enrollment in this country (Wiley 2005a: 599). In addition, the 2006 College Board survey reported that, out of the fifty US states, only thirty three have established Chinese programs in elementary and secondary schools, with a total of 313 in the entire nation, ranging from fifty six in Massachusetts to one in Utah and zero in others.

A survey of two-way bilingual immersion programs[1] (Center for Applied Linguistics 2006a) revealed no better results. Specifically, there were only thirteen partial or total Chinese immersion programs across the country (including one Cantonese program), accounting for 4.2 percent of all two-way immersion programs. When we consider that Chinese has the second largest non-English speaking population in the USA, its enrollments are strikingly low at all levels. They are certainly not a mirror image of English enrollments in China, where hundreds of millions of children are studying English.

In 2005, the Asia Society asked an ambitious hypothetical question (Stewart and Wang 2005): What would it take to have 5 percent of all US high school students learning Chinese by 2015? One answer was to ameliorate the severe shortage of certified Chinese teachers. That is, the quantity and quality of Chinese-language teachers remain a key bottleneck (Asia Society & the College Board 2008). Although a few initiatives are underway, such as alternate route teacher licensure programs, there are only a few universities in the USA which are able to offer NCATE (National Council for Accreditation of Teacher Education) accredited Chinese teacher licensure, such as Ohio State University, New York University, University of Iowa, and University of Massachusetts at Amherst. At the strategic meeting held by the Asia Society and the College Board in May 2006, it was found that, unfortunately, only a handful of certificates had been granted by these universities in the previous five years.

However, there seems to be a slightly different story at the postsecondary level. Data show that Chinese enrollments at the university level have gained momentum much sooner and more quickly (although they are still low; see Table 5.4). Nonetheless, the number of students studying Chinese has been rapidly increasing since 1980. The 2006 MLA survey shows that there was a 20 percent increase in 2002 (over 1998) and a 51 percent increase from 2002 to 2006 (Furman *et al.* 2007).

Table 5.4. *Chinese enrollments at university level*

Year	Number of Chinese students	Percentage of all foreign language enrollments
1980	11,366	1.2
1990	19,490	1.6
1998	28,456	3.6
2002	34,153	2.4
2006	51,582	3.3

Source: Furman *et al.* 2007.

Moreover, a large number of the highest degree grantees in the USA are Chinese students. It is estimated that more than half of the currently received doctoral degrees in sciences and technology granted by US universities are to foreign students, out of whom the largest contingent are from China (Li 2002: 29). For example, there were 2,408 Chinese students who earned doctoral degrees in the USA in 1997, of whom 55.2 percent specialized in physical sciences and engineering. Furthermore, the majority of these Chinese students chose to remain in the USA after they earned their doctorate degrees, partly because they believe that China's existing technological capacity cannot meet their high expectations and what they learned in the USA cannot be applied in China immediately (Li 2002: 27). In other words, the USA is, to them, a land of opportunity and promise, which can realize their dreams and offer them a better future.

Evidence of language shift to English and of Chinese maintenance

Signs of shift

Extensive studies of heritage language (HL) issues report that immigrant children's heritage language literacy is lost after they enter mainstream schools (Wong-Fillmore 1991), where they are swept away by "an abrupt shift" from the heritage to the dominant language (Bougie *et al.* 2003: 349) and often encounter an intense disconnection between home and school literacy practices (McCarthey 1997). To gain acceptance, immigrant children typically drop their heritage language and make English their primary language (Pease-Alvarez *et al.* 1991; Li 2003, 2006a). In this section, I will present findings from studies on literacy, grammar, and identity that all point toward a similar loss of Chinese in the USA.

Li (2003) found that many Chinese immigrant children experienced discontinuity between home and school, and that their home literacy was incongruent with their school practices and was not valued by their school teachers. As a result, many were struggling with reading and writing in Chinese, which presented a significant dilemma for their parents. In another example, Xu (1999) found a remarkable disparity between Chinese and English literacy materials and activities in the homes of six kindergartners. Resources for English were abundant, yet those for Chinese were minimal, and the parents engaged their children in extensive English literacy activities with minimal attention to Chinese literacy. Although they agreed that their heritage was important, the parents believed that children needed strong English to earn college degrees in order to obtain decent jobs. In such home environments, the children's oral use of Chinese gradually decreased.

In another study of literacy, Xiao (2008b), using surveys and interviews, studied the correlation between the home literacy environment and Chinese heritage language (CHL) maintenance among 127 university CHL learners. Like Xu (1999), she found that the CHL home literacy environment contained inadequate reading materials and literacy activities for CHL maintenance. Most of the parents were concerned more about their children's English proficiency and schoolwork than with their CHL literacy development. Another significant finding was that, although CHL learners used Chinese with their parents, they did so only when the parents did not know English, and with their siblings they tended to use English even at home. Moreover, community CHL schools had restricted operations of two to three hours per week, insufficient funding and makeshift classrooms and facilities, and out-of-date teaching practices carried out by untrained volunteer instructors. The majority of the participants in the study complained about boredom and age- and level-inappropriate tasks in CHL schools.

In a study of eighty-five recent Chinese immigrants in New York City, Jia (2008) asked participants to rate their CHL speaking, reading and writing skills for each two-year interval of their residence in the USA, as well as their CHL use in various situations. Findings revealed that (1) with an increasing exposure to English and a steady growth of English skills, CHL skills increasingly declined over time, and (2) CHL reading and writing skills experienced larger scale attrition than speaking skills. In another study that connected length of residence in the USA to attrition of Chinese, Jia and Bayley (2008) investigated the acquisition of the Mandarin perfective aspectual marker *-le* by thirty-six CHL children and adolescents and found that the use of *-le* declined as the length of residence in the USA increased, especially among adolescents. The researchers suggested that as learners moved into adolescence, the demands on their time for school success (in English) increased, and their social lives increasingly took place in English outside of the home. As a result, their language use largely shifted to English.

Koda *et al.* (2008) explored CHL development among third through fifth grade CHL students on morphological awareness and reading comprehension. The researchers found that, as the students entered higher grade levels, they did not perform significantly better on either type of task. The researchers also found that these children received primary literacy instruction in English at school and pursued ancillary literacy in weekend CHL school, where the input available to the children was heavily restricted in quantity. Such results supported Wang's (2004) observations in her longitudinal four-year study of CHL schools that "there was no sense of progress or achievement. Students basically stay at the same level, unable to move forward in their heritage language proficiency or literacy" (p. 368).

Immigrant parents' dilemma in preparing their children for adult life has been found to significantly contribute to their children's language shift. On the one hand, parents desire to maintain their heritage language and culture; on the other, they learned from their own experience that English was the only ticket to the mainstream society and to socioeconomic mobility in the USA. In contrast to their first-wave counterparts, who prepared their children with Chinese-language and job skills to return to China, contemporary Chinese immigrants, like other immigrant groups, view their primary responsibility as providing their children with the mainstream skills with which to compete for desirable social and economic roles in the dominant culture when they grow up (Ogbu 1977).

Li (2006b) reports that Chinese parents engage their children in Chinese use only when their children have trouble with school work and need English–Chinese translation to help understand the assignments. Such Chinese use was immediately stopped once the children no longer needed translation to help with their school work, because many parents believe that Chinese is a hindrance to their children's English development, especially accent acquisition and grammar learning. Thus, it is not surprising that Chinese immigrant parents are reluctant to provide CHL literacy-related materials and activities at home, or that CHL learners typically drop out of community CHL schools between 5 and 7 years old when they start kindergarten or grade school (Xiao 2008b).

Finally, CHL learners' marginalized ethnic identities also have a significant impact on their language shift. As they grow up, CHL learners – like most minority groups – experience a process of forming and transforming their ethnic identities, in which they negotiate multiple identities across languages, cultures, and generations (He 2008). As such, CHL learners typically perceive their own ethnic identities in very different ways. While some of them identify themselves with Chinese culture, the rest identify with either American, both Chinese and American, or neither. Moreover, they often feel excluded, as expressed in the following quote: "Those in America see me as Chinese, while those in China see me as an American" (Dai and Zhang 2008). It has been found that those who experience ethnic ambivalence hold a negative attitude toward their CHL maintenance and have significantly lower self-rated Chinese proficiency (Jia 2008).

Collectively, these studies provide empirical data to show that Chinese language shift in the USA is real and is happening rapidly.

Signs of maintenance

As shown above, Chinese language shift is prevailing and widespread; however, there seems to be a silver lining in CHL, given its unique context associated with Chinese immigration and China's economic development. First, the pioneer Chinese immigrants, who viewed returning to China as their ultimate goal and prepared their children with native-like Chinese-language skills, left the legacy of building and expanding the community Chinese schools, which have involved almost all Chinese immigrant youth born in the USA or arriving at a young age. As of 2004, there were approximately 600 community CHL schools across the country enrolling 160,000 students (McGinnis 2005a). Moreover, these schools are no longer isolated but are now well-organized entities, led by two nonprofit organizations in recent years: the National Council of Associations of Chinese Language Schools (from Taiwan and Hong Kong) and the Chinese School Association in the USA (from the People's Republic of China). These organizations supervise the curricula, communicate with mainstream schools, and provide information and advocacy. One of their outstanding achievements is that, in many parts of California, students' learning in CHL schools is now accredited by some mainstream schools. That is, some students can receive high school credit for their studies in a Chinese heritage language school. Such institutional support will certainly empower Chinese-language development and CHL maintenance.

Second, over 75 percent of the contemporary Chinese immigrants are first generation or 1.5 generation immigrants, who have either fully or partially developed Chinese as their L1 and continue to be active members of the Chinese-speaking community. They have extended families on both sides of the Pacific Ocean, and their family members travel back and forth, thus building a socially connected migrant network spanning national boundaries (Liu 2002: 15) and expanding the Chinese speech community from China to the USA, where the Chinese language is used as the vital communicative tool. Such cross-ocean connections and communication have been and will continue to be the driving force of CHL maintenance.

Third, a number of top-down federal initiatives have taken place in recent years. For instance, the federal Foreign Language Assistance Program established that Chinese is a "critical language" and as such is entitled to priority in funding decisions. The National Security Education Program has established a number of Chinese Flagship Programs which provide a model for

K-16 articulation and immersion. Moreover, the National Foreign Language Center has undertaken the initial planning phase of a multiyear project entitled "STARTALK," a multiagency effort to expand foreign language education in undertaught critical languages by funding new and existing programs throughout students' learning careers, kindergarten through university, and to provide incentives and rewards for foreign language learning and use in the work force (National Foreign Language Center 2008). In the summer of 2007, STARTALK involved over twenty institutions and supported twenty-five summer Chinese programs, in which 944 high school students and 427 high school teachers across the country participated. And in the summer of 2008, it is expected fund fifty-five Chinese programs, servicing 1,884 students and 688 teachers nationwide (Asia Society 2008). These initiatives have greatly boosted the campaign for CHL maintenance and made it part of the national agenda.

Finally, with China's growing role in the international arena, the need for Chinese language proficiency is becoming a top priority for the nation. Learning Chinese is the interest not only of Chinese immigrant families but also non-Chinese speakers in the USA. The author's own experience is a living example. When she first became a Chinese pedagogy specialist for a well-established flagship university campus on the East Coast in 1999, there were only a dozen Chinese students at the beginning level and just four students majoring in Chinese. Now there are hundreds of students at the first year and over fifty Chinese majors. The same is true of many other universities and K-12 schools, where Chinese programs are vigorously expanding. To meet the special needs of CHL learners, more and more colleges and universities have established dual-track (non-HL and HL) Chinese programs, or even triple track (non-HL, HL-Mandarin, HL-Cantonese) programs, such as at the University of California at Davis.

In the summer of 2007, Chinese Advanced Placement courses and exams made their first national appearance, in which 3,261 Chinese students participated (Asia Society and The College Board 2008). So far, over 2,400 high schools have expressed interest in establishing AP programs and offering these courses (Stewart and Wang 2005). Moreover, Chinese immersion programs have sprung up all over the nation, with children starting as early as in kindergarten. In Portland, Oregon, the Chinese immersion program for K-12 has nearly quadrupled in size. It is now common for CHL learners who dropped their Chinese studies at a young age to return to the classroom and relearn what they lost. Santos (2007b) describes a typical example, that of Mr. Yang. Upon his arrival in the USA as a kindergartener, he discontinued his Chinese studies and lost his Chinese proficiency. He later realized that, as a Chinese man, he needed his heritage language to connect with a big part of who he was. As a result, he began to take Chinese classes and eventually gained advanced Chinese proficiency. Enthusiasm like this, inspired by being part of one's Chinese heritage, makes CHL maintenance meaningful and compelling.

Conclusion

As advocated by the National Security Education Program (2005), maintaining and developing CHL should be one of the highest priorities to meet the vital needs for more advanced skills in languages critical to US national security. Considering the factors favoring shift to English, CHL development will be no easy task, yet it is possible due to the increased interest in Chinese, China's increasing economic development, the advantage of early language exposure, and the unique Chinese immigrant parents' dedication to community Chinese weekend schools. Chinese-specific trans-Pacific family ties will keep the Chinese language and culture alive and growing, and China's growing economy will increasingly make the Chinese language a must, not only for Chinese speakers but also for English speakers and speakers of other languages. With a head start in the home language and culture, CHL learners have distinct advantages. Ample evidence from language acquisition studies shows that an early start in language learning is most effective and that early exposure to a language has a positive effect on subsequent learning (Au and Romo 1997; Stowe and Sabourin 2005; Xiao 2007; Ming and Tao 2008).

However, Chinese skills will not grow naturally in an English-speaking setting given the fact that language learning takes place best in a context where a natural speech community exists. Deliberate and collective efforts are hence needed to nurture and foster the maintenance and development of heritage languages in the USA. To do so, interventions should start at all levels, including learners' homes, communities, and mainstream schools. While parents should be actively and diligently involved in the process, the Chinese community HL schools should be strengthened and supported financially and administratively by the mainstream system. Mainstream schools should not only provide level-appropriate Chinese-language programs, but also educate their teachers to build up the connections between school and the home for HL students and appreciate their prior linguistic knowledge and heritage values.

DISCUSSION QUESTIONS

1. The author posed this question in the chapter: "What factors contribute to the highly congregated and heritage-loyal Chinese immigrants and their descendants losing the battle to maintain their heritage language, just like other immigrant groups in this country?" Make a list summarizing the most important factors, based on the research presented in this chapter.

2. Many have said that the twenty-first century will be "the Chinese century" (e.g. T. C. Fishman 2004). How do you think China's emerging status on the world stage will impact the maintenance of Chinese in the USA?

---

6 Tagalog in the USA

Elvira C. Fonacier

Introduction

Tagalog is one of the top twelve non-English languages spoken at home by people over the age of 5 in the USA (US Census 2000a). Ranking third in the list, with more than 1.4 million speakers, it also ranks second to Chinese among Asian languages spoken in the USA. Tagalog has experienced an increase of over 45 percent in its population from 1990 to 2000, and an increase of another 21 percent from 2000 to 2007. This can be attributed mainly to the immigration of Filipinos who speak Tagalog, either as a first or second language. On a global scale, including the US Census, the Filipino language is primarily referred to as *Tagalog*. Therefore *Tagalog* is the term that will be used in this chapter, and the terms *Filipino(s)* or *Tagalogs* will refer to the people who speak the language.

Of the 171 languages spoken across the Philippine islands (Gordon 2005), Tagalog is the most widely spoken. Campbell (1995) estimates that there are approximately 20 million speakers of Tagalog as a first language around the world, and around 43 million who speak it as a second language. In the 1987 Philippine Constitution, Article XIV (Education, Science and Technology, Arts, Culture, and Sports) establishes "Filipino," a Tagalog-based language, as the national language, and Filipino and English as the official languages of the Philippines. Hence, every Filipino who is educated up to at least primary level may be assumed to have been taught in or exposed to the Tagalog language. A later section of this chapter will describe the relationship between "Filipino" and Tagalog.

In comparison to other Asian languages spoken in the USA such as Chinese, Vietnamese, and Korean, Tagalog has the highest number of speakers claiming to speak English "well" and "very well." This is likely due to the strong presence of English as an official language and educational medium in the Philippines. It is certainly spoken by many Filipino immigrants. Tagalog ranks second to German, with 93 percent of its more than 1.4 million speakers claiming to speak English "well" or "very well."

History

Tagalog belongs to the family of Austronesian languages, which extends from Malaysia and Indonesia to parts of New Guinea, New Zealand, the Philippines and Madagascar (Katzner 2002: 24). It is native to the central and southern area called Luzon, and has various dialects that are spoken in different provinces in the Philippines including Batangas, Lubang, Manila, Tanay-Paete, and Tayabas (Grimes 1995). A common group of Malayo-Polynesian root words provides the central lexical core of Tagalog, but the language has been exposed to several cultural influences that are now reflected in the loanwords it contains from Sanskrit, South India Dravidian, Arabic, and Chinese (Campbell 1995). In addition, the more than 400 years of contact with the Spanish language resulted in the assimilation of many Spanish loanwords. Its syntax, however, remained unchanged.

As the basis of the national language (Filipino), Tagalog has been a political focus in the Philippines even before the country's independence from the USA in 1946. In 1936, the Institute of National Language (INL) was established in the Philippines to study the country's dialects "for the purpose of evolving and adopting a common national language based on one of the existing native tongues" (Rubrico 2007: 2). In 1939, the INL recommended Tagalog as the country's national language, which was then taught in Philippine schools soon thereafter. Thompson (2003) believes that Tagalog was recommended, in part, because it was the lingua franca in the southern part of the nation and "was in an intermediate position geographically and linguistically" (p. 28). It should be noted here, though, that there are at least two other major languages in the Philippines which were well qualified at the time to be considered for the national language given the number of speakers: Cebuano and Ilokano (Crystal 1987). However, due to the influence of the governing body, which was comprised mostly of Tagalogs, these languages were not chosen.

In 1959 the Philippine Department of Education renamed the national language *Pilipino* rather than Tagalog as part of an effort toward removing its close association with Tagalog speakers and, consequently, making the national language more acceptable to speakers of other Philippine languages. Then the 1973 Constitution mandated the formation of the Philippine National Assembly, which was to develop and formally adopt a common national language, to be called Filipino (Rubrico 2007). But it was in the 1987 Constitution that the language was formally renamed Filipino (spelled with an "F" rather than a "P"), essentially to integrate elements from other principal languages whose alphabets are not entirely the same as Tagalog's, and to accommodate the many Spanish and English loanwords that have become part of the people's daily lives.

Tagalog is perhaps the first of the many Philippine languages that reached American shores from as early as the sixteenth century. It was spoken by the Luzon Indians who were reported to be crew members on board the Spanish galleon that docked off the coast of what is now called Morro Bay in California in 1587 and then began to spread to different regions in the USA (Wagner 1929). Between 1565 and 1815, numerous galleons traveling between Manila and Acapulco included Filipinos as crew members (Posadas 1999), which also facilitated the spread of Tagalog. Later, in 1883, a *Harper's Weekly* edition wrote of "Malay fishermen – Tagalas from the Philippine Islands" living in the bayous of Louisiana (Posadas 1999). These were the residents of the "Manila Village" in Jefferson Parish who popularized effective shrimp-drying techniques in the area.

The USA's colonization of the Philippines in 1898 triggered the flow of laborers who spoke various Philippine languages such as Ilokano, Visayan, and Tagalog. For example, the first Filipino plantation workers were recruited to work on Hawaiian farms in 1906, which was considered the first wave of Filipino migration to the USA and which lasted until the 1930s (Filipino-American Centennial Commemoration 2005). Most of these Filipino workers were illiterate and poor laborers from an agricultural background (Takaki 1989: 58). A 100-person annual quota was imposed on the Philippines when it gained its independence in 1946. Okamura (1998) noted many of the entrants were wives of American servicemen and Filipino Americans. And, like many Asian immigrants, they were restricted to unskilled and semiskilled work, especially agricultural labor, and worked multiple low-paying jobs while trying to integrate into the American mainstream (Okamura 1998: 41).

After 1965, the number of Tagalog speakers in the USA steadily rose along with the flow of immigrants from the Philippines. Between 1990 and 2000, the population grew by more than 30 percent. This growth may be attributed to two factors. First, the US Immigration Act of 1990 restructured the immigrant categories of admission and provided for increased immigration of certain categories, including family members (US Citizenship and Immigration Services, n.d.1). Second, new legislation provided permanent resident status for undocumented aliens who had resided in the USA since 1982. Filipino immigrants took advantage of these changes and were able to register as permanent residents and bring over their immediate relatives (including spouses, children, and parents) to the USA. Furthermore, increased Filipino immigration between 1990 and 2000 may also be partly due to the Filipino government's promotion of highly skilled labor exports overseas (Schneider 2000).

Many who immigrated during this time were medical professionals such as nurses, physicians, surgeons, and pharmacists. In fact, even in the 1960s and 1970s, the Philippines sent more professional immigrants to the USA than to any other country in the world (Revilla 1996: 290).

Table 6.1. *States with the largest Tagalog-speaking populations*

	Ages 5+	Percentage of all US Tagalog speakers
California	668,073	48.60
New Jersey	80,996	5.89
Illinois	77,512	5.63
New York	72,174	5.25
Texas	56,752	4.12
Hawaii	55,657	4.04
Florida	49,475	3.59
Washington	49,348	3.59
Nevada	45,459	3.30
Virginia	32,819	2.38
Total in USA	1,480,429	

Source: Modern Language Association 2009, US Census Bureau 2007c.

Demographics

The Filipino-American community is the largest Asian-American group in the USA, after the Chinese-Americans. In 2000, the US Census reported that over 2.4 million Americans identified their ancestry as "full Filipino" (1.9 million) or "part Filipino" (0.5 million). It should be noted here that even though Filipinos identify themselves as being of "full-" or "part-Filipino" ancestry, this does not necessarily mean that they speak Tagalog (Filipino) as their first language or mother tongue. More likely, many of them who claim to be "full-" or "part-Filipino" may actually speak a first language other than Tagalog or English. More often than not, besides English, Filipinos speak at least two languages at home: the language of their parents or of their regional origin and Tagalog.

Filipino-Americans comprise 1.5 percent of the total population of the USA, and they are found in many states across the nation, with the highest concentration in the west. Table 6.1 shows the ten states with the largest populations of Tagalog speakers.

The State of California has the largest Tagalog-speaking population in the USA, with Los Angeles as its principal enclave, followed by San Diego, Santa Clara, and the San Francisco Bay area. In the 2000 Census profile of general demographic characteristics of California, there were 918,678 Filipinos, and perhaps more because some may have claimed their ethnicity under "two or more races" (US Census Bureau 2000c). This number comprises 2.7 percent of the population of the state of California. The States of Hawaii and Alaska also ranked Tagalog speakers as their largest ethnic group based on population

Table 6.2. *Settlement states where Filipino immigrants live (ranked by state immigrant population)*

State	1990 Filipino population	2000 Filipino population	Percentage growth
Nevada	7,339	33,046	77.8
Alaska	4,773	9,555	50.0
Maryland	12,473	23,276	46.4
New Jersey	38,043	70,670	46.2
Washington	27,621	46,382	40.4
Virginia	22,416	36,548	38.7
West Virginia	955	1,531	37.6
Illinois	47,370	67,840	30.6
Hawaii	74,957	104,862	28.5
California	484,277	670,560	27.8

Source: Center for Immigration Studies 2003.

figures, and they are concentrated in the counties of Honolulu and Anchorage. The high concentration of Tagalog speakers in Nevada and Washington is also visible in Table 6.1.

In terms of population growth of Filipino immigrants in the USA, Table 6.2 shows the number of Filipino immigrants between 1990 and 2000. The state of Nevada recorded a 77 percent increase in population, followed by Alaska with an increase of 50 percent, and New Jersey and Maryland with over 46 percent growth each. The states of Hawaii and California, which have the highest concentrations of Filipino population, recorded a growth of approximately 28 percent.

It is important to reiterate here what was mentioned earlier: 93 percent of Filipino-Americans in the USA claim to speak English "very well" and "well" (US Census Bureau 2007c). This high percentage is largely due to the American colonization of the Philippines, which revolutionized the education system. Public schools were transformed and changed into the American system, and English was imposed as the medium of instruction. Forbes (1945: 313) claims that, "by 1913, there must have been passed through the schools well over a million Filipinos who had learned enough English to communicate with each other." Over the years, the presence of English in the country grew and it is now in every domain in the Philippines: in mass media, education, government, and business, domains which influence and sometimes shape the language of the Filipino people, including the language of the immigrants to the USA. This also explains why Filipinos are typically more fluent in English than citizens of neighboring countries in Southeast Asia.

Public presence of Tagalog

The previous section showed that Tagalog speakers are growing in number and are spreading in many parts of the nation. Although they are not as numerous as the US Chinese-speaking population, in states where they are concentrated Filipinos can be attended to in Tagalog over the telephone and in person for various basic services including the police, hospitals, utility companies, banks, fast-food restaurants, supermarkets, many libraries, and airports. It is certainly advantageous for immigrant Filipinos and locally born Filipino-Americans to live in Filipino communities where goods and services provided are not too distinctly different from what they are in the Philippines. Local public and private organizations in places where there is a high concentration of Tagalog speakers also tend to employ people who are able to speak the language and relate to their Filipino clients, in order to provide better service to them in the language with which they are more comfortable. In this section we will focus on the presence of Tagalog in the media, religion, and education.

Media

Local newspapers and other print media use the Tagalog language or Tagalog combined with English or another Philippine language. There are also Philippine-based news and/or print media which use Tagalog as their medium of expression, many of which are found on the internet. Some examples include the newspapers *Abante* and *The Philippine Star*, which can be found online or on news stands at local Filipino stores in US communities. In Hawaii, there is the *Hawaii Filipino Chronicle*, which features a regular Tagalog language column and special feature articles in Tagalog from time to time, and *The Philippine Courier*, which includes advertisements in Tagalog. In California, the *Philippine News*, which is circulated nationwide, maintains a section in Tagalog that focuses on issues of teaching the Tagalog language. The presence of Tagalog in the USA is also felt through daily newspapers and popular weekly magazines that arrive straight from the Philippines shortly after appearing in Manila (Okamura 1998: 107). These print materials are often found in local Filipino stores, restaurants, and Filipino-owned businesses.

Some states in the USA have regular radio or TV broadcasts that focus on Filipino culture, and Tagalog is used in these broadcasts as a medium of communication along with English. In many states where there is a high concentration of Filipino-Americans, satellite feeds of the two popular Filipino TV channels, that is, *The Filipino Channel* (more commonly referred to as TFC) and *GMA Pinoy TV*, serve as the main sources of television broadcasts and entertainment from the Philippines. All Filipino households in states where they are available may now be able to subscribe to *TFC* and/or *GMA Pinoy TV* in the USA and watch their favorite Tagalog soap operas (*telenovelas*), movies, newscasts, and other favorite shows in their own homes.

All the major Tagalog newspapers in the Philippines are also now available on the internet and accessible to Tagalog speakers anywhere in the world. Numerous websites carry podcasts and video files of Philippine newscasts, documentaries, investigative journalistic reports, and interviews, in both Tagalog and English. Youtube.com, for example, carries a wide range of Tagalog movies, some documentary films, and theatrical productions, which used to be of limited availability or accessibility to Tagalog speakers. For Filipinos who want to keep up with the current political climate in the Philippines, the website for the Philippine Center for Investigative Journalism provides more objective reporting, including updates on politics and the Philippine government in English, and some audio interviews and reports in Tagalog.

With the growing number of Filipino podcasts, online newspapers and magazines, and other online media and portals, the internet has undoubtedly not only removed the geographical boundaries that kept Tagalog speakers in the USA separated from their counterparts outside the country, but in fact has made the presence of Tagalog in the media stronger and more accessible than ever.

Religion

When Filipinos immigrated to the USA they also brought with them their religious practices and observances as collective expressions of the immigrant Filipino ethnicity. Filipinos typically observe Roman Catholic religious holidays and celebrations, which is a result of the extended contact between the Philippines and Spain. Protestantism, Islam, and Buddhism are also present in the Philippines, but in much smaller numbers. Christianity in the Philippines started in the sixteenth century, when the first Spanish fleet landed in the southern part of the islands. Since then the Christian faith has spread, mostly northwards, and different types of Christian faiths, including Catholicism and Protestantism, are represented in the Philippines today.

The religious rituals practiced in quite a number of Filipino communities in the USA are mainly organized by Catholic churches and community organizations for their Filipino membership, and here we find Tagalog in use. For example, there are Sunday masses and religious services that are mainly for Filipinos because they are celebrated in Tagalog. Some examples would be Saint Patrick's Church and Saint Boniface Church in San Francisco, as well as Holy Angels Church in Colma, CA. These churches hold at least one Sunday mass in Tagalog. Gonzalez also reports that the Filipino-American Jehovah's Witnesses have grown from two congregations in the 1970s to twelve, and one has to know Tagalog to attend their Filipino services (Gonzalez 2001: 4).

US Tagalogs, like their counterparts in the Philippines, are well known for their reverence of Christian saints and observances, for which they hold annual *fiestas* "celebrations." In the San Francisco Bay Area, seven parishes are reported to celebrate the *Simbang Gabi* "Midnight Mass" while *Flores de Mayo* "Flowers of May" and the Easter *Salubong* "The Meeting" are slowly being integrated into regular church activities (Gonzalez 2001). Okamura's (1998) study of the Filipino-American diaspora also noted similar events happening in a populous Filipino community in Kalihi in Honolulu, HI.

The most popular of these observances are Easter and Christmas celebrations. Easter is a community event that is celebrated by Tagalogs with the reading of the *Pasyon* (Passion and Life of Christ), a text in Tagalog that recounts in verse the life and death of Jesus Christ, which readers deliver in a chant. The reading of the *Pasyon*, called *pabasa*, involves a family that provides the facility for the *pabasa* and serves food and refreshment to the readers and the many guests. The reading may stretch on for days, depending on the speed of reading, or more accurately, the pace of chanting or singing. Many *pabasa* are held indoors, by invitation to a private home, and are carried out as solemnly as they are in the Philippines. One may wonder how much of the *pabasa* is understood by Filipino-Americans; it is perhaps more the annual observance and traditional practice that matter to Filipinos than the meaning of the words of the *Pasyon*.

Besides its common use in religious observances, Tagalog is also found in many religious printed materials such as the Bible, prayer books, and hymnals. The Philippine Bible Society has the oldest and most widely sold translation of the Holy Bible in Tagalog, *Ang Biblia*, and more recently, has published the Old and New Testament in separate Tagalog editions. There is also a bilingual version of the Holy Bible (King James Version) in English and Tagalog. With the help of internet-based businesses, these publications are available to Filipino-Americans for purchase online.

Education

Despite Tagalog's ranking as the third most common non-English language spoken at home in the US, it does not have the status or visibility of other Asian languages like Chinese, Japanese or Korean in terms of foreign language study. Unlike these Asian languages, which are fairly widely offered as foreign language courses in universities and in some high schools, Tagalog courses are confined to communities where there are high concentrations of Filipinos, such as in California and Hawaii. Tagalog does not seem to be a foreign language that is attractive enough to foreign language learners, except to those who have some heritage background or social affinity with the language. A survey of students at the University of Hawaii at Manoa enrolled in its Tagalog (Filipino) courses showed that many of them are indeed heritage speakers, a term defined in Chapter 1 of this book as referring to bilingual[1] individuals who grow up in households where a minority language is spoken, yet schooled in the country's majority language.

Besides school- or university-based language programs, there are other projects that promote Tagalog as a foreign or heritage language. The University of Hawaii at Manoa administers the Fulbright-Hays-funded Advanced Filipino Abroad Program (AFAP), an eight-week immersion program in the Philippines which brings advanced, non-Tagalog-speaking students from different US universities to the country, and through immersion teaches them the language and culture of the Tagalogs. On average, around ten to twelve students a year have been awarded a Fulbright-Hays grant to participate in the program over the last seventeen years (Galang 2006). More recently, AFAP has been awarded another term of four years which will allow it to continue offering the program until 2011.

Some educational resources are also available in Tagalog, including textbooks, do-it-yourself language resource materials, and English–Tagalog dictionaries. There are also several websites that focus on promoting the teaching of Tagalog, including the US Department of Education-funded Northern Illinois University's Southeast Asian Languages and Cultures website, which provides an excellent and comprehensive resource for teachers and students of Tagalog (SEAsite n.d.).

Evidence of language shift to English and of Tagalog maintenance

Before we discuss evidence of shift to English and of maintenance of Tagalog, we will first offer a few general details about the Tagalog language as it is spoken by the various immigrants from different Tagalog-speaking regions in the Philippines. This may shed light on the characteristics of Tagalog as it is spoken in Filipino communities in the USA.

As mentioned above, Tagalog is a language with multiple dialects spoken in different areas of the Philippines. Speakers from different regions can understand each other, but they notice marked differences, more in vocabulary than in pronunciation. There are several dialects of Tagalog, found in Bataan, Batangas, Bulacan, Lubang, Manila, Marinduque, Tanay-Paete, and Tayabas (Grimes 1995), which are undoubtedly represented in many US Filipino communities.

Perhaps the most noticeable trait of Tagalog in the USA, as well as Tagalog in the Philippines, is code-switching – the combination of Tagalog and English in the same conversation exchange – commonly referred to as "Taglish" (Bautista 2004; Cordova 2000; Johnson 2000; Thompson 2003). Due to high proficiency in both languages, Tagalog speakers code-switch even in many formal contexts. As discussed in Chapter 2 of this volume, code-switching is often not due to a lack of vocabulary, but rather is one variety in a bilingual speaker's repertoire. Here is an excerpt from a Tagalog novel by Bautista (1983), *Bata, Bata . . . Paano ka ginawa?* ("Child, child . . . How were you created?"), which was later made into a movie, that shows how code-switching occurs naturally, almost as if Tagalog and English were one language. In this excerpt, two women (Lea and Pilar) are arguing about life's priorities and Lea's decision to allow her daughter to join a beauty contest at her school. (The translations in parentheses are provided by the author of this chapter.)

LEA: Look what's happening around us: war, hunger, poverty, epidemics . . . *tapos, ang iniisip natin, pagandahan* ("then, all we think about are beauty pageants")? My God, Pilar; *ang importante sa tao'y ang kabuuan niya bilang tao . . .* ("what's important to people is the person").

PILAR: Look who's talking! *Ganoon pala ang paniwala mo* ("So, if that is what you believe"), how come *na pinasali mo si Maya* ("you allowed Maya to join in")?

LEA: *Dahil gusto niyang sumali . . .* ("Because she wants to . . . ") *at hindi sa pagandahan kundi dahil sa mga* ("and not because of the pageant, but of the many") activities. She wanted to take part in the program . . . *ang ibig naman ng titser niya'y isali siya sa* ("but her teacher wants for her to join the") contest. (pp. 16–17)

"Taglish" may have started and become prevalent in the Philippines soon after the USA made its presence more visibly felt with the establishment of the military bases in Luzon. With more US service members and their families stationed in strategic bases in the Philippines, and the close affinity of the Filipino people with American media and culture, "Taglish" became a lingua franca in the country. In the 1960s a popular magazine decided to publish some of its articles using a combination of Tagalog and English to boost its sales and reach a wider readership. But it was not until the 1970s, the same time the Bilingual Education Policy was established in the Philippines, when "Taglish" became more popular, so popular in fact that it is now the lingua franca in the Philippines (Thompson 2003).

In the USA, Filipino immigrants and even the locally born Filipino-American Tagalog speakers naturally code-switch in their conversations with other Tagalog speakers. This is also a characteristic of the Tagalog language that the children learn from their immigrant parents, and from being exposed to Tagalog-based media. It is important to note that whenever languages come in contact and become an essential part of daily life, it is likely that code-switching will take place.

In addition to code-switching, Tagalog has incorporated a large number of English loanwords, For example, English verbs are sometimes conjugated using Tagalog affixes to indicate grammatical aspect and focus and are also spelled phonologically in Tagalog. The verb *compute* (phonologically spelled as "kompyut") may be used as *magkompyut* "to compute," *nagkompyut* "computed," *nagko**kompyut*** "is computing," or *magko**kompyut*** "will compute," all with a focus on the actor/doer of the action. In a similar manner, the same verb may be used to indicate a focus on the object or goal of the statement and appear as ***kompyut**in* "to compute," ***k**in**ompyut*** "computed," *kino**kompyut*** "is being computed," or *ko**kompyut**in* "will be computed." In addition, the Tagalog alphabet, which used to have twenty letters, now has twenty-eight letters, which are read like the English letters of the alphabet as pronounced by Filipinos.

Signs of shift

Despite the presence of Tagalog in media, religion, and education, it tends to be lost among many children of Filipino immigrants. Ilano-Tenorio (1997) found that many Filipino children express discouragement, frustration and sometimes anger at not being able to speak the language. Fluent Tagalog speakers were found to be "unsupportive" and indignant at efforts by non-fluent speakers' attempts to speak and/or learn the language. This explains why Filipino-Americans who are learning the language lose their motivation and harbor a feeling of segregation. Instances were also reported where classroom teachers discouraged immigrant parents from speaking to their children in Tagalog. Those teachers were reported to have claimed that using Tagalog impedes the children's integration in school, and slows down their pace in learning English. Cordova (2000: 345) reported that, in schools that work to eradicate immigrant students' home language and culture, many second generation Filipino Americans grow up speaking only English. There are certainly many other reasons why children of second generation immigrant parents tend to speak more English than Tagalog, but what is important to point out here is the fact that there exist misguided notions about the supposed negative effect of the use of the first language on the learning of English, which were also presented in Chapter 1 of this volume.

A study of English language acquisition by young immigrants showed that 5 to 17 year olds reported much more use of English than speakers over 18 years old (Bayley 2004). Of the 59 percent of the sample who were of Filipino ethnic background born in the USA, Bayley noted that 95 percent of 5 to 17 year olds use "English mainly" or "English only," and that 5 percent speak mainly their mother tongue. Bayley, in support of Veltman's (2000) findings, claims that were it not for high levels of immigration, the number of speakers of the most common languages other than English would decline rapidly (p. 273). In fact, Rumbaut *et al.* (2006: 458) note that this decline of non-English language use is particularly pronounced among Filipinos, since, when considering linguistic life expectancy (which they define as the retention of the ability to speak a language), "[t]he lowest life expectancies are observed among immigrants from the Philippines" and the average mother tongue life expectancy is 1.6 generations, fast even by the standards of speakers of other Asian languages, who tend to shift to English quickly.

Prohibiting the use of Tagalog in the workplace is also a factor that contributes to language shift. For example, in 1964 a federal court upheld an "English-only" rule instituted by many healthcare providers, which prohibited its Filipino nurses and workers from speaking Tagalog in the workplace (Aspen Health Law Center 1998). The English-only policy in healthcare institutions certainly pushes speakers of languages other than English to shift to avoid being punished by their employers.

In Hawaii, Alaska, and California, Tagalog has long been associated with speakers who work in service-oriented jobs. It is the language of many hotel workers, restaurant waitstaff, busboys, cleaners, gardeners, cannery workers, and fishing boat crews. San Buenaventura (1995) observed that local Filipinos in more prestigious occupations look down on immigrants who speak Tagalog because they "remind [them] of what they were before" (p. 38), that is, of poor education and a low socioeconomic background. Cordova (2000) confirms this, saying, "those who speak variations of Filipino English often experience discrimination" (p. 343). Thus, many Tagalog speakers themselves, especially new immigrants, not only want to become proficient in English as quickly as possible so that they can get ahead in life, but also to escape the stereotype associated with low-paid, poorly educated workers.

Signs of maintenance

US Tagalog is demographically restricted, but many Filipinos have taken strong initiatives to promote Tagalog language learning to ensure its maintenance for future generations in their geographic locations. As a response to growing Filipino communities, several high schools and universities in California offer Tagalog language and/or culture courses in their curriculum. Cordova (2000) reviews the spread of Tagalog as a foreign language subject and certificate course, as well as Tagalog as a full BA degree in the USA. She found at least ten universities across the USA offering Tagalog language and culture courses, and the University of Hawaii at Manoa offers the only BA in this field. In addition to the academic landscape, students and local youth also demonstrate their interest in the language and culture of Filipinos through annual regional youth summits conducted by academic organizations, such as the University of Hawaii system, and by the local community, such as Hampton Roads in Virginia Beach, supported by many Filipino-American youth in the area. The youth summit of Hampton Roads started in the early 1970s, and sought to provide a venue for the young Filipino-Americans in the local community to raise awareness of their Filipino heritage and culture. These summits, along with other cultural activities and gatherings, certainly contribute to the awareness of Filipino-Americans about their language, heritage, and culture.

With the small but growing number of courses offered in several universities, there is also a growing need for more qualified Tagalog teachers and quality language programs that will service the population. This scenario certainly encourages and pushes for the maintenance of the Tagalog language. Professional organizations have also supported Tagalog maintenance. For example, in 1999, the American Council on the Teaching of Foreign Languages created the Tagalog version of the Oral Proficiency Interview (OPI), a nationally known foreign language standardized test. This confirms the increasing importance of Tagalog not only in the academic field, but also in professional and career-oriented domains. Additionally, the international presence and prestige of Tagalog is on the rise; for example, New Zealand recently announced that it would "adopt the Filipino language as the chosen foreign language to be taught" in its schools (ABS-CBN News 2008).

According to J. A. Fishman (2004), the maintenance of a heritage language should begin at a young age with the family and local community through saturation in the language. The creation of early childhood language experiences outside of the family, and an increase in language programs in both elementary and secondary levels, will contribute to the longevity of the language. This is a reality for Asian languages such as Chinese and Japanese, where after-school and Saturday programs are designed to teach these languages. It seems that maintaining Tagalog as a heritage language faces more challenges ahead because most of the current efforts in language maintenance occur with and are targeted toward speakers at the secondary level or higher, when language is less easy to acquire (J. A. Fishman 2004). Tagalog, seen in this light, is standing on precarious ground. Therefore, Tagalog speakers might follow the example set by speakers of other Asian languages by establishing after-school programs and activities that will promote Tagalog and its maintenance among young Filipino-American children.

Although there have been anecdotal reports of churches offering after-school Tagalog language programs, not much has been written about these in the literature, nor has any empirical study been conducted to demonstrate the effect of such programs on language maintenance. The current offerings of courses at the secondary and university level, although important, do not in and of themselves provide the answers to Tagalog language maintenance. Anecdotally, many of the current language learners registered in classes at these levels take the course in order to fulfill the language requirement of their degrees, rather than due to a genuine desire to learn the language and culture of the Tagalogs.

Conclusions

US public school policies do not typically allow heritage Tagalog-speaking children the opportunity to develop age-level appropriate communication and literacy skills in Tagalog, nor is its use in public always welcomed by the general public. Immigrant languages in the USA have traditionally been "transmitted incompletely if at all into the linguistic repertoire of the grandchildren of immigrants" (Finnegan and Rickford 2004: 115). Despite its relatively strong public presence stemming from demographic concentration, there are clear indications that the future vitality of Tagalog in the USA is precarious, and will rely not only on continued immigration, but also on community and government efforts in promoting and maintaining the language. J. A. Fishman (2004) strongly advocates the maintenance of non-English languages in the USA, and says that:

> without self-supported, self-protected, and self-initiated islands of demographically concentrated local non-English language and culture transmission, non-English mother tongues lack "safe harbors" wherein the young can be socialized according to the languages, values, and traditions of cultures. (p. 123)

Tagalog speakers need "safe harbors" to maintain their heritage language, not only to surmount the pressure of language shift, but also to thrive in a multicultural, multilingual society.

DISCUSSION QUESTIONS

1. How might the Philippines' unique history, including its history of colonialism, affect the maintenance of Tagalog in the USA?
2. In what ways is the situation of Tagalog different than other Asian languages in the USA? In what ways is it similar? Comparing Tagalog to another Asian language in this volume. Which is more likely to be maintained? Why?

---

7 French in the USA

Albert Valdman

Introduction

French is the fourth most common non-English language spoken in the US (Table 1.1).[1] However, it is also one of the four languages among the top twelve that experienced a decline in the number of speakers between 1990 and 2000, and again between 2000 and 2007. This is due to both low levels of immigration of French speakers to the USA and also low rates of intergenerational transmission of the language. This chapter provides a general presentation of French in the USA with a focus on two communities established in the eighteenth and nineteenth centuries that have endured to the present: the New England and Louisianan Franco-American communities, where there still exists some severely limited intergenerational transmission of the local vernacular bolstered by grassroots efforts to maintain and revitalize these varieties. Brief mention will be made of small geographically isolated communities where the local vernacular is moribund. After exploring the history of French in the USA, this chapter provides demographic information about the various communities, the public presence of French, and aspects of language shift and language attrition that affect these various communities.

History

Numerous French place names including Butte, Des Moines, Eau Claire, Terre Haute, and Baton Rouge serve as an eloquent testimony to the former French presence on the territory that forms a large part of the present-day USA. But even though French *coureurs des bois*, (adventurers, hunters, and fur traders) from present-day Québec province criss-crossed much of the territory during the seventeenth and eighteenth centuries, they have left few linguistic traces except for these toponyms.

The major and relatively cohesive present-day francophone communities in the USA spread from two original settlements: New France (part of which is present-day Québec Province) and Acadia (present-day Nova Scotia and New Brunswick). Samuel de Champlain first established a trading post on the tiny island of Sainte-Croix (in present-day Maine) in 1604. From an original group of seventy-nine settlers, by 1755 the Acadian population had grown to 14,000 residents. That community has had an influence on the expansion of French far greater than its original low demographic weight. Victims of a brutal expulsion from their native land, which their descendants label *le grand dérangement* (the great removal), Acadians were scattered in France, in the West Indies, and in the American colonies. Between 1765 and 1780, about 4,000 Acadians found a permanent refuge in Louisiana which, at that time, was under Spanish rule.

But it is New France that constituted the principal bastion of francophony in North America. The first French settlement in New France was established in 1608 near the present site of Québec City (Québec) by Champlain. In 1642, a second settlement was established at the site of present-day Montréal. It was from the Montréal and Québec regions that expeditions were launched along the Great Lakes region, the Illinois country, and the banks of the Mississippi down to the Gulf of Mexico. Although the colonists of the original French settlement in Louisiana came directly from France rather than down the Mississippi, they were led by a Canadian, Lemoyne d'Iberville. It is also from Québec province that the demographic streams, driven by economic hardships, originated, that in the nineteenth and early twentieth centuries settled in the New England textile mill towns and, to a lesser degree, in the upper Midwest.

Demographics

Three fundamental features distinguish the francophone communities in the USA from other communities such as Spanish speakers. First, current migratory currents bringing francophone speakers to the USA are limited. Second, the presence of standard French (SF),[2] reinforced by its use in schools, negatively affects the maintenance of indigenous vernacular varieties. Third, in any case, these varieties assume a limited functional role.

With regard to current migratory currents, except for very small numbers of expatriate groups living in the New York area, California, and major cities like Atlanta, Chicago, and Philadelphia, the francophone communities are not renewed by a large and steady flow of immigrants. In 2005, only 4,399 permanent immigrants arrived from France out of a total of 1,122,373 holders of permanent resident cards (Lagarde 2007). To be sure, there are large cohesive Haitian diaspora communities in Boston, the New York area, and southern Florida totaling more than one million persons that are bolstered by new arrivals (Zéphir 2005). But most of these immigrants, especially those newly arriving, are primary speakers of Haitian Creole, not of French.

French migratory currents toward the North American continent, particularly the Canadian part of "New France," were not substantial. In the late seventeenth and in the eighteenth centuries, French colonial policy favored the plantation

Table 7.1. *Language spoken at home for selected areas: 1990 versus 2000*

	Census 1990		Census 2000	
State/Region	French	French creole	French	French creole
LA	227,376	34,797	194,100	4,470
New England	338,923	18,554	263,125	56,265
NY	183,868	52,208	174,080	114,745
CA	129,986	3,393	134,405	4,105
FL	110,725	83,121	125,650	208,485
TX	57,081	7,233	61,770	3,505
Total	1,047,959	199,306	953,130	391,575
US total	1,701,655	220,626	1,624,030	453,370

Source: US Census Bureau 2000a: Population 5 years and over.

islands of the Caribbean with their potential for lucrative cash crops to the "acres of snow" of Canada referred to by Voltaire. For example, between 1663 and 1679, only 2,000 French migrated to New France (Charbonneau and Guillemette 1994: 163). At the time of the conquest of New France by the English in 1760, its population had reached only 70,000. However, by the middle of the nineteenth century, a high birth rate which the French Canadians call *la revanche des berceaux* (the revenge of the cradles) fueled a demographic expansion, and the population of former New France had risen to nearly a million (Thibault 2003: 899). It was this demographic vitality combined with economic difficulties that spurred migration in all directions from the province of Québec.

Beginning in the early 1960s, a new francophone community termed Floribec was established north of Miami by retiring Québécois "snowbirds" fleeing the icy winters of their homeland. This community of about 60,000 retirees, supplemented by Haitian immigrants, accounts for Florida's standing as the American state with the largest combined francophone and creolophone population. Between 1990 and 2000, there was approximately a 4.5 percent reduction in the number of persons declaring the use of French at home, but a 100 percent increase in the number of those declaring the use of French Creole, as displayed in Table 7.1. Most of the latter are speakers of Haitian Creole living mainly in Florida, New York, and Massachusetts. The figure for French Creole in Louisiana refers most likely to speakers of Louisiana Creole (LC), an indigenous variety differing from Haitian Creole that developed in the early years of the eighteenth century. Research by Klingler (2003) confirms that LC is moribund. The two long-established communities, New England and Louisiana,

Table 7.2. *States with the largest French-speaking populations*

	Ages 5 +	Percentage of all US French speakers
New York	141,017	10.64
Louisiana	129,910	9.80
California	129,454	9.76
Florida	103,095	7.77
Massachusetts	58,308	4.39
Texas	57,992	4.37
Maine	54,599	4.11
Maryland	46,959	3.54
Pennsylvania	42,732	3.22
New Jersey	41,243	3.11
Total in USA	1,355,805	

Source: Modern Language Association 2009, US Census Bureau 2007c.

show sharp declines in the use of French, whereas there are slight increases in California, Florida, and Texas.

Table 7.2 shows the ten states with the largest French-speaking populations. That New England and Louisiana remain the communities with the highest concentration of French speakers is obvious because Louisiana and Maine are near the top of the list, despite having much smaller total populations than some of the other listed states. The relatively high numbers in Florida are also evident, and California can be seen to have a large number of speakers though, with its large population, this accounts for a relatively low concentration.

Vernacular French communities

The six New England states, northern New York state, and south Louisiana (the latter region often referred to as Acadiana or the Francophone Triangle) constitute the bastions of francophony in the USA. It is not so much because of their demographic preponderance – together they account for only about a quarter of US users of French at home – but because they have preserved indigenous vernacular varieties of the language. These varieties are being eroded, primarily by language shift to English, and they show language contact phenomena that will be discussed ahead. The other major concentrations of French speakers are in the New York City area, southern Florida, and southern California, as shown by the cited US Census. Most of the speakers of French in southern Florida are most probably bilingual members of the Haitian diaspora. Some reported home users of French in New York state are also bilinguals of Haitian

Table 7.3. *The complex diglossia of the "Francophone Triangle"*

English *Dominant language*	**Louisiana French** *Vernacular varieties including Plantation French, Colonial French, Cajun French*	**Louisiana Creole** *Lowest level vernacular*	**Standard French** *Limited official status*
He had a car.	Il avait un char.	Li **te** gẽ ẽ ʃar.	Il avait une voiture.
He was playing when I arrived.	Il était après jouer quand j'ai venu.	Li **t ap** ɣue kõ mo vini.	Il était en train de jouer quand je suis arrivé.
He would be fishing now if it weren't raining.	Il serait après pêcher asteur s'il serait pas après mouiller.	Li **s ape** peʃe astɛr, si la pli **se** pa tõbe.	Il serait en train de pêcher maintenant s'il ne pleurait pas.

Note: There is no standard spelling for Louisiana Creole. The International Phonetic Alphabet is used here.

origin, and others are members of the expatriate French community. Persons who declare the use of French at home in California are mostly expatriates or relatively recent immigrants from francophone countries (Lindenfeld 2000).

Louisiana

The French presence in Louisiana dates back to the beginning of the eighteenth century when, sailing from France, the Canadian Lemoyne d'Iberville and his brother established settlements first in Mobile, Alabama and Biloxi, Mississippi, then in New Orleans about a decade later, in 1718. It was not until the French ceded Louisiana to Spain in 1763 that the colony experienced a significant demographic increase with, in particular, the arrival of Acadian refugees between 1764 and 1783.

The linguistic situation of Acadiana is characterized by a complex hierarchical diglossic relationship involving four languages: English, the dominant language; standard French (SF), which still has a limited official status and enjoys prestige; vernacular indigenous varieties of French, collectively referred to as Louisiana French (LF); and Louisiana Creole (LC) (Picone and Valdman 2005), as displayed in Table 7.3.

There is no full agreement about the genesis of Louisiana Creole. Evidence suggests that it resulted from the attempt on the part of slaves speaking a variety of African languages to acquire the form of vernacular French (not standard French) spoken by European settlers, indentured servants, military personnel, etc. However, following the Saint-Domingue slave revolt, a large group of French settlers (about 10,000) from that colony arrived in Louisiana with their slaves in 1809.[3] This group constituted about 25 percent of the population of Louisiana at that time. Thus, Saint-Domingue Creole spoken by these immigrants may have influenced the indigenous creole.

As for LF, three vernacular varieties of French are generally recognized: Colonial French, which evolved from the variable usage of the founding period; Plantation French, closer to SF, which reflects the speech of settlers that immigrated directly from France attracted by Louisiana's flourishing economy in the first half of the nineteenth century; and Cajun French, the evolved speech of the original Acadian settlers.[4] Today, these three varieties are neither neatly localized nor easily distinguishable from one another. The label "Cajun" is generally used to subsume all three because features associated with that variety differ most from corresponding features of SF and, furthermore, it is the best preserved variety because of the relative isolation of its original speakers. For that reason, I will refer to these three varieties globally as Louisiana French (LF). In regions where LC and LF coexist, speakers, both whites and blacks, may frequently switch between them. LF and LC differ primarily at the grammatical level, and they are not mutually intelligible. Also, Louisianans who use these two varieties will often switch between them with the result that a continuum forms between them.

LF is fairly well described. Descriptions include the pioneering study of Conwell and Juilland (1963) and several more recent studies with more solid empirical bases (Brown 1988; Byers 1988; Dubois 2000; Rottet 2001, 2005), the latter focusing on the issue of language shift and loss. The lexical resources of the language, first described in the 1930s (Read 1931; Ditchy 1932), are now well documented by inventories of progressing thoroughness and adherence to standards of lexicographic research (Daigle 1984; Griolet 1986; Lavaud-Grassin 1988; Valdman *et al.* 2009). From a structural viewpoint, two major variables distinguish areas settled by Acadians from other parts of the Francophone Triangle: (1) the interrogative pronoun referring to inanimates *qui* (*Qui tu vois?* "What do you see?") that refers only to humans in non-Acadian areas; (2) the third person plural verb ending – *ont* (*ils chantont* /ʃãt-õ/) versus Ø (*ils chantent* /ʃãt/) in other parts of Acadiana. At the phonological level, dental and velar stops may be palatalized, as shown by the pronunciation of *cadien* /kadʒɛ̃/. In the Ville Platte region, in the northern part of Acadiana, /t/ and /d/ are assibilated before high front vowels, as they are in Québec and in most varieties in New England: *tu dis* [t^{s}yd^{z}i] "you say." In Lafourche parish, in the southern coastal area, the voiced postalveolar fricative /ʒ/ is replaced by the glottal aspirate /h/: *j'ai jamais mangé* /he hame mãhe/ "I never ate." This local particularity reflects an origin in the regional dialects of the western French province of Saintonge.

LF shows features surviving from the speech exported to North American and Caribbean French colonies of the seventeenth and eighteenth centuries, notably the progressive periphrastic structure *être après*, also found today in French regional speech: *je suis après travailler* "I'm working" (*je suis en train de travailler*).[5] In comparison to SF, the lexicon of LF shows numerous particularities, some of which are shared with other North American varieties, such as *catin* (*poupée*) "doll," *chassis* (*fenêtre*) "window," *bessons* (*jumeaux*) "twins," *char* (*voiture*, *auto*) "car," *graffigne*r (*égratigner*) "to scratch," and others that are shared with French-based creoles, notably Haitian Creole: *chérant* (*cher*) "expensive," *siau* (*seau*) "bucket," *quitter* (*permettre*, *laisser*) "to allow," *rester* (*habiter*) "to reside."

New England

An estimated 900,000 immigrants from Québec province and the Maritime Provinces of Nova Scotia and New Brunswick began to stream into New England and northern New York state between 1840 and 1930, attracted by the labor needs of textile mills and shoe factories. In the various mill towns in which they settled, these francophones formed tight-knit self-contained communities, referred to as *Petits Canadas*, served by a Catholic church and a parochial school offering bilingual education. The use of French was also fostered by the establishment of numerous associations, including mutual aid societies, and art and musical clubs, and was enhanced by a wide variety of newspapers and periodicals. But after 1930, various social movements and political events, such as access to higher education on the part of the second and third generations and World War II, eroded the relative self-sufficiency of Franco-American communities and increased the social mobility of their members, who became progressively assimilated into mainstream American society (Miller 1969; Quintal and Cotnoir 1983; Richard 2002).

As pointed out by Fox (2007: 1279), research on the linguistic situation of New England French (NEF) has been sporadic and narrowly focused. Most studies, beginning with Sheldon (1887) and continuing with Locke (1946) have dealt with borrowing and the pronunciation of small numbers of speakers. Although beginning in the 1990s there appeared articles resting on more solid empirical grounds and dealing with morphosyntactic and lexical issues (Charbonneau 1997; Fox 1998; Russo and Roberts 1999), there exist neither major descriptions of the structure nor documentation of the lexical particularities of the various local varieties of NEF comparable to what has been accomplished in Acadiana. A major collaborative project undertaken by the State University of New York at Albany and the University of Maine has begun to fill the many gaps in our knowledge (Fox and Smith 2005; Fox 2007). That study focuses on eight communities, half in northern New England and half in southern New England, differing with regard to the proportion of speakers declaring francophone ancestry and use of French at home (Table 7.4).

Table 7.4. *Use of French at home in eight New England communities*

	Community	French ancestry (%)	Use of French at home 1990 (%)	2000 (%)
North	Van Buren, ME	82	76	75
	Berlin, NH	65	38	32
	Biddeford, ME	60	32	21
	Waterville, ME	39	13	8
South	Woonsocket, RI	55	20	10
	Gardner, MA	37	10	5
	Southbridge, CT	41	9	5
	Bristol, MA	24	7	5

Source: Fox and Smith 2005.

The high level of use and retention of French in Van Buren, located in the Upper Saint John River Valley that borders New Brunswick, Canada, stems from the constant contact with French speakers across the border (Price 2007). Elsewhere, despite the sizeable proportion of persons declaring French ancestry, Table 7.4 shows a sharp decline in the use of the language. Fox and Smith (2005: 123) posit two geographical axes determining variation in the speech of these communities resulting from patterns of migration: a north/south axis characterized by the level of English influence, greater in the South than in the North; an east/west axis wherein eastern varieties are more likely to show features associated with Acadian French, such as the palatalization of velar stops before front vowels.

Francophone isolates

There exist a number of francophone isolates in the USA in addition to these two primary bastions of francophony, which cannot be examined in detail here due to space constraints. Nonetheless, they provide valuable insight into the use of French in the USA and deserve mention. The nature of the French imported into North America in the seventeenth and eighteenth centuries – Colonial French – may be inferred from local varieties experiencing severe language loss in Old Mines, Missouri (Dorrance 1935; Carrière 1937; McDermott 1941; Thogmartin 1970, 1979; Thomas 1981), and Red Lake Falls, Minnesota (Benoit 1975, 1988; Creagh 1988; Papen 2005). A related variety imported from the islet of Saint Barth, a dependency of Guadeloupe, in the late nineteenth century exists in a section of the harbor called *carénage* or Cha-Cha Frenchtown in Charlotte-Amalie, the main town of Saint Thomas, in the US Virgin Islands (Highfield 1979; Calvet and Chaudenson 1998). A variety of French historically distinct from Colonial French was introduced in the central Pennsylvania hamlet of Frenchville by settlers from eastern areas of France in the mid-nineteenth century (Caujolle 1972; Uritescu and Mougeon 2003; Bullock and Gerfen 2004). Another isolate, Valdese, North Carolina, features a variety of Occitan (southern French dialects), the vernacular language of Waldensian settlers from the mountainous western part of Piedmont, Italy (T. G. Pons 1973; C. R. Pons 1990). Valdman (1979) provides further details on these varieties.

Public presence of French

Media

Though not nearly as omnipresent as Spanish-language media, there are important sources of francophone media in the USA. In New England in 1937, there were twenty-one French-language newspapers and four monthly publications (Ham 1938). At present, the only existing periodical in that region is the *Forum*, published quarterly by the Franco-American Center at the University of Maine, which contains articles in French and English. In Louisiana, Centenary College publishes *Tintamarre* which, although it is widely distributed in the Francophone Triangle, appears irregularly. The newspaper *France-Amérique*, published twice monthly in New York, provides French-language news coverage to an estimated 60,000 readers. It is the largest US-based French-language newspaper and is also the international version of *Le Figaro*, a daily newspaper in France. Interestingly, the French-medium print media outlets with the broadest impact are two weekly newspapers serving the Haitian diaspora, *Haïti Progrès* and *Haïti en Marche*, most of whose articles are in French rather than Haitian Creole. For example, of the twenty pages of *Haïti en Marche*, only one contains material in Haitian Creole.

For the two indigenous francophone communities, radio stations appear to be the main French language media vectors. In New England, WNRI in Woonsocket broadcasts two programs on weekends totaling five hours. In Louisiana, access to French via the airwaves is far easier. For example, KRVS, the Lafayette public radio station, provides thirty hours weekly of material in LF and LC and one hour in SF. Ten hours weekly of SF and LF programs are broadcast by KBON and KEUN (Eunice), KVPI (Ville Platte), and KLRZ (Lafourche parish) and two hours weekly by WWNO (New Orleans), WYNK (Baton Rouge), and KSCL (Shreveport). With regard to television, three Lafayette stations, Channel 3, Channel 10, and the Cox Cable Acadiana Open Channel provide access to weather information and some news on a regular basis. However, it seems that most people in Louisiana are exposed to French and local culture, particularly Cajun music, via the internet, particularly

Radio CODOFIL, Radio Louisiane, and the site of the French consulate in New Orleans.[6]

Education

In New England, until the 1960s, schooling largely took place in parochial schools and the language of instruction was French. At that time, many parochial schools closed due to a variety of external forces, and francophone students entered the public school system, many facing difficulty because use of French was stigmatized and punished (Hagel 1981; Jacobson 1984). In Louisiana, during the nineteenth and early twentieth centuries, parochial school, whose main language of instruction was French, did not reach the majority of speakers of LF relatively isolated in the bayous and marsh areas, among whom the rate of illiteracy remained high. The constitution of 1921 instituted English as the sole language of instruction in all of Louisiana, and Cajuns of that generation who had to write numerous times "I shall not speak French on the school grounds" were shamed into not passing on to their children a stigmatized tongue (Ancelet 1988). Following the enactment of the Bilingual Education. Act in 1968, the language maintenance or transitional programs it funded were stretched in both New England and Louisiana to attempt to rejuvenate the eroding vernacular French varieties and LC.

The most striking difference between these two bastions of US francophony is the depth and intensity of discussion about which variety of French should be taught. As Ancelet (1988) stresses, after World War II, Cajun soldiers whose knowledge of their community language translated into positive experiences in France contributed to a revalorization of their language and culture. Perceiving the advantage for the tourist industry of a revived competence in French, James Domengeaux, an influential Lafayette lawyer and former US congressman, persuaded the Louisiana legislature to establish and fund the Council for the Development of French in Louisiana (CODOFIL). Interestingly, the original mission of CODOFIL was defined as: "do any and all things necessary to accomplish the development, utilization, and preservation of *the French language as found in Louisiana* (emphasis mine) for the cultural, economic and touristic benefit of the state." The mission was later changed to the development of French *in Louisiana.*

Proclaiming *L'école a détruit le français, l'école doit reconstruire le français* (Schools destroyed French, schools must rebuild French), CODOFIL launched a massive program for the teaching of SF at the elementary school level throughout the state. Because most Louisianan elementary teachers lacked proficiency in SF, CODOFIL began importing French, Belgian, and Québécois instructors, referred to collectively as the "International Brigades." But another slogan of CODOFIL announced *Tu sauves la langue, tu sauves la culture* (You save the language, you save the culture). This strategy triggered a reaction from local Cajun activists who failed to see how an imported variety not mastered by most Franco-Louisianans could revive their culture. They prepared materials for the teaching of LF for use at school and, especially, at university levels (Faulk 1977; Abshire-Fontenot and Barry 1979) or those focusing on SF but incorporating features of LF (Gelhay 1985). For example, the latter author provides matching SF and LF lexical equivalents, for example, *fenêtre* and *chassis*, respectively, for "window." Except for Faulk, who devised an autonomous spelling difficult to decipher for users of SF, Cajun activists wisely adhered to the conventional French spelling but retained local grammatical and lexical particularities (Ancelet 1993).

In high school French courses and in immersion programs, the introduction of LC and LF is hampered by the dearth of native Louisianan teachers mastering these varieties. Tornquist (2000) found that of 110 instructors teaching in immersion programs in Acadiana only three were Louisiana natives and twenty eight were naturalized residents of the state. On the other hand, one detects among all teachers a growing interest in local language and culture that translates into the introduction of LF in the classroom. In addition, local universities, in particular Louisiana State University, have introduced classes in LF as an option for fulfilling the language requirement.[7]

Regarding the teaching of French as a foreign language, of the 1.4 million students in US colleges and universities studying a foreign language in fall 2006, 13 percent (more than 200,000) were studying French, making it the second most popular language of study after Spanish (Modern Language Association 2007). This number is up 2.2 percent since 2002. French is also the second most studied language at the secondary level, with 8 percent of language students choosing French, for a total enrollment of more than 1 million (National Center for Education Statistics 2002b). There are also ninety total or partial French immersion programs in the USA spread among many states, of which twenty seven, the largest number in any state, are located in Louisiana (Center for Applied Linguistics 2006a).

Religion

The Catholic church has played an important role in the history of French in the USA. The intimate link between Catholicism and the French language is symbolized by the motto *Qui perd sa langue, perd sa foi* (Losing one's language is losing one's faith). From the first waves of francophone immigration until the 1960s in New England, the church played a particularly important role in the maintenance of French. Brault (1972) notes that Catholicism was integral in defining Franco-American identity in New England, and Fox (1995) claims that francophone communities centered on the church, which offered services in

French and ran parochial schools where the language of instruction was French. As parochial schools lost influence and closed in the 1970s, though, this impact waned. In Acadiana, French-speaking priests were no longer replaced and the Catholic church moved toward the exclusive use of English in religious services (Ancelet 1988).

Evidence of language shift to English and of French maintenance

Signs of shift

Few speakers of vernacular varieties of French in the USA do not possess competence in English as well. In fact, around 92 percent of Census respondents who speak French at home claim to speak English "well" or "very well" (US Census Bureau 2007c). Bilingualism, which entails a high level of language contact, leads to borrowing, calquing, and code-switching, phenomena amply discussed in Chapter 2 of this volume. Moreau (2000) suggests that in a bilingual situation, these phenomena may also reflect a conscious choice on the part of speakers, akin to the switching between styles and registers. For example, for a speaker of LF, the use of *elle est **gone** à la **grocery*** instead of SF *elle est allée à l'épicerie* (she went to the grocery store) may stem from a conscious choice that has sociolinguistic significance. The period during which a form adopted from the dominant language is considered external may be relatively short, as is attested by the rapid grammatical assimilation of borrowings. For example, in Red Lake Falls French, the inflections for plural on nouns and the past participle of verbs are eliminated in loanwords: *les farms* /farm/ rather than /farmz/ and *self propel* rather than *self propelled*. Picone (1996) interprets such accommodations, which often result in forms that differ from both the external language and the home language, as part of an intercode from which bilingual speakers may draw to enrich their vocabulary or effect stylistic distinctions. For example, in the LF sentence *Ils voulaient **check** sur la situation* "They wanted to check out the situation," the verb *check* is neither assimilated to SF, *ils voulaient **checker***, nor does it preserve the correct English form, *ils voulaient **to check***.

Borrowing is predictable when speakers of French vernaculars which have evolved in a rural context are exposed to terms absent from the traditional culture. For example, in Frenchville French, which lacks the word *usine*, speakers have adopted *factory*.[8] Calques, on the other hand, involve expressing a concept from English with vocabulary from French, resulting in expressions that are often not comprehensible to nonbilinguals. For example, in Old Mines French, Thogmartin (1979: 116) notes the use of *courir* modeled on the polysemous verb *to run* instead of SF *opérer* [*une machine*] "to run a machine," *tenir* [*un magasin*] "to run a store" and the compound *to run out of* for *manquer de:*

Table 7.5. *Use of French varieties in Louisiana*

	Age group				
	0–19	20–29	30–44	45–64	≥65
	N = 14	N = 56	N = 128	N = 176	N = 147
Louisiana Creole (%)	7.1	5.3	8.5	10.8	8.8
Cajun French (%)	35.5	57.2	57	58.5	59.2
Standard French (%)	57.1	37.5	34.4	30.7	32

Source: Henry 1994.

il[s] ont couru ennehors de sel "they ran out of salt" (*ils ont manqué de sel*), *i'courait une groc'rie* "he ran a grocery store" (*il tenait une épicerie*).

Code-switching involves inserting multiword segments from the external language into sentences of the home language. Clear-cut examples are offered by New England French (NEF) ***What for you*** *m'a vendu une hache non-garantie?* "sold me an ax not guaranteed" (Locke 1946: 420), and Frenchville French ***Oh, it's better for you, well, I come up on sixty-three***, *il y a vingt-cinq ans* "25 years ago" (Caujolle 1972). But it is often difficult to distinguish between one-word code-switches and borrowings, for example, LF: *On communiquait sur* ***le shortwave****, sur le radio,* ***FM frequency****, on parlait en français sur l'air* "We used to communicate on the shortwave radio, FM frequency, we spoke in French on the air."

It is a truism that the survival of language varieties fundamentally depends on their transmission through communicative networks anchored in daily use in the home. For all US francophone communities, there is scant intergenerational transmission of vernacular varieties of French. In a study conducted in thirty-five Acadiana communities in which subjects were asked which language they spoke better, Trépanier (1993) found that French was chosen by 41 percent of the young adults, compared to 92 percent for their grandparents, 84 percent for their parents, and only 3 percent for their children. Also in Louisiana, the only community for which solid data exist, there appears to be considerable use of LF on the part of older speakers but, a shift to SF on the part of the younger generation; see Table 7.5 (Henry 1994).[9]

LF and NEF became endangered with the onset of modernization of the US, especially after World War II. In New England, as the textile industry moved to the southern states, Franco-Americans left the *Petits Canadas* to seek broader economic opportunities, and they had greater access to higher levels of education conducted exclusively in English. In Louisiana, with the economic boom triggered by the development of the oil industry, Cajuns progressively abandoned traditional occupations that involved close social networks, such as

Table 7.6. *Forms of the third person plural subject pronoun + verb in LF*

	ils: total (%)	eux-aut' (%)	eusse (%)	ça (%)
55+	27	31	33	9
30–54	5	14	66	15
<30	1.5	1.5	79	19

Source: Adapted from Rottet 2001.

farming, ranching, fishing, trapping, and fiber crafts, as well as cultural events based on cooperation with neighbors, such as *boucheries* (slaughtering cattle and sharing the meat) and *bals de maison* or *fais-dodo* (dances organized in the home).

Because of their limited intergenerational transmission, vernacular varieties of French in the USA are experiencing severe attrition which, ultimately, is leading to their loss of true functional value and is threatening their survival. They also show features of language attrition whose study proves difficult for the vernaculars spoken in most of the isolates because the lack of sufficient data gathered over an extended period of time makes impossible the comparison of language structures over several generations. But the more thorough and revealing studies conducted in the two US communities where some intergenerational transmission still perdures, New England and Louisiana, have yielded robust data, particularly in the case of the latter community (Rottet 2001).

Language attrition is often accompanied by a reduction of stylistic variation. Research on this phenomenon in LF (Rottet 2001, 2005) has shown that extensive variation in the pronominal and verbal systems tends to be reduced among younger speakers with limited competence in the vernacular. The excerpt below produced by an older LF fluent speaker reveals four variants of the third person plural pronoun and verb form:

*Mais sho', **eux-autes** serait contents, tu les appelle 'oir, parce que **ça travaille** tard, **eusse** a ein grand jardin en arrière, et **ils travaillont** tard, des fois **ils** sont tard dans la maison, so tu peux les appeler quand-ce que/'oir équand tu pourrais les prendre.* (Rottet 2001)

(But, sure, they would be happy, you call to see them, because they work late, they have a large field in back, and they work late, at times they are (come back) late at the house, so you may call them to see when you can get them.)

As Table 7.6 indicates, there is a decrease in the number of variants directly related to age group: whereas older speakers use three forms with nearly the same frequency, the youngest groups have narrowed down the variants to one, *eusse*. Younger speakers, who are in fact semispeakers rather than fluent speakers, possess a more limited repertoire of forms that could be used potentially to effect stylistic shifts.[10]

Signs of maintenance

Because the LF community is more cohesive, it has been possible to launch initiatives for the preservation and renaissance of the traditional culture. The combined action of educators and researchers, at the school and university levels, combined with the reorientation of the policy of CODOFIL, now staffed by Cajun activists, toward valorizing local varieties of French, have had a positive effect on the maintenance of LF. Of particular importance has been the rejuvenation of Cajun culture, particularly in the musical and culinary spheres. It has contributed to a grassroots movement toward the valorization of that culture and attracted tourists from francophone countries, thus providing native Louisianans an incentive for maintaining or re-acquiring a mastery of French. Of particular importance in efforts for the revalorization and maintenance of LF is the production of literary works (Gravelles 1979; Ancelet 1988).

It has been more difficult for New England Franco-American activists, scattered across six states, to launch a cohesive set of initiatives. In 1947, leaders of various organizations and representative of some postsecondary institutions (but not the prestigious Ivy League universities) founded the Comité de la Vie Franco-Américaine (Committee for Franco-American Life) designed to coordinate the activities of member associations (Quintal and Cotnoir 1983). The initiatives of these associations were generally top-down, and failed to generate the type of grassroots support enjoyed by Cajun activists (Richard 2002). They tended to stress the historical and culture link with Québec province (Brault 1986). One of the more successful initiatives of the Comité was to persuade state legislatures to create local commissions for the promotion of Franco-American culture. The New Hampshire Commission attempted to launch the CODOFINE (Council for the Development of French in New England) on the model of the CODOFIL, but without success because of the lack of funds (Quintal and Cotnoir 1983). The film *Réveil* (Levine 2003) documents other French revitalization efforts in this part of the USA.

The question of French-language maintenance among the francophone African communities in the USA has only barely begun to be addressed. Current research in Chicago (Cornell 2008) has found that many African-origin immigrants studying at local universities find ways to use French to their professional advantage. It remains unclear to what degree French survives in these communities by way of intergenerational transmission. Upon arrival in the USA, parents who were educated in French and speak one or more regional language from their native country in Africa must choose how often and in what situations to use which languages with their children. Perhaps they choose English, the new language of their children's education, or they try to pass on the French they learned in school, or they use the regional language(s) they grew up speaking.

Language and identity

Attitudes toward SF and local varieties constitute a major factor in the use and maintenance of French in Louisiana and New England. Fox (2007) reports that some speakers are intimidated when confronted with SF, whereas others are reluctant to converse with interlocutors whose speech they perceive as marked by vernacular features, such as the use of /we/ for /wa/ in the pronouns *moi* "me" and *toi* "you" (/mwe/, twe/ versus SF /mwa, /twa/, respectively). Particularly negatively marked are borrowing and code-switching. On the other hand, many fluent speakers do not consider that these strategies affect the quality of their speech, as is demonstrated by the following excerpt (Fox 2007: 1289):

> *Parfois elle mêlait des mots d'anglais avec des mots de français pis quand j'essayais de la corriger elle me reprochait "je parle un aussi bon français que vous hein parce que j'ai étudié avec les Sœurs de la Présentation quand j'étais jeune."*
>
> (Sometimes she would mix English with French words and when I tried to correct her, she reproached me "I speak as good a French as you, you know, because I studied with the sisters of the Presentation Order when I was young.")

Although SF is the preferred variety in most of New England, in areas such as the Upper Saint John Valley where Québécois and Acadian French are available, either from the media or Canadians, the latter varieties tend to be preferred (Price 2007).

With the decrease of the use of French at home, schools constitute a primary vector for the maintenance of French. The crucial factor in the debate about the choice between SF and local vernacular varieties in school programs is the attitude of parents. In a survey involving about 800 parents of pupils in immersion programs in Acadiana, Tornquist (2000) reports that, although most favored the use of SF, these parents, most of whom do not possess competence in the local vernaculars, nonetheless are prepared to accept the use of these varieties in the classroom provided that SF remains the main target; see Tables 7.7 and 7.8.

Conclusion

In the absence of constant demographic renewal, the presence of French in the USA is expected to diminish. The considerable increase in speakers of Spanish, Chinese, Tagalog, Vietnamese, Korean, and Russian in the USA between 1990 and 2000 and between 2000 and 2007 shown in Table 1.1 is due to recent immigration. In comparison, the flow of primary immigrants from France or other

Table 7.7. *Parental opinions on teaching local vernaculars*

	Yes (%)	No (%)
Teach LF	45	19
Teach LC	38	21

Source: Adapted from Tornquist 2000.

Table 7.8. *Parental opinions on the variety of French they would like their children to speak*

Variety (or varieties)	Percentage
SF	38
SF+LF	29
LF	10
LC	2
SF+LF+LC	9

Source: Adapted from Tornquist 2000.

French-speaking regions is negligible. Although immigration from Haiti is significant and will no doubt continue, these immigrants are primarily speakers of Haitian Creole, not French. Their linguistic impact is reflected by a nearly 100 percent increase of speakers of that language between 1990 and 2000, as noted in Table 7.1. But the small proportion of habitual users of French in that diaspora cannot be expected to have any significant impact on the maintenance of French. The low level of intergenerational transmission in New England and south Louisiana is leading to serious attrition of the endogenous varieties of French. At best, in these two traditional bastions of francophony in the USA, there might be an increase in school acquirers of SF. However, there are hopeful signs, especially in Louisiana where there is a valorization of the indigenous vernacular varieties as part of an educational strategy focusing on the teaching of SF in schools.

From a scholarly perspective, the study of indigenous vernacular varieties of French is of particular interest for specialists in the language sciences. It contributes to a better understanding of the various interrelated phenomena that language shift triggers (such as borrowing, calquing, and code-switching) as well as of language attrition and loss. For specialists in French studies, it makes it possible to reconstruct the varieties of French exported to the American colonies and, given that they evolved independently of SF, they reveal the evolutionary tendencies of spoken French. US vernacular varieties also serve as repositories for linguistic forms and structures that have been eliminated in France by the diffusion of SF and the resultant elimination of regional dialects.

DISCUSSION QUESTIONS

1. Compare and contrast the prospects for French maintenance and shift in the two primary endogenous francophone communities in New England and Louisiana. Which factors are the same and which are different? Do you think differences in the situations of these communities will differentially impact the maintenance of French?

2. How do status and ideology play a role in language maintenance or shift? Specifically, consider the case of standard French (SF) versus vernacular varieties in US francophone communities. Why do parents in Louisiana want their children to speak SF, a variety that they themselves do not speak? What does this augur for maintenance of LF and LC? How have community activists approached the issue of status? Can you think of similar situations in other communities?

---

8 Vietnamese in the USA

Vy Thuc Dao and Carl L. Bankston III

Introduction

Vietnamese is the third most widely spoken language Asian language in the USA, spoken at home by an estimated 1,207,004 people in 2007, or about 2.2 percent of all of those who spoke a non-English language. Only Chinese, with 4.5 percent of non-English speakers, and Tagalog, with 2.7 percent of non-English speakers, were used by more Americans. As shown in Table 1.1, by 2007 Vietnamese ranked fifth among all the nation's non-English languages and it was one of the fastest growing. Vietnamese use has increased dramatically over the years. Spoken by only around 3,000 Vietnamese people in the USA in 1970 (Rumbaut 2007), by 1980 the number of speakers over the age of 5 who reported speaking Vietnamese at home had grown to close to 200,000, according to data from the US Census. By the time of the 1990 Census, this number had increased to 507,069 and then to 1,009,627 in 2000 and 1,207,004 in 2007.

History

From about 100 BCE until the tenth century CE, Vietnam was under Chinese rule. Throughout the Chinese period, classical Chinese, known in Vietnamese as Chũ-nho (pronounced roughly "chew nyahw"), was used for writing. From about the time of independence until as recently as the early twentieth century, the Vietnamese wrote their language in an adapted version of Chinese characters, known as Chũ-nôm (pronounced roughly "chew nohm"). During the seventeenth century, Jesuit missionaries, mainly of French origin, began arriving in Vietnam, and these missionaries began developing a new Vietnamese writing system, which came to be known as Quốc Ngũ (roughly, "gwhok ngeu"), or the "national language," which eventually became the modern Vietnamese writing system.

Over the course of Vietnamese history, three separate regions emerged. These three regions became the bases of the primary dialects of the Vietnamese language, and all three dialect varieties are mutually intelligible. Northern Vietnamese, or the Hanoi dialect, is regarded as the official dialect.

During the late nineteenth century, France colonized Vietnam and gradually established control. The French maintained their colonial domination of Vietnam until World War II, when it fell to Japan. Following the war, the French fought Communist-dominated Vietnamese forces in an effort to re-impose some measure of French control. Following military defeats, France was forced to grant independence, but it managed to limit the Communists to the northern part of the country by splitting Vietnam into two parts along the seventeenth parallel. Two provisions prescribed by the Geneva Convention included an agreement to 300 days of unencumbered movement between North and South as well as elections held within two years. While some Southerners traveled to the North, the bulk of migration resulted in nearly one million Northern Vietnamese settling in the South. Many Catholics and others opposed to the socialist government of what became known as North Vietnam moved to the South. The Northern Vietnamese and some allies in the South retained a determination to re-unite the country. Gradually, the USA became involved in supporting the southern part of the country in order to prevent what American policy makers during that Cold War period saw as the spread of international Communism. Thus, entire villages of speakers of the northern dialect became residents of South Vietnam.

In 1973, with growing unwillingness among the American people for continuing the war in Vietnam, the USA withdrew nearly all of its forces from Vietnam, Cambodia, and Laos. In the spring of 1975, South Vietnam fell to the forces of the North, beginning a flow of refugees to the USA over the course of the following two decades. Immediately following the fall of South Vietnam, the US government rapidly created a program known as Operation New Life, which moved refugees to American military bases to prepare them for temporary resettlement in the USA. Among this first wave of refugees, a large segment included educated Vietnamese from the middle class, academics, Vietnamese government and military personnel, and others who had worked for the American military in both direct and support capacities. Thus, in this way 126,000 Vietnamese became the first wave of refugees from Southeast Asia. During the late 1970s, Vietnamese continued to leave their country by boat or on foot across Cambodia to Thailand, and the exodus continued into the 1990s.

Initially, American policy makers attempted to scatter the deluge of new arrivals from Vietnam around the nation in order to encourage assimilation and provide manageable numbers for social service agencies charged with service and support of the refugees. However, many refugee organizations found it easier to settle them as groups. In addition, the Vietnamese themselves began to cluster into ethnic communities for the sake of cultural similarity and mutual support. As a result of the early efforts at scattering, the reliance on a variety of organizations for resettlement, and Vietnamese desires to form communities in the new homeland, the Vietnamese language became dispersed around the USA, but also concentrated in a handful of metropolitan areas and distinctive neighborhoods.

Demographics

The most striking demographic characteristic of the Vietnamese American population is its newness. According to Rumbaut (2007), there were probably only about 3,000 Vietnamese in the entire USA in 1969, including wives of US military personnel who had served in Vietnam. During the next half-decade, the worsening war situation promoted increasing immigration from Vietnam. Zhou and Bankston (1998) give an estimate of about 15,000 during the early 1970s. By the beginning of 1975 there were reportedly as many as 30,000 Vietnamese in the USA (Rumbaut 2007). Following Operation New Life, the Vietnamese-American population began to grow rapidly. After 1975, 1980 saw the largest number of refugee admissions from Vietnam, with over 95,000 refugees arriving in the USA.

According to the 2000 US Census, people of Vietnamese ethnicity made up about 0.4 percent of the US population. As we have described above, the process of settlement during the late twentieth century resulted both in dispersal around the country and in concentration in ethnic communities. Montana, North Dakota, and Wyoming were the only states in the USA to hold fewer than 100 Vietnamese in the 2000 US Census, and identifiable Vietnamese communities could be found around the country. This pattern can be seen in Table 8.1, which shows the ten states with the largest Vietnamese-speaking populations.

In addition to the data from this table, the MLA's language maps (Modern Language Association 2008) show a tendency toward clustering on the West Coast. Indeed, about 40 percent of Vietnamese speakers are located in California, and the third largest population is in Washington. This was largely a result of the secondary migration following settlement in the USA, in which Vietnamese sought to form ethnic communities. However, clusters of Vietnamese can be found throughout the USA, as is obvious from the presence in the top ten of states as diverse as Georgia, Pennsylvania, and Texas, in the pattern of dispersed concentrations that we have just discussed.

As Table 8.2 shows, the Vietnamese are generally underrepresented within the largest American cities. Only in San Diego, where they are 2.3 percent of the city population, and in Houston, where they are 1.6 percent of the population, do they show percentages much over their proportion of the American population as a whole. This is a reflection of two related tendencies on the part of the new Vietnamese-American population. First, they have formed in many of the newer, growing localities such as South Texas, the Atlanta region, or Southern

Table 8.1. *States with the largest Vietnamese-speaking populations*

	Ages 5+	Percentage of all US Vietnamese speakers
California	459,587	40.04
Texas	139,534	12.15
Washington	49,104	4.27
Florida	40,811	3.55
Massachusetts	39,876	3.47
Virginia	38,965	3.39
Pennsylvania	35,834	3.12
Georgia	30,487	2.65
New York	27,886	2.42
Louisiana	21,081	1.83
Total in USA	1,207,004	

Source: Modern Language Association 2009, US Census Bureau 2007c.

Table 8.2. *Ten largest urban areas in total population and in Vietnamese population*

City and state	Rank by total population	Rank by Vietnamese population	Percentage Vietnamese of total population
New York, NY	1	5	0.2
Los Angeles, CA	2	2	0.4
Chicago, IL	3	9	0.3
Houston, TX	4	17	1.6
Philadelphia, PA	5	12	0.7
Phoenix, AZ	6	42	0.5
San Diego, CA	7	23	2.3
Dallas, TX	8	35	0.6
San Antonio, TX	9	63	0.2
Detroit, MI	10	*	*

Note: * Not available. Estimated Vietnamese population is less than 50.
Source: US Census Bureau 2000a.

California, rather than in the old northeastern immigrant magnets. Second, Vietnamese communities have generally formed in metropolitan regions, but not within urban centers. As we can see in Table 8.3, Vietnamese settlements in the USA can be seen more clearly in the Metropolitan Statistical Areas (MSAs) of the Census than in cities.

Table 8.3. *Fifteen metropolitan statistical areas with the largest Vietnamese populations in 2000*

Metropolitan Area	Vietnamese population
1. Los Angeles-Riverside-Orange County, CA	234,150
2. San Francisco-Oakland-San Jose, CA	144,234
3. Houston-Galveston-Brazoria, TX	64,155
4. Washington, D.C.-Baltimore, DC-MD-VA	45,741
5. Dallas-Fort Worth, TX	45,488
6. Seattle-Tacoma-Bremerton, WA	38,819
7. San Diego, CA	34,496
8. Boston	33,145
9. New York-Northern New Jersey-Long Island, NY-NJ-PA-CT	26,606
10, Atlanta, GA	24,248
11. Philadelphia-Wilmington-Atlantic City, PA-NJ-DE-MD	23,359
12. Portland-Salem, OR-WA	20,605
13. Sacramento-Yolo, CA	18,454
14. Chicago-Gary-Kenosha, IL-IN-WI	16,024
14. Minneapolis-St. Paul, MN, WI	15,498
15. New Orleans, LA	15,376

Source: US Census Bureau 2000a.

In Southern California, for example, the Vietnamese settled in the region of Los Angeles, but also in newer neighborhoods outside of even this highly dispersed city. Although only about 19,500 Vietnamese lived in Los Angeles itself in 2000, as seen in Table 8.3, an estimated 234,150 lived in the larger Los Angeles–Riverside–Orange County metropolitan area. Orange County was the site of the largest Vietnamese community in the USA, with an estimated Vietnamese population of 136,197, making Orange County home to over 12 percent of all the Vietnamese in the USA. The city of Westminster, within Orange County, the center of "Little Saigon," is sometimes regarded as the cultural capital of Vietnamese America. In 2000, Westminster contained an estimated Vietnamese population of 27,121, out of a total population of 87,884, so that Vietnamese made up nearly one third of the city's people.

A sizeable American-born generation has only begun to emerge in the dispersed Vietnamese-American concentrations. In 1980, 95 percent of the Vietnamese in the USA were first generation. Only 3 percent were second generation and only 2 percent were third generation; counting as third generation anyone born in the USA with at least one parent who was also born in the USA. By 2006, as a result of the continuing flow of refugees, 77 percent of the now much larger Vietnamese-American population was still first generation. The second generation had increased to 19 percent, but the third generation was still a miniscule 4 percent of the total Vietnamese population in the USA. Native-born Vietnamese-Americans were limited to young people. Only one third of those under 21 were first generation in 2006, while 55 percent were second generation and 12 percent were third generation (Ruggles *et al.* 2009).

Both the settlement of the Vietnamese in ethnic communities and the continuing arrival of newcomers have helped to maintain the Vietnamese language in the USA. A native-born generation has only recently emerged and third generation Vietnamese-Americans are still few in number. It may well be that as Vietnamese population growth from migration slows and members of native-born generations move away from ethnic neighborhoods, Vietnamese will become less widely spoken than it is today. Nevertheless, it appears that Vietnamese communities and people with memories and active links to Vietnam will continue to be part of American society for the foreseeable future.

Public presence of Vietnamese

Although knowledge of the Vietnamese language is much less common than knowledge of Spanish or other European languages in the American public at large, Vietnamese has been gaining a public presence in the USA. Most state Departments of Motor Vehicles provide informational literature in Vietnamese and several offer at least part of the driving test in Vietnamese. Vietnamese is now taught at many colleges and universities, but it is rarely taught as a foreign language in secondary schools. Many primary and secondary schools in areas with large Vietnamese populations do have Vietnamese-speaking counselors, and Vietnamese bilingual education is available in Boston and several other cities around the USA. While Vietnamese can often be heard in public places throughout the nation, Vietnamese still has more of a private presence, rather than a public presence, as a means of communication among family and community members. Nevertheless, one can see some influences of Vietnamese speakers on American government, media, and education.

Government

Early Vietnamese arrivals in the USA were much more concerned with political events in Vietnam than in the USA. In addition, since most arrived in this country as refugees, they were often reluctant to become involved in American politics. The most visible form of Vietnamese involvement in American politics around the nation has taken place through the Vietnamese-American Voters' Associations that mainly came into existence in the 1980s. The primary functions of these associations have been to encourage Vietnamese-Americans to become citizens, to learn about the American political system, and to register to vote.

While Vietnamese-Americans continue to have a low-key presence on the American political scene, they have become participants in American civic life. Foreign-born people of Vietnamese ethnicity show a higher rate of naturalization than other immigrants. The 2000 Census showed that 58 percent of foreign-born Vietnamese-Americans were naturalized citizens, compared to 40 percent of all foreign-born people in the USA (see Figure 1.2 in Chapter 1 of this volume). Over one third of the Vietnamese who had arrived in the USA between 1990 and 2000 were naturalized citizens, compared to only 13 percent of all immigrants who arrived during the 1990s.

The Vietnamese language has been much less of a political issue in the USA than Spanish has. A number of Vietnamese-American political leaders emerged in the 1990s, but they generally have not involved themselves in language politics. The most prominent Vietnamese-American politicians in the early twenty-first century are Van Tran, a Republican member of the California State Assembly for parts of Orange County, and Hubert Vo, a Democratic Representative from Houston in the Texas State Legislature. It is also notable that recent entries into political and governmental arenas include members of the younger generation. Madison Nguyen and Lan Nguyen (no relation) became the first two school board officials of Vietnamese-American descent in the USA for their respective school districts. Madison Nguyen was later elected to the San Jose, California, City Council in 2005.

Media

Most of the print and electronic media in the Vietnamese language can be found in the fifteen metropolitan areas listed in Table 8.3. While still small relative to English-language or Spanish-language media in this country, newspapers, radio stations, and television stations have been growing rapidly around the country. One sign of this growth was the appearance of the first annual Vietnamese-American Media Expo in Houston in 2006. Held for the second time in May 2007, the goal of the exposition has been to provide a networking event for Vietnamese-American media, businesses, advertisers, and for members of the public interested in the Vietnamese media.

Several Vietnamese language television stations have come into existence in the USA. The best known and most influential of these is probably the Saigon Broadcasting Television Network (SBTN), based in Garden Grove in Orange County's Little Saigon. Viet-Nam Public Television (VPTV) operates out of Falls Church, Virginia, in the Washington, DC, area. A number of localities around the country have Vietnamese-language programs available through community access television.

Radio stations in Vietnamese, such as the Tieng Nuoc Toi (TNT) and Little Saigon Radio (LSR) station in Houston, have spread around the country. While the rise of internet radio, such as SaigonBao.com, has made it possible to hear news in Vietnamese almost anywhere, the local stations provide valuable information to their own communities.

Started in the late 1970s, *Nguoi Viet* was the first Vietnamese-language newspaper to be published in the USA. Still in operation, *Nguoi Viet* has since customized its operation to accommodate the changing demographic trends of the Vietnamese community, adding an English-language edition as well as an online repository of news. Vietnamese-language newspapers have since become widely available. Most of these are local, with small circulations, but some have reached large numbers of readers. The San Jose *Mercury* began publishing the *Viet Mercury* in Vietnamese in the late 1990s, and the Santa Clara County publication became one of the country's best known Vietnamese-language newspapers before it ceased publication in 2005. The *Viet Mercury* was followed by another California paper, the *VTimes*.

Increasingly, new publications being distributed in Vietnamese communities are not solely restricted to Vietnamese speakers and focus less on local news. *Yellow* magazine in Houston, Texas, or *Nirvana Fashion and Lifestyle* magazine in Mountain View, California, cater aggressively to the youthful, upwardly mobile panethnic Asian market. Heavily retail oriented, *Yellow* and *Nirvana* feature articles on high fashion, entertainment and lifestyle, arbitrating taste and style for affluent, urban Asians. Articles are in English with occasional phrases and references from all Asian subgroup languages. This is a practical choice given the mission of securing readership from a linguistically diverse group, yet this may signal a larger trend in the future of language maintenance for the group of young Vietnamese who have attained high levels of education and high earning capacities. They, along with their affluent Chinese, South Indian, and Southeast Asian counterparts, may adopt a panethnic, linguistically neutral identity that resonates most closely to their middle- to upper-class lifestyle and aspirations.

Education

The Preparation for American Secondary Schools (PASS) program, begun in refugee camps in Thailand and the Philippines in the mid-1980s, constituted one of the first American educational programs directed specifically at Southeast Asian refugee children. PASS established American-style schools in the camps. The curriculum emphasized mathematics and English-language skills, along with cross-cultural training (Peterson and Sosnowski 1985).

Upon arrival in the USA, Vietnamese families frequently settled in low-income neighborhoods and therefore often attended schools characterized by economic disadvantage. In San Diego, for example, the Children of Immigrants Longitudinal Survey (CILS) (Portes and Rumbaut 2008) found that most of the

Vietnamese families lived in mixed neighborhoods with mostly other immigrants and with nonwhite native minorities. Over 60 percent of the Vietnamese adolescents attended schools where white students were the numerical minority, 49 percent were enrolled in inner-city schools, and 48 percent were in schools where over half of the students qualified for subsidized lunch, an indicator of poverty.

Lack of facility in English has been one of the greatest handicaps of Vietnamese-American students. Recall from Table 1.2 in Chapter 1 that 69 percent of Vietnamese immigrants reported speaking English "well" or "very well" in 2007, which was the lowest rate for all the languages profiled in this book. According to Rumbaut (1995), the San Diego school district classified over 40 percent of its Vietnamese students as Limited English Proficient (LEP) in 1992. In that same year, only 16 percent of the children of other Asian immigrants were so classified. In a study of Vietnamese students in Orange County's Little Saigon, Saito (1999: 3) noted, "the targeted FEP (Fluent English Proficient) population encompassed approximately 54 percent of the total 12th-grade Vietnamese students at the six high schools included in the study." In a study of high school students in a Vietnamese community in New Orleans (Zhou and Bankston 1998), the students were concentrated in two schools. Close to 70 percent of the Vietnamese pupils in the school located inside the Vietnamese neighborhood were classified as LEP as were nearly 30 percent of those at the nearby school outside of the neighborhood.

Even though many Vietnamese children faced the challenge of the English language, grew up in poor families, lived in inner-city neighborhoods, and attended urban public schools that many American middle-class families had abandoned, they made remarkable progress in education during the late twentieth century. As of 1990, Vietnamese adolescents were less likely than their American peers to drop out of high school, and Vietnamese young adults were more likely than their American peers to attend college. For example, in the Los Angeles metropolitan region, the dropout rate among US-born Vietnamese aged 16–19 was 5 percent, compared with 8 percent among whites; the high school dropout rate among US-born Vietnamese adults aged 18–24 was 9 percent, compared with 11 percent among whites; and the college attendance rate among US-born Vietnamese was 50 percent, compared with 38 percent among whites (Cheng and Yang 1996).

At the close of the twentieth century, young Vietnamese-Americans were still showing high rates of educational achievement and attainment. The 2000 US Census showed that both Vietnamese men and women in the 18 to 24 age group had higher rates of college attendance than the American population in general. A majority (52 percent) of Vietnamese men in this age group were attending college or graduate school in 2000, compared to under one third (32 percent) of all 18- to 24-year-old men. Women showed similar gaps:

55 percent of women in this age range were in college, compared to 37 percent of all women (US Census Bureau 2000a).

Relatively high rates of academic achievement and attainment have sometimes led to popular stereotypes of "the Vietnamese valedictorian."[1] Such stereotypes can lead to overlooking the many young people who do not fit into them, and this can cause those concerned with Vietnamese in American schools to ignore risks and problems. Zhou and Bankston (2000b) warned that the fact that many Vietnamese-American youth were apparently doing well in American schools could cause some to overlook the point that doing well and being well may be two entirely different matters. In their monograph, Zhou and Bankston (2000b) reported that student responses to psychological and emotional measures in the 1994 National Longitudinal Study of Adolescent Health suggested that contemporary Vietnamese-American students were prone to greater uncertainties, self-doubts, and emotional difficulties than other American adolescents.

Researchers have found school performance to be associated with Vietnamese-language abilities and usage. Bankston and Zhou (1995) surveyed Vietnamese students in a high school in New Orleans. They found that literacy in Vietnamese was related to overall scholastic performance, even though instruction in the school was primarily in English. They suggested that this could have been a result of transference of cognitive development, of the contribution of literacy in any language to general intellectual preparation. However, their evidence suggested an explanation rooted in social relations. According to Bankston and Zhou, Vietnamese-language skills were connected to ethnic self-identification, which was in turn connected to relations with adults in the social group, and that having a strong sense of ethnic identification, combined with support from Vietnamese adults, promoted academic achievement.

Vietnamese-language skills promote academic achievement because they connect children to social resources available in the family and community in three ways. First, in learning to speak, read, and write the language of their elders, children are socialized into accepting the goals and ambitions of their elders. Achieving places of respect in the new country through intergenerational mobility is a fundamental goal among these displaced people (Bankston and Zhou 1995, 2002). Second, language use gives children a sense of continuity with the cultural traditions that are felt to be basic to Vietnamese-American identity. Although the Vietnamese have drawn upon their traditions selectively in reconstructing social institutions in the new country, they still see tradition as the basis of their ties to one another. As Wharry (1993) found, maintaining the Vietnamese language is seen by Vietnamese students as a way of maintaining a distinctive culture. Third, learning the parental language involves children in organizations and activities that promote scholastic endeavors.

The association between Vietnamese-language abilities and overall school performance supports the view that Vietnamese bilingual education, in which students are encouraged to maintain their parental language, can contribute to academic excellence. Thus, the findings of Miller Maloof, Rubin, and Neville Miller (2006), that a Vietnamese heritage language school led to increased Vietnamese proficiency, suggests that such schools (usually offered on Saturday mornings) can have a positive influence on Vietnamese students' academic performance. There is also some evidence that Vietnamese-American parents agree that language maintenance should be part of the mainstream American school environment. In May 1997, Russell L. Young and MyLuong T. Tran surveyed 106 Vietnamese parents in San Diego on their attitudes toward bilingual education. Parents in this survey tended to favor making Vietnamese a part of the school curriculum, regardless of the English proficiency of their own children (Young and Tran 1999).

The role of language in school raises the empirical question of how likely it is that Vietnamese-American youth will continue to maintain the language of their parents into the future. As we discuss below, language maintenance may be increasingly problematic for American-born members of this group.

Evidence of language shift to English and of Vietnamese maintenance

Signs of shift

Adopting English and dropping a heritage language is a standard, almost stereotypical, part of the experience of ethnic groups established in the USA by immigration. There are variations in the extent and speed with which young members of these groups move away from the languages of their ancestors though, and there have been situations in which non-English languages have been retained and transmitted for generations. In their study of Vietnamese children in the USA, Zhou and Bankston (1998: 112) noted, "despite the recency of immigration, Vietnamese children have rapidly shifted their primary language use toward English, as have other immigrant children from non-English-speaking countries." In fact, in a study of immigrants in Southern California, Vietnamese, like other Asian languages, was found to have a linguistic life expectancy (defined as retaining the ability to speak the language) of between 1.3 and 2.0 generations of US residence, among the shortest of the groups studied (Rumbaut *et al.* 2006: 458), presenting evidence that a shift to English is taking place at a fairly rapid pace. Even when looking only at second generation members, though, Zhou and Bankston found that Vietnamese youth were less likely than Chinese, black, or white children of immigrants to become monolingual English speakers. They attributed this to language environments at home, ethnic density in neighborhoods, and limited socioeconomic status. Taking the last into consideration, they still found that "advantageous socio-economic status accelerates the shift to English but does not sever the tie to Vietnamese" (Zhou and Bankston 1998: 115).

As we have seen above, the most striking fact about the Vietnamese population in the USA is how recently it was established. Questions remain, therefore, about the extent to which a shift away from Vietnamese toward English will occur and about the form such a shift could take for members of this particular group. Assimilation theories posit that language shift among immigrants occurs in a linear fashion, where non-English speakers will, within a generation or two, progressively learn and use English so as to eventually replace their native language altogether. Yet the manner and details of this transition remain unclear (Bean and Stevens 2003). Language shift for the Vietnamese is mediated by two factors: one is a particular feature of the language itself and the other is the different social contexts in which young Vietnamese people speak the language.

Two significant characteristics of the Vietnamese language are its tonality and monosyllabic nature. The tonality of Vietnamese means that words take on meaning according to the tone with which they are pronounced. A third grammatical trait is its use of pronouns as forms of status indicators. Pronouns are parts of speech that replace nouns, such as *I*, *me*, *you*, *him*, or *her*, and in Vietnamese, personal pronouns serve as forms of address that describe the social positions of the speakers as well as their relationship. For example, in speaking to a grandparent, parent, or close elderly relative, a child, no matter their age, must refer to themselves as *con*, but if the elder person is a stranger, this renders the interaction formal and the speaker specifies they are *em* (that is, if they are a substantially younger male or female) or *toi* (if they are a middle-aged to comparably aged man or woman). The highest forms of address are reserved for the eldest and most respected individuals in Vietnamese society, such as *Ông* "grandfather" and *Bà* "grandmother," and both are used universally by all speakers whether or not there are actual familial ties. However, these universal titles are exceptional in that, principally, Vietnamese relies on very specific forms of address such as *chú*, an uncle who is your father's younger brother, and *gau*, your mother's younger brother.

Further, each of these titles is applied differently depending on the speaker's age and status, and it is important to correctly label oneself and one's conversation partner. This principle is often seen by non-Vietnamese as extraordinarily subtle and subjective. Between women of *approximately* similar age, no matter the formality, the term *chi* "sister," is appropriate when the women are unrelated friends, acquaintances, or strangers engaged in an informal transaction, but if the women are related, only the younger woman addresses the elder sister as *chi*, while the older woman also refers to herself as *chi* but calls her younger sister *em*, a more diminutive endearment. *Em* is also used to label younger brothers in reference to themselves toward older sisters and brothers, husbands refer to their wives as *em*, and best female friends will both use *em* in referring to themselves and their friends. Yet, wives call husbands *ahn* (an endearment of "brother" or "male loved one") as well as their older brothers, same-age or older male acquaintances, or same-age male cousins.

These rules form a complicated matrix of hierarchical labeling, and terms must be applied with a high degree of precision in order to avoid offense. First and 1.5 generation Vietnamese, who were children born in Vietnam or who settled in the USA between the ages of 5 and 13, respectively, are fluent in the social context of the language. They become skilled at an early age in discerning the subtleties of these status pronouns, and by the time they are teenagers rarely make mistakes in labeling. This is likely due to the consistent reinforcement of parents, family and the society at large. Vietnamese people replace all personal pronouns such as *I*, *me*, and *you* with these titles during conversation and bookend the talk by greeting and saying good-bye using status pronouns, such as *chào bàc* (greeting to an elder man by a low-status person) or *chào chu* (greeting to the same gentleman by a middle-aged family member or high-status person). The continual and consistent reproduction of this grammatical principle serves to reinforce values emphasized in Vietnamese society: respect and honor for elders, esteem for parents and other respected authority figures, and conscientious attention to humility and submission to family.

Even as use of Vietnamese continues, young Vietnamese growing up in the USA generally use English in most spheres and therefore their intuitive grasp of how to use the multiplicity of status pronouns becomes weaker. In transitional generations of immigrants such as the first and 1.5, where English is learned and may eventually erode the use of Vietnamese, there can be a symbolic wearing away of the knowledge of these pronouns as form of address. Without continual practice, young Vietnamese people find themselves out of form for applying the complex application for titles. Additionally, dispersed families and smaller, more homogeneous ethnic communities in the USA provide Vietnamese speakers with a limited arena to perform the nuanced evaluation and the rehearsal of these status pronouns. Young and Tran (1999) have noted that few scholars have investigated how elder generations as well as younger generations of Vietnamese, who manage to retain facility with their language, may hold negative, possibly shaming attitudes toward those who have allowed their heritage language to evaporate. Those who allow their Vietnamese to lapse are no longer "real" Vietnamese; thus, language loss may be identity loss.

Another area where language shift may be revealed is in differential domains of use, specifically, domestic versus nondomestic. Vietnamese in the USA is

Table 8.4. *Vietnamese and English ability of Vietnamese-American minors, by generation, 2006*

Language ability	Total	First (foreign-born)	Second	Third
Speaks only Vietnamese	0.5	1.1	0.3	0.0
Does not speak English well	5.5	6.5	6.0	0.2
Speaks English well	15.0	18.7	15.5	2.4
Speaks English very well	41.5	26.9	58.3	6.0
Speaks only English	37.5	46.8	19.9	91.3

Source: Ruggles *et al.* 2009.

increasingly used only to describe matters of the home and household for new immigrants who must make their way out into the larger society in English. Thus, language shift is less a transition from the native tongue toward the dominant language but rather a divergence between the Vietnamese spoken at home with family and English spoken everywhere else. However, this bifurcation may be complicated by the need for Vietnamese children to serve as translators of outside matters for their parents. For example, the domain of the home may revolve around family and domestic matters, but one particularly intimate home matter may be parental expectations regarding education. While Vietnamese may be spoken exclusively within the home, and English at school, most Vietnamese children must translate school notes and convey report card scores. Vietnamese parents who harbor high educational goals for their children will make their expectations known. But it is the children who must interact with teachers and schools.

These two areas, the erosion of the social concepts inherent in Vietnamese and the restriction of Vietnamese to the domestic sphere, may be the early signs of the particular way in which a language shift may be occurring even among the majority of Vietnamese-American young people who, as Table 8.5 shows us, seem to be retaining the language of their heritage.

Despite some apparent language maintenance, discussed below, the evidence suggests that a very rapid shift to English, delayed by the continuing arrival of new immigrants, is beginning to occur among young Vietnamese-Americans as a substantial second generation emerges and as most members of the first generation grow up in the USA with limited contacts with Vietnam. Table 8.4 uses American Community Survey Data of the US Census to look at the language use of Vietnamese-Americans under age 21, the people who will be the language users and the parents of the language users of the twenty-first century.

The data indicate a trend consistent with language assimilation theories. Vietnamese immigrants adopt English in place of their native language successively over three generations until 91.3 percent of those born in the USA speak exclusively English. This is an expected movement toward integration that is supported by social and familial conditions for third generation Vietnamese. However, the resulting reliance on English is only part of the picture of assimilation. Second generation Vietnamese have a comparably low rate of speaking only English, about 20 percent, while the first generation reports a 46.8 percent reliance on English exclusively. At first glance, this is a surprising development since one would expect a progressive increase in English-only reliance with every succeeding generation. This finding supports the notion that language maintenance among the Vietnamese is robust into the second generation, signifying that there are factors that buffer against dramatic language loss, at least before the rapid English adoption by the third generation.

Recent research by Young and Tran (1999) gives some details as to the familial dynamics that affect this trend. They note that "the longer a family lived in the United States, the greater the shift toward English use (from all Vietnamese, to bilingualism to English only)" (p. 80). Intriguingly however, Young and Tran state further that while there is strong initiative and motivation among first generation Vietnamese to learn English quickly, Vietnamese parents will then encourage their children to maintain their native tongue as the family lives longer in the USA. Thus, length of residence is correlated with both the external pressures to adopt English and familial support to preserve and speak Vietnamese.

The evidence, then, shows some clear signs of a shift to English among Vietnamese-Americans. However, there are also signs that the Vietnamese in this country are maintaining their ancestral language. In order to look at both sides of this complex issue, we turn now to evidence of Vietnamese maintenance.

Signs of maintenance

Understanding and investigating how language maintenance occurs for the Vietnamese is complicated by two characteristics of the Vietnamese immigrant population. First, there has been an especially lengthy migration process where the first Vietnamese groups arrived in 1975 and have continued to steadily increase in number into the 1990s. Second, as mentioned earlier, native-born and second generation Vietnamese have yet to become the large majority of Vietnamese-Americans, although evidence of a population explosion of this group is imminent. These two factors indicate special circumstances for the language maintenance of Vietnamese; specifically, the long settlement process may have slowed down the language shift to English and supported a longer maintenance of Vietnamese, especially among younger Vietnamese people.

Table 8.5. *Vietnamese and English ability, by generation, 1980 and 2006*

	Total		First (foreign-born)		Second		Third	
Language ability	1980	2006	1980	2006	1980	2006	1980	2006
Speaks only Vietnamese	8.3	5.5	8.4	7.1	9.6	0.2	1.2	0.0
Does not speak English well	27.2	23.3	28.0	28.7	23.5	5.9	1.6	0.2
Speaks English well	34.6	27.7	35.8	32.2	20.8	14.9	4.7	2.4
Speaks English very well	20.6	31.6	20.8	25.7	21.4	60.8	8.9	7.1
Speaks only English	9.4	11.8	7.0	6.4	24.7	18.1	83.7	90.2

Source: Ruggles *et al.* 2009.

Recent research explores these differing patterns of language maintenance, and Tannenbaum (2003) specifically explores the communication between immigrant parents and children, and whether preferences for native language use reflect actual-use patterns. Tannenbaum finds that parents consistently report an alignment between the actual use of their native language and their expressed preference for doing so, while their children state that they are speaking their native language more than they prefer to, especially to their mothers. This finding suggests that in the home, where domestic matters such as relationships, household tasks, and familial expectations reside, children interact with their mothers and fathers and more often speak their native language, whether they are inclined to do so or not.

Consistent with Tannenbaum's findings, Zhou and Bankston (1998) found in their community study that use of Vietnamese in the home and in the community were primary factors in the maintenance of the language. These have interacted with the continuing migration we discussed above to support the continuing use of Vietnamese even as Vietnamese-Americans have become increasingly fluent in English. Table 8.5 gives percentages of Vietnamese in the USA who spoke only Vietnamese, only English, and percentages of those at different levels of English ability who spoke both languages. This table indicates that the percentage of Vietnamese in the USA who spoke only English and did not speak Vietnamese increased only slightly during the quarter of a century from 1980 to 2006, from 9.4 percent to 11.8 percent. At the same time, those who were fully bilingual, who spoke English very well and also spoke Vietnamese, increased greatly, from 20.6 percent to 31.6 percent. It would appear, then, that with the support of family and community, reinforced by continuing immigration, as suggested by the literature, Vietnamese-Americans show a pattern of maintaining Vietnamese while developing fluent bilingual skills.

If we look at the generational language use in Table 8.5, we may well wonder how long the maintenance of Vietnamese alongside English will last. Numbers of second generation Vietnamese were tiny in 1980 and primarily children of highly assimilated individuals who had settled in the USA before the end of American involvement in Vietnam. It makes sense, then, that nearly one quarter would speak only English. However, by 2006, when a sizeable second generation had begun to emerge from the population created by the refugee waves, over 18 percent of those born in the USA spoke only English, even though they were children of relatively recent immigrants from Vietnam. The third generation was still quite small even by 2006, but over 90 percent of them spoke only English. This raises the distinct possibility that the present pattern of Vietnamese-language maintenance alongside increasing English fluency may not continue long into the present century.

A possible buffer against language loss is an increase in language awareness and activism. Language awareness is already evidenced by Vietnamese parents' expressed support of bilingual education (Young and Tran 1999) as well as young Vietnamese people themselves (Wharry 1993). Vietnamese media, profiled earlier, play a role in Vietnamese cultural preservation, and by extension, would support language maintenance measures by broadcasting exclusively in Vietnamese to densely populated regions. Two prominent examples would be Saigon Radio, broadcast throughout Orange County and San Jose, and RadioSaigon of Houston, Texas.

Conclusion

The presence of the Vietnamese language in the USA is characterized by a swift and assertive appearance, followed by a lengthy plateau of language preservation over two generations of Vietnamese. This period is sustained by the combined efforts of parents, who advocated for a bilingual proficiency in their children, and environmental factors such as the establishment of densely populated ethnic communities in major metropolitan centers. There have been positive by-products of this persistent bilingualism for Vietnamese children and adolescents in the form of high rates of educational completion and attainment as compared to other select Southeast Asian groups with similar refugee characteristics and settlement patterns (Kim 2002).

Recent trends, however, threaten an exponential erosion of the Vietnamese language in the form of a burgeoning native-born population of young people. It is a fitting circumstance that it is this younger population that will have the most profound impact on the future of the language. Whereas before, the bilingualism of Vietnamese young people served to preserve their heritage language and slowed the pace of attrition, it will be another, younger generation of Vietnamese that will likely speed up the pace of replacement.

DISCUSSION QUESTIONS

1. The Vietnamese community offers a variety of media outlets such as newspapers, magazines and internet resources. Describe some of the websites that are available for the Vietnamese online. What are the characteristics of these sites and what does this tell you about the community?

2. Compare the language shift among younger Vietnamese to the language shift of the larger Vietnamese group. How are they different? How are they similar? What are the implications?

9 German in the USA

Renate Ludanyi

Introduction

German presence in the USA dates back to colonial times. In 1608, German craftsmen, mostly carpenters, helped create the first American settlement in Jamestown. In 1683, thirteen families of Mennonites and Quakers arrived in Pennsylvania and created Germantown, the first German settlement in the USA (Faust 1912, II: 7). Many of the immigrants during these early days came for religious reasons. They continued to settle in Pennsylvania, but also in New Jersey, Maryland, Virginia, and North Carolina and mainly came from the western part of today's Germany. Later, they came for economic reasons or were political refugees. They all brought their faith, their belief in hard work, and, of course, their language.

Today, more than 400 years later, the USA has the largest concentration of German speakers outside of Europe. According to the 2007 American Community Survey conducted by the US Census Bureau, German is the sixth most commonly spoken non-English language in the USA (Table 1.1), though the number of US German speakers declined by 11 percent between the 1990 Census and the 2000 Census, and by a further 20 percent between 2000 and 2007. This chapter presents a brief historical overview of German ancestry and language, as well as some demographic and recent immigration information, followed by some thoughts about the future of the German language in the USA.

History

German, like English and Dutch, belongs to a handful of West Germanic languages which originally were mutually intelligible. By the fifth century CE, some continental West Germanic tribes (Saxons, Angles, Jutes) had invaded the British isles and replaced the Celtic languages with their own. Also, between the third and the fifth centuries CE, the High German consonant shift began to take effect, and the early Germanic languages in the south shifted away from those in the north. West Germanic dialects on the continent largely changed into Low and High or Upper Germanic varieties, which eventually developed into standard German, Dutch, Afrikaans, and a number of regional forms (mostly nonstandardized and without written forms) within a dialect continuum that still exists today. This continuum spans the political borders of countries as well as the borders of some German federal states. Before it was unified under Bismarck in 1871, Germany consisted of independent principalities and feudal districts. During the early (and later) immigration to the USA, German-speaking people arrived from all parts of this divided Germany and from outside it as well. They were a diverse group, with many local dialects and identities (Luebke 1990: XIII). If this led to communication difficulties in the USA, they were overcome by the use of English (Adams 1993: 4). Eventually, some German dialects in the USA began a process of leveling – a simplification that makes unintelligible or partially intelligible regional dialects mutually intelligible – creating, in fact, new German dialects in the USA (Eichhoff 1985: 231).

It is difficult to determine an exact count of German settlers before the first official US Census in 1790. In 1775, the number of German settlers in the thirteen colonies was given as 225,000, which today is considered to be a low estimate (Faust 1912, II: 12). Fifteen years later, the first US Census reported about 600,000 Germans in the New World (Faust 1912, I: 24).

Unimpeded immigration to the New World started after the Napoleonic Wars in 1815. Improved organization of immigration (Moltmann 1985: 14), a major crop failure in 1816–17, and a potato rot in 1846 were some contributing factors. The new, large wave of emigration originated mainly from western Germany. The immigrants were small farmers, craftsmen, and laborers. Also, after 1830, when reactionary forces began to persecute liberals, and particularly after the failed German Revolution of 1848, some 6,000 political refugees (the so-called Forty-Eighters) came to the USA. They were well educated, liberal, and often wealthy, and did not see themselves as immigrants, but rather as asylum seekers (Adams 1993: 7). Later in the nineteenth century, despite the German unification in 1871 and an economic boom after the Franco-Prussian War, 1882 marked the highest number of German arrivals, with 250,000 persons in that year alone (p. 4). Immigrants now included those who arrived from territories that are today Austria, France (Alsace Lorraine), Switzerland, and the Balkans, as well as from Eastern European borderlands with Germany and German ethnic enclaves and settlements in Russia (Totten 1983: 195). In this chapter, they all are called German or German-speaking.

This widespread immigration created the so-called German Belt from Connecticut to California and Washington, with heavy settlements in the South as well. By the beginning of the twentieth century, Germans could be found in every US state (Moltmann 1985: 21). Later, that century experienced two world wars and massive devastation. Between 1930 and 1960, Germans once

Table 9.1. *Total German immigration into the USA 1820–1988*

Decade	Total immigration	German immigration	Percentage of total
1820–9	128,502	5,753	4.5
1830–9	538,381	124,726	23.2
1840–9	1,427,337	385,434	27.0
1850–9	2,814,554	976,072	34.7
1860–9	2,081,261	723,734	34.8
1870–9	2,742,137	751,769	37.4
1880–9	5,248,568	1,445,181	27.5
1890–9	3,694,294	579,072	15.7
1900–9	8,202,388	328,722	4.0
1910–9	6,347,380	174,227	2.7
1920–9	4,295,510	386,634	9.0
1930–9	699,375	119,107	17.0
1940–9	856,608	117,506	14.0
1950–9	2,499,268	576,905	23.1
1960–9	3,213,749	209,616	6.5
1971–80	4,493,000	66,000	1.5
1981–8	4,711,000	55,800	1.2
Total	49,753,412	7,028,258	14.1

Note: 1970 was omitted from the source.
Source: Adams 1993: 6.

more came in large numbers, and immigration in the 1950s nearly matched that of the 1860s. After 1970, German immigration to the USA subsided. Table 9.1 summarizes the trends of German immigration from 1820 through 1988.

The concept of ethnicity and language maintenance was discussed widely by German newcomers in the nineteenth century, particularly after the mid-1840s. The word *Schmelztiegel* (melting pot) was first used in 1857, half a century before it became customary in English (Conzen 1985: 138). And although many German immigrants were willing to quickly give up their native tongue, there were those who dreamed of creating areas where the German language and way of life would be preserved. By their efforts a number of towns in Missouri came into being, among them Hermann, which is still a well-known tourist attraction for its German heritage and quaintness. But no "new and free" Germany was created. In another example, in 1842, when Texas was still a part of Mexico, a union of German aristocrats purchased land with the intent to create German societies, and between 1845 and 1847, 5,247 immigrants landed in Galveston. By the beginning of the Civil War, Texas had 30,000 Germans (Eichhoff 1985: 232), yet this attempt to create a "new Germany" failed as well. Nonetheless, the Texas Germans retained a German way of life quite divergent from the rest of Texan life. Both Kloss (1963 [1998]: 221) and Gilbert (1981: 269) agree that German in Texas was relatively well preserved until recently.

Two groups of immigrants in the USA who spoke German-language variants were more successful, in that they were indeed able to create lasting social and linguistic communities: the German-speaking Anabaptist groups (Amish, Hutterites, Mennonites, and others), discussed further below, and Yiddish-speaking communities centered mostly in New York (who will not be discussed in this chapter). Yiddish was the medieval German dialect of Jewish communities in the Rhineland; it became their lingua franca during their migration eastward.

As mentioned previously, Germans who came to the USA in earlier centuries did not come as a homogeneous group, but rather from various German regions and European countries with different German dialects. Settlers in Wisconsin came mostly from northern regions speaking Low German dialects (*Plattdeutsch*), and no dialect leveling took place there (Eichhoff 1985: 233). The settlers in Texas arrived from central Germany (particularly from Nassau), and the immigrants in Pennsylvania mainly came from the Rhineland.

As shown in Table 9.1, after 1900, large-scale German immigration to the USA slowed. Booming European industry began providing satisfactory employment and offered fewer incentives to leave. More importantly, new US immigration quota laws in 1924 and 1929 limited immigration in general. The entry quota for persons from the Weimar Republic totalled just over 25,000, which was not changed even for the rescue of German Jews from Nazi persecution in the 1930s and 1940s (Adams 1993: 4, 36). However, there were new arrivals in the 1930s, and among them were thousands of intellectuals, writers, artists, actors, and musicians. It was one of the greatest "brain drains" Germany had ever experienced, as the US welcomed physicist Albert Einstein, architect Ludwig Mies van der Rohe, writer Thomas Mann, actress Marlene Dietrich, and Secretary of State Henry Kissinger, among many others. After World War II, a second "brain drain" occurred, from which Wernher von Braun, the missile scientist, is one of the best known.

A discussion of the history of the German language and culture in the USA would be incomplete without mentioning the discrimination against German and German-Americans in the early part of the twentieth century, even though – or partially because – they were the largest ethnolinguistic community in many of the large cities and states. In 1916 the National Council of Defense and numerous local council affiliates were established, including the Victoria Council of Defense in Texas, which in 1918 mandated that all people should abandon the use of German in public and private life. Following suit in other parts of the country, thousands of German schools were closed, as well as many German newspapers, social centers, associations, and clubs. In Findlay, Ohio, the town council imposed a fine of $25.00 for the use of German in the streets

Table 9.2. *Comparison of German ancestry and German speakers*

	Total German-ancestry population per state		Percentage German ancestry		Total German speakers per state		Percentage of state's population
1	North Dakota	642,200	43.9	1	North Dakota	14,925	2.32
2	Wisconsin	5,363,675	42.6	2	South Dakota	13,425	1.78
3	South Dakota	754,844	40.7	3	Montana	9,410	1.04
4	Nebraska	1,711,263	38.6	4	Wisconsin	48,305	0.90
5	Minnesota	4,919,479	36.7	5	Indiana	44,135	0.73
6	Iowa	2,926,324	35.7	6	Colorado	30,820	0.72
7	Montana	902,195	27.0	7	Minnesota	35,030	0.71
8	Wyoming	493,782	25.9	8	Washington	39,660	0.67
9	Kansas	2,688,418	25.8	9	Ohio	72,570	0.64
10	Pennsylvania	12,281,054	25.4	10	Kansas	16,820	0.63

Sources: US Census Bureau 2000a and Modern Language Association 2008.

(Kloss 1963 [1998]: 61). In addition to "patriotic" book burnings, the windows of German businesses and families were smashed, and citizens perceived as having only lukewarm patriotism were persecuted. This new American patriotism, à la Theodore Roosevelt (whose quote about the "polyglot boarding house" is cited in the introductory chapter to this book), now required the total assimilation of Germans into American language and culture. Fortunately, the laws that had been enacted to limit German use were eventually rescinded. One of the more important rulings, not so much in defense of language rights but of individual liberties, was *Meyer v. Nebraska* (1923), the Supreme Court ruling that struck down as unconstitutional a Nebraska law that prohibited the spoken use of any language other than English in schools. But much damage had been done and the German language never recuperated as a vital, integral part of everyday American life.

Demographics

According to the 2000 Census, 15.2 percent of all US residents (42.8 million) claim German heritage, making it by far the largest ancestry group in the country. Where do the people claiming German heritage live? Do these German-heritage claimants still speak German? How many of the German speakers in the USA today belong to the group of German-ancestry claimants, and how many are newcomers to this country?

Table 9.2 displays the top ten states with German ancestry. Census statistics indicate that German ancestry leads in twenty-three states. In the vast majority of all other states, German occupies a substantial position as well. In fact, there

Table 9.3. *States with the largest German-speaking populations*

	Ages 5 +	Percentage of all US German speakers
California	113,924	10.22
Florida	73,398	6.58
New York	70,886	6.36
Texas	61,316	5.50
Pennsylvania	58,015	5.20
Illinois	57,608	5.17
Ohio	50,837	4.56
Michigan	45,913	4.12
Wisconsin	38,566	3.46
Washington	35,481	3.18
Total in USA	1,104,354	

Source: Modern Language Association 2009, US Census Bureau 2007c.

are only two states, Maine and Rhode Island, where it does not represent one of the five most common heritages.

While ancestry may affect life experiences ranging from food choices to preferences in music, it is not necessarily an indication of language use and language retention. Indeed, a large shift to English usage is apparent. Table 9.3 displays the ten states with the largest German-speaking populations.[1] In terms of overall numbers, as seen in Table 9.3, California (113,924), Florida (73,398), New York (70,886), and Texas (61,316) contain the largest number of German speakers – hardly surprising, as these states also represent the four most populous states in the USA. On the other hand, in Table 9.2 we saw that the concentration of German ancestry in the top ten states corresponds with the concentration of German speakers reasonably well. Six of the top ten states for German ancestry appear on the top ten states for concentration of German language speakers, while Iowa (eleventh) and Pennsylvania (tied for twelfth), also have a relatively high concentration of German speakers.

Despite this apparent correspondence, though, it is obvious that the overwhelming majority of German-ancestry people in these states no longer have a connection to the German language, and that a shift to English has long since taken place. As noted by Wiley (Chapter 16, this volume), Veltman (2000: 60) points out that in the 1990 Census, of the "Americans who reported their ethnic ancestry, 58 million people claimed German ancestry in whole or part, whereas German was only spoken by 1.5 million people." Though nearly half of North Dakota residents claim German ancestry, for example, a mere 2 percent of the population there speaks German today. Additionally, as will be explored more extensively below, the states with large German-ancestry populations are no longer the destinations of significant numbers of modern German immigrants.

World language speakers in the USA may or may not be foreign born, and often they are not. Astoundingly, German-language usage in the USA still includes many heritage speakers of the second generation and beyond. But it also includes people newly entering the country. The Census and MLA data do not differentiate between American-born and foreign-born German speakers. The German Federal Statistical Office provides yearly figures of persons entering the USA, including German citizens and noncitizens. From 2000 to 2006, there were 209,803 such migrants (Statistisches Bundesamt Deutschland 2006: 11). A similar number of persons per year entered during the ten years from 1990 to 2000.

US immigration statistics corroborate the fact that the number of Germans entering the USA has remained relatively stable in recent years. Comparing Census data state-by-state shows that, of the fifteen countries sending the most immigrants to the USA, Mexico became the largest sending country in 2000, replacing Germany's number one position in eight states in the 1990 Census. Germany is now the leading source of immigrants only in West Virginia. It is, however, still high on the list in many states, and it also shows an increase in total immigrant population growth in thirty states and a decrease in the other twenty states (Carmarota and McArdle 2003: Table 1). The 2006 *Yearbook of Immigration Statistics* indicates that the combined number of German-speaking legal permanent residents from Austria, Germany, and Switzerland from 2000 to 2006 is the fifth largest of all Europeans, after those from the UK, Poland, Yugoslavia, and Russia (US Department of Homeland Security 2007: 10). Germany occupies fourteenth place worldwide as a sending country of US legal permanent residents (Rytina 2006: 4). Further data from the 2006 *Yearbook of Immigration Statistics* reveal that, in addition to the legal permanent residents, in 2000 an additional 4,508 Germans became citizens, and there were 2,139,191 German visitors to the USA (US Department of Homeland Security 2007). According to a Migration Policy Institute report, half of all visitors to this country were nationals of the UK, Mexico, Japan, and Germany (Meyers and Yau 2004: 4).

Although the settlement pattern for German newcomers is still fairly dispersed, and they are listed in first place among the most diffuse immigrant groups (Carmarota and McArdle 2003: 6) – which has implications for the ability to maintain ethnic identity and language – data also strongly suggest that Germans who come to the USA today no longer prefer the farms of the Midwest as destinations, as did their forerunners. Instead, they prefer the large economic centers, and in particular California, as do immigrants and visitors from other countries. California had early German settlements but, as indicated in Table 9.2, it is not one of the ten states with a large percentage of German ancestry. Nevertheless, Los Angeles has traditionally been a haven for German-speaking intellectuals and artists fleeing Europe or seeking fame in Hollywood. Today, California accounts for the highest number of German immigrants (98,160 in 2000) and also receives the highest number of German visitors (395,999 in 2000), mostly traveling for business or visiting family and friends (CIC Research, Inc. 2007). As a consequence, California also has the largest number of German-speaking persons applying for adjustment of their legal status from a temporary (visiting) visa to become permanent residents. These persons are called "adjusts."

Cognizant of immigration trends shifting to centers of commerce and research, a recent article by the German Federal Institute for Population Research, using data from the US Census, discussed a German concern about a possible new "brain drain" to the USA, prompted by a significant percentage of highly skilled German scientists, researchers, and managers entering the USA and becoming "adjusts," many of them after only two years. Such persons now account for about half of the German-born immigrants admitted to the USA annually (Diehl 2005: 4). They speak standard German, are fluent in English, are often multilingual and successful, and do not see themselves as immigrants.

The fluency in English by this group is reflected by some fairly astounding statistics provided by the US government from the 2000 Census, where 40.9 percent of new immigrants from Germany reported speaking English at home. New immigrants from Austria reported an even higher level of English use (42.1 percent). Additionally, 95 percent of German speakers reported speaking English "well" or "very well" (US Census Bureau 2007c). How this relates to German-language shift or retention will be discussed later in this chapter.

Concomitant with this relatively novel situation of well-trained, bilingual (standard-German–English) persons entering the USA, the traditional US German dialects are in the process of disappearing, with only a small number of older people still speaking them. Texas German, the language of the German settlers in Texas Hill Country in the nineteenth century, is almost extinct. Pennsylvania German (PG) or Pennsylvania Dutch, also *Pennsylvanish* or *Pennsilfaanisch-Deitsch*, a Central German dialect and the closest to Standard German (SG), once used by one of the largest groups of immigrants, is dying in the secular community as well, as are other regional versions of German, since they no longer have their own domains (Eichhoff 1985: 233, 234; Huffines 1985: 248; Fuller 1999: 38).

On the other hand, German-language variants spoken by the conservative religious separatist groups show great success in survival. *Plautdietsch* or Mennonite Platt, a Low German dialect that is mostly intelligible only with other Low German dialects, was, as of 2000, the first language of 11,974 people in

Kansas, California, and Oklahoma (Gordon 2005). Hutterite German or *Hutterisch*, an Upper German dialect descended from a regional German spoken in Carinthia, Austria, is still spoken by the Hutterite colonies and some Mennonite groups. *Hutterisch* is also spoken by the *Bruderhofer*, newer communities in New York, Connecticut, and Pennsylvania, who follow some Hutterite practices and teach this language to their children. According to Kloss (1963 [1998]: 178), the most popular and frequently used of the German dialects, PG, is still the conversational language of numerous "Plain People" in Ohio, Indiana, and Pennsylvania. We will return to these communities in a later section of this chapter.

Public presence of German

As discussed above, public awareness of German in the USA has risen and fallen throughout the country's history, from relative insignificance before the nineteenth century to a rise in prominence that culminated in the anti-German backlash of the early twentieth century, which in turn (along with decreased immigration) precipitated a decline in the public presence of German. Today, despite the considerable financial and commercial presence of Germany in the USA, the public presence of Germans has returned to being relatively insignificant politically and socially.

Nonetheless, important venues for the public presence and use of German remain. Fishman (1985: 142) points to the church and the school as the bedrock institutions of ethnicity and language. With this in mind, the following two sections will address the presence of German in religion and education, while the third section will briefly describe the media.

Religion

The Anabaptist movement began in Switzerland in 1525. By refusing to obey the church and baptize their babies, this group also rejected the power of the authorities to tax and conscript. This group shook the foundations of civil authority by declining to swear oaths of allegiance, believing in a "free church," independence from state control, and freedom of individual conscience. They later split into the Hutterites, Mennonites, Amish, and Brethren (Kraybill 2003: 6). Motivated by missionary ardor and persecution, they left Switzerland and settled in other areas of Europe to practice their faith (Kraybill 2003: 5). After difficulties in their new homes, they finally migrated to the USA and Canada[2] in the eighteenth and nineteenth centuries to acquire farmland and create communities based on their religious, social, and linguistic traditions.

Along with many aspects of their lifestyle, dress, and physical appearance, these groups consider their traditional German dialect to be a barrier between themselves and the world of people who do not share their beliefs. German continues to connect them to the values of the *Alte Ordnung* (Old Order). They use it for daily communication with each other and their children, although English is taught as well out of practical necessity. However, to "go English" entirely would mean to want things from the English-speaking world. Thus language is more than a means of communication. For the Old Order communities, it symbolizes self-definition and self-preservation. They speak PG, read and understand Biblical High German, and use their hymnbook, the German *Ausbund* of the sixteenth century, for singing in church. They also know English and, as yet, do not intend to give up their long-lived multilingual tradition.

PG, considered "a German dialect which originated in America" (Kloss 1963 [1998]: 187), has been spoken for almost four centuries in the USA and Canada. Different from High German, it never had a standard orthography, and, spoken or written, it is not easily understood by speakers of modern SG. No longer replenished by an influx of new immigrants, it has become a language in isolation, though still in wide use. Continuing to flourish for so long in close proximity to a language to which it is genetically related and by which it has been influenced (English), it has become an intriguing laboratory for comparative and historic linguists.

The question of what happens when one Germanic language affects another (Aikhenvald 2006: 51) has encouraged a multitude of studies. One of them is Burridge's work on the language of today's Mennonite Anabaptists in Canada, who left Pennsylvania after the American War of Independence. It shows that Mennonite PG has experienced a number of internal and external influences (Burridge 2006: 188). English is recognized as a catalyst that accelerated developments already, some of which had also occurred in English and in other Continental German versions over the course of history (similar to Silva-Corvalán's (1994) claims for Spanish in the USA). In a comparable study, Fuller (1999) describes the relationship between English and PG as "complex and varied" (p. 51). She also compares the developments of certain grammatical features of PG to developments in SG and some dialects in Germany and finds that across this even larger scenario, overlapping and similar modifications have occurred.

Yet, linguistic changes, particularly those that are contact induced, must also be seen in their social, and here, in their cultural–religious context. Along with the use of many English discourse particles, interjections, loan words, and calques in Mennonite PG, which is typical of most situations of bilingualism, an additional phenomenon became evident: need-borrowing. The introduction of the telephone, for example, required the addition of new English lexical items (Burridge 2006: 189).

The PG-speaking sectarians are alleged to be quite aware of their special dialect and accept the "'hybrid' nature of their language." Without conscious language engineering, they are accepting "the low status of the dialect variety . . . [as] an appropriate symbol of their humility" and as a gesture of affirming their "identity of the Traditional Mennonites" (Aikhenvald 2006: 41). English plays a less emotional role in their communication and is acquired in a formal school setting after their PG vernacular is already "deeply anchored" (Burridge: 2006: 194), which is why it remains fairly "intact" (Aikhenvald 2006: 41).

We know a lot of details about their language, we have fewer details about the number of people who actually speak it. The collection of objective data is made difficult by the unwillingness of many Old Order residents to be counted (Johnson-Weiner 1998: 376). *Raber's Almanac* (based on voluntary information; German since 1930, English since 1970) gives a yearly count of the Amish districts, their leaders, and their congregations. According to Hostetler (1980: 100), the total number of districts of Old Order Amish has grown from 22 in 1890 to 526 in 1979 with an estimated population of 85,783 in that year. For 2000, *Raber's* estimates 1,204 Old Order Amish congregations, with a population of 180,750, 75 percent of the settlements in Ohio, Pennsylvania, and Indiana (Kraybill and Bowman 2001: 105), and the Young Center for Anabaptist and Pietist Studies estimates the 2008 population at 230,850 (YCAPS 2008).

The population of Old Order Mennonites who use PG (except in Virginia, where they communicate in English) was estimated at 24,000 in 1997 (Kraybill and Bowman 2001: 67). It was forecasted to double every sixteen years. Additionally, as mentioned earlier, Gordon (2005) reports 11,974 speakers of a Low German Plautdietsch, another form of Mennonite German spoken in Kansas, California, and Oklahoma. 5 percent of its users also speak SG, and 98 percent speak English as a second language.

The 116 Hutterite colonies in the USA live in segregation from the rest of society, mainly in Minnesota, Montana, North and South Dakota, and Washington. Typically, ninety people live in a colony (Kraybill and Bowman 2001: 23, 25). Attention is also drawn to the rapid growth of these communities, with large families and a low infant mortality rate. The average number of live births per Amish family is seven, and 22 percent of Amish women in Pennsylvania give birth to ten or more children. Among Hutterite woman, 48.2 percent give birth to ten or more children, though this has recently declined slightly (Kraybill and Bowman 2001: 49). Loss of church members is said to be fluctuating, and an exact number does not exist, with estimates between one tenth and one third (Crowley 1978: 263). However, it is not large enough to offset the population increase (Hostetler 1980: 104–7).

Unlike the conservative Old Order groups, some of the more progressive sectarians are adopting English. As a consequence of public education, and as the influences of the outside world, such as technology and transportation, become more accessible to them, these church communities have to make mindful choices. As change to English is seen as a chance for church renewal and a commitment to evangelism, which requires the removal of the language barrier. Language shift here does not represent a passive occurrence of cultural assimilation but an active selection. It also signifies a spiritual break from the Old Order congregations (Johnson-Weiner 1998: 386). As a result, New Order congregations, despite their remaining religious and retaining their communal cohesiveness, are said to have fared no better than other immigrant groups in maintaining their language (Huffines 1985: 53). Fuller (2001: 358) noted that "English is gradually taking over as the in-group language" and that "the next generation is English-dominant."

In addition to these Anabaptists, later German-speaking settlers in the USA included Catholics, Lutherans, and other Protestants. These "church" Germans all formed their congregations and maintained their language via the pulpit, as well as in the classroom, first in monolingual German and later in bilingual schools. But as time went on, particularly after World War I, the language of the church became English. For example, in 1910, only one sixth of the Missouri Synod Lutheran churches held one English service per month. By 1917 this had increased to three quarters. Despite this apparent sudden change around the time of World War I, however, Schiffman (1998) presents evidence that English was in fact in widespread use by these groups in "unofficial" contexts as early as the mid nineteenth century. In 1985, Fishman *et al.* reported 196 Catholic and 65 Protestant German-speaking local religious units, and lamented that these ethnic mother-tongue bastions have been little studied "of late" as centers of non-English language use (page 251).

Education

German companies and citizens are present in many parts of the world. The 2007 *Online Membership Directory* of the German American Chamber of Commerce (GACC) in New York lists 1,800 German firms in the USA (based on voluntary membership in the GACC). There are 2,111 Germans connected to these businesses in New York City alone. Many of them are very interested in language and culture maintenance, and this has led to the creation of the private all-German *Deutsche Schule* in White Plains, NY. Additional *Auslandsschulen* (German schools abroad), partially supported by Germany, exist in Washington, DC, on the West Coast, and in Boston. Another educational alternative for these "expats" (and others) are supplementary private German-language schools.

As German in the USA has disappeared from the public ear and declined in the American school system, parents of school-age children and friends of the German language have created private solutions in the form of German *Sprachschulen*, mostly Saturday schools. Most of these institutions belong to a national umbrella organization, the German Language School Conference (GLSC). Many schools date from after World War II, but the oldest in the Northeast began in 1874 (Boston) and 1892 (New York). National student enrollment is estimated at 6,000 students, with larger schools (Atlanta; Boston; Stamford, CT; Washington, DC) teaching up to 300 students. The majority of the students, from pre-school to adults, are American-born, including many heritage learners of first, second, or later generations (GLSC n.d.). The schools also include students born in German-speaking countries abroad. Students vary in language proficiency, and natives as well as heritage learners typically have stronger oral than literacy skills in German. For the most part, the attainment of native fluency is not a primary goal. Instead, many students seek to prepare for national tests such as that of the American Association of Teachers of German and the German Advanced Placement exam, while others study German to qualify for demanding German examinations that allow entrance to German universities, in preparation for studying abroad. Furthermore, the majority of the students wish to keep a linguistic connection to the homeland and relatives living there.

Clearly, the variety of ages, proficiencies, learning levels, and learning needs puts a high demand on curriculum planning, the choice and use of teaching materials, and teacher selection and development. McCarthy (1985: 271) speaks of the concerns of German teachers in a shrinking job market, yet many of these community schools find it difficult to locate teachers with the necessary linguistic ability, pedagogical background, and dedication to the task of language maintenance and instruction required by these programs. In addition, there is a total lack of empirical research and commercial material to support teaching the various levels of the bilingual continuum in these schools. A measure of financial assistance is often available from the German State Department, which also provides pedagogical consultants. What keeps these institutions strong is, above all, the powerful commitment and support of the students' parents.

Though private language instruction in the USA has a long tradition, the future of these institutions (and German teaching in general) will depend on a variety of factors, including professional, institutional, political, financial, and private support. For the first time, the GLSC has started collecting data on student and parent demographics (Mischner-Bang 2005; Opaka 2006) to highlight these schools, which are seldom cited in the professional literature (Eichhoff 1985: 248; Fishman *et al.* 1985: 364; McCarthy 1985: 275).

In addition to private ethnic community initiatives, the public and private school sector also offers German, though with reduced enrollment. For 2000, the

American Council for the Teaching of Foreign Languages (ACTFL) reported that German high school enrollments have declined again, bringing the percentage of all German students down from almost 3 percent to 2 percent (Draper and Hicks 2000). In postsecondary institutions, a look at German enrollments yields somewhat better results. As shown in Chapter 1 of this volume, German was the third most commonly taught non-English language in USA. Colleges and universities have experienced a 3.5 percent increase from 2002 to 2006. Still, the gradual increases experienced by German and French have not restored them to the levels they held in the 1970s (Furman *et al.* 2007: 7, 19).

Media

The German language press in the USA was one of the pillars of language maintenance for the new settlers and assisted them in adjusting to life in their new country (Huffines 1985: 241). In 1732, Benjamin Franklin was involved with the publication of the first German-language newspaper in Philadelphia. Before World War I, every American town with a high concentration of Germans had at least one German-language newspaper, often several. At their peak, there existed nearly 800 German daily and weekly periodicals (Wittke 1973: 208). The *Staatszeitung,* which appeared first in 1834 with a circulation of 60,000, is still published today as the *New Yorker Staats-Zeitung*. In 1892 the German-American Hermann Ridder bought this paper and co-started the American media empire Knight-Ridder, Inc. The Austro-Hungarian Joseph Pulitzer, after whom the coveted journalism prize is named, began working at the *Westliche Post* in St. Louis before buying that paper and several others. From 1848 to 1880, after the arrival of the Forty-Eighters and additional well-educated and intellectual Germans, German newspaper and book printing flourished and reached its peak by 1914 (Huffines 1985: 246).

In 1917, neutrality in the USA came to an end and war was declared not only on Germany but also on the German language and the German press. Some dailies changed into weeklies, and many disappeared. The New York Jewish-German newspaper *Aufbau* was bought by a Swiss publisher to merge with a Jewish German-Swiss weekly, which like *Aufbau* started publication in Berlin, Germany. In his 1985 statistics, Fishman reports two dailies, twenty-three weeklies, fifteen monthlies, four other periodicals and eight with no data (Fishman 1985: 258). However, Baroni (2001) points to a study of the same year for the *Westfälische Wilhelms-Universität*, where only sixteen German-American weeklies were counted. For the year 2001 he counts merely eight remaining weeklies (Baroni 2001: 22), among them the *Amerika Woche* (Chicago), the *New Yorker Staats-Zeitung*, the *Washington Journal*, the *Nordamerkanische Wochenenpost* (Troy, Michigan), and the *California Staatszeitung*

(Los Angeles). A list published by the Press Guide (2007) counts forty-nine publications altogether, including those that often serve a very small, localized, and special-interest audience, but not publications of the religious communities.

Recently, a number of newer German-English magazines with websites have become available (*German Life, German World*). Other newspapers, e.g. the *Herald-Zeitung*, which was created in 1852 as the first German newspaper in Texas under the name of *Neu Braunsfelser Zeitung*, are now published totally in English. The *Atlantic Times* (first edition in October 2004), also in English, is a free, monthly publication with articles on German American relations, business, cultural topics, and politics. The German-language press in the USA as it existed in the past has disappeared.

Evidence of language shift to English and German maintenance

Luebke (1990: 175) comments that there is almost no demographic, sociological, or historical research on the Germans and German immigration to the USA in recent history and thus the "persistence of German ethnicity and culture in contemporary US society is *terra incognita*." As language and culture are interdependent, and no up-to-date studies exist exploring these elements, either alone or in their relationship, it is difficult to offer well-substantiated facts on present evidence or future prospects for German-language maintenance or language shift to English, although statistics from both the MLA and the US Census presented earlier do provide compelling evidence of shift.

Evidence of shift

As has been shown in this chapter, language shift or maintenance depends on a multitude of historic, sociological, political, religious, regional, and private elements. Although German bilingualism thrived until World War I, the main reasons for its final decline and the shift to English have been discussed previously in this chapter, including the xenophobic attack on German; restrictive language policies; the subsequent almost total loss of the use of German in the home, school, churches, the press, and in public in mainstream US culture; and, finally, the end of large-scale immigration.

Of the 1,104,354 German speakers in the USA, the majority speaks English "well" or "very well," as noted previously (US Census Bureau 2000). Equally noteworthy, this high percentage holds among German speakers of age 65 or higher. A similar picture appears for French and only slightly less so for Korean, as compared to Spanish or Chinese, where only 59.6 percent or 34.3 percent, respectively, of the older speakers reported a high English proficiency. One explanation for the high percentage of English speakers among the elderly Germans, certainly, is the similarity of the two languages, which was alluded to at the beginning of this chapter. Another reason can be found in the fact that Germans above 65 who reside in the USA today are often refugees from the World War II situation. A large number of them are well educated and bilingual, and in many cases would not have left Europe had circumstances at that time been different. There are signs that, although there is a shift among these people to English for everyday use, there is also a fear of becoming monolingual in the next generations, which is one of the reasons that prompts many of them to send their grandchildren to private German-language schools. The newer and younger German-speaking settlers in this country no longer flee hardship, destruction and war, or persecution. They follow the economic lure of a flat world with the USA in its center. They are the descendants of a World War II and post-World-War-II generation, who, although to a lesser degree today, still have a somewhat uneasy relationship with the political past of their country and thus to their own ethnicity. Even if they enjoy and often seek the company of their compatriots, often for the sake of their children, they belong, for the most past, to the postethnic generation. Language has lost the romantic significance it had for their elders, and they do not see its retention in a Fishmanesque sociopolitical light. Maintenance or shift for them signifies an individual and personal decision or requirement. In addition, German (like other languages) is well known for its predilection to accept items from other languages and in particular from English, a trend that is creating an ambivalent reaction from German experts and citizens alike. So-called Denglish *Deutsch-Englisch*) is heard on both sides of the Atlantic. This is hardly surprising since both languages have a 60 percent lexical similarity (Gordon 2005).

Signs of language maintenance

Although it is rare, lengthy intergenerational minority language retention is possible, as proven by the conservative German religious groups in the USA. According to Veltman (2000), only the highly isolated communities of the Amish and the Hassidic Jews have been successful in minority language preservation for more than three generations in the USA. The stability of German dialects in the Amish, Hutterite, and Mennonite communities over a period of centuries represents the greatest area of success in language maintenance in the USA, and there is no sign that this situation will discontinue in the near future.

On the other hand, the lifestyle today of most mainstream foreign-born as well as of recent generations' heritage German speakers in the USA has different requirements. Determined strongly by commercial endeavors, it no longer calls for the German language as a source of separatist identity. Instead, it relies on German for connection and communication, not only locally but also across political, institutional, and ethnic borders. These new German speakers (including Austrians and Swiss), the "expats," "transfers," or "adjusts," will continue to arrive, typically as professional and multilingual individuals. The distance for them to the home country, physically as well as emotionally and financially, has become short, and they maintain regular and frequent contact by travel, telephone, and the internet. While the immigration experience in general points to a shift to English in the subsequent generations, it is possible that in the new, highly mobile and interconnected world, some of the "new immigrants," including German-speaking people, have an advantage in providing a basis for not only their own language maintenance, but intergenerational maintenance as well. Only time will tell, as this is still a very new development.

What might contribute to the continued acquisition of German in the USA is its international status. In view of transatlantic trade and investment, "Europeans and Americans literally own each other" (Hamilton 2008: 1). America's investment in Europe of $1.2 trillion in 2006 was 53 percent of its total global investment. German-owned affiliates in the USA were selling $343 billion in exports in 2005. Hamilton (2008: 3) notes that transatlantic markets are the laboratory of globalization, and Germany is playing a key role. These markets may also be a laboratory for the creation of a new multilingual society, such as the Common European Framework for Languages by the Council of Europe (2008) endeavors to achieve.

Globally, there are about 100 million native speakers, and another 20 million nonnative speakers, who use German on a regular basis. Today, SG is the most frequently spoken mother tongue in the European Union (18 percent) (Special Eurobarometer 2006: 7), and it was voted the most useful language after English in fourteen out of twenty-nine European Union nations (p. 32). German is the national language of Austria, Germany, Liechtenstein, and Luxembourg, the largest official language in Switzerland, and an official language also in Belgium, Denmark, Italy, and Poland, as well as a minority language in many other countries around the world. The *Frankfurter Buchmesse* (Frankfurt Book Fair) is the world's biggest international trade fair for publishing. According to the German Information Center (2008) in Washington, with more than 80,000 titles published each year, Germany's international ranking is third after the USA and China, which makes German one of the world's most widely read languages. It is also the sixth-most widely used language on the internet, despite German speakers accounting for only 4.2 percent of all internet users (Internet World Stats 2008).

Conclusion

Fishman's (1985) prediction for a continued role of German "when the quatricentennial of German immigration [2008] is being celebrated" was correct. What remains to be seen, however, is how accurate his additional contention is that there is "far more life on the German scene" in the USA than meets the eye (pp. 251, 267), for how long, and to what degree.

DISCUSSION QUESTIONS

1. How does German's long history in the USA make its position different from those of other common non-English languages spoken here?

2. What is your prediction for the future of German in the USA? Do you have different predictions for Pennsylvania German (and related varieties) and standard German? If so, what factors make them different?

10 Korean in the USA

Hae-Young Kim

Introduction

Koreans are the fifth largest group of Asians in the USA, after Chinese, Filipino, Indian (South Asian), and Vietnamese (US Census Bureau 2000a). As shown in Table 1.1, the number of Korean speakers in the USA grew by 43 percent from 1990 to 2000, and by another 19 percent from 2000 to 2007, mainly due to new immigration from Korea. With the enactment of the Immigration and Nationality Act of 1965, which abolished discrimination based on national origin, particularly Asian exclusion, Asian immigration to the USA dramatically increased, and today Korea is one of the major Asian source countries of immigrants (Min 2006). The flow of immigrants reached a peak in the 1970s and 1980s due to political turmoil and rapid industrialization under military rule in South Korea. Similarly to other immigrants to the USA, many Koreans sought better economic opportunities, social and political stability, and accessible college education for their children (Yoon 1997; Min 2006).

Located on a peninsula between China and Japan, contemporary Korea has been divided into the communist North and the capitalist South since the end of World War II which ended the decades-long Japanese colonial rule. North Korea and South Korea, however, share the same language, traditions, and history of successive dynasties over two thousand years. There are 23 million people living in the North, and 49 million living in the South (US Census Bureau 2007b). There are also 7 million Koreans living outside of Korea, including over 2 million in China, almost 1 million in Japan, 1 million in the USA and half a million in Russia and Central Asia (Overseas Koreans Foundation 2007). Korean is ranked as eleventh among languages of the world in terms of number of speakers (Sohn 1999: 4; Song 2005: 14). Korean was first taught as a foreign language at St. Petersburg University in Russia in 1897 (Sohn 1999), and is now taught in forty-one countries at the postsecondary level (Song 2005).

History

Contemporary Korean is believed to descend from the language of the Unified Shilla kingdoms (668–918 CE) and the succeeding dynasties (Sohn 1999:

40). Regional dialects with different sounds and words have developed as a result of various geographical, historical, and political factors, and North Korea and South Korea have established different standard dialects. However, they are mutually understandable, and in fact Korea today is one of the most linguistically homogeneous countries in the world (Sohn 1999; Song 2005).

It is generally believed that Korean is genetically affiliated with the Altaic languages, which include Turkish, Mongolian, Machu-Tungus, and Japanese (K. M. Lee 1976; Miller 1979; B. H. Kim 1984; Sohn 1999). Linguistic features commonly shared by Altaic languages include subject-object-verb (SOV) word order, agglutinative morphology, and vowel harmony (Sohn 1999). Korean's agglutinative characteristics include that one or more suffixes are added to an unchanged stem to form a word. For example, a verb stem can be affixed with an auxiliary, subject honorific, tense, mood, and discourse markers. The Korean expression for "Would (you) like to try to put (it) on?" would be "*ib* (wear) – *ŏbo* (attemptive) – *si* (subject honorific) – *ket* (future) – *sŭmnikka* (polite interrogative)." However, vowel harmony is no longer strictly adhered to in contemporary Korean due to a vowel shift that took place in the seventeenth century and the influence of a large-scale influx of Chinese vocabulary that does not have vowel harmony (Sohn 1999: 54).

The extent of Chinese borrowing is so great that Chinese-origin vocabulary exceeds that of native Korean. Some estimate that between 52 percent and 60 percent of the contemporary Korean lexicon is Chinese-based (Sohn 1999: 87; Song 2005: 83). A large number of Chinese words have entered Korean since the Koryŏ dynasty (918–1392) when the civil service exam was introduced from China with Chinese classics as its basis (Sohn 1999: 103). China was the major political and cultural influence in Korea until the Japanese colonial power arrived in the early twentieth century. Many Chinese words at that time were imported from Sino-Japanese, since Japan was modeling their modernization on European thinking and technology and had modern scientific and technical terms available in Japanese (that also used Chinese extensively). Native Korean words that survived the encroachment of Chinese borrowings include body parts, natural objects, flora and fauna, as well as cultural elements such as kinship terms and honorific expressions (Sohn 1999: 94).

The Korean alphabet, *hangŭl*, is probably the only indigenous writing system that can be dated and whose creator is known. Chinese was the language of writing used in Korea before the invention of *hangŭl* by King Sejong in 1443. Working with a group of scholars, King Sejong studied Chinese linguists' work on consonants, syllables, and tones, and conducted systematic research on the phonology of Korean (Sohn 1999: 129). The outcome was a set of consonant symbols shaped after articulatory organs and vowel symbols based on yin/yang philosophy, which combine into syllable-unit letters. The symbols are featural in that they are systematically distinguished from each other in terms of phonological features, such as point of articulation and aspiration. The Korean alphabet is praised as "one of the greatest intellectual achievements of humankind" (Sampson 1985). However, *hangŭl* was rejected by the ruling elite of the Chosŏn dynasty (1392–1910), who would not give up their cultural capital of Chinese learning. It was not until Chosŏn was on the verge of becoming a Japanese colony at the turn of the twentieth century that *hangŭl* was promoted as a medium and symbol of Korean modernity and national sovereignty by intellectuals (Schmid 2002: 64–72). Both in North and South Korea, *hangŭl* is now used in administration, media, and education (Song 2005).

Prior to 1965, there were two distinct waves of Korean immigration to the USA. The first large wave, consisting of young working-class males, reached Hawaii in 1903 as labor on sugar plantations. The second wave, a result of the Korean War, consisted of Korean wives of American servicemen, war orphans, refugees, and some professionals (Hurh 1998). After the Immigration and Nationality Act of 1965, more than 250,000 Koreans immigrated to the USA by 1979, and in the 1980s Korean immigrants maintained an annual flow of 30,000 (Min 2000: 308). Kinship-centered migration of relatives of permanent residents who had originally come as students and professional workers accounted for the largest share of the surge (Hurh 1998: 39).

Post-1965 Korean immigrants were better educated than their compatriots in Korea: 46 percent had college degrees and 90 percent had a high school diploma (Min 2006: 249). Upon arriving in the USA, a large number of Korean immigrants go through downward job mobility from professional occupations to small business entrepreneurship or mechanical and manual occupations. For example, in a 1986 sample, 46 percent of Korean immigrants had held professional jobs and 14 percent had been business owners in Korea, but in the USA, only 26 percent held professional jobs while 30 percent owned small businesses (Hurh 1998: 43). According to the 1990 Census, an unusually high proportion of Korean-Americans are self-employed workers in small businesses (17 percent) when compared to the US population as a whole (7 percent) (p. 55). However, labor-intensive small businesses owned by Korean immigrants are not usually passed down to their children. In the 2000 Census, while 23 percent of first generation Korean immigrants are self-employed, only 9 percent of second generation Korean-Americans are self-employed, indicating second generation Korean-Americans' integration into the mainstream economy (Min 2006: 250–1).

Demographics

In the 2000 Census, Koreans constituted less than one half of one percent (0.4 percent) of the US population, totaling just over one million (1,076,872). The number of people 5 years and older who reported speaking Korean at

Table 10.1. *States with the largest Korean-speaking populations*

	Ages 5 +	Percentage of all US Korean speakers
California	345,024	34.26
New York	105,425	10.47
New Jersey	69,656	6.91
Illinois	53,672	5.33
Virginia	46,848	4.65
Texas	45,272	4.49
Washington	39,894	3.96
Georgia	33,118	3.28
Pennsylvania	32,827	3.26
Maryland	32,649	3.24
Total in USA	1,062,337	

Source: Modern Language Association 2009, US Census Bureau 2007c.

home was 894,065, which increased to 1,062,337 by 2007. Table 10.1 shows the ten states with the largest Korean-speaking populations. In fact, 90 percent of Korean speakers reside in eighteen states, while the remaining 10 percent are distributed among thirty-two states and Washington, DC. Seven states alone account for 69 percent of Korean speakers: California (34% of Korean speakers), New York (10%), New Jersey (7%), Illinois (5%), Virginia (5%), Texas (4%), and Washington (4%). On the other hand, otherwise highly populated states such as Florida, Ohio, and Pennsylvania have Korean populations of less than 3 percent. In terms of concentration, Hawaii has the highest percentage of Korean speakers, followed by the District of Columbia, California, and Alaska.

Koreans are almost exclusively concentrated in urban areas: 97 percent live in metropolitan areas, and 38 percent reside in a central city (US Census Bureau 2000a). As shown in Table 10.2, there are large populations in New York, Los Angeles, Chicago, and Philadelphia, but a smaller presence in other major cities in Texas, Arizona, and Michigan. Los Angeles and its vicinity, including Orange County and Riverside, has the largest Korean population, and the New York area, including Bergen-Passaic, NJ, Newark, NJ, and other cities in New Jersey, has the second. The third largest Korean population center is Washington, DC, and its vicinity, including Baltimore. However, Koreans are not evenly represented in the nation's ten biggest metropolitan areas, in that Houston, Phoenix, Detroit, and San Antonio have relatively few Korean residents.

Table 10.2. *The ten US cities with the largest Korean American populations*

City and state*	Rank by Korean population	Number	Percentage Korean of total population
Los Angeles, CA	1	186,350	2.0
New York, NY	2	92,942	1.0
Washington, DC	3	56,327	1.1
Orange County, CA	4	55,573	2.6
Chicago, IL	5	45,371	0.5
Bergen-Passaic, NJ	6	37,561	1.7
Seattle, WA	7	27,786	2.1
Philadelphia, PA	8	26,805	0.5
Atlanta, GA	9	22,317	0.5
Honolulu, HI	10	21,681	2.5

Note: * For lack of single city data, the data for Los Angeles are of Los Angeles and Long Beach PMSA (Primary Metropolitan Statistical Area) and the data for Phoenix are of Phoenix and Mesa MSA.
Source: US Census Bureau 2001b.

Table 10.2 also shows that other urban centers, such as Seattle, Atlanta, and Honolulu, have fairly large Korean populations. Not shown in the table are ten other cities that boast a Korean population larger than 10,000; these include San Diego, San Jose, San Francisco, Oakland, Portland, Tacoma, Boston, and Minneapolis. More than twenty other cities have a Korean population of larger than 3,000, including Miami, Orlando, St. Louis, Kansas City, Austin, Denver, Las Vegas, and Anchorage.

The high concentration of Koreans in Honolulu and Southern California, particularly around Los Angeles, originates from the earliest Korean immigration to Hawaii and the West Coast for agricultural labor in the late nineteenth century and for political asylum from Japanese annexation of Korea in the early twentieth century (Min 2006). Immigration to the New York and New Jersey area, on the other hand, began after the Immigration and Nationality Act of 1965, when Korean international students arrived at East Coast universities and medical professionals came to the area (Min 2006). The Washington, DC, area rose to third place, which used to be held by San Francisco and its vicinity, only recently (Min 2006). Earlier immigration to Washington, DC, was due to Korean embassy employees, Korean international students, and wives of American servicemen. More recently, there has been an increase in Korean residents who work for the US federal governments or run business in downtown Washington, DC, but live in Fairfax County (Min 2006).

Public presence of Korean

Government

The US government's view of the importance of the Korean language is mainly related to national security. Since the divided military occupation of the Korean peninsula at the end of World War II, the USA has been deeply involved in the military, political, and economic affairs of the peninsula (Cumings 1997). The USA aided the military build-up and economic development of South Korea as protection against communist North Korea, China, and the Soviet Union. Even after the end of Cold War and the demise of communist regimes, the USA perceives North Korea to be a major threat as it staunchly upholds a communist ideology and opposes American "imperialism." American military bases, which were established after the Korean War, remain in South Korea and occupy the largest land area of its bases in all countries (Moon 2005). Dispute over North Korean development of nuclear weapons has been the thorniest issue in the region. Destitute in the 1990s after draughts, famines, and the discontinuance of economic relations with former communist countries, as well as fearful of an American offensive against its regime, North Korea bet its survival on the development of nuclear weapons and waged a "war of nerves" with the USA (Park 2002). Furthermore, it was believed that North Korea was engaged in trading counterfeit US currency and exporting weaponry to countries hostile to the USA. The US government has also been vigilant about successive South Korean governments, which were authoritarian until the 1980s and more democratic since the 1990s, and which maintain delicate relationships with the USA over many contentious issues, although the country remains a military ally.

For these reasons, the US federal government has invested in training government employees and soldiers in Korean-language skills. The Foreign Service Institute, Central Intelligence Agency, National Security Agency, and Defense Language Institute all offer Korean programs. The Defense Language Institute in particular teaches Korean to about 600 soldiers in an intensive program lasting more than a year (Sohn 2000). In 2002, the National Security Education Program in the US State Department began funding two Korean programs, one at UCLA and one at the University of Hawaii, for the purpose of producing potential government employees with superior knowledge and proficiency in Korean. These programs provide a small cohort of college graduates with two years of intensive instruction in Korean, including one year of immersion in Korean. Given that the US government interest in Korean is restricted to security and intelligence concerns in relation to North Korea, these investments are not likely to have a broad impact on motivation to learn or maintain Korean among the general public. In the US, government-sponsored programs for civilians recruit a very small number of students (for example, the Flagship program at the University of Hawaii admits about ten students each year) and may not do enough to dispel the pervasive perception of North Korea as a rogue regime which will or should collapse any time soon. Korean-Americans, most of whom have roots in South Korea, will probably not be motivated to learn Korean under such circumstances.

Media

The Overseas Koreans Foundation (2007) counts 217 Korean newspapers, magazines, TV channels, and radio stations altogether in the USA. In New York alone during 1997–1999, there were five Korean-language TV programs, two radio programs, three Korean-language dailies, and several weeklies (Min 2001). Local weeklies are freely available at Korean retail stores, while daily newspapers are bought or subscribed to. Three major South Korean dailies, *Hankook Ilbo*, *Joongang Ilbo*, and *Segye Ilbo* are distributed in most metropolitan areas. Each branch duplicates newspapers via satellite from Korea and distributes them around the same time. They also carry local sections including news, classifieds, notices of sales of businesses, and information on church services. A survey of Korean immigrant families in Queens, New York, shows that 68 percent of them subscribe to at least one Korean newspaper (Min 2001). TV stations air several programs from South Korea via satellite including news and other shows, as well as a small portion of locally produced programs (Min 2001). Unlike TV stations, radio stations create their own programs, directly targeting and involving immigrant audiences, and thus have a more powerful influence than other Korean media (Min 2001). For example, Radio Seoul, an AM station based in Flushing, New York, has developed programs that provide information and counseling about health, family, education, and real estate, while airing news from Korea at regular intervals.

Although the large amount of Korean language media in urban centers should be a positive factor in the maintenance of Korean, Min (2006) calls these Korean language media "a mixed blessing" to immigrant communities. They provide crucial help for monolingual Korean immigrants in their daily lives, but they are largely inaccessible to the second generation. Designed to be consumed by monolingual or native-like Korean speakers, the available media do not seem to appeal to second generation Korean-Americans who have not attained a high enough level of Korean proficiency or knowledge about Korean current affairs and issues.

Business

Other than a handful of high-tech entrepreneurs, Koreans are concentrated in small businesses. In the New York City Metropolitan area in late 1990s, there were 350 garment manufacturing firms, 3,000 grocery stores, 2,000 dry cleaners, 800 fish markets, 2,500 nail salons, and 1,400 retail produce stores owned by Koreans (E. Lee 2004: 125). In Los Angeles' Koreatown in 2002, thousands of such Korean businesses were estimated to exist, along with 34 Korean bookstores, 116 travel agencies, 193 law firms, 184 accounting firms, 410 medical offices, and 41 nightclubs (Min 2006: 237). In other major cities such as Atlanta, Chicago, and Philadelphia, Korean-owned businesses are also highly visible.

Korean immigrants go into these businesses for several reasons, including lack of access to professional jobs due to the language barrier, nontransferability of educational credentials and occupational skills acquired in Korea, availability of ethnic resources such as start-up funds from *kye* (rotating credit associations), and market demands from fellow Koreans for cultural goods and products, as well as from other minority ethnic groups such as African-Americans and Hispanic-Americans who are not catered to by mainstream businesses that do not wish to enter high-risk and low-profit underdeveloped minority markets (Hurh 1998). As a result, Korean immigrants serve the role of a "middleman minority" distributing the goods produced by the ruling group to underprivileged groups (Hurh 1998; Min 2006). Conflicts of interests inherent in this arrangement sometimes flare into serious clashes such as the African-American boycott of Korean stores in New York and Los Angeles (Min 2006).

Education

Educational options in Korean are extremely limited at the elementary school level. There exist four Korean–English dual-language programs at the elementary level and one at the middle school level, all of which are located in Southern California, except for one in New York (Center for Applied Linguistics 2007). Therefore, Korean immigrant parents mostly rely on community weekend schools for their children's Korean maintenance and literacy development. There are 976 weekend Korean schools in the USA (Overseas Koreans Foundation 2007), many of which are affiliated with Korean ethnic churches. These community-based Korean programs, however, are far from offering an age-appropriate literacy curriculum, due to the small scale of operation and a lack of instructional resources, curricular models, and teacher expertise (Shin 2005).

Korean is taught as a foreign language at many US secondary schools and universities, predominately in New York and Los Angeles. In 2006, fifty-four of sixty-four high schools in the USA that offered Korean-language classes were located in California, New York, and New Jersey (Foundation for Korean Language and Culture in the USA 2007). For second generation Korean-Americans from areas other than these, however, university Korean classes are the only opportunity to learn Korean. Universities offering Korean, altogether eighty-two, are located in various areas including California, New York/New Jersey, and Washington, DC (American Association of Teachers of Korean 2007). There is evidence that a very high percentage of students enrolled in university classes are Korean-American heritage speakers. You (2001) cites an unpublished survey conducted by member institutions of the American Association of Teachers of Korean, which reported that between 70 and 80 percent of first-year Korean classes and 90–100 percent of second-year Korean classes were populated by heritage students. High school enrollments are likely to have a similar pattern. Although only a few programs offer separate tracks for traditional foreign language learners, there is still a need to develop curricula that effectively meet the needs of Korean-American heritage speakers (King 1998; You 2001; Lee and Kim 2008).

Evidence of language shift to English and of Korean maintenance

Signs of shift

As shown in the introductory chapter, 71 percent of Korean speakers 5 years and older reported that they speak English "well" or "very well" (Min 2000). As is common among first generation immigrants, Korean is used in most aspects of their lives due to their high concentration in small businesses, strong affiliation with Korean ethnic churches, and the availability of Korean ethnic media. In one survey of Koreans living in Queens, New York, 97 percent reported they almost always spoke Korean at home (Min 2000). In another survey of Koreans living in Baltimore, Chicago, Houston, and New York, 56 percent spoke Korean and 38 percent spoke both Korean and English to their children (Shin 2005: 131–2). This would seem to bode well for Korean-language maintenance by the second generation.

However, second generation adults do not use as much Korean as their immigrant parents. In a 5 percent sample of the 1990 Census, 43 percent of the second generation and 90 percent of the third generation of Korean-Americans spoke only English at home (Alba *et al.* 2002), and, in a study of immigrants in Southern California, Korean, like other Asian languages, was found to have a linguistic life expectancy (defined as retaining the ability to speak the language) of between 1.3 and 2.0 generations of US residence, among the shortest of the groups studied (Rumbaut *et al.* 2006: 458). Dramatically reduced Korean-speaking ability among second generation Korean-Americans is also evidenced in survey and interview studies (Cho and Krashen 1998; Shin 2005; Lee and Kim 2008). Many second generation Koreans have very low confidence in their Korean (Lee and Kim 2008), and there are reports of communication breakdowns with parents (Cho and Krashen 1998; Min 2000). However, Lee and Kim (2008) report that 47 percent of college students studying Korean claimed that the language was the main connection to their roots and their family, and 30 percent claimed it to be a marker of their cultural and ethnic identity. Thus, they see the language as fulfilling important family and personal functions.

In addition, whereas the immigrant generation's affiliation with Korean churches maintains a bond of ethnicity, language, and culture, Christianity among second generation Korean-Americans has little to do with shared language or cultural heritage (Min 2006). Korean ethnic churches conduct their service and social activities in Korean, but provide separate services in English for second generation Korean-Americans who do not speak fluent Korean. Many Korean-American college students join co-ethnic campus ministries, but they disavow their parents' churches as ethnic institutions (R. Kim 2006). They perceive the first generation's churches to be "hierarchical" and "patriarchal" (p. 43), their services "static, antiquated and inexpressive" (p. 45), and their relation to larger society "ethnically exclusive and too self-contained" (p. 47), lacking in commitment to proselytizing and involvement in the surrounding non-Korean community. Youths thus leave their parents' church and establish or join groups consisting of second generation Korean-Americans and model their religious services after mainstream evangelical organizations. Interestingly, though they proclaim to place their Christian identity above their ethnic identity, many prefer Korean-American groups to pan-Asian or multiracial Christian groups (R. Kim 2006: 9).

An inevitable question arises: Why is maintenance of Korean poor among the second generation, given the relative homogeneity of Korean language and culture, geographic and social segregation, and prevalent use of Korean among their first generation immigrant parents? In attempting to find answers, one should keep in mind the language policy, culture, and ideology of the USA (explored in Chapter 1) that are antagonistic to minority languages. Despite ostensible tolerance for minority languages and some progressive legislation and court decisions in the 1960s and 1970s, the US linguistic culture is decidedly monolingual (Grosjean 1982; Schiffman 1996; Wiley 1999). Exerting pressure on "the children and grandchildren of immigrants to speak not just English, but *only* English" (Portes and Hao 1998: 269), assimilationism is the norm in educational policy, leaving little room for minority languages in formal schooling. We also saw above that the presence of Korean in public spheres such as media and education is very limited and geographically constrained. With this caveat in mind, I will now focus on how larger social conditions translate into or interact with more specific conditions of the Korean community that contribute to language shift.

The dominant US pattern of English monolingualism has led Korean immigrants to prioritize acquisition of English for their children, often at the expense of Korean (Shin 2005; Shin 2006; Jeon 2008). As mentioned above, many Koreans experienced downward job mobility upon immigration and regard limited English proficiency as a major cause (Hurh 1998: 58). Almost without exception, higher education at an elite university and a professional job are the main aspirations of Korean parents for their children; hence their preoccupation with their children's success at school, where they perceive that Korean has no place. Emphasis on English development both by school and parents inevitably leads to loss of what little Korean the child has acquired in a pattern of subtractive bilingualism.

A factor specific to Korean is the high proportion of self-employment among Korean immigrants mentioned earlier. Small businesses are usually run by both parents, and they work long hours with little time to spend at home with children (Min 2000; E. Lee 2004). Typically, the initial few years of the business establishment is especially hard on the owners, with heavy loans and no hired labor, and therefore the married couple put in long hours (E. Lee 2004). This is usually when their children are young and is thus a critical time for language development at home. Unless there are other caretakers who speak Korean or childcare facilities where Korean is spoken, the chance of full development of Korean is small. Weekend Korean schools supplement Korean-language development, but cannot be the sole source. In addition, the teachers at weekend schools are mostly volunteers without expertise in language teaching or understanding of children's cognitive development or educational experiences (Shin 2005), which leads to high dropout rates as children get older.

Transmission of the language to third generation Korean-Americans seems further curtailed by marriage patterns of the second generation. Exogamic marriages to whites are very common among second generation Asian-Americans, which reduces the chance of transmission of the heritage language to the third generation. In the 2000 Census, which allowed a selection of more than one racial category, 7 percent of Asians and 5 percent of Latinos also claim a white identity. More than 25 percent of native-born Asians and Latinos marry outside their own race, whereas just 6 percent of whites and 10 percent of blacks do so (Lee and Bean 2006: 27). There is no separate count of Korean-Americans, but they probably participate in the exogamic trend to the same extent. When only one parent speaks a minority language, the language at home is usually English and thus the chance is very slim that the child will learn the minority language (Alba *et al.* 2002).

Signs of maintenance

The pictures drawn above are rather bleak for the prospect of maintenance of Korean among second and third generation Korean-Americans, like most other immigrant languages. However, there are several developments that could slow the pace of the shift to English or revive interest in maintenance. These include reclamation of Korean language and cultural heritage by second generation Korean-Americans in their young adulthood, an influx of 1.5 generation Korean-Americans (who immigrated between 5 and 15 years of age), and other Korean youths of affluent family background coming to the USA for higher education, the availability of online communities and the soaring popularity of Korean popular music (e.g. Fin, K. L., Boa, Rain), TV dramas (e.g. *Winter Sonata*, *My name is Kim Samsoon*, *Jewel in the Palace*, *Full House*), films (e.g. *Shiri*, *My Sassy Girl*, *April Snow*, *Lady Vengeance*) and online games (e.g. Lineage, Ragnarok) in East Asia, which are also spreading to Asian-Americans.

A large number of Korean-American youths flock to Korean classes when they enter college. According to Brod and Welles (2000), there was a 34 percent increase in enrollment in Korean between 1995 and 1998, making it the third largest increase after American Sign Language and Biblical Hebrew. Furthermore, between 2002 and 2006, Korean enrollment again rose greatly, with a 37 percent increase in those four years (Furman *et al.* 2007). As mentioned earlier, over 80 percent of the students in Korean-language classes are from Korean ethnic backgrounds (King 1998; You 2001), as in other less commonly taught language programs in US colleges, where heritage language learners make up a growing proportion of enrollees (Gambhir 2001). Unfortunately, negative perceptions exist that Korean-American students enroll in Korean courses for easy grades. This perception may be in part related to the fact that some students have very low estimations of their Korean proficiency and attempt to enroll in lower level courses; proper placement procedures and appropriate curricula are necessary to address this issue. In fact, taking Korean is a serious choice and personal investment for most Korean-American students that requires foregoing other course options (Lee and Kim 2008). One student I interviewed mentioned that he would not have chosen to come to the university he was attending if Korean were not offered there. The motivational orientation of second generation Korean-American students is predominantly personal and symbolic. They regret not having had the chance to fully develop Korean-language proficiency and an ability to relate to their parents and their culture, thus they try to gain as much Korean-speaking ability as possible. The effect of such efforts to (re)learn Korean in college will depend in part on the degree of contact that students establish with Korean speakers and media.

Opportunities to interact with Korean-speaking peers have increased for Korean-American youths due to the increased presence of international Korean students and students of transnational backgrounds[1] in secondary schools and colleges as well as 1.5 generation Korean-Americans who immigrated to the USA between the ages of 5 and 15 (Jo, to appear). This trend is due to the increased involvement of the Korean economy in the global marketplace and greater freedom in the international movements of Korean capital and people, which has had greater impact on the upper echelon of the Korean population. As of 2007, 62,359 Korean postsecondary students studied in the USA, making South Korea the third leading place of origin for international students in the USA after India and China (Institute of International Education 2007). This was a 6 percent increase from the previous year, and the largest group (45.2 percent) were undergraduate students. An increasing number of K-12 students from Korea arrive in the USA as well, with 14,474 attending US schools in 2006, marking a 19 percent increase from the previous year (Korean-American Education Commission 2007). The increased presence of these Koreans might augment the opportunity and motivation to speak Korean on the part of Korean-American students (unless they separate themselves from the new group socially – see Gorman and Potowski 2009).

Many of these newly arriving youths are active participants in online communities where they socialize with Korean peers and pursue their interests in contemporary Korean popular culture (Lee 2006; Yi 2008). In South Korea, 66.5 percent of the population (compared to 69.5 percent of the US population and 67.1 percent of Japanese) is online (Internet World Stats 2008), and most of them are on high-speed broadband connections. Korean youths in the USA often have their own social network websites to interact with co-ethnic peers, as well as connecting to social, informational, and entertainment websites in Korea. Instant messaging and online postings in the Korean alphabet (*hangŭl*) are highly interactive and immediate, so the types of Korean language used in them are very close to spoken forms. Online communities or real-time interaction with the 1.5 generation, international, and transnational Korean youths can provide second generation Korean-Americans with the much-needed peer network crucial for Korean maintenance and development.

Korean popular culture is enjoying unprecedented popularity in Asia, earning the name *hallyu* or Korean Wave (Dator and Seo 2004; J.-S. Park 2006; Shim 2006). The popularity of Korean TV dramas, popular music, and films in China, Indonesia, Japan, Singapore, Taiwan, Thailand, and Vietnam has manufactured Korean celebrities and heartthrobs, stepped up sales of Korean paraphernalia and electronic and other industrial products, brought hordes of tourists to filming sites in Korea, and increased enrollment in Korean-language programs in the Asian region (Shim 2006). This phenomenon invites much speculation about its causes and theorization about popular culture and globalization, and can only be explained properly when specific local conditions are considered. One speculation that seems relevant to the current discussion is that it is because Korean popular culture relates to cultural sensibilities of Asians better than American popular culture (Dator and Seo 2004; J.-S. Park 2006). The Korean Wave may not reach the mainstream USA, although remake rights for many Korean films are bought by Hollywood (e.g. *The Lake House*) and Korean dramas (e.g.

Winter Sonata, Jewel in the Palace, Stairway to Heaven) and films (*Old Boy, Joint Security Area, Untold Scandal, Spring, Summer, Autumn, Winter... and Spring*) have gained popularity among some non-Korean-Americans in Hawaii and the West Coast (Chang 2006; Dickie 2006). This phenomenon is likely to increase second generation Korean-Americans' interest in Korean popular culture and consumption of Korean media, not only because of its exalted status but also because of a sense of cultural affinity as experienced by other Asians.

Conclusions

This chapter described the general trend of Korean-language transmission and maintenance in relation to immigration and settlements patterns and in reference to US language policy. To recapitulate the main points, although first generation Korean immigrants remain mostly monolingual and maintain a high level of ethnic attachment, language shift is taking place quickly among the second generation. Intergenerational transmission at home is often disrupted by parents' work conditions, and the English monolingual educational system and Korean parents' prioritization of their children's success in school leave little room for Korean maintenance. The informal, community-based Korean schooling on the weekends usually has limited effects.

This description is intended as a broad stroke picture of the state of Korean maintenance in the USA, to explain why it is that 43 percent of second generation Korean-Americans and 90 percent of the third generation end up speaking only English at home (Alba *et al.* 2002). Of those who do speak Korean, their level of proficiency probably varies over a wide range, and only a small fraction may have advanced proficiency. Successful maintenance of Korean in a society where minority languages are accorded lower status and visibility can, however, result, when there is a combination of favorable circumstances, resources and efforts. Examples of these include three-generational homes with monolingual Korean-speaking grandparents (E. Park 2006), parents who are determined in enforcing Korean use at home, schools that are more accepting of languages other than English, extra-curricular Korean instruction such as private tutoring or weekend schools, and frequent travel back to Korea (Lee 2002).

Focusing on structural factors that account for general patterns of language maintenance and loss, this chapter attributes the lack of Korean maintenance to the existing social climate and the adaptation of Korean-Americans to it. In order to reverse this shift, both the expansion of the teaching of Korean at schools and universities in more diverse geographical areas and improvement in the types of curricula offered are needed. These actions will enhance the status of the language in the eyes of the second generation while increasing opportunities to learn the language. In addition, use of Korean among peers for social and cultural purposes needs to be promoted to help second generation

Korean-Americans attain functional proficiency in Korean (see Tse 2001b for the importance of peer influence in language maintenance). In this regard, the recent influx of school- and college-age Korean speakers into the American education system and the spread of Korean popular culture outside the country present opportunities to revitalize Korean among youth. Research on real and virtual interaction within and between various Korean and Korean-American student social groups, and imaginative and innovative instructional approaches that utilize the new venues will help to maximize these opportunities.

DISCUSSION QUESTIONS

1. As mentioned above, while 97 percent of Koreans live in a metropolitan area, only as many as 38 percent reside in a central city. In fact, there are many Korean immigrants with professional jobs and good command of English who settle in a white or mixed-race suburban neighborhood. What would the prospect of Korean maintenance of their children be?

2. Compare the chances of maintenance of Korean among second generation speakers born of Korean immigrants who arrived in the USA in the early 1960s and those who arrived in the 1990s. Focusing on groups of similar socioeconomic status and areas of settlement in the USA, consider similarities or differences of the two periods with respect to:
   i. US educational policies and societal attitudes towards immigrants and minority languages,
   ii. Korean immigrants' and their children's perceptions of the status of the Korean language and culture as a function of political and social changes in Korea.

---

11 Russian in the USA

Olga E. Kagan and Kathleen Dillon

Introduction

Russian ranks eighth among the most commonly spoken non-English languages in the USA (Table 1.1). The 2007 American Community Survey conducted by the US Census Bureau lists 851,174 home speakers of Russian. A comparison of the 1990 and 2000 Census figures indicates that the number of Russian speakers increased by 191 percent (up from 1990's figure of 243,904), the greatest increase of all the languages included in the Census. This upward trend continued, albeit less dramatically, between 2000 and 2007, with an increase of 20 percent. Immigration increases are especially noticeable from 1988 to 1994, when more then 300,000 immigrants arrived from what is now the former Soviet Union.[1] According to the data of the US Department of Justice, 80 percent of these immigrants were Jewish (Chiswick 1997: 233). These increases can be explained by the relaxation of emigration policies in the former Soviet Union while the USA continued granting refugee status to immigrants from former Communist countries.

History

The Russian language belongs to the Slavic branch of the Indo-European language family and is an East Slavic language, along with Belarusian and Ukrainian. The three East Slavic languages share a common linguistic history.[2] Russian is the most geographically widespread language of Eurasia and the most widely spoken of the Slavic languages. It was the state language of the Russian Empire (1721–1917) and the Soviet Union (1924–91). As a result, it was spoken in fifteen different areas that were vastly different ethnically, culturally, and linguistically: Armenia, Azerbaijan, Belarus, Estonia, Georgia, Kazakhstan, Kyrgyzstan, Latvia, Lithuania, Moldova, the Russian Federation, Tajikistan, Turkestan, Ukraine, and Uzbekistan.

More than one hundred different languages were spoken in the Russian Empire and the Soviet Union. Each Soviet republic had two national languages: the local language and the official language, which was Russian. With the exception of Ukrainian and Belarusian, none of the local languages bear any resemblance to Russian. They belong to a variety of linguistic groups and are not mutually comprehensible. The Soviet government established a language policy (Grenoble 2003: 3–4) for all fifteen republics that imposed Russian as the official "top tier" language to be taught in all schools.

Both the local language and Russian were used in some republics such as Armenia, Georgia, Estonia, and Lithuania, but in the other republics, the national language was largely subsumed by Russian in official, educational, and even personal spheres. Thus, in some republics, many people speak only Russian and do not know the local language. Efforts are being made in many of the former republics, especially Ukraine and Central Asian countries, to revive the use of their national languages in all spheres, but the process is slow. For now, Russian remains the lingua franca in this part of the world. Russian is also one of the official languages of the United Nations.

Russian explorers may have reached Alaska as early as 1648, but the first documented settlement was on the Aleutian island of Kodiak in 1784. Unlike other European explorers in America, the Russian settlers were not colonists or pioneers. They were "motivated entirely by profit," and most were employees of the Russian-American Company (Hardwick 1993: 51). These fur hunters and traders gradually extended Russia's possessions along the Pacific Coast to within 100 miles of San Francisco. Czar Alexander II sold Alaska to the USA in 1867. After the sale of Alaska, most of the Russians returned to their homeland, but many Aleuts and Eskimos had converted to Russian Orthodoxy, and many Russian Orthodox "Old Believers" who emigrated from the Soviet Union have their own old-style Russian villages in Alaska today (Alaska Office of Economic Development n.d.). In 1882, there were 16, 918 Russian-speaking residents in the USA, and by 1899 there were 387,416, which was the highest total for any year in the nineteenth century.

Severe shortages of farmable land forced farmers and peasants to leave the Russian Empire, and over several decades hundreds of thousands of Ukrainians, Belarusians, Lithuanians, and Poles emigrated from the Russian Empire and arrived at Ellis Island in the USA. The imperial Russian government, however, prohibited ethnic Russians from emigrating; the 1910 Census identifies fewer than 60,000 Russians in the USA. Many of these Russian Empire immigrants headed west to take advantage of the Homestead Act. Some small pacifist sects settled in Oregon and California and have preserved their traditional culture and music into the twenty-first century. Other Russian-speaking immigrants found work in the mines, sweatshops, and mills burgeoning on the East Coast and the Great Lakes regions. Additionally, many Jews fled the Russian Empire near the turn of the twentieth century. For example, almost five million Jews lived in the Russian Pale of Settlement, an area in the western part of Imperial Russia where permanent residence of Jews was allowed between 1791 and 1917.[3] Jews fled from the Pale of Settlement in large numbers because of anti-Semitism that culminated in pogroms (violence directed against a particular group, in this case Jews) following the assassination of Czar Alexander II in 1881, which became especially violent in the period 1903–5. Russian Jews constituted 78 percent of the Jewish immigration from Europe from the end of the nineteenth century and beginning of the twentieth (Nadell 1990: 11). Even though they came from the Russian Empire, many of these immigrants spoke Yiddish rather than Russian.

A pivotal event in world history provoked what is known as the first wave of Russian immigration to the USA in the twentieth century. In 1917, the communist revolution terminated the imperial era of Russian history and plunged the empire into civil war until 1922. An estimated one million Russians, most of whom had engaged in the struggle against the Bolsheviks, fled the country. Most settled in Europe and China, though many also came to the USA. According to the 1920 US Census, there were 392,049 Russian-born US citizens. This figure contrasts starkly with the records from ten years earlier that identified just 57,926 foreign-born Russians in the USA (Davis 1969: 9). The majority of the émigrés of this period were members of the aristocracy and intelligentsia, but many accepted humble jobs in their new country.

The US Immigration Act of 1924 reduced the number of US immigration visas and allocated them on the basis of national origin. This law placed the first permanent limitation on immigration and established the "national origins quota system" that governed American immigration policy until the passage of the Immigration and Nationality Act of 1952, which broadened the grounds for exclusion and deportation (US Citizenship and Immigration Services, n.d.2). But immigration from the Soviet Union slowed down in the 1930s and 1940s mainly due to the restrictions imposed by Stalin's government. The US Immigration and Naturalization Service's records list only 14,016 Russian immigrants from 1930 to 1944 (Hardwick 1993: 111).

The second wave of Russian immigrants arrived after World War II. Details about this wave, according to a Hoover Institution researcher, are "almost impossible to document" (Shmelev 2006: 6). The vast majority had been brought out of the Soviet Union by the German army as forced labor or were prisoners of war, and they refused to return to their homeland after the war. They tended to change their names and identities for fear of persecution by the Soviets. In addition, very few wrote about their histories, and those who did mainly wrote under pseudonyms. The letters and publications that would have documented this era were for the most part left behind since the immigrants could bring only sparse belongings when they came to America.

The third wave of twentieth-century immigration from the Soviet Union began in the early 1970s, when Soviet Jews, as political refugees, were granted virtually unlimited immigration by US authorities, who pressed the Soviet government to release them. The 1974 Jackson–Vanik amendment (Trade Act 1974) led to this change in Soviet emigration policy. For details of the history of Soviet-Jewish emigration starting in the 1970s see Lazin (2005). This amendment required the Soviet Union to permit ethnic minorities (Jews and some others) to emigrate in exchange for obtaining most favored nation status in trade with the USA.

In 1980, the USA passed the Refugee Act, which set a limit of 50,000 refugee-immigrants from all over the world, but also defined refugee as a person being persecuted for religious or political reasons, thus tilting the immigration quotas in favor of Soviet citizens and citizens of other Communist countries. This wave continued until the Soviet Union began to collapse in the late 1980s, when Soviet President Mikhail Gorbachev initiated the policies of *glasnost* ("transparency") and democratization.

In 1987, Gorbachev launched the fourth wave of Russian immigration when he announced that victims of religious persecution had permission to leave the Soviet Union for the first time in seventy years (Hardwick 1993: xi). Many Soviet Jews who had been denied permission to leave for many years (they were known as "refuseniks") finally obtained exit visas and emigrated to the USA as well as other countries, most notably Israel. Estimates by the US Immigration and Naturalization Service in 1990 indicate that one-quarter million Soviet Jews were living in the USA. According to unofficial estimates, however, the number of people who relocated to the USA from the Soviet Union approaches 1 million (Kishinevsky 2004: 5).

In the process of immigration – application for refugee status, temporary housing in transit centers in Europe prior to entry into the USA – Jewish refugees from the former Soviet Union had considerable help from Jewish nonprofit agencies, such as the American Jewish Joint Distribution Committee and The Hebrew Immigrant Aid Society. Help was also provided by non-Jewish organizations like the Tolstoy Foundation and the International Rescue Committee. In the USA, Jewish Federations offered services such as financial aid, assistance with finding an apartment, learning English, and enrolling children in school. Jewish Vocational Services assisted immigrants in finding jobs. American Jews were happy to help, but misunderstandings and resentments arose because they expected Soviet Jews to be like earlier Jewish immigrants to the USA who embraced religion once they were free to practice it. But most of the Soviet Jews knew little about Judaism, and their priority was to learn English, obtain well-paying jobs and integrate themselves in the new society – not to pursue religion (Jacobs *et al.* 1981).

A conflict between some Jewish organizations and the refugees also concerned professional expectations. Soviet Jews expected to be treated as professionals, but American Jewish organizations believed that Soviet education was vastly inferior and therefore expected the immigrants to start their new lives in the USA at the bottom of the pay and social scales. Although some did begin in unskilled jobs because of limited English skills and inadequate understanding of American life, many moved ahead quickly. Simon (1997: 161) notes that the Soviet Jews did in one generation what generally takes immigrant families three generations to achieve, namely reaching educational and occupational parity with the native-born.

The majority of immigrants of the third and fourth waves were well educated, had studied English, possessed professional skills, and acclimated rapidly to the US lifestyle, finding good jobs in the legal economy. This "rapid linguistic and economic mobility" has enabled most to become invisible in American society (Kishinevsky 2004: 5). The demographic tables in the next section of this chapter mainly reflect the composition of the two most current waves of immigration from the Soviet Union and the post-Soviet geopolitical space.

Demographics

According to the 2000 Census, almost three million US residents describe themselves as having Russian ancestry. They include those whose ancestors came from the Russian Empire in the nineteenth or early twentieth century or from the Soviet Union after World War II, as well as those who arrived with the most recent waves of immigration. In the case of Russian immigrants, identity is often far more complex than the Census form can accommodate. In the 2000 Census, ancestry is determined by the question "What is your ancestry or ethnic origin?" and respondents have the option of indicating a single ethnic identification or multiple ethnic origins. However, former citizens of the former Soviet Union identified themselves as having both ethnic and geographic affiliations in addition to Russian, including Azerbaijani, Belorussian, Cossack, Estonian, Mordovian, German from Russia, Volga (not an ethnicity, but location), Kalmyk, Latvian, Lithuanian, Moldavian, Muscovite (not an ethnicity, but location), Soviet Turkic, Tatar, Soviet Central Asia, Turkestani, Uzbek, Georgian, the Commonwealth of Independent States (CIS), Ukrainian, and Tajik. Those who self-defined as "Russians" constitute 49 percent and "Russian/other ethnicity" (for example, indicating Russian and French) constitute 51 percent (see Table 11.1).

Particular attention needs to be paid to Jews, who form 80 percent of immigration from the former Soviet Union. Because the Soviet government's official policies prohibited the practice of religion, and particularly because of official and unofficial policies of anti-Semitism, the designation "Jewish" referred to an ethnicity, not a religion. For example, one of the categories on the Soviet internal passport was "nationality." Included could be Russian, Georgian, Armenian, Estonian, etc., that is to say, all the ethnicities that had their own territories,

Table 11.1. *Russian ethnicity and language*

Home language use	Claim Russian ethnicity	Claim Russian plus another ethnicity
Russian	71.8% (278,424,674)	0.5% (7,571)
No Russian	28.2% (338,663)	99.5% (1,381,793)
Total	100% (278,763,337)	100% (1,389,364)

Source: US Census Bureau 2000a.

Table 11.2. *States with the largest Russian-speaking populations*

	Ages 5 +	Percentage of all US Russian speakers
New York	232,434	27.94
California	147,312	17.71
New Jersey	45,783	5.50
Washington	44,629	5.36
Pennsylvania	34,887	4.19
Massachusetts	34,869	4.19
Illinois	34,700	4.17
Florida	34,087	4.09
Maryland	21,200	2.54
Oregon	17,581	2.11
Total in USA	851,174	

Source: Modern Language Association 2009, US Census Bureau 2007c.

but also others such as the Jews, who did not. Understandably, Jews may self-identify as "Russian," "Georgian," "Lithuanian," etc. on the Census form depending on the part of the former Soviet Union they emigrated from.

What Table 11.1 highlights is that claiming Russian ethnicity is not equated with being a speaker of Russian. We see that almost 100 percent of those who claim an additional ethnicity (or geographical location) in addition to Russian do not speak Russian, and approximately a third of those US residents who claim only Russian ancestry do not speak the language or do not speak it at home. Table 11.2 shows the ten states that have the largest populations of speakers of Russian, as opposed to Russian ancestry.

Table 11.3. *Increase in Russian-speaking population by US state*

State	1990	2000	Percentage change
New York	73,822	212,913	288
California	49,582	116,609	235
Pennsylvania	11,538	39,483	342
Illinois	15,075	37,490	249
New Jersey	18,707	36,354	194
Massachusetts	10,907	32,474	298

Source: US Census Bureau 2000a.

According to figures from 1990 and 2000 (see Table 11.3), there has been a significant increase in the Russian population in several states, with the greatest concentration in the Eastern and Western states, as is generally the case with other US immigrant populations. New York and Los Angeles are home to the greatest concentrations of Russian speakers. In all the states, in fact, concentrations of Russian speakers are found in urban centers. This phenomenon can be explained by the nature of immigration from the former Soviet Union. Tolts (1997) indicates that the majority of Russian immigrants came from urban centers and therefore tended to settle in the large US cities, and many have occupations that require living in or near a city. In addition, in the Soviet Union, urban life has traditionally held strong appeal even to the rural populace. Since the nineteenth century, Russians commonly felt an imperative to live in Moscow, or at least in some other major city. Another factor contributing to the Soviet immigrants' tendency to remain in the large US cities where they first settled was the effect of the Soviet system of *propiska* (a registration of the residence component of an internal passport) that restricted every citizen to a particular location. A "Catch-22" law required that a citizen have a new job in order to relocate, but to get a job a person had to have a local registration. The resulting habit of remaining in one place may have contributed to the trend among immigrants from the former Soviet Union to be less mobile than typical Americans.

Finally, we offer a brief description of the socioeconomic and educational status of Russian speakers in the USA. According to the 2000 Census, Russian speakers are generally a well-educated population with 51 percent having at least the equivalent of a bachelor's degree and 92 percent having at least a high school diploma. Additionally, 75 percent of Russian speakers over the age of 5 report speaking English "well" or "very well" (US Census Bureau 2007c). Regarding employment, all Russian speakers independent of ethnicity or language are more likely to have jobs requiring a higher level of education when compared to the general US population. Among Russian speaking immigrants, 18 percent are in management and 36 percent are in professional occupations (compared to 13 percent and 20 percent of the general population). They are also less likely to be in construction and production (5 percent and 7 percent, versus 10 percent and 15 percent in the whole of the USA). In addition, Russian speakers in the USA tend to work in the for-profit sector of the economy, and only 10 percent are self-employed. According to Portes and Rumbaut's (2006) more recent data, however, the number of self-employed among Russian immigrants is 18 percent. This may be due to the fact that the newest post-Soviet immigration comes from a market economy and is more business oriented.

Public presence of Russian

In a number of US cities, especially New York and Los Angeles, there are Russian immigrant communities that preserve elements of Russian everyday life and culture. As in other ethnic communities, immigrants have established businesses that cater to the community and make the newly arrived feel at home by employing Russian speakers and offering services such as legal and medical practices, restaurants, grocery stores, and drugstores. But the most prominent public face of Russian in the USA is within academia. The next sections describe the public presence of Russian in media, business, and education.

Media

The first Russian-language newspaper in the USA was published from 1868–71 and was called *Svoboda* (Freedom). A bilingual, semi-monthly periodical, it was known in English as the *Alaska Herald* (Hardwick 1993: 76). Before 1921, fifty-two other newspapers were published, eighteen of which were discontinued after one year, and by 1921 only four Russian dailies were being produced in the USA. A fifth, *Novi Mir* (The New World), was suppressed by the US government because of its affiliation with the Communist Party (Davis 1969: 124). In total, Harvard University lists fifty-seven Russian language émigré publications from 1900 to 1940 (Whittaker 2006: 57).

Today, Russian-language print and media resources are abundant and easily available in the post-Soviet and digital era. Magazines are available in the USA by subscription and in Russian bookstores and grocery stores. The daily newspaper that has served the Russian community in the USA the longest is *Novoe russkoe slovo* (The New Russian Word), which has been published continuously since 1910. Russian-language newspapers are published in the areas of the USA with high concentrations of Russian speakers, and several newspapers have a nationwide and even international readership. The weekly *V Novom Svete* (In the New World), which covers international current events, is available throughout the USA as well as Canada, while *Vecherniy New York* (The Evening New York), targets the Russian speakers of the New York metropolitan area. A Russian-language weekly, *Panorama*, has been published in Los Angeles since 1980. There are also examples of Russian-language newspapers in the USA that are targeted primarily at Jews, such as *Evreiskii Mir* (The Jewish World), which covers Jewish issues and events in Israel.

Russian-language radio, broadcasting from Russia as well as locally, is also available in the USA. *Radio Mayak* and *Radio Baltica* are delivered by providers of Russian-language media. In addition, there are several local Russian-language radio stations throughout the USA, including New York-based *Davidzon Radio* and Chicago-based *New Life Radio*. A number of radio stations broadcasting from Russia can also be streamed online.

Russian television networks include *Russkii Mir* (Russian World), *RTR-Planeta*, *RTVi*, and *Pervyi Kanal* (Channel One), which broadcast around the world. *NTV America*, based in both Russia and New York, is broadcast throughout North America. Its programming is based on the programming of the Russian network *NTV* but also includes a daily edition of US news and some programs on topics of interest to those living in North America. *RTN* (Russian Television Network of America) is a US-based network serving the Russian-American community.

Business

There are Russian-oriented small businesses such as groceries, bookstores, and beauty salons in areas where there is a relatively large population of Russian speakers. There are also real estate and insurance agencies that employ many Russian speakers. A Russian-language yellow pages directory has print and online versions and lists a full spectrum of businesses and services (*Russian Yellow Pages: All States* 2008). The print versions of the yellow pages are often available in Russian bookstores and grocery stores. A broad range of businesses and services can also be located through Russian-community websites. However, it is not clear either from their names or advertised services that they cater exclusively to Russian clientele or that all employees are Russian speakers. Food services such as restaurants and markets are typically owned and staffed by Russian speakers.

In major cities, many medical offices advertise that either the doctors or their staff speak Russian. There is a Russian-American Medical Association (RAMA) and Russian-American Dental Association (RADA) that hold annual meetings. Founded in 2000, RAMA has a membership of over four hundred professionals, representing forty US states and Canada (RAMA, and RADA n.d.). Russian business associations have also been established. For example, the Russian-American Business and Arts Council is a nonprofit organization aimed at strengthening business and cultural ties in Southern California (RABAC 2008), the American-Russian Business Council was founded in 1994 to promote trade and investment in Russia (ARBC 2006), and the Mid-Atlantic–Russia Business Council conducts seminars for its members who conduct business in Russia (MA-RBC 2007).

Education

Russian is classified as a Level III language in terms of difficulty for native English speakers (Omaggio 2001: 26). This is according to research conducted at the Defense Language Institute in the 1970s that assessed the number of hours of study that are required for English speakers to reach a certain degree of language proficiency. Spanish and French are in Group I, German is in Group II, Russian is a Group III language, and Chinese, Korean, Arabic, and Japanese are in Group IV. This indicates that Russian is generally a more difficult language for English speakers to master.

Russian was not widely taught in the USA before the 1960s. Prior to World War II, only 19 US universities offered Russian courses. Fewer than half a dozen universities had formal Russian or Slavic departments, and only three offered doctoral programs. As a result of the US–Soviet alliance during World War II, Russian teaching expanded so that by 1946, 190 academic institutions offered Russian, as reported by the Committee on College and Pre-College Russian (n.d.). When the Soviet Union launched the first Sputnik in 1957, the US government quickly reacted by passing the National Defense Education Act, with the goal of improving instruction in the sciences and promoting the study of Russian. The establishment of many new departments of Russian at US universities was a direct consequence. From 1958 to 1969, enrollment in college Russian courses doubled, and doctoral programs were expanded. There was another growth spurt in the 1980s when Gorbachev promised reform and democratization. In 1980 approximately 24,000 students were studying Russian at the college level. By 1990 that number had almost doubled to over 44,000, the highest number of enrollments in Russian in US history (Furman *et al.* 2007).

As the USA began to perceive the former Soviet Union as no longer a threat to security or a challenge in the economic sphere, enrollments began to decrease again, and many of the high school programs collapsed. From 1998 to 2007, 189 programs in forty states were terminated (Brecht *et al.* 1995). By 2005 there remained 126 programs that enrolled 7863 students. In 2007 in the city of Los Angeles, there were no K-12 institutions, either public or private, that taught Russian. A cautiously heartening observation can be made, however, from the MLA enrollment data published in 2007: in contrast to the low 0.5 percent increase between 1998 and 2002, Russian enrollments in 2006 showed a 3.9 percent increase from four years previously (Furman *et al.* 2007). In addition, in the past several years Russia has been attaining prominence as an economic and political force. This change may be contributing to restoring motivation to study Russian as a foreign or heritage language. Russian also remains in the top tier of strategic languages for the US government; for example, through its inclusion in the Language Flagship initiative funded by the National Security Education Program.[4]

Unlike some other languages (notably Chinese and Korean) that have a system of community/church schools whose goal is to preserve immigrant children's home language and culture, there are few schools for Russian-speaking children. There are some schools affiliated with Russian Orthodox Churches and a few proprietary Saturday schools. An interesting example is a school established by the Russian-speaking faculty at the University of California, Irvine, in 2003. The school's mission is "to provide a unique opportunity for children to be exposed to the rich Russian culture and to develop and maintain their Russian language skills" (*Karandash* 2007). The school offers Russian language and literature, math, physics, Russian history and geography, art, theater, and music. All classes are taught in Russian.

As a consequence of increased immigration from the Soviet Union, heritage learners began to appear in large numbers in college Russian classes in the late 1980s. The level of competence in Russian of these children of the third and fourth waves of immigration is directly tied to the amount of education they had received prior to immigration (Kagan and Dillon 2006). Russian heritage language learners can be divided into four groups according to their age at the time of emigration, linguistic biographies, and their resulting language competence (Table 11.4).

By the late 1990s, due to understanding that heritage learners' instructional needs differed widely from those of foreign language learners, some colleges began to offer special courses for these students. Many descendants of Russian immigrants choose to enroll in heritage Russian courses at the university level, and a survey is being conducted by the National Heritage Language Resource Center (Carreira *et al.* 2007) to discover the main reasons why they have chosen to study Russian. The most common motivating factor, cited by 90 percent of the respondents, is a desire to communicate better with their families in the USA. A third are motivated by plans to travel to the former Soviet Union. Notably, only 14 percent of the respondents indicate their motivation as "because it is easy for me," which is contrary to the idea held by some Russian instructors that heritage speaker students hope to get an "easy A" in Russian courses.

Three major professional organizations serve the needs of researchers, teachers, and students in the Russian field: the American Association of Teachers of Slavic and East European Languages, founded in 1941, the American Association for the Advancement of Slavic Studies, founded in 1948, and the American

Table 11.4. *Groups of heritage Russian-language learners*

	Education	Russian proficiency
Group 1	Graduated or almost graduated from high school in Russia or a former Soviet republic.	Fully developed grammatical system, native range of vocabulary, full understanding of and connection to Russian culture.
Group 2	Attended school in the former Soviet Union for five to seven years, therefore experienced an interruption in Russian-language development in adolescence.	Strong knowledge of Russian grammatical system but without the same range of vocabulary or register as educated native speakers.
Group 3	Attended elementary school in the former Soviet Union	Have some Russian literacy but their language development was interrupted at an early age (7–9) so range of vocabulary is limited. When they take Russian classes, they often recover some of the "lost" language.
Group 4	Emigrated as pre-schoolers or were born in the USA to Russian-speaking parents and have been educated primarily or solely in English.	Never use Russian outside of home. Consequently vocabulary is limited to home sphere; typically do not have a strong control of Russian grammar. Reanalyze their language at a later age to arrive at a different grammatical system (Polinsky 2000).

Sources: Kagan and Dillon 2001; Kagan 2005.

Council of Teachers of Russian, founded in 1974, which expanded its focus to become American Councils for International Education in 1987.

Evidence of language shift to English and of Russian maintenance

Shift to English has been rapid among Russian-speaking immigrants in the USA. Russian, like other immigrant languages, is used primarily in the home. But, unlike many other immigrants groups, the majority of Russian-speaking immigrants do not live in an ethnic community. They tend to disperse very quickly into the general population. Several factors help to explain this phenomenon. Gitleman (1981) explains that there were many cultures within Jewish immigrant groups from the Soviet Union. From the point of view of Americans, "the class, educational, and linguistic differences" that set these groups off from one another were irrelevant, whereas for the immigrants they became even more important after the immigration (p. 15). The same can be said not only about Jews but about all immigrant groups from the former Soviet

Union. The Soviet Union was a vast empire that united diverse populations by political means. Once the political restraints were lifted, unification also disappeared. There are some small neighborhoods that preserve a Russian-speaking environment such as in Brighton Beach, New York, but most Soviet immigrants have dispersed in the general population, where they have fewer opportunities or need to use their mother tongue outside the home.

Another factor that contributes to the lack of ethnic neighborhoods derives from the Russian culture's attitude towards socializing and friendship. Traditionally, Russians develop and maintain very close friendships, but they are not likely to socialize with people outside their own close circle. The Russian word *svoj* meaning "one's own" expresses this attitude. All people are divided into *svoi* and *čužie* "outsiders, others." Because of the political conditions in the Soviet Union, it was unwise to trust anyone not belonging to one's immediate circle. While this may appear irrational outside of the former Soviet Union, the attitude is still prevalent among first generation immigrants.

Along with a shift to English as the dominant language, Russian speakers in the USA have also introduced English language features into their Russian. Sociopolitical factors have had a very direct and immediate impact on the Russian language as spoken in the USA. For the third wave of Russian immigrants (1970–90), entering the USA meant moving from a closed society with a state-controlled economy to an open society with a market economy. As a result, Russian speakers had to find ways to express notions that either did not exist in Soviet society or were not commonplace. For example, real estate was an unknown and uncharted territory, given that most apartments in the Soviet Union were owned by the state and allocated to its citizens. Consequently, Russian speakers in the USA would use the word "mortgage" either as a quotation pronouncing it as in English or they would Russianize it phonetically and morphologically (*morgidž*). In the new post-Soviet Russia not only is there a Russian word for "mortgage" (*ipoteka*) but it is in everyday use, so present-day immigrants can be expected to use the Russian word that is unfamiliar to earlier immigrants.

A common language contact phenomenon described in Chapter 2 of this volume is calquing, or direct translations, which is very common in Russian-American due to the dominance of English among Russian speakers in the USA. Andrews (1998) explains the tendency to calque as a consequence of the vast differences between Russian and American lifestyles.[5] However, some common calques may be the result of the prevalence of English idiom. Some notable examples involve usage of the verb "to take," which in Russian has numerous equivalents depending on the context. Many Russian speakers in the USA use only one Russian verb that is the direct calque of "to take" to cover many situations; for example, "to take a class," "to take an exam," "to take a shower," or "to take a trip" (Zemskaia 2001; Kagan and Dillon 2001, 2002).

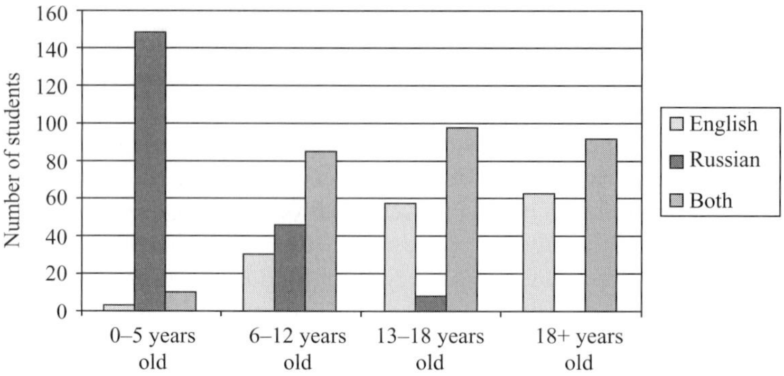

Figure 11.1. Language use at various periods in life
Source: Adapted from Carreira *et al.* 2007

Semantic extensions are also common, such as using the Russian word for K-12 school, *škola*, to refer to college and even graduate school. Similarly, the Russian word *klass* has a much more limited meaning than its English equivalent "class," but Russian-speaking students tend to translate every instance of the word "class" with the Russian *klass*.

There is a spectrum of attitudes toward the preservation of Russian in the USA. At one polar end are those who insist on the preservation of "pure" Russian, and on the other are the majority of speakers who incorporate some English into their speech, particularly words and expressions (e.g. "politically correct," "sexual harassment," "diversity"), that do not exist in Russian or would require a lengthy explanation. Some immigrants or heritage speakers use code-switching, calques, and semantic extensions to such a degree that monolingual Russian speakers find it challenging to understand them. In sum, the impact of the dominant English language on the Russian proficiency of heritage students is similar to that in other immigrant languages.

Signs of shift

As noted previously, in the 2007 American Community Survey, 75 percent of US Russian speakers claimed to speak English "well" or "very well." The National Heritage Language Resource Center Survey (Carreira *et al.* 2007) also offers some insight into Russian use among members of the 1.5 and second generations. Figure 11.1 compares English and Russian language use at different ages, as reported by 160 college Russian heritage language students. As is the case with other immigrant groups, immigrant Russian children typically speak Russian almost exclusively until they start school at the age of 5, when they begin to switch to the dominant language, English. After the age of 18, almost 50 percent reported exclusive use of English, and very few reported use of Russian exclusively. This is a very clear sign of shift away from Russian and to English.

Additionally, according to Rumbaut *et al.* (2006), 35 percent of Mexicans in the USA retain strong heritage-language skills beyond the second generation, while only 3 percent of European immigrants do. We expect the offspring of Russian speakers to fall into this latter category. As explained above in the section on education, there are very few Saturday schools for Russian-speaking children. There are no immersion programs, and Russian is not taught in many schools. It falls to families to teach their children Russian if they feel it is important to preserve the language. However, Lavretsky *et al.* (1997: 337) note that Russian parents generally do not insist on speaking Russian to their children and grandchildren, and that it is common for children who came to this country before entering school not to have speaking, reading, or written knowledge of Russian.

Signs of maintenance

The most salient indication of the motivation to preserve and advance Russian-language proficiency in the immigrant population is the heritage learner phenomenon. The number of students at the college level has grown steadily, providing the impetus for the development of a textbook designed to meet the learning needs of the Russian heritage language learners at the college level (Kagan *et al.* 2003). In a recent development, some publishers in Russia are beginning to publish textbooks targeting children of immigrants (Russkij Jazyk Publishers n.d.). There are enough Russian heritage learners at the high school and college levels to warrant the creation of special categories in national language competitions. A landmark effort to produce advanced competence in Russian is the Flagship Program, established by the National Security Education Program. Heritage students are in the fast track in these programs, which may result in increased interest in language preservation among members of generations 1.5 and two.

In 2007, Russian President Vladimir Putin launched a new organization, *Fond Russkij Mir* (The Russian World Foundation). The goals are similar to those of the German Goethe Institute, the French Alliance Française, the Spanish Cervantes Institute, and the Chinese Confucius Institute. The main purpose is to promote and support the study of the Russian language and culture abroad. One aim is to help Russian speakers abroad maintain their language proficiency. Thus, the organization is directly aimed at Russian heritage speakers all over the world. One of the grants awarded by the Foundation in 2008 was for the development of a textbook for Russian-speaking children aged 8–12 (Miznik *et al.* 2009). The project brought together a group of authors from Israel, Russia,

Germany, and the USA. It remains to be seen whether such new initiatives will have a significant impact on the maintenance of Russian in diaspora or among those who study Russian as a foreign language.[6]

Conclusions

Zemskaia (2001) argues that the first wave of twentieth-century Russian immigrants preserved Russian better than the subsequent waves because only the first wave left Russia fully intending to return. It is true that the fall of the Soviet Union opened the possibility of return for all Russian/Soviet immigrants, many of whom travel often and conduct business there. It is also true that because of Russia's strengthened political and economic influence during the Putin era, more first, second, and 1.5 generation speakers travel to Russia and go on study abroad programs there. But not many intend to return permanently. While the National Heritage Language Resource Center Survey, mentioned above, indicates that college students who grew up in Russian-speaking families are well disposed to preserving the language and are almost unanimous in their desire to teach Russian to their children, the question is, of course, whether it is likely to happen. Despite the various promising preservation efforts, we think it is unlikely that the Russian language will survive beyond the second generation in the USA. The dominance of the English language throughout the world and the challenges to bilingualism in the US educational system will likely overpower the good intentions of a relatively small number of families and individuals who imagine they can preserve their home language and culture.

DISCUSSION QUESTIONS

1. Summarize and analyze the main differences between the waves of Russian immigration in the twentieth and twenty-first centuries. How might the different circumstances contribute to language use among Russians in the USA?

2. Compare the reasons for immigration between Russians and any other immigrant group. How might these differences contribute to language use?

12 Italian in the USA

Anna De Fina and Luciana Fellin

Introduction

Italian Americans constitute one of the earliest and most important immigrant communities in the USA, with their presence felt around the country both culturally and economically. Today, Italian ranks ninth among the non-English languages spoken in the USA, with nearly 800,000 persons still using it as their home language. Although the number of US speakers of Italian has been continuously declining (as shown in Table 1.1), interest in the Italian language and culture has been rekindled by recent changes in Italy's public image in the USA as well as by increased opportunities for contact with Italy through travel and the global media.

Although most Italian Americans moved out of "Little Italy" communities in the 1950s, Italian neighborhoods in many cities are still significant sites for the transmission and enactment of cultural traditions throughout the generations. Italians are often considered a primary example of an immigrant community that successfully left behind the poverty and the social stigma experienced by the early settlers (Alba 2000). In fact, as we will note below, the median income and educational attainment of Italian-Americans today are equal or superior to the national average, and their degree of adaptation to US society has been extraordinary. Nonetheless, Italian-Americans are still a very distinct community with their own traditions and moral values and a strong attachment to their culture. Their influence on US society has been felt in many areas, from politics to the arts, and their language has gradually risen to the status of one of the most commonly studied in the country. In the following sections we will present a more detailed picture of the social and cultural presence of Italians in the USA and of the transformations that their linguistic identity has experienced since their arrival in a massive immigration wave in the late nineteenth and early twentieth century.

History

The Italian language spoken in Italy today derives from the Florentine dialect of the fourteenth century, which, in turn, developed from the Vulgar Latin commonly spoken in the fifth century CE in the geographical area that corresponds to modern-day Italy. The process which led to the development, standardization, and diffusion of Italy's official national language was complex, with a history that spread over centuries. Although many early varieties of Italian were born from Latin, with some written texts documented as early as the ninth century CE, the Tuscan dialect took the lead around the fourteenth century. This is largely credited to the renowned poet Dante Alighieri, who first codified the Florentine dialect, giving the language a vehicle of wide diffusion and legitimacy *vis à vis* Latin, the then-dominant written language of culture (Migliorini 1987). At the time Dante wrote *The Divine Comedy*, Florence held a prosperous economic and political position, which undoubtedly fostered acceptance of its dialect outside of Tuscan borders.

With the political unification of Italy in 1861, the Tuscan-based variety of Italian began to be actively promoted as the national language through the establishment of mandatory schooling and the creation of a centralized bureaucratic apparatus for the newly established national institutions. However, it is estimated that at the time of Italy's unification, only 2.5 percent of the population spoke the national language (De Mauro 1963) and that the rest of its citizens were monolingual in their local dialects – which were mostly not mutually comprehensible with Italian.[1] In addition, primary access to Italian was through the written word, which was only accessible to the 22 percent of the population who was literate at the time. It was only in the decades after World War II, with increased interregional communication and the development of radio and television broadcasting, that Italian began to turn into a real national language spoken across the country. In recent years, Italian has turned into the first language of the majority of the Italian nation's population, with local dialects losing their primacy as varieties spoken at home.[2] Currently, Italian is spoken primarily in Italy, in the Ticino Canton of southern Switzerland, in San Marino, and in Corsica, as well as in immigrant communities in North and South America, Europe, and Australia.

Demographics

According to data from the 2000 Census, there are 16 million individuals of Italian ancestry in the USA, constituting almost 6 percent of the total population and forming the fifth largest ethnic group in the country; after people of German (19.2%), African (12.9%), Irish (10.8%) and English (7.7%) descent. Statistics published by the Order of the Sons of Italy in America (2007) estimate the number of people in the USA with at least one Italian grandparent at about 26 million.[3] Table 12.1 shows the five states with the largest numbers and those with the largest percentages of Italian-Americans, who we can see are primarily

Table 12.1. *States with the largest Italian-ancestry populations*

State	Number with Italian ancestry	Percentage of population in that state
New York	2,737,146	14
New Jersey	1,503,637	18
California	1,450,884	4
Pennsylvania	1,418,465	12
Florida	1,003,977	6
Rhode Island	199,077	19
Massachusetts	860,079	14
Connecticut	634,364	19

Source: US Census Bureau 2000a.

Table 12.2. *States with the largest Italian-speaking populations*

State	Ages 5 +	Percentage of all US Italian speakers
New York	222,704	27.83
New Jersey	89,044	11.12
California	66,193	8.27
Pennsylvania	54,658	6.83
Florida	52,050	6.50
Massachusetts	46,162	5.76
Illinois	44,173	5.52
Connecticut	41,017	5.12
Ohio	24,494	3.06
Michigan	24,154	3.01
Total in USA	798,801	

Source: Modern Language Association 2009, US Census Bureau 2007c.

located in the Northeast. The northeastern states are, in fact, where most of the immigrants from the late eighteenth and early nineteenth century settled.

Although the number of US citizens of Italian ancestry is relatively high, those who actually speak Italian are much fewer. Approximately 800,000 US residents of Italian descent speak Italian. This number represents only 1.4 percent of US residents who speak a language other than English at home, yet Italian occupies ninth place among the non-English languages spoken in the country. Table 12.2 displays the ten states with the largest populations of Italian speakers. Italian speakers in the USA are concentrated in four urban centers, three of which are in the Northeast. New York City (140,000), Philadelphia (15,000), Chicago (12,000), and Boston (7,000).

In 1910, the 1.4 million speakers of Italian made it the third largest mother-tongue group in the USA (Stevens 1999). However, as shown in Table 1.1, the number of people who speak Italian declined by 23 percent – from approximately 1,300,000 to 1,000,000 – between 1990 and 2000, and again by 21 percent – from 1,000,000 to 800,000 – between 2000 and 2007. This decline can be partly explained by the reduced number of immigrants from Italy. According to a report on the US foreign-born population, immigration from Europe is now significantly less than from countries such as Mexico, Cuba and the Philippines (US Census Bureau 1993). More than 70 percent of Italian immigrants counted in 1990 had arrived before 1970, while the percentage of foreign-born Italians had fallen from 41 percent of the total foreign-born population before 1960 to just 6 percent in 1990. Importantly, almost 80 percent of those born in Italy reported speaking a language other than English at home. It must be emphasized however, that in the case of Italian, the Census does not distinguish between standard Italian and other dialects spoken in Italy. This is significant because, particularly among many members of older generations of immigrants, the local dialect (and not Italian) is the home language, and when these individuals report speaking Italian on US Census forms, they may in fact mean a dialect. Italian-Americans descend from families that originated in different regions of Italy, and although the majority of them come from the south, their dialects of origin are varied and often not mutually comprehensible (see Correa-Zoli 1980). We will return to the important effects of the sociolinguistic complexity of Italian and its related dialects in a later section.

Public presence of Italian

Pasquandrea (2007: 20) notes that the Australian government promoted Italian-language maintenance through school bilingual programs and support for Italian-language media. Unlike Australia and Canada, however, the US government has not offered assistance in the conservation of Italian as a heritage language. On the contrary, the use of Italian has been ignored at best, and at worst openly discouraged (which will be discussed in more depth). As a result, the public presence of the language today is limited. However, in recent years the Italian Ministry of Foreign Affairs has begun a campaign to promote Italian language and culture abroad, including the establishment of such a mission for its *Istituti Italiani di Cultura* in 1990, the launch of Italian radio and television (*RAI International*) within immigrant communities, and the establishment in 2000 of an "Italian Language in the World Week," which takes place each October.

Media

The presence of Italian media in the USA is linked to areas where there are large concentrations of Italian immigrant communities, particularly California and the Northeast and a few areas in the Midwest such as Chicago and St. Louis. The only US daily newspaper in Italian is *America Oggi*, published in New Jersey with an average daily circulation of 34,400. The remaining Italian dailies come directly from Italy and target the foreign-born. The bulk of the Italian-American press consists of weekly, monthly, and bimonthly publications directed to local communities concentrated in urban areas. However, these are usually either bilingual or entirely English publications. A notable exception is the Italian language weekly *L'Italo-Americano*, published in the Los Angeles area, catering to northern and southern California residents of Italian descent, and which has an average weekly circulation of 30,000 (*L'Italo-Americano* 2003). A number of regional monthly magazines published in Italy (*Puglia Emigrazione*, *Veronesi nel Mondo*, *Sicilia Mondo*, *Trentini Mondo*, and others) dealing with issues of immigration, regional folklore, and heritage, are also sent by regional government agencies to subscribers abroad.

As for radio, there are currently five stations in the New York area transmitting daily programs in Italian. However, the bulk of Italian-American presence on the radio consists of programs hosted by local AM and FM channels. These programs are mostly bilingual or English-only. An important presence since 1995 is the international branch of Italy's national radio and television broadcasting agency, *Radiotelevisione Italiana*, or *RAI*. *RAI* offers, via cable and satellite, radio and television programs across the USA. Typical offerings include daily newscasts, talk shows, sports programs, and documentaries on Italian culture (e.g. *La vita di Dante*). Its programs are also accessible on the web, which, in recent years, has become a major source of Italian-language contact and exposure for the younger generation of Italian-Americans as well as for recent immigrants from Italy.

Business

According to a report by the Order of the Sons of Italy (2003) in America, and based on Census 2000 data, two thirds of Italian-Americans today occupy white-collar positions in business, medicine, law, education, and other professions, and their median income is $61,297 (compared with a national median of $50,000). Italian-Americans also have a slightly greater college graduation rate than the national average (18.5 percent college graduates v. 15.5 percent), and a greater than or equal rate of advanced degrees compared to the national average. There are more than a thousand US Italian-owned firms in the country in a variety of commercial areas such as food, clothing and textiles, furniture and

Table 12.3. *Enrollment in Italian in US K-12 programs, 2005*

	Pre-elementary	Elementary	High School	Adults	Other courses	Total
Courses	307	1,484	1,437	358	30	3,616
Students	5,308	31,572	29,472	4,453	372	71,177

Source: Italian Embassy.

design, household goods, chemicals, and precision machinery. The estimated number of American companies doing business with Italy is 7,500, and more than a thousand US firms have offices in Italy, including IBM, General Electric, Motorola, and Citibank. Trade with Italy and the increasing presence of Italian firms in the USA have given impulse to the study of Italian at the postsecondary level and to the creation of opportunities for study abroad programs launched by US universities for students – who are the focus of the next section.

Education

Table 12.3 presents data provided by the Italian Embassy on enrollment in Italian language courses across US K-12 classrooms. The Embassy calculates over 71,000 students of Italian enrolled in over 3,500 courses in US schools. In Table 12.3, pre-elementary school refers to pre-school programs addressed to children below 6 years of age. Adult and other courses refer to classes for adults that are offered outside the regular high school curriculum, including language courses and content courses taught in Italian. The most significant numbers of courses and students are concentrated in large urban centers of the North such as New York, Detroit, Chicago, and Boston, which are also cities with significant Italian-American communities. Although Italian is the fourth most commonly taught spoken language in the US today, it is still underrepresented among the foreign languages taught at the secondary level. In response, the Italian Ministry of Education has worked in conjunction with local Italian-American organizations to promote Italian by sending a limited number of qualified Italian teachers to US schools every year and by providing an annual contribution for the hiring of local Italian teachers. In 2006 the Italian version of the high school Advanced Placement exam was first offered, and was taken by slightly over 1,500 students (College Board n.d.). This prestigious exam, for which associations such as the National Italian American Foundation have been lobbying for years, is an important step in the diffusion of Italian teaching in schools, since it will constitute an incentive for the introduction of new Italian-language courses at the high school level. Students can earn credit at most universities by attaining a certain score on this exam.

While Italian does not appear to be widely taught at the elementary and secondary level, it has been increasingly taken up by university students. In the 1960s just 11,000 students were enrolled in Italian at the college level nationwide. This number rose to 34,000 in 1970, almost 50,000 in 1990, and almost 64,000 in 2002. Between 1998 and 2002, enrollment in university Italian courses grew by nearly 30 percent, and 2006 data from the Modern Language Association show that Italian enrollments are still increasing, having reached 78,368 (Furman *et al.* 2007). Italian is now the fifth most studied language, as American Sign Language has taken fourth place. This positive trend is also seen at the level of graduate studies. Goldberg and Welles (2001) show that Italian and Spanish were the only foreign language Master's programs that had not declined between 1995 and 1999. In addition, the number of students enrolled in Italian Master's and doctoral programs has increased slightly from 925 in 1998 to 1,100 in 2007 (Calabrese 2007).

This recent interest in Italian is due to different factors that will be discussed ahead, including a positive change in Italian-Americans' attitudes towards their language and culture that has motivated many heritage learners to study Italian at the college level, as well as the attraction that Italy exerts at the cultural level for non-Italian US students.

Evidence of language shift to English and of Italian maintenance

Signs of shift

The Italian speech community in the USA fits the textbook model of linguistic assimilation (Fishman 1991b; Alba 2004). Most Italian immigrants of the first migration wave, spanning the late 1800s and early 1900s, arrived in the USA as monolingual speakers of their regional dialect (Correa-Zoli 1980). In subsequent waves, they arrived bilingual in their local dialect and Italian. Most of these immigrants, particularly women, learned just enough English to get by, which in general with most other immigrant groups has been attributed to factors including isolation within the immigrant community, difficult working conditions, and limited resources. Parents typically spoke their mother tongue to their children, who in turn typically spoke English with their siblings and peers and, in many cases, responded in English to their parents. When children of the second generation raised their own families, they spoke English with their offspring, giving rise to the first English monolingual generation. In many cases, monolingual third generation children picked up fragments of Italian from their grandparents and parents, but their competence remained receptive only. In sum, following a classic pattern, Italian immigrant families typically experienced language shift in the span of three generations (Alba and Nee 2003).

An explanation for the high level of English proficiency among Italian-Americans who speak Italian (89 percent of speakers claim to speak English "well" or "very well" [US Census Bureau 2007c]) is due to the fact that the bulk of the community is made up of second, third, and fourth generation members whose language of socialization was in fact English, to the waning presence of first generation elders with lower levels of education and exposure to the dominant language, and, finally, to the inclusion in the statistics of the recent wave of émigrés who are typically multilingual professionals who are already fluent in English upon arrival in the USA.

Among the major European immigrant groups of the early twentieth century, Italians showed a rather fast pattern of assimilation to English, with few attempts at language maintenance when compared to, for example, German speakers, who founded numerous bilingual schools in the Midwest and who were successful in maintaining their mother tongue across generations until World War I (Alba 2004; Chapter 9, this volume). French-Canadians living in New England also managed to keep French alive until the 1950s through parochial schools (Gerstle 1989), while Greek communities still maintain their language through schools organized by the Orthodox Church (Constantakos and Spiradakis 1997).

A distinctive factor that contributed to Italian immigrants' language loss was their more complex situation of diglossia between Italian (the "High" code; see more about diglossia in Chapter 2, this volume), and regional dialects (the "Low" code) that they experienced in the homeland and imported to the new country (Bettoni and Gibbons 1988; Rubino 2006). As noted above, the first language of most early immigrants was their regional dialect and, quite often, their competence in the national code, standard Italian, was weak. The need for the High variety (Ferguson 1959) became more urgent, and the diglossic division even more relevant, in the new immigrant context where the national code (generally its less educated variety, i.e. "italiano popolare," cf. Cortelazzo 1972) assumed the function of lingua franca for communicating with Italians from other regions. Speakers' insecurity in the standard code, together with the low prestige of dialects as compared to the higher value of Italian and English, discouraged efforts to maintain them.[4] Instead, many Italians simply shifted to English in order to communicate with other Italians and with other English-speaking groups in the USA. Haller (1987, 1993) documented three language varieties spoken by US Italian immigrants: (1) a lingua franca consisting of a common variety of Italian highly influenced by southern dialects, (2) Italianized archaic dialects, and (3) pidginized forms of Italian.[5] Thus, regional and linguistic fragmentation contributed to low levels of national identification and weak language loyalty.

Heritage language loss in the Italian community also went hand in hand with the group's deracialization. During the nineteenth and twentieth centuries,

Southern Italian immigrants to the USA were considered somewhere in between white and black, which Richards (1999) terms "nonvisibly black." The resulting strong degrees of discrimination by white Americans led to a desire for quick assimilation and abandonment of Italian ethnic markers more quickly than other peer immigrant groups. As the Little Italy communities dismantled and Italian-Americans moved to the suburbs and adopted the lifestyle of mainstream America, both their ethnic racialization and their language faded (Nelli 1983). The abandonment of Italian peaked during World War II, when Italians and Germans became particularly suspect. One government poster depicting caricatures of Mussolini and Hilter read "Don't Speak the Enemy's Language! Speak American!" (Di Stasi 2001; Carnevale 2003).

Finally, another crucial factor in the process of language shift was the lack of institutional support. Whereas other European language groups could rely on the church, school, or governmental agencies to provide linguistic and cultural education in the mother tongue, these institutions in Italian-speaking communities did not provide such services. The Catholic Church, although promoting associations and cultural activities for many Italian immigrants, did not pursue a specific Italian-language policy. It is interesting to note that the church has played an important role in the maintenance of other immigrant languages in the USA, but the Italian communities in general have engaged in less active intervention and lobbying for language politics and support from the church. Schools typically did not offer Italian as a subject even in areas with very high concentrations of Italian residents, where instead French, German, and Spanish were made available to students (Tursi 1983). As for state institutions, the Italian government did not consistently invest in the diffusion of Italian language and culture as did, for example, the governments of Germany and France. To this effect, compare the traditionally strong role in language diffusion of the *Alliance Française* for French and the *Goethe Institute* for German. It was only in December 1990 that the Italian government passed specific legislation for the promotion of Italian language and culture abroad through the *Istituti Italiani di Cultura*, a move which supports language maintenance, to which we now turn.

Signs of maintenance

The Italian government's initiative to promote Italian language and culture abroad began in the 1990s, a period coinciding with growing interest in the USA towards Italy and things Italian. The activities of the *Istituti Italiani di Cultura* comprise, for example, the organization of Italian cultural events, such as film festivals, concerts, and symposia with invited scholars and artists (musicians, filmmakers, writers), and the co-ordination and exchange of visiting Italian teachers in American public schools. The image of Italy spread by the media is no longer restricted to poor immigrants, the mafia, and pizza; it is one of refined appeal associated with Italy's rich historical, cultural, artistic, and culinary heritage. For example, on American coffee tables, the 1990s book *A Year in Provence* (Mayle 1989) extolling the virtues of French living is now outsold by *Under the Tuscan Sun* (Mayes 1998), which sold over two million copies and was on the *New York Times* bestseller list for over 126 weeks.

As mentioned earlier, many third generation Italian-Americans are now enticed to rediscover their Italian identity, heritage, and language. For example, after his first visit to Italy to see his grandfather's town, author Fred Gardaphe claimed that he "became a born-again Italian" when he returned to the USA (Amella 2007). This renewed interest can be seen, on the one hand, in the increased presence of heritage speakers in Italian courses taught at the college level (although no concrete figures on the numbers/percentage of heritage speakers are currently available) and, on the other hand, in third generation members' novel and creative use of their limited competence in Italian. Although the grandchildren of immigrants are monolingual in English, they often pick up expressions and a few Italian "chunks" from their grandparents and parents. In a study of third generation Italians, Fellin (2007) shows that their use of code-switching from English into Italian (or dialect) tends to be conscious, intentional, and metaphorical. In fact, younger members of families of Italian origin use Italian words and dialect expressions in discourse in order to convey multiple meanings and connotations related to their sense of identification with certain aspects of the culture of origin. Token expressions in Italian or dialect are used to mark boundaries of interaction – for example, in greetings (e.g. *ciao*, *buona notte*) and ritualized sequences (e.g. *buon appetito*, *salute*) – as well as to signal beginning and end of turns, shift of topic (e.g. *capisci*, *aspetta*), and group affiliation through the use of Italian and dialect for familial terms (e.g. *nonna*, *zio*) and culinary terms (Fellin 2007).

The use of fragments of Italian or dialect as an index of identity is not exclusive to the younger generations. Recent studies on language alternation among Italian-Americans show that code-switching into Italian or dialect may take up a symbolic value among other groups as well. In a study of an Italian-American card-playing club, De Fina (2007a, 2007b) illustrates how even the use of limited Italian within English utterances by second or third generation immigrant Italian-American men is instrumental to the construction of individual and collective identities centered on "Italianness." De Fina found that, like members of the younger generations studied by Fellin, these men also tend to use stock Italian expressions such as greetings, ritualized sequences, and fillers to signal their ethnicity.[6] More importantly, the Italian origins and affiliation of the club are constructed through the teaching and use of Italian at the card-playing table. These examples indicate that individuals and communities of Italian origin may still index their Italianness through language use, no matter how well they speak Italian.

Conclusion

In sum, loss of Italian in the Italian immigrant community hinged on a combination of various factors that, briefly summarized, include discrimination, pressure to assimilate, exogamous marriages, lack of institutional support, and ideologies of language relegating Italian to a position of low prestige and utility in the linguistic marketplace (Bourdieu 1977, 1991). All this was compounded by and set within a national context where the dominant language ideology followed the monoglot standard (Silverstein 1996), also known as the "one language, one nation" principle. Such language ideology, described in Chapter 1 of this volume, is characterized by dedication to the correctness and pureness of language, together with the view of monolingualism as the norm and multilingualism as a deviation. In the melting pot model of American society that constitutes itself as unified through one language ("English-only"), Italian immigrants had little motivation to socialize their children in Italian and to pursue language-maintenance efforts. Thus, Italian and its varieties had few chances of survival in the immigrant community. The Italian-American community has in fact experienced a definite shift towards English that makes it similar to most of the other national groups that formed the migration wave of the late eighteenth and early nineteenth centuries.

However, recent generations are showing an increasing interest in the Italian language. Along with the growing prestige of things Italian in the mainstream US culture, third generation Italian-Americans are enrolling in language courses and employing creative ways to manipulate their limited Italian repertoire for socially meaningful purposes, while members of the older generations are no longer ashamed to use their language in public. These new attitudes can hardly reverse the language shift, especially if we consider the small number of new Italian immigrants to the USA, but they point to the fact that language maintenance is just one of the possible strategies to encode ethnic belonging and membership, and that limited language use and proficiency can still play a role in maintaining a sense of "Italianness" for people of Italian origin in the USA.

DISCUSSION QUESTIONS

1. What unique characteristics of the Italian-American immigrant community fostered its members' rapid shift to English?
2. Do you think that the fact that Italian immigrants spoke (and speak) different dialects affects language shift to English? In what ways?

---

13 Arabic in the USA

Sonia Shiri

Introduction

The US population claiming roots in the Arabic-speaking world has doubled in the last few decades. As shown in Table 1.1, the Arabic-speaking population grew by 73 percent between 1990 and 2000, and a further 25 percent between 2000 and 2007. This increase places Arabic as the tenth most commonly spoken non-English language in the USA, in spite of representing just 0.5 percent of the total population. Overall, this group is better educated and wealthier than the average US population at large. With a history of over five generations of active immigration to the USA, those with connections to the geographically and culturally diverse peoples of the Arab world present a varied profile both linguistically and in terms of identity. While predominantly originating in the Middle Eastern Levant region, Egypt, and Iraq, the Arabic heard in the USA today represents the diverse dialects and cultures of the twenty countries officially recognized as Arabic-speaking, as well as the types of Arabic spoken natively by communities elsewhere. The language shift to English that occurred among earlier immigrants and their descendants is now being offset with more efforts toward Arabic-language maintenance among the more recent waves of immigration. This chapter explores the presence and use of Arabic in the USA with an eye toward understanding its future longevity.

History

Arabic is a Semitic language that originated in the Arabian Peninsula. With the emergence of Islam in the seventh century and the launch of the Islamic Conquests, speakers of various Arabic dialects spread out of the Arabian Peninsula into almost all of the Middle East and northern Africa, and west into the Iberian Peninsula and gradually all the way eastward to China. Over time, as the incoming Arabic speakers intermarried with indigenous peoples in the Middle

East and North Africa, the Arabic language became the prominent language of these regions.

Arabic is spoken today by over 300 million people in the Middle East and North Africa. It is also used as a liturgical language by over one billion Muslims throughout the world, mainly in Asia and Africa. Arabic is considered a *diglossic* language, i.e. two forms of the language are used for different purposes by the same community: one form is used for everyday talk, and the other for religious, educational, and other formal contexts. The spoken language used in everyday exchanges is commonly referred to as "dialect," although "regional varieties" might be more accurate. The other form of the language, considered to be "higher," is called "standard" Arabic. Standard Arabic is primarily written, but is also spoken in the media today. Standard Arabic is primarily acquired through schooling, and dates back to pre-Islamic times. Standard Arabic is held in high regard by Arabic speakers because of the large body of religious, literary, and scientific texts that has been produced in this form, particularly around the Golden Age of the Islamic civilization during the Middle Ages. Most students learning Arabic as a foreign language today, however, tend to study Arabic in the reverse order from the way native speakers learn it: they study standard Arabic in school before they learn dialects, typically while studying abroad.

The regional varieties or dialects are divided into four major categories: Arabic of the Maghreb (North Africa), Egyptian Arabic (Egypt and the Sudan), Levantine Arabic (Lebanon, Syria, Jordan and Palestine/Palestinians in Israel), and Iraqi/Gulf Arabic. While some of these varieties are mutually intelligible, others, especially geographically distant ones, are not.

Of the numerous regional varieties or dialects, Egyptian Arabic is considered one of the most commonly understood in the Arab world, due to decades of a prolific Egyptian cinema and entertainment industry. However, none of the dialects of Arabic is officially recognized as a model or lingua franca for all Arabic-speaking communities. Each country, though, tacitly recognizes its own "standard" or model variety, which tends to be located in its capital city (Holes 1995).

As a result of the contact between Arabic and other languages over the last fifteen centuries, many languages of the world have borrowed words from Arabic. Spanish and Portuguese contain a large Arabic vocabulary dating back to the eight centuries of Muslim rule in the Iberian Peninsula. English also borrowed many words starting with "al" such as "alchemy" and "algebra." Arabic has also borrowed words from other languages: from Greek during the vast translation effort of the Golden Age of Islam, and from European languages (particularly French) in the nineteenth century. Standard Arabic continues to borrow today with the active and close contact with the modern world media.

Each spoken dialect of Arabic, too, has borrowed from the languages with which it has come in contact over the centuries.

Although Arabic is used as a liturgical language by non-Arab Muslims in the USA, the focus in this chapter will be on the use of Arabic among Arab-Americans.[1] There have been five identifiable waves of Arabic-speaking immigration to the USA. Arabic is believed to have first reached the "New World" with Arabic-speaking crew members on explorer ships in the sixteenth century despite the Spanish ban on transporting Muslims (Arab and non-Arab) to the Americas during the first fifty years after Columbus. Arabic then arrived in the USA with enslaved African Muslims who had knowledge of Arabic. An estimated 10 percent, or 18,000, of the 180,000 Africans brought in as slaves between 1711 and 1775 were Muslim, according to Austin (1984). Austin (1984, 1997) and Diouf (1998) document the lives of literate enslaved African Muslims who continued to read and write in Arabic during their decades of captivity in what became the USA; original documents written in Arabic by these Muslims continue to surface today. It is suggested that Arabic served as a unifying element among these African-Muslims, who came mainly from West Africa and spoke different local languages.

The first voluntary wave of Arabic speakers can be traced to the 1880s. These immigrants came primarily from Greater Syria, which was then under the rule of the Ottoman Empire. This wave consisted mostly of Christian, unskilled, and illiterate males (Abraham and Abraham 1981: 18, Hitti 1924: 58). Arab immigration to the USA continued throughout the twentieth century mainly for political and economic reasons. After slowing down as a result of the immigration quotas of the 1920s, the immediate post-World War II period witnessed a second wave of Arab immigrants that included Christian Iraqis and Muslims from Lebanon, Palestine, and Yemen (Abraham and Abraham 1981). Students and professionals from these same countries and from Egypt began arriving in the USA during the 1950s and 1960s, forming the third wave of Arabic-speaking immigrants. A fourth wave, resulting primarily from the Lebanese civil war and the Palestinian–Israeli conflict, brought in more educated Arabs, both Muslim and Christian, to the USA in the 1970s and the 1980s. The fifth wave throughout the 1990s brought speakers of dialects from the eastern part of the Arab world. Educated, primarily male Muslim speakers of the western Arabic dialects (Moroccans, Algerians, and Tunisians) also began to arrive during this period. The 2000 Census reported a doubling in the number of Arabs in the USA between 1980 and 2000 (from 610,000 in 1980, to 860,000 in 1990, to nearly 1.2 million in 2000). After September 11, 2001, Arab immigration slowed down, although thousands continue to be admitted through the Diversity Immigrant Visa Program, also known as the "green card lottery," and a limited number of refugees from the Iraq war continue to arrive as of 2008.

Demographics

Before reporting on self-reported Arabic speakers, I will briefly discuss US Arabic-ancestry communities in general, not all of whom are necessarily still Arabic-speaking. The 2000 Census counted about 1.2 million persons who self-identify as having an "Arabic-speaking" origin. This constituted an increase of 38 percent over 1990 (860,000) and represents 0.42 percent of the total US population, compared with 0.27 percent in 1980. The Census acknowledges that this question encompasses people whose geographical origins are in an "Arabic-speaking country or region," but who might ethnically and linguistically identify with another group in that region, such as Berbers or Kurds. The way the question is formulated also excludes people who would identify themselves as Arab such Mauritanians, Sudanese, and Somalis. The Census also acknowledges that, for various reasons, people might not report or identify themselves as Arab in origin. This possible underreporting is suggested when we compare Census results with estimates presented by the Arab American Institute, based on a Zogby poll, that places the US Arabic-origin population at 3.5 million, double what the Census reported (Arab American Institute 2007).

The US Census also reports the following. People of Arab descent are 57 percent male and have a median age of 33, two years younger than the US population overall. The majority of Arab-Americans (63 percent) are Christian. Within this group, Catholics represent 35 percent, Orthodox Christians 18 percent and Protestants 10 percent. Muslims represent 24 percent (Sunni, Shia, and Druze) while 13 percent are of other religions or report no particular denomination (Arab American Institute 2007).

People of Arab ancestry are twice as likely to have a college degree (41 percent, compared to 24 percent among the general population). This high level of education will translate, among the more recent immigrant groups, into a strong knowledge of the dialects as well as the standard Arabic language, it will also mean a reasonably good knowledge of English. Their median income of $52,300 is about $2,300 more than the median income for other families. Specifically, about 64 percent of US residents with Egyptian ancestry have a college degree, the highest among Arab groups. The Lebanese have the highest median family income (nearly $61,000). People of Arab ancestry also have a greater chance of working in management jobs than the US average (42 percent compared to 34 percent).

Individuals of Arab origin are evenly distributed across the four regions of the USA. However, almost half of all US Arabic-origin people (48 percent) are concentrated in five states: California, Florida, Michigan, New Jersey, and New York (see Table 13.1). The state with the largest number of Arab-Americans is California, mostly in the Los Angeles and San Diego areas. Michigan, however, is the state with the greatest concentration of Arabs in the country, followed

Table 13.1. *States and urban areas with largest populations of Arab descent*

States	Total (percentage) of total local population	Cities	Total (percentage) of total local population
California	191,000 (1.2)	New York, NY	69,985 (0.87)
New York	120,000 (0.63)	Los Angeles, CA	25,673 (0.69)
Michigan	115,000 (1.16)	Chicago, IL	14,777 (0.51)
Florida	77,461 (0.48)	Houston, TX	11,128 (0.57)
New Jersey	71,770 (0.85)	San Diego, CA	7,357 (0.60)
Texas	63,046 (0.30)	Detroit, MI	8,287 (0.87)
Ohio	54.014 (0.48)	Boston, MA	5,845 (0.99)
Massachusetts	52,756 (0.83)	Jacksonville, FL	5,751 (0.78)
Illinois	52,191 (0.42)	Jersey City, NJ	6,755 (2.81)
Pennsylvania	48,678 (0.40)	Dearborn, MI	29,181 (30)

Source: US Census Bureau 2003b.

by New Jersey and Massachusetts. While more than half the states in the USA counted a low Arab-American presence, of the order of 0.1 percent, many states had one or two counties with between 0.7 percent and 1.1 percent of residents of Arab descent, primarily in the Northeast and the Midwest. Dearborn, Michigan, a city of just under 100,000, is about 30 percent Arab. The first immigrants to this city were attracted by jobs in the automotive industry. New York City is the US city with the largest number of Arab-Americans. Large numbers of people of Arab descent also populate large cities such as Los Angeles, Chicago, and Houston, but the corresponding percentages remain low.

Almost every state in the country witnessed an increase in its Arab population between 1990 and 2000. California topped the list with an increase of 48,000 people, followed by Michigan at 39,000 and Florida at 28,000. The Census informs that approximately 60 percent of the US population of Arab ancestry has origins in three countries: Lebanon, Syria, and Egypt (see Table 13.2). This strong Lebanese presence dates back to the early immigrants of the late nineteenth century, Christians from Mount Lebanon, and the wave that followed about a hundred years later during the Lebanese civil war of the 1970s and 1980s. The next largest group is Palestinians, who showed a 50 percent increase from 1990. Among North Africans, Moroccans are the group with the largest presence in the USA.

Of the US population reporting Arab ancestry, it is estimated that 54 percent are foreign-born and 46 percent are born in the USA, according to Brittingham and de la Cruz's (2005) report based on the 2000 Census. Of the foreign-born, Iraqis constitute the largest group (61%), followed by Moroccans (59.6%), then Jordanians and Egyptians (43.8% each).

Table 13.2. *Seven largest groups of Arab descent by country of origin*

National origin	Total number	Percentage of US population
Lebanese	440,279	0.16
Syrian	142,897	0.05
Egyptian	142,832	0.05
Palestinian	72,112	0.03
Jordanian	39,734	0.01
Moroccan	38,923	0.01
Iraqi	37,714	0.01

Source: US Census Bureau 2000a.

Table 13.3. *States with the largest Arabic-speaking populations*

Arabic	Ages 5 +	Percentage of all US Arabic speakers
California	125,697	18.53
Michigan	93,845	13.84
New York	73,657	10.86
New Jersey	40,682	5.99
Illinois	39,963	5.89
Texas	39,570	5.83
Florida	38,377	5.65
Ohio	31,289	4.61
Virginia	24,923	3.67
Massachusetts	20,516	3.02
Total in USA	767,319	

Source: Modern Language Association 2009, US Census Bureau 2007c.

Slightly different from the Arab-origin population are the data on self-reported Arabic-language use in the home. Table 13.3 displays the ten states with the largest populations of Arabic speakers. According to the 2000 Census, approximately 50 percent of US-born Arab-Americans are bilingual, and Arabic ranked seventh among all foreign languages spoken by American school-aged children. However, as pointed out in Chapter 1 of this volume, the vast majority of people of Arab descent living in the US – 89 percent – report speaking English "very well" or "well" (US Census Bureau 2007c). Among the population aged 18–64, the percentage of people who reported speaking English "not well" or "not at all" does not exceed the 10 percent mark. The only exception is in Michigan where the ratio is closer to 20 percent, most likely because it is home to the highest concentration of Arabic-speakers in the country (as mentioned earlier, Arabs form 30 percent of the total population in Dearborn, MI).

This bi- or multilingualism among more recent waves of immigration makes the issue of Arabic-language maintenance for the next generation even more problematic past the pre-school age. As children start to shift to English in response to school socialization, their educated, bilingual or multilingual parents either gradually follow suit when interacting with them or stop expecting them to respond in Arabic. Arabic use is also related to place of birth. Moroccans, Iraqis, and "other Arabs" constitute the groups with the largest proportion of foreign-born members, experiencing a tenfold increase on average since before 1970. About 15 percent among the other groups (with a high proportion of foreign-born) report speaking English only at home. Approximately half of the longest established groups (53.5 percent of the Lebanese and 45.8 percent of the Syrians) are now monolingual in English. What is noticeable here is that while the foreign-born infuse the US Arabic-identifying community with their native diglossic Arabic skills, their high level of education and proficiency in English conversely constitute factors that do not promote maintenance in the following generation.

Public presence of Arabic

This section offers a brief description of the presence of Arabic in public life in the USA, focusing mainly on the presence of Arabic in government, the media, business, and education.

Government

The Arabic language so far has only been relevant to the US government in that has been designated as "critical" to national security at various points in history, particularly so after the attacks of September 11, 2001. Arab-Americans, however, regardless of religion and of their fluency in Arabic, are an emerging political group in the USA. Their role in the 2000 presidential election was noted as they were courted by the Republican Party. A large number of Arab-Americans saw a better partner in the Republican candidate in domestic matters pertaining to civil rights and in Middle East foreign policy and consequently voted for him. That support was withdrawn in 2004 out of disillusionment with the government's foreign policy in the Middle East and the feeling of persecution and racial and religious profiling suffered by many in the

Arab-American community in the aftermath of September 11, especially after the USA PATRIOT Act was passed[2] (Curtiss 2004 and Murray 2004).

A poll conducted by Zogby International in 2000 indicated that 88.5 percent of Arab-Americans are registered to vote, that they vote in larger numbers than other communities, and that they are active and contribute financially to presidential campaigns. About 82 percent reported watching a presidential debate (Hanley 2004). Their organizing efforts are particularly visible in counties with higher concentrations of Arab-Americans, such as in Wayne County, MI, or Los Angeles, CA. Although they did not run on an Arab-American platform, some Arab-Americans have become well-known politicians in the USA: Green Party presidential nominee and leading consumer advocate Ralph Nader, former US Secretary of Energy Spencer Abraham, former US South Dakota Senators James Abourezk and James Abdnor, and Helen Thomas, dean of the White House press corps, are a few prominent names.

Media

Since the late 1990s, the USA has witnessed a large increase in Arabic-language media. Whereas a variety of printed and other media are produced in the USA, the majority is satellite television-based or web-based and is imported from the Arab World and Europe. The audience for these Arabic media remains primarily foreign-born. In the aftermath of September 11 and the launch of the wars on Afghanistan and Iraq, the market for Arabic media grew among Arab-Americans, spreading to even fluent speakers of English who used to get their news from English-speaking sources. The rise of the Qatar-based *Al-Jazeera* Arabic television on the international media scene as a credible, professional, and objective first-hand source of world news and Arab news made it a strong rival of English US-based television stations. Its open and critical talk shows and discussions made it attractive to Arab-American audiences seeking diverse opinions. With correspondents dispatched everywhere in the world and in places where no other correspondents ventured (for example, during the invasion of Afghanistan and later the invasion and occupation of Iraq), the *Al-Jazeera* logo started appearing on international television, with Arabic reports or speeches translated and dubbed into the languages of the world. According to Dignam (2006), a survey by Interbrand named *Al-Jazeera* as one of the world's five most recognizable brands behind Apple, Google, Starbucks, and eBay, and ahead of brands such as Virgin, Nokia, and the *BBC*. For many Arabic-speaking viewers in the USA, watching original *Al-Jazeera* programming meant a renewed pride in their language and in their ability to get information about the Arab world at its source with no mediation from other television stations. *Al-Jazeera* also has a number of dedicated specialty channels such as the sports channel, the children's channel, and the documentary channel. The most notorious, however, is the English *Al-Jazeera* news channel, which started broadcasting in 2007. With an estimated audience of about 100 million households around the world, it now rivals the *BBC* and *CNN*. In the USA, however, the *Al-Jazeera* English channel is not carried by the larger satellite networks.

In addition to *Al-Jazeera*, many Arab-Americans subscribe to a package comprising a variety of entertainment and news channels originating in the Arab world or in Europe (primarily the UK). Arabic versions of US programs captivate viewers worldwide, including "Star Academy" (an "American Idol" equivalent), a host of talk shows similar to "Oprah." Arabic speakers thus started to feel connected in a novel way with other Arabic-speaking communities by sharing in this programming and by increasing their knowledge of other Arabic dialects as a result of this media exposure. The satellite channels consequently became a rich source of linguistic input not only in standard Arabic but in the various dialects as well.

While younger Arab-Americans have been exposed to this Arabic-speaking media, they are often unable to follow the news programs fully because the broadcasters speak in standard Arabic which, as mentioned earlier, is acquired through schooling. While US-born Arabic speakers may retain proficiency in their family's regional dialect, it is not possible to acquire standard Arabic without being formally trained. This diglossic situation has contributed to the generational shift along linguistic lines, highlighting the younger generation's distance from the language of their ancestors, especially the standard form. For many, therefore, the English-speaking internet, blogs, and Arab-American television programs constitute a source of information and a medium for community building.

US-based and foreign-based Arabic newspapers and other print forms such as women's magazines are also available, especially in locations with higher concentrations of Arabic speakers. Most of the printed media originating in the Arab world and Europe such as the London-based *Al-Hayat* and *Al-Quds* or the Egyptian *Al-Ahram* have been readily accessible online. This is a far cry from the 1890s, when the only media some immigrant communities could rely on for local and homeland news on was a local four-page bilingual publication (Tayash and Ayouby 1992). In fact, those newspapers themselves inadvertently contributed to bringing about their own demise and that of the language that they represented by advocating Americanization and failing to transcend the old country's (Greater Syria) divisive self-identifications that characterized that time (Tayash and Ayouby 1992). The post-World War II Arab immigrants, who were mainly literate and politically conscious supporters of pan-Arabism, revived the press and injected the community with their enthusiasm for preserving their language and heritage (Tayash and Ayouby 1992). As an awareness of Arab ethnic identity emerged, uniting the fourth generation Arab-Americans and the newer waves of immigrants, a need for a bilingual media that serves the greater community emerged. Advertisements for Arab-American services and businesses abound in these publications. Local productions across the nation flourished over the following decades until new technologies came about that created connections across the globe. The impact of these new technologies on language maintenance is most noticeable among the foreign-born but may be of little consequence for the US-born generations. This point will be revisited in the section on language maintenance below.

Business

As mentioned above, the US population of Arab descent is socioeconomically better off than the population at large. About 30 percent have an annual household income of more than $75,000 compared with 22 percent of the rest of the population. A large number of them are employed in the private sector, running their own businesses – a sign of autonomy and self-sufficiency in this community. Around 73 percent work in managerial, professional, technical, or administrative fields (Brittingham and de la Cruz 2005). In cities with high concentration of Arab-Americans, businesses advertise their services in the local Arabic or bilingual newspapers, and business "yellow pages" are generated for the community. Arab commodities are either locally manufactured or imported from the Arab world for local and national consumption. In the businesses located in these areas, the Arabic language (through the regional dialects) enjoys a great vitality. Signs in Arabic are a common feature in the streets of some areas that are densely populated by Arab-Americans, such as Dearborn, Michigan and Anaheim, California.

Education

This section will examine the teaching and learning of Arabic both as a foreign language and as a "heritage" language. As a politically and economically "strategic" language in the USA, Arabic has attracted a steadily growing number of learners in higher education during the last few decades. Graduate students of North Africa and the Middle East studies, undergraduates looking for a linguistic challenge or a potential business career, and students of Arab and Muslim descent traditionally populated Arabic classrooms in the USA. The numbers have grown slowly but steadily since the 1980s (see McCarus 1992 on the history of Arabic-language study in the USA). As the number of Arab and (non-Arab) Muslim communities grew in the USA, and as more and more of their children attended college, this group started to become more visible in Arabic classrooms. This group is commonly designated "heritage learners." According to a 2002 survey conducted by the National Middle East Language Resource Center (NMLRC) and that involved self-reports collected from Arabic students attending eight universities, 13 percent are categorized as heritage learners. Informal data collected by this contributor suggest that 25 percent of US college Arabic students are heritage speakers.

The years that followed September 11, however, and the designation of Arabic as a "critical need language" triggered a serious jump in interest in the language from the general population and a greater flow of resources to its study and instruction. This increase in interest and funds is not unlike those during World War II or the 1980s. McCarus (1992) reports the occurrence of "a revolution in Arabic studies" during World War II, explaining that the "immediate need to train combat infantrymen and intelligence personnel to function in, and do research on, the Arab world revealed how woefully unprepared the nation was in terms of this and other languages of the world" (p. 208). In response, the federal government put resources into designing textbooks and crash courses that taught Arabic and other languages to military and intelligence personnel. Just over a generation later, in 1979, President Jimmy Carter appointed a commission to examine the state of language studies and international studies. The report declared the nation's language readiness "scandalous" (Allen 1992: 233). A 1984 report corroborated their findings. These reports engendered "a great deal of activity on the national level involving the need to enhance and transform how US citizens learn and are taught foreign languages" (p. 234). That activity brought together government agencies and the academic system and culminated in the issuing of the first American Council on the Teaching of Foreign Languages Generic Guidelines and the establishment of procedures for "training academic language teachers in the art and science of the oral proficiency interview" (p. 235).

Another generation later, according to a 2006 survey, Arabic has for the first time reached the top ten most studied foreign languages at US colleges and universities (Modern Language Association 2007). The number of students taking Arabic as well as the number of institutions offering it doubled since the previous survey in 2002, reflecting the US population's rekindled interest in Arabic after the 2001 attacks. This number actually quadruples in 2006 compared with 1998, going from 5,505 to 23,974 students nationwide. Whether attracted by the prospects of better career opportunities, prompted by curiosity about the language of the "other," or the wish to promote more peaceful relations with Arab nations through mutual understanding, the numbers of non-Arabic students who chose to study Arabic during this period visibly increased.

Higher education institutions have responded to the demand for Arabic by starting or expanding programs in the study of this language and its culture, and the number of institutions offering Arabic almost doubled from 264 in 2002 to 466 in 2006 (Modern Language Association 2007). Language Flagship programs for the study of "strategic" or "critical need languages" such as Arabic and Chinese also emerged around the country with the aim of graduating students with a superior command of the language. The Language Flagship, administered by the National Security Education Program (NSEP) in the US Department of Defense and forming part of the National Security Language Initiative (NSLI), includes State Department summer immersion study programs, increasing support for immersion language study centers abroad for students and teachers, and support for teachers and students of Arabic K-12. The Department of Education FLAP program (Foreign Language Assistance Program) is set up under NSLI to "address the shortage of critical foreign language speakers by supporting new and expanded programs in grades K-12" (US Department of Education 2007). Among the seventy grants awarded in 2006, however, only five funded K-12 programs, and in 2007 only three FLAP grants funded K-12 programs. The 2009 request for FLAP proposals, however, specified critical need languages such as Arabic and Chinese, so it is likely that more programs will be funded in the near future.

The Center for Advanced Study of Language, established in 2003 in partnership with the University of Maryland, is another well-funded federal government program with Arabic offerings. One of this center's main aims is to provide the tools for achieving advanced levels of language proficiency through in-depth study of all the dialects and forms of Arabic as well as the cultures associated with them (CASL n.d.).

The continued dearth of students reaching advanced fluency in Arabic is evident, however, in the fact that advanced level enrollments in Arabic make up no more than 12.8 percent of all enrollments (Modern Language Association 2007). These numbers place Arabic among the four languages with the smallest numbers of advanced level learners among the top fifteen languages taught in the USA. The percentage of advanced enrollments is almost double in other "critical need languages" such as Korean (25%), Chinese (22%), and Russian (30%). We should also note that all four of these critical need languages are considered difficult to learn by the Foreign Service Institute with Korean, Chinese, and Arabic being assigned the highest "Type III" rating (Jackson and Kaplan 1999). A possible explanation for this situation, other than the relative novelty of this renewed interest in Arabic, is that there may be more heritage language learners among the advanced students of these other languages. Some also suggest that schools and colleges need greater resources and support to address the deficit in advanced Arabic speakers.

Although Arabic attracts its share of heritage learners, higher education programs that cater specifically to this group of students remain limited. A burgeoning program of this nature was launched by the University of California at San Diego in 2001. A more recent program was adopted by the Arabic Language Flagship (administered by NSEP), with the goal of bringing these heritage language learners to advanced levels of competence. In secondary education, it is noticeable that few schools with a high Arab-American student ratio offer Arabic instruction. Even in the Dearborn, MI area, where schools can be up to 95 percent of Arab descent, only 1,000 of the 17,600 students in the district typically enroll in Arabic classes (Zehr 2004). Where available, such Arabic courses offer little to heritage learners because they do not address their specific needs and usually cater to the total beginner. Community-run ethnic or religious after school and Saturday/Sunday Arabic programs often suffer from the same problem except in reverse: the curricula often adopted in such programs are created for native speakers of Arabic living in Arab countries such as Jordan or Saudi Arabia, and thus do not serve the needs of the heritage learners. The teachers often receive limited or no training. While in the earlier days these classes were often held in churches for a predominantly Christian Arab origin constituency, many of these after-school Arabic programs are now available at mosques or at Islamic schools (where the instruction of Arabic forms an integral part of the curriculum). For the many secular families and the non-Muslim communities, these programs are therefore not viable. A good number of US-born heritage learners of Arabic, regardless of denomination, do usually attempt Arabic study in college, where available. As stated earlier, however, only a relatively small proportion of students reaches the advanced level.

As far as offering Arabic to the total beginner, programs known as Foreign Languages in the Elementary Schools (FLES) are bringing Arabic to some schools around the country. 25 percent of elementary schools in the USA offer FLES programs (Center for Applied Linguistics 2008); however, the number of schools that provide Arabic instruction remains negligible. According to the Center for Advanced Research on Language Acquisition, no more than sixty-six schools offer Arabic in the USA (CARLA n.d.). In addition, there has been some controversy around the idea of teaching Arabic in US schools, particularly to children of non-Arab ancestry as was the case with the Khalil Gibran International Academy, a public secondary school founded in Brooklyn, NY in 2007.

Evidence of language shift to English and of Arabic maintenance

An examination of the situation of Arabic in the USA suggests that, despite some Arab-Americans' conscious effort to maintain their ancestral language, Arabic is slowly but indisputably disappearing into the melting pot along with other minority languages. The conditions determining the vitality of Arabic in the new millennium echo those that led to the decline of Arabic among the descendants of the earlier waves of immigration over a century ago. At both points in history, Arabic in the USA faced the repercussions of stricter immigration laws and negative attitudes towards languages other than English in general and toward Arabic in particular (especially at the turn of this century).

Signs of shift to English

As indicated in the demographics section above, the vast majority of Arabs claim to speak English "well" or "very well." They enjoy a higher level of education than the average for the rest of the population. The new immigrants among them, overall, fit this profile as well, since they tend to hold college or graduate diplomas. As is the case with other languages, this close contact with English has led to linguistic practices that bilinguals and multilingual speakers display: borrowing from English as well as Arabic–English code-switching (see articles in Rouchdy 1992 for a detailed discussion of these phenomena in different Arabic-speaking communities in the USA). Although new immigrants will invigorate and revitalize their communities at least initially, many of them do speak other native or European languages in addition to Arabic and English, thus heightening the competition with Arabic. Many will have practiced code-switching Arabic and their other languages. They will therefore quickly pick up the borrowings and the "rules" for Arabic–English code-switching in their new community. This usually occurs regardless of negative attitudes toward this practice. As was discussed by Romaine in Chapter 2 of this volume, code-switching cuts across gender, age, socioeconomic and religious boundaries; it is just a matter of degree for bilingual individuals, being more or less present depending on the addressees and subject. Although it is a normal practice that is typical of bilingual and multilingual contact situations, code-switching is considered by some to be an indication of linguistic attrition for minority languages.

Sawaie (1986, 1992) and Sawaie and Fishman (1985) examine the use of Arabic in institutions such as places of worship, the media, ethnic schools, and ethnic societies among the early immigrants and during the 1980s. They argue that the gradual shift to English that was evident among the descendants of the first immigrants was likely to be repeated in the 1980s as a result of continued social and geographical mobility of Arabs, their intermarriage with non-Arabic speakers, and the social advantage of English. The 2000 Census seems to support this prediction as about 76 percent of the people of Arab ancestry reported speaking English only at home or speaking English "very well" (31.5 percent and 44.5 percent respectively).

In the case of Arabic, this situation is further complicated by both the co-existence of multiple, diverse Arabic dialects within this community as well as the existence of diglossia. In situations of cross-dialectal contact, Arabic speakers will use code-switching into a foreign language as one of the strategies for successful communication with other Arabic speakers that they do not understand or who they think will not understand them (Shiri 2002). This is a strategy that fluent native speakers of Arabic will use when confronted with other fluent native speakers of distant dialects or dialects that are perceived as distant. Arabic speakers in cross-dialectal situations also use another successful communication strategy called "converging accommodation." When engaging in converging accommodation, speakers will try to sound more like their addressees. They will use what they consider typical features of their addressees' dialects and leave out what they perceive as idiosyncratic linguistic features of their own. In Arabic, this usually translates into speech that sounds more Eastern (specifically urban Egyptian and Levantine) (Shiri 2002). It might be argued that there is a shift in the making to these Eastern dialects of Arabic, particularly urban Egyptian and Levantine, among speakers of other Arabic dialects as a result of the convergence of the latter to the former in cross-dialectal situations. Certain dialects of Arabic might therefore face attrition while their speakers still interact in Arabic – an Arabic that is not their own but is adopted for the sake of communication. Because the idiosyncrasies that distinguish these dialects are avoided in communication across dialects in favor of "more commonly understood" forms, the vitality of these dialects rests on the community of speakers of that same national or regional dialect.

The Arabic diglossic situation further complicates the retention of dialects and the acquisition of standard language for the group commonly known as "heritage learners." Heritage learners are usually taught the standard language, ignoring their proficiency in their home dialects, which usually stagnates. In some cases, it might even cause attrition as they start speaking more standard and less dialect to their families as a result of schooling. In those classrooms where a dialect is selected for instruction instead of standard Arabic, other dialects spoken by students are inevitably excluded. Unless this issue is addressed by educators and curriculum designers of Arabic courses, the experience of schooling in Arabic will ironically contribute to shift within the different varieties of Arabic itself, as one form of Arabic is emphasized and another is neglected.

Since September 11, 2001, US Arabic speakers have been conscious of the ambivalence that has enveloped the country regarding proficiency in Arabic. While declaring Arabic a "critical language" made proficiency in this language a desirable asset, for many it also highlighted its status as the "language of the enemy." The written Arabic word itself acquired highly political and negative undertones in public places. US news accounts reported that people were not allowed on planes and other public transportation or removed from some public places because they spoke Arabic, carried Arabic books, or wore clothing inscribed with Arabic (NBC11.com 2006). As a group that has been targeted by racial profiling practices, Arabic speakers are more wary of speaking in public a language that is perceived in a negative light, especially in the years immediately after September 11.

Signs of maintenance

As stated in the introduction, the language shift that was noticeable among the earlier immigrants and their descendants is now being counterbalanced by more efforts toward Arabic-language maintenance among the more recent waves of immigration. This change might be associated with two factors. The first is the emergence of a social and political discourse that is more open toward multiculturalism and hyphenated identities in general during recent decades in the USA (Jacoby 2004). The second is that many new Arabic-speaking immigrants have college degrees and a political consciousness imbibed with a sense of national identity.

As mentioned earlier, the new millennium brought Arabic to the fore of languages designated by the US government as "critical" to national security. Arabic, therefore, became one of the most desirable languages to acquire and maintain in the country. After an initial phase of self-reflection and ambivalence among the speakers of this language and the rest of the population in the USA, both groups showed a greater interest in Arabic. A large number of Arabs resumed efforts to maintain the language and support the hyphenated identity that nurtures it. Cultural activities where Arabic can be heard and spoken resumed or intensified. Arab film festivals, for example, bringing the latest from the cinemas of the Arab world, grew in number and in size. Musicians, singers, and dancers from the Arab world conducting tours in the USA catered to the tastes of the older and the younger generations alike, regardless of their proficiency in Arabic. Mosques and churches where sermons are conducted in Arabic in addition to English (and/or Greek in the case of the latter) continued to spread. Demand for courses about the history and culture of the Arabic-speaking region grew. The number of non-Arabic students enrolling in Arabic programs also soared, nationwide. However, in addition to the new political overtones that Arabic study is now acquiring – on the one hand encouraged among the general population, yet somehow unappreciated when spoken natively – the issues of diglossia in Arabic and the co-existence of multiple dialects in this language community present a challenge to both groups in their efforts to learn and maintain Arabic in the USA.

Conclusions

At first sight, Arabic looks like it ought to be thriving in the USA. Its acquisition is being encouraged, government resources are flowing into its instruction, and opportunities for revitalizing it are afforded by a vibrant satellite and computer-mediated media and an active (albeit reduced) immigration rate. The linguistically, religiously, ethnically, and culturally diverse communities of Arabic speakers are now consolidating their sense of identity in an ambivalent political climate. On the other hand, this community is long-standing in the USA, with generations of assimilated, English-speaking members and a relatively small number of highly educated new immigrants, many of whom are multilingual. More importantly, it is a community that understands that speaking the heritage language is not a prerequisite for citizenship in the multicultural, hyphenated-American world that they now inhabit. Speaking the heritage language is an asset, perhaps a luxury, but not a necessity for Arab-Americans. The study of Arabic is likely to benefit – at least relative to where it was at the turn of the century – as a result of its current position in the spotlight, but it appears unlikely to interrupt the widespread three-generation pattern of shift to monolingualism in English.

DISCUSSION QUESTIONS

1. Examining Table 13.1 and the discussion preceding it, can you predict whether a child of Arab descent is more likely to learn Arabic when born in Los Angeles, California or in Dearborn, Michigan?
2. What are the prospects for maintenance of Arabic in the near future in the USA?

14 Portuguese in the USA

Ana Maria Carvalho

Introduction

Portuguese is the eleventh most commonly spoken non-English language in the USA, with the 2007 American Community Survey conducted by the US Census Bureau recording 687,126 speakers, making up 0.24% of the population and 1.24% of US LOTE speakers. As noted in Table 1.1, the Portuguese-speaking population officially grew by 31 percent in the decade between 1990 and 2000, and a further 22 percent from 2000 to 2007. US Census numbers undoubtedly represent an extreme undercount, however, given that the Brazilian government estimates that the number of Brazilians alone living in the USA surpasses one million (Lokensgard 2007: 1).

Besides Brazilian immigrants, Portuguese speakers in the USA are mainly Portuguese (from the Azores Islands and mainland Portugal) and Cape Verdeans, and on a much smaller scale, immigrants from Mozambique and Angola. Although immigration from Portugal has practically halted and third generation Portuguese-Americans very rarely maintain productive skills in Portuguese, Cape Verdeans and Brazilians continue to arrive in the USA, perpetuating the language. Indeed, in certain areas with high concentrations of Portuguese-speaking immigrants, such as Massachusetts, Portuguese is the second most spoken foreign language, preceded only by Spanish (US Census Bureau 2009). As long as the influx of Portuguese-speaking immigrants continues, Portuguese will continue to thrive in US territory. Otherwise, only robust and efficient institutional initiatives will succeed in maintaining Portuguese among American-born generations and in reversing the usually inevitable path to language shift.

Outside the USA, Portuguese is spoken in Brazil, Portugal, Mozambique, Angola, Guinea Bissau, Cape Verde, São Tomé and Príncipe, and East Timor, all members of the Community of Portuguese Language Countries (CPLP). With approximately 250,000,000 speakers, it is the sixth most widely spoken language in the world by number of speakers, after Mandarin Chinese, English, Spanish, Hindi, and Arabic (Crystal 1997: 289). Portuguese has recently improved its unity and political force due to its new and unified Orthographic Reform, recently signed by eight of the CPLP members.

Within the USA, there is a demand for schools to serve the growing community of Portuguese heritage speakers by offering K-12 language courses. According to the US Census, 85,000 school-age children spoke Portuguese at home in 2000, and in 2008, 14,829 students were taking Portuguese classes in K-12 schools (Vicente and Pimenta 2008). With regard to postsecondary education, a 2006 Modern Language Association (MLA) report pointed out that the availability of Portuguese instruction increased 22.4% between 2002 and 2006. It ranks thirteenth on the list of the most taught languages and is currently offered in 226 postsecondary institutions. On the national level, Portuguese is considered a preferred language by the National Security Education Program (NSEP), is taught at US Army and US Air Force military academies, and is protected as a critical language and less commonly taught language (LCTL).

History

Portuguese, like Spanish, is a Romance language derived from the colloquial Latin spoken by the Romans when they were in the Iberian Peninsula. More specifically, it originated from the Latin spoken in the part of the peninsula then called Lusitania, which makes up most of modern Portugal. After separating from Galician, Portuguese became the official language of Portugal and by the late twelfth century a considerable body of literature had already been produced in that language. Portuguese became the official language of Portugal and acquired its first grammar in 1536. In the fifteenth century, Portugal began an unprecedented exploration oversees that reached Asia, Africa, and the Americas. By the sixteenth century, the Portuguese language had already been established on five continents.

In US territory, Portuguese has been spoken since the seventeenth century, when a group of self-exiled Portuguese Jews from Brazil landed in New Amsterdam (today's New York City) in 1654 (Jouët-Pastré and Braga 2005: 864), but the bulk of Portuguese presencc in the USA can be traced to the late nineteenth and twentieth centuries (Azevedo 2005: 16). Whalers from the archipelago of the Azores, a Portuguese territory in the Atlantic, began to settle in New England early in the nineteenth century, soon followed by immigrants from Cape Verde and continental Portugal. California was also a common destination for immigrants from continental Portugal, the Azores, and Madeira (another Portuguese territory in the Atlantic Ocean) (Azevedo 2005: 16). The influx of Portuguese immigrants continued during the twentieth century but decreased significantly by the 1980s. Nonetheless, the continued arrival of Cape Verdeans and Brazilians has accounted for a steep increase in the number of Portuguese speakers in the USA over the last twenty years.

Table 14.1. *States with the largest Portuguese-speaking populations*

State	Ages 5 +	Percentage of all US Portuguese speakers
Massachusetts	205,778	31.03
New Jersey	82,362	12.42
Florida	72,400	10.91
California	71,026	10.71
New York	36,987	5.57
Rhode Island	33,915	5.11
Connecticut	29,763	4.48
Georgia	17,615	2.65
Texas	12,612	1.90
Maryland	11,327	1.70
Total in USA	687,126	

Source: Modern Language Association 2009, US Census Bureau 2007c.

Demographics

Although Portuguese speakers are found in every state of the USA, some regions have historically hosted population concentrations due to social networks that gradually formed immigrant enclaves. Table 14.1 displays the locations of the nation's highest concentrations of Portuguese speakers.

Massachusetts has by far the highest density of Portuguese speakers in the USA. Having been a traditional destination for Portuguese and Cape Verdean immigrants, Massachusetts began to attract Brazilians arriving in USA at the end of the twentieth century, as they gravitated to towns where Portuguese-speaking communities were well established (Rubinstein-Avila 2005: 875). Framingham, Massachusetts, one of the first places where Portuguese immigrants settled, is considered today "the most Brazilian town in the United States" (Siqueira and Jansen 2008: 105). Outside of New England, California constitutes an important locale for Portuguese speakers. Whereas Portuguese, mostly Azoreans, have established communities in the San Francisco Bay Area, including San Jose and the San Joaquin Valley (Azevedo 2005: 206), Brazilians are concentrated in the cities of Los Angeles and San Francisco. More recently, Portuguese-speaking communities have been rapidly growing in the South, with Georgia, Florida, and Texas receiving the most recent wave of Brazilian immigrants. Margolis (2009: 6) estimates that the suburbs of Atlanta alone contain 30,000 Brazilian residents. Recent reports on Brazilian immigration trends show a tendency to spread to other areas as well, including, for example, a rapidly growing community in Utah (Silva 2006).

Table 14.2. *Largest Portuguese-speaking groups by country of origin*

Country of origin	Population
Brazil	288,620
Portugal (including the Azores)	174,268
Cape Verde	17,110
Africa (non-specified)	6,140

Source: Ruggles *et al.* 2009.

As mentioned, US Census counts of the numbers of Portuguese-speaking individuals in the USA are gross underestimates (Margolis 2009: 5). For example, the 2000 US Census reported the presence of 231,270 Brazilians in the USA, while the Ministry of Foreign Affairs in Brazil claimed that there were 799,000 US-resident Brazilians in that year. In 2005, the Brazilian government estimated that this number had increased to 1.1 million Brazilians, surpassing by far the US Census estimate for the total number of Portuguese speakers in the USA of all nationalities. The primary reason behind this undercount may be that many Brazilian immigrants are undocumented and try to maintain a low profile. It is estimated that, as a whole, one in every three immigrants to the USA is undocumented (Camarota 2007), and during her ethnography of Brazilians in New York, Margolis (2009: 7) found that more than half of her participants were undocumented. The Census Bureau is trying to correct the undercount by connecting with the Brazilian community, the Brazilian Embassy, and media and faith-based organizations for the 2010 Census (US Census Bureau 2009).

According to the 2000 Census, the three largest Portuguese-speaking groups in the USA are, in order of size, the Brazilians, the Portuguese, and the Cape Verdeans (see Table 14.2). Note that African immigrants are not specified by country, but one may assume the respondents are from Mozambique, Angola, Guinea Bissau, and São Tomé and Príncipe. The following sections present a brief history and demographic sketch of each group, by order of arrival in the USA.

Portuguese

The Portuguese presence in the USA dates back to the time when Europeans first arrived in the New World. A Portuguese navigator, João Rodrigues Cabrillo, led the first European expedition to California (Jouët-Pastré and Braga 2005: 864). During colonial times, several Portuguese communities settled in the USA and Canada. Mostly Azoreans, they arrived in Massachusetts and California on whaling vessels, and were later attracted to California by the gold rush. By

1860, the Portuguese constituted a significant and stable ethnic community in America (Stephens 1989: 716). After both whaling and mining faded, the Portuguese turned to agriculture, fishing, and the dairy industry (Williams 1980: 724).

Portuguese immigration continued throughout the twentieth century, picking up after 1960. According to Vieira (1980), between 1966 and 1975, 113,733 immigrants arrived in the USA from Portugal. By 1975, half a million Portuguese were concentrated within a radius of fifty miles in southern New England (Vieira 1980). A typical Portuguese-American fishing village in New England, and the contact between Portuguese-Americans and Anglo-Americans, are portrayed in Julia Roberts' first movie, *Mystic Pizza* (1988).[1] In addition, the Portuguese-American experience has been chronicled by a well-established corpus of literary production (see Almeida 2005).

In the wake of the National Bilingual Education Act of 1968, a series of Portuguese–English bilingual education initiatives took place in the 1970s, and a handbook for teaching Portuguese-speaking students was published in 1983 (California State Department of Education 1983). Over the last 25 years, however, the Portuguese influx to the USA has ceased (Borges 2009). Although much Portuguese culture is preserved and performed during annual celebrations, third generation Portuguese speakers are hard to find. Jouët-Pastré and Braga (2005: 864–5) report on research that indicates a high level of assimilation among Portuguese immigrants, who are willing to blend in to escape negative stereotyping. As a result of this assimilationist ideology, lack of institutional support, and decrease in first generation arrivals, one may assume, albeit without documented evidence, that European Portuguese is in the process of shifting to English.

Cape Verdeans

The Republic of Cape Verde, situated in the Atlantic Ocean on the west coast of Africa, gained independence from Portugal in 1975. Since the eighteenth century, its harsh environment, including severe and recurrent draught, has propelled emigration to several countries; it is believed that there are around 500,000 Cape Verdeans oversees, exceeding the resident population of 460,000 on the islands. Cape Verdean presence in the USA dates back to crew members of whaling ships arriving in the eighteenth century. Nowadays, it is estimated that the number of Cape Verdeans and their descendants living in the USA reaches 400,000, mostly in New England (Halter 2005). The experience of Cape Verdeans living in America is chronicled in the feature-length documentary about the Cape Verdean community in Rhode Island entitled *Some Kind of Funny Porto Rican?: A Cape Verdean American Story* (2006), directed by Claire Andrade-Watkins.

The sociolinguistic profile of the Cape Verdean community is very different from that of other Portuguese-speaking groups. A Portuguese-based Creole, not Portuguese, is the native language of the Cape Verdean population. Portuguese is spoken by bilinguals after being acquired through schooling, and is used for government, literature, mass media, and formal communication purposes (Carvalho 2009: 2). This diglossic situation has consequences for the maintenance of Portuguese outside Cape Verde, in places where no schooling in Portuguese is available. Ferreira (2005: 849) reports that Cape Verdean learners of Portuguese in Massachusetts were more comfortable with receptive skills, including reading and listening, than productive skills, whereas Azorean and Madeiran learners controlled writing and speaking better. Thus, Portuguese proficiency is variable among Cape Verdean immigrants: those who were schooled in Cape Verde come to the USA practically bilingual in creole and Portuguese, but children who were schooled in the USA speak English and creole, and acquire Portuguese as a third language when placed in Portuguese classes (Rubinstein-Avila 2002), although they are familiar with the Portuguese lexicon (Ferreira, personal communication). Outside the family sphere, the maintenance of Portuguese among the Cape Verdean immigrant communities in the USA relies solely on institutional support.

Brazilians

According to the Brazilian government, there are approximately one million Brazilians – or Brazucas, as they are popularly called – in the USA, a population that has been portrayed in US literature (see Tosta 2005). Unlike Portuguese, Brazilians are overwhelmingly recent immigrants. The first great migratory wave took place between 1984 and 1987, and migration picked up in the 1990s, when economic conditions in Brazil deteriorated and inflation and unemployment were extremely high. These first immigrants were mostly young, educated, middle-class men and women who entered the USA on tourist visas and overstayed (Bensabat-Ott 2000: 86). They were followed by working-class Brazilians from small towns and rural areas, many of whom entered the USA by crossing the US–Mexico border, a saga portrayed in the movie *A Fronteira* (2003).

In 2007, Brazil was placed twenty-third among countries of birth for foreign-born US residents (Camarota 2007). Despite increasing immigration controls in recent years, in which Brazilians have been deported, apprehended at border crossings, and turned away at US ports of entry, Brazilians have continued to migrate to the USA (Martes 2008: 127). They hold jobs in the construction trades, sales, production, and professional occupations (Siqueira and Jensen 2008: 117), but most work in service industries, especially in restaurants, housecleaning, painting, landscaping, and carpentry (Margolis 2009).

As far as language behavior is concerned, Bensabat-Ott (2000) observed that bilingual Brazilians in Washington, DC, preferred Portuguese for intragroup communication, considering it of much integrative value and an integral part of their Brazilian identity. Reportedly, their desire to retain Portuguese stems also from the hope that one day they will return to Brazil (pp. 92–3). As Braga and Jouët-Pastré (2008: 14) point out, however, after twenty years of Brazilian immigration, a generation of children has been born in the USA. There is still a dearth of research about this new group of American citizens, who, together with generation 1.5 (those who were born in Brazil but emigrated as children and were schooled in the USA), are the ones who will preserve, or not, the Portuguese language.

Public presence of Portuguese

This section will present a brief description of the presence of Portuguese in US public life. Contrary to what speakers of more widely spoken languages in the US experience, basic services are rarely available in Portuguese, excepting in areas heavily populated by Portuguese speakers, which in recent years have had to comply with Title VI of the Civil Rights Act of 1964 by ensuring meaningful access to healthcare for limited English-speaking patients. In these areas, in addition, one finds dentists' offices, hair salons, bakeries, restaurants, and large grocery stores that cater to the community.

Margolis (1994), in her seminal work on Brazilian immigrants in New York City, noted the general invisibility of the Brazilian community. Their desire to maintain a low profile results not only in Census undercounts, but also in an absence of community organization. While the lack of secular organizations to assist Portuguese-speaking immigrants that Margolis observed in the 1990s still holds true nowadays (Margolis 2008: 347), Souza (2000: 9) claims that one sees more social activism in some areas, such as Boston, where "local grass-roots movements are pressing for language and cultural rights such as bilingual services in schools, hospitals, courts, etc., and government agencies are being forced to recognized the unique needs of this population." A noteworthy initiative of this type is the Massachusetts Alliance of Portuguese Speakers (MAPS), a private, non-profit, community-based organization. This organization offers health and social services for Portuguese speakers in Massachusetts, provided by bilingual staff from the local Portuguese-speaking community.

Media

The first US newspaper printed in Portuguese dates from 1880. *A Voz Portuguesa*, published in San Francisco, was followed by several other newspapers catering to the Portuguese-speaking community that proliferated in California

Table 14.3. *Enrollments in Portuguese courses in postsecondary institutions in selected years*

	1960	1970	1980	1990	1995	1998	2002	2006
Enrollment	1,033	5,065	4,894	6,211	6,531	6,926	8,385	10,267

Source: Furman *et al.* 2007.

and New England throughout the nineteenth century (Borges 2008). According to a website about Brazilian émigrés sponsored by the Brazilian Government (Ministério das Relações Exteriores, n.d.), there are forty-six printed magazines and newspapers and eight online news sources by and for Brazilians in the USA. Several radio stations in California and New England broadcast in Portuguese, in addition to stations airing individual radio shows (Borges 2008; Ministério das Relações Exteriores n.d.). Halter reports on the presence of Cape Verdean press in the USA as early as the 1920s, and the inclusion of broadcast programming on radio and television in the 1940s (Halter 2005: 620). In addition, satellite-based transmissions allow the real-time reception in the USA of television programs from leading networks in Brazil and Portugal, providing Portuguese-speaking families with daily exposure to their home language and culture. The daily presence of national television in the immigrants' homes is particularly important for youth, as it showcases contemporary pop culture in Portuguese, adding a certain prestige to what otherwise might seem the unappealing language of their parents.

Education

The first documented Portuguese program in the USA dates back to 1658, when a group of self-exiled Jewish immigrants from Brazil established a language school in New York City, according to Tesser's (2004) detailed history of the teaching of Portuguese in the USA. By the end of the nineteenth century, the University of Virginia and Columbia and Harvard Universities began offering Portuguese classes geared toward the study of medieval manuscripts. As early as 1919, John Casper Branner published an article in *Hispania* about the importance of studying Portuguese and, in 1944, ninety-two universities in thirty-five states were offering Portuguese, although that number declined in the 1950s (Tesser 2004).

Since 1960, the MLA has published enrollment figures periodically, as shown in Table 14.3. The table shows that enrollment in college-level Portuguese courses has been increasing in the last twenty years. The thirteenth most studied language at university level nationwide, it is taught at 226 universities.

Table 14.4. *Universities with the highest enrollments in Portuguese courses*

Rank	University
1	Brigham Young University
2	North Carolina at Chapel Hill
3	University of Massachusetts at Dartmouth
4	University of Georgia
5	Florida International University
6	University of Arizona
7	US Military Academy
8	University of California at Berkeley
9	Boston University
10	University of Wisconsin at Madison

Source: Pacheco 2008.

The teaching of Portuguese is supported by academic associations such as the American Association of Teachers of Spanish and Portuguese (AATSP) and the American Portuguese Studies Association (APSA), and a Special Interest Group of the American Council for the Teaching of Foreign Languages (ACTFL). Table 14.4 shows the ten universities with the largest numbers of students enrolled in Portuguese classes, based on the 2006 MLA report.

In terms of primary and secondary education, the Luso-American Foundation (FLAD, or Fundação Luso-Americana de Desenvolvimento) has launched an initiative to investigate and document the current state of the teaching of Portuguese in the USA. The foundation has identified several K-12 public and community schools that offer Portuguese in Massachusetts (52), California (25), New Jersey (20), Rhode Island (17), Connecticut (13), New York (10), Florida (5), and Georgia (1) (Vicente and Pimenta 2008). In addition, Vicente and Pimenta report on other initiatives to enhance the teaching of Portuguese, such as Portuguese weekend schools in New Jersey, a recent agreement between the Brazilian Consulate in Miami and Broward County schools to found a Portuguese language program, and a grant by FLAD to Middlebury's Portuguese Language School to train teachers to teach Portuguese in Cobb County, Georgia. FLAD is also seeking approval from the College Board to make an Advanced Placement test in Portuguese available to high school students (Vicente and Pimenta 2008: 15).

Despite increasing demand for bilingual and heritage language learning at all school levels, few studies have investigated this group of learners and their acquisition process (Silva 2008: 2). In what follows I review the studies that are available. Rubinstein-Avila (2002) analyzed issues of language variety and language use in a dual-immersion English–Portuguese program in a K-8 school in a Portuguese-speaking neighborhood in Massachusetts, where students were Azoreans, Luso-Americans, Brazilians, and Cape Verdeans. She observed a rise in awareness of dialectal differences among teachers, parents, and staff, and discussed the complex sociocultural and historical tensions that these differences aroused.

Ferreira's 2005 study focused on the learning experiences of Cape Verdeans and second generation Portuguese learners from the Azores and Madeira in a college in Massachusetts. She observed a marked linguistic prejudice against heritage varieties of Portuguese, leading to insecurity in those speakers, and emphasized the importance of addressing sociolinguistic issues when teaching these populations. In 2007, also in Massachusetts, Ferreira analyzed the differences between heritage language learners and traditional second language learners taking Portuguese classes. She found that third generation Portuguese had the lowest proficiency level among heritage language learners, equivalent to that of traditional second language learners, whereas first generation Cape Verdean and Brazilian and second generation Portuguese learners rated similarly on a recall test. These preliminary results pointed to a third generation language shift in which the ancestral language is lost.

Rothman (2007) compared knowledge of inflected infinitives among educated native speakers of Brazilian Portuguese, advanced adult L2 learners, and heritage language learners, finding that, unlike the other two groups, heritage speakers did not demonstrate knowledge of the inflected infinitive, probably because it is absent in colloquial Brazilian Portuguese. His results underscore the need to analyze linguistic input in heritage language acquisition before making generalizations about language attrition or incomplete acquisition. Continuing this line of inquiry, Pires and Rothman (2009) compared the production of inflected infinitives among European Portuguese versus Brazilian Portuguese heritage speakers, contributing to our understanding of the native acquisition of a heritage grammar and comparing this process to L1 native acquisition. They conclude that the different grammars result from exposure to distinct primary linguistic inputs rather than from a difference in the process of acquisition.

Gláucia Silva (2008) also analyzed the perception and production of a particular grammatical feature, the subjunctive mood, by heritage and non-heritage language learners of Portuguese. Specifically, she was interested in investigating whether heritage learners of Portuguese differed from foreign language learners in their perception and production of this form in written tasks, and how this changed with length of formal Portuguese instruction. She concluded that heritage learners did perform better than foreign language learners. She also found that foreign language learners performed better with longer instruction whereas heritage learners did not (Silva 2008: 17). Finally, these differences demonstrate the need to teach heritage learners with appropriate methods and to separate them from foreign language classes so that their specific needs may be targeted.

Based on this incipient line of research, together with the large body of literature about the acquisition of other heritage languages in the USA, specific teaching practices and materials clearly need to be used in teaching speakers of Portuguese as a heritage language, in order to optimize learning. In addition, linguists, educators, administrators, and community leaders should collaborate to find the optimal ways to serve the community of Portuguese heritage speakers in the USA and to familiarize themselves with the principles of heritage language teaching in general, about which much research is already available.

Evidence of shift to English and of Portuguese maintenance

There is a complete lack of large-scale studies about patterns of language choice among Portuguese-speaking immigrants and their descendants in the USA that could provide us with evidence of either language shift to English or Portuguese maintenance. In this section, I review some small-scale studies that have explored these questions, and, based on these results and some community-led initiatives, make tentative predictions about the linguistic vitality of Portuguese in US territory.

Before beginning this discussion, though, I will offer a brief overview of some aspects of the Portuguese used in the USA. As is true in any language-contact situation, the Portuguese dialects spoken in the USA are replete with instances of (1) lexical borrowings, or the incorporation of lexical items from one language into the other (in this case, from English into Portuguese); (2) semantic extensions, or the incorporation of the meaning of a lexical item from another language; and (3) code-switching, or the alternating use of two languages in the same utterance, both within sentences (intrasentential) and between sentences (intersentential). Table 14.5 illustrates some of these phenomena, drawn from available studies.

These linguistic phenomena are inevitably present in linguistic varieties that co-exist with other languages, as discussed in Chapter 2, and should not be viewed as a degradation of Portuguese. One of the aims of bilingual and heritage language education is bidialectalism – that is, to teach individuals to expand their bilingual dialects, usually colloquial varieties used in informal situations, to incorporate more formal and standard varieties into their linguistic repertoires. The aim, thus, is not to replace US Portuguese (or any bilingual variety) with standard Portuguese, because the former has value as a group dialect, and as such carries strong ties with ethnic and cultural identification.

Signs of shift

The clearest sign of language shift in immigrant communities is when the minority language ceases to be used at home. When this happens, children stop acquiring the home language and gradually stop using it altogether. Obviously,

Table 14.5. *English-contact phenomena in US Portuguese varieties*

Phenomenon	Examples from US Portuguese	Standard Portuguese	Source
Borrowing	bisado (from Eng. *busy*)	ocupado/a	Mota 2008: 237
	parquear (from Eng. *to park*)	estacionar	Mota 2008: 237
	estopar (from Eng. *to stop*)	parar	Meihy 2004: 228
	rentar (from Eng. *to rent*)	alugar	Azevedo 2005: 210
Semantic extensions	teatro (from Eng. *movie theater*)	cinema	Meihy 2004: 228
	enforçar (from Eng. *to enforce*)	fazer cumprir	Azevedo 2005: 210
	pretender (from Eng. to pretend)	fingir	Meihy 2004: 228
Intrasentential code-switching	*I twisted my ankle again* no futebol	Torci meu tornozelo no futebol	Bensabat-Ott 2000: 121
Intersentential code-switching	Ohhh . . . *Who told you that?* Como você sabe?	Ohhh . . . Quem te disse? Como você sabe?	Bensabat-Ott 2000: 121

when they in turn become parents, they raise their children speaking English, the only language they feel comfortable with, completing the language shift cycle. This cycle usually takes three generations: the first generation is dominant in the home language, their children are bilingual, and their grandchildren monolingual in the majority language.

Portuguese-speaking families seem to be following the standard path to language shift. Among the 687,126 Portuguese speakers recorded in the 2007 American Community Survey (see Table 1.1), 77.8 percent reported speaking English "well" or "very well," suggesting that 22.2 percent of Portuguese speakers (most likely first generation immigrants) are not comfortable speaking English. Among Brazilians in Connecticut, both generations 1.5 and 2 are reported to be bilingual by Menezes (2003: 165), and often serve as interpreters for their parents in public domains. As Mota (2008) observes, this practice causes a problematic inversion of the family hierarchy as children must assume adult roles and responsibilities their parents cannot manage due to lack of language proficiency. In addition, Mota (2008: 325) finds the following very typical language-choice patterns among Brazilian immigrant families in Washington, DC: communication among siblings tends to be exclusively in English, whereas children's communication with parents tends to depend on birth order and gender; older children and girls tend to address their parents in Portuguese, younger children and boys in English. Sales and Loureiro (2008: 307) observed a similar pattern among second generation Brazilians in Massachusetts: in community gatherings, adults speak Portuguese amongst themselves while children and adolescents speak English.

Among Portuguese-Americans, language shift has typically been completed by the third generation, who are either English monolinguals or English-dominant bilinguals (Azevedo 2005; Ferreira 2005). As early as 1980, Williams noted that language maintenance was low among the Portuguese community in California, with even some Portuguese-born individuals no longer speaking Portuguese (p. 729).

Signs of maintenance

Ethnic pride functions to promote language maintenance. Despite the lack of instrumental value assigned to Portuguese because it does not have a clear capital value in US society, Portuguese holds strong integrative and emotional value among immigrant families (Bensabat-Ott 2000: 148–149). Ferreira (2005: 851) also found that her students "had mostly intrinsic and integrative motivations rather than instrumental ones for taking the Portuguese class," indicating that positive feelings towards the language motivate students to take Portuguese classes and to continue to develop their proficiency. It is important to remember, however, that Cape Verdean students have fundamentally different motivations for learning Portuguese than their peers do, since it is Cape Verdean Creole, not Portuguese, that is the language of ethnic identity and group solidarity (Ferreira 2005: 852).

Another factor that leads to language maintenance among Brazilian families is the desire to return to Brazil someday. Regardless of the actual likelihood of being able to return, many Brazilians see their stay in the USA as temporary (Siqueira 2008: 175). According to Mota (2002: 2), the expectation of returning to Brazil provides an incentive for language maintenance, since the parents want to ensure that their children maintain their Portuguese proficiency so that they can continue their schooling on the family's return to Brazil. A desire to return home was, according to Stephens (1989: 719), also the main reason for the maintenance of the home language in Portuguese communities in the USA.

Even more essential to the maintenance of a minority language than ethnic pride or plans to return to the home country is a constant influx of first generation immigrants. Although language shift may continue to happen within the family domain, language maintenance is observed in the society at large when new immigrants continuously arrive in the community and interact with previous generations of immigrants. This phenomenon, called *recontact*, may in fact slow down the process of language shift. Ferreira (2005: 849) claims that it is indeed the constant influx of new immigrants in Massachusetts that has greatly slowed rates of acculturation and language shift to English there, allowing for the preservation of both Portuguese and Cape Verdean Creole in the state.

Indeed, recontact contributes to the status of Portuguese as the third most spoken language in Massachusetts, a frequent destination for the three main Lusophone ethnic groups: Portuguese, Cape Verdeans, and Brazilians. Cross-dialectal differences among these Portuguese dialects should not present an obstacle for language maintenance. The concentration of these groups provides Portuguese speakers, regardless of their background, with Portuguese-speaking contacts and networks that enhance the maintenance of the language. Dialectal differences, although perceived as socially significant, do not pose a communication barrier for speakers, as reinforced by both Rubinstein-Avila (2002) and Ferreira (2005), who did not see any instances of communication breakdown between various groups of students.

Among community-based events that promote the use of Portuguese, Mota (2002: 5) points to the role of Portuguese-speaking churches in reinforcing the use of Portuguese among young people, both during rituals and in church social activities. An initiative sponsored by Georgetown University and the Brazilian Embassy in Washington, DC, recently gathered linguists, teachers, and parents to discuss strategies for teaching Portuguese to Brazilian offspring, which included the development of pedagogical materials and a resource website (Vivaldo Santos, personal communication). Moreover, MAPS has advocated for the maintenance of Portuguese in Massachusetts, and FLAD has worked intensively to enhance the visibility of the language and its diffusion in the USA.

Despite the positive effects that ethnic pride, recontact, and community-based initiatives have on language maintenance, bilingual and heritage language education is essential for slowing down the language shift process. During her ethnographic observations of Brazilian immigrant families, Mota (2002: 5) noticed that despite parents' efforts to maintain Portuguese proficiency among their children, both to assert their authority and to preserve cultural identity, children in her sample demonstrated a gradual decrease in productive skills in Portuguese. Souza pinpointed the importance of bilingual programs when she noted, based on her experience as a school counselor in the Boston area, "how quickly children tend to lose their native language, as well as cultural ties and values, when placed in mainstream classrooms" (Souza 2000: 8). She observed, in contrast, that children who attended bilingual classes for an extended period and spoke Portuguese at home did indeed become fully bilingual.

Conclusion

It would be premature to predict the future of the Portuguese language in the USA. At the moment, the available facts indicate that language shift is near completion among third generation Portuguese-Americans, that Cape Verdeans born in the USA depend on the availability of bilingual education to learn

Portuguese, and that a significant population of second generation Brazilian immigrants has just started to emerge and be investigated. It is also too early to know how the factors that usually determine a minority language's vitality will influence Portuguese maintenance. Based on the evidence from the few available studies of Portuguese speakers in the USA and on the vast corpus of research about language shift in immigrant communities in general, it is safe to say, however, that unless new immigrants continue to arrive in places populated by earlier settlers, and a national and effective standard and official bilingual education program in Portuguese is put in place, the language shift to English will complete its cycle.

DISCUSSION QUESTIONS

1. Consider the Cape Verdean sociolinguistic situation, in which creole is the language spoken at home and in all informal communication, while Portuguese is the language used by government agencies, the school, and a communication media. What is your prediction about the likelihood of Portuguese maintenance among Cape Verdean communities in the USA, where English is the public language?

2. *Recontact* is a language phenomenon that interrupts the process of language shift in a community as a result of the ongoing arrival of first generation immigrants. In areas such as California, where the influx of Portuguese immigrants has practically halted but Brazilian immigration has increased rapidly, will recontact be sufficient to maintain Portuguese ethnolinguistic vitality?

15 Polish in the USA

Bożena Nowicka McLees and Katarzyna Dziwirek

Introduction

Poland is the sixth largest country in Europe and possibly the most homogeneous in its linguistic, cultural, and religious makeup. There are approximately 50 million people worldwide who speak Polish, including 38 million living in Poland and approximately 12 million forming the Polish diaspora. Most Poles living abroad reside in the USA, and in fact the largest Polish city after Warsaw in terms of numbers of Polish speakers is Chicago (Stecuła 2007). As shown in Table 1.1, Polish currently occupies the twelfth spot on the list of the top twelve non-English languages spoken in the USA.

This chapter explores the history of Polish immigration to the USA, current demographics, changes in Poland and in US immigration policy, and the role of the media, business, and education in keeping Polish among the most common languages other than English spoken in the USA today.

History

Polish belongs to the family of Indo-European languages and to the subgroup of Slavic languages of Central and Eastern Europe. The core of the Polish lexicon is Slavic, but a considerable number of words in the Polish vocabulary are derived directly from Latin or have origins in Latin or Greek. Over the past ten centuries, German settlers from across the border to the West established artisan guilds and helped develop cities and commerce. Polish-Germans are credited with operating the first printing shops in the Renaissance Kingdom of Poland and they became instrumental in codifying Polish orthography and grammar. As a result, many German words were incorporated into the Polish language, especially those referring to commerce, crafts, industry and urbanization. Poland's historic neighbors such as Czechs, Ukrainians, Russians, Hungarians, and Turks also enriched the Polish lexicon. Major European cultural trends such as the Italian Renaissance, the Spanish Baroque, and the French Enlightenment contributed to Polish vocabulary in the areas of literature, art, architecture, home furnishings, and fashion.

German borrowings remained prominent in science and technology until the late twentieth century when English became the dominant language in information technology, commerce, marketing, and popular culture (Klemensiewicz 1980; Dąbrowska 2004).

The earliest Poles to immigrate to the USA were a small group of craftsmen invited by the British Virginia Company to settle in Jamestown in 1608 (Haiman 1974). In the eighteenth century, the once vast and powerful Commonwealth of Poland and Lithuania fell to its stronger neighbors Russia, Prussia, and Austria, resulting in the partitioning of Poland and many drastic changes in its economy. Several unsuccessful national uprisings for Poland's independence in the nineteenth century, followed by political oppression and economic hardship, prompted exoduses of Polish nobility and peasants alike. The initial tendency for Polish immigrants, who arrived in huge groups and settled together, was to preserve their Polish identity by separation and self-reliance. In this spirit they established three national fraternal organizations: the Polish Roman Catholic Union of America (1873), the Polish National Alliance (1880), and the Polish Women's Alliance (1898) (Wachtel 1913; Pienkos 1984; Pienkos and Pienkos 2003). These organizations provided life insurance for their members, as well as support for Polish education and various Polish causes. The church was often the center of the immigrants' life and a foundation of the Polish neighborhood (Galush 1996).

US Census statistics from 1900 and 1910, when Polish immigration reached its peak, indicate no listing for Polish nationals because they were counted as residents of the partitioning states and held documents issued by Germany, Austria, or Russia. When the Treaty of Versailles reinstated Poland as an independent state in 1919, some immigrants returned to Poland. The 1930 US Census numbered the first and second generation Poles at almost 3.5 million. This is the group that is often referred to as the first wave of Polish immigrants to the USA (Bukowczyk 1987). Several prominent Polish-American politicians emerged from this first wave of immigration, including Chicago Democrat Dan Rostenkowski, who served for many years (1981–94) as an influential chairman of the US Congress Ways and Means Committee; senior Democratic Senator Barbara Mikulski from Maryland, Republican US Senator and Governor of Alaska Frank Murkowski, and Democratic Congressman John Murtha, the former chairman of the House Appropriations Defense Subcommittee.

Poland remained sovereign for twenty years, but World War II had a devastating effect on its population. Nearly 6 million Polish citizens (almost 18 percent of its prewar population) were killed, and one third of its territory was annexed by the Soviet Union. Nearly 250,000 Poles found refuge in the West, either enlisting in the Allied Forces, being freed from concentration and labor camps, or receiving a Displaced Person status. They were generally fearful or unwilling to return to a Soviet-dominated Poland. In the late 1940s and early 1950s, over 200,000 Poles came to the USA. They are referred to as the second wave of Polish immigration (Pula 1995).

The third and smallest wave resulted from protests against Soviet rule in 1968, 1970, and 1976, which culminated in the massive, ten million strong labor movement of 1980 known as the *Solidarity* Free Trade Union. In the 1980s over 62,000 Poles immigrated to the USA (Erdmans 1998). After the first semidemocratic elections in June 1989 and the consequent fall of communism, Poland began its transformation into a free democratic society. There was a sense of hope and opportunity and, consequently, less drive and fewer reasons for immigration, though the uncertainty about the new economic model and the fast-changing reality continued to add to the number of potential immigrants until the situation stabilized and Poland joined the European Union in 2004.

In the USA, beginning in the late 1970s under President Carter, when a first generation Polish-American, Zbigniew Brzezinski, served as National Security Advisor, more attention was given to Poland and Polish-American issues. The heightened interest in Poland was also stimulated by compelling events in international affairs. In 1978 Cardinal Karol Wojtyla was elected the first non-Italian Roman Catholic Pope in modern times. Then, in 1980, the *Solidarity* movement shook the foundation of the "iron curtain" behind which Poland had been trapped since 1945. These events openly challenged Soviet domination in Central and Eastern Europe and encouraged Americans of Polish descent to feel proud of their heritage and become more interested in the "old country" (Bukowczyk 1987). During President Reagan's administration (1981–9), there was a noticeable shift in the Polish-American community from the Democratic to the Republican Party (Blejwas 1996). Reagan's bold stance toward Soviet leaders rallied Polish-American politicians as well as activists in the staunchly anti-communist Polish American Congress (established in 1944), the Polish National Alliance, the Polish Roman Catholic Union of America, and the Polish Women's Alliance.

The culmination of this extraordinary period of renewed Polish American pride came in 1989, when the iconic leader of the *Solidarity* movement, Lech Wałęsa, addressed a joint session of the US Congress five months after the first semidemocratic elections had ended the Communist Party's monopoly on power in Poland. For the first time ever, the Polish language had been used at this level of American political life.

The next big political achievement was Poland's entry to the North Atlantic Treaty Organization in 1997. Poland joined the European Union on May 1, 2004, and since then Poles seeking employment and career opportunities are permitted to work legally in other European Union countries. At the same time, the US Homeland Security Office excluded Poland from the visa program because the number of Polish immigrants exceeded 50,000 during the preceding five-year period. Poland's admittance to the European Union, combined with the borderless movement of its citizens as stipulated in the Schengen Agreement (implemented in 2007) and its steadily improving economy, plus a more restrictive US immigration policy, suggest that the 2010 Census might show a further decline in Polish immigration to the USA. On the other hand, findings of the 2005 American Community Survey as reported in Stecuła (2007) show an increase in the number of Polish speakers in the USA of close to 10 percent. We will address these findings shortly.

Demographics

There are 8.5 million Americans of Polish descent according to the 2000 US Census, and 9.8 million according to the 2005 American Community Survey (Stecuła 2007). Most Polish-Americans live in suburbs of large cities such as Chicago, New York, Buffalo, Los Angeles, Pittsburgh, and Detroit. Table 15.1 shows the top ten states for Polish ancestry residents; Table 15.2 lists cities with 10,000 or more residents of Polish ancestry.

Table 15.1. *States with largest numbers of residents with Polish ancestry*

State	Number of Polish residents	Percentage of state population
New York	986,141	5.12
Illinois	932,996	7.30
Michigan	854,844	8.44
Pennsylvania	824,146	6.63
New Jersey	576,473	6.61
Wisconsin	497,726	8.99
California	491,325	1.35
Ohio	433,016	3.77
Florida	429,691	2.41
Massachusetts	323,210	5.05

Source: US Census Bureau 2000a.

The disintegration of Polish churches and ethnic neighborhoods combined with upward mobility of Polish-Americans and the different character of Polish immigrants in the 1960s–1980s contributed to the relocation of Polish speakers outside the big cities. These immigrants were better educated and earned more, enabling them to move to the suburbs as part of the "white flight" characteristic of the late 1960s and 1970s (Erdmans 1998). This trend continues as newly arriving Poles look for better public schools and a suburban lifestyle over the coziness of an urban ethnic enclave. For example, in Illinois, 65 percent of those who identified themselves as Polish in the 2000 Census live in the suburbs,

Table 15.2. *Cities with over 10,000 residents of Polish ancestry*

	City	State	Number of Polish residents	Percentage of population
1	New York	NY	213,447	2.7
2	Chicago	IL	210,421	7.3
3	Milwaukee	WI	57,485	9.6
4	Cheektowaga	NY	37,560	39.9
5	Buffalo	NY	34,254	11.7
6	Toledo	OH	31,792	10.1
7	Pittsburgh	PA	28,178	8.4
8	Cleveland	OH	22,978	4.8
9	Detroit	MI	18,992	2.0
10	Grand Rapids	MI	15,442	7.8

Source: US Census Bureau 2000a.

Table 15.3. *Metropolitan areas with largest Polish-speaking populations in 2000*

	City	Number of Polish residents
1	Chicago	831,774
2	Detroit	479,659
3	Philadelphia	288,440
4	New York	268,228
5	Buffalo-Niagara Falls, NY	209,303
6	Pittsburgh, PA	209,032
7	Milwaukee-Waukesha, WI	190,076
8	Cleveland-Lorain-Elyria, OH	186,571
9	Minneapolis-St. Paul, MN	148,876
10	Los Angeles	122,680

Source: Stecuła 2007.

23 percent in Chicago, and 12 percent in other parts of the state. Table 15.3 (Stecuła 2007: 9) includes people living outside city limits in the suburbs of large metropolitan areas.

According to Stecuła (2007: 9), Polish Americans have higher levels of education and income than the average US population: 88 percent are high school graduates (v. 80 percent of the general population), and 33 percent hold a bachelor's degree (v. 24 percent overall). More Polish Americans are also homeowners, 73 percent compared to 66 percent in the general US population.

Table 15.4. *States with the largest Polish-speaking populations*

	Ages 5 +	Percentage of all US Polish speakers
Illinois	193,018	32.05
New York	94,584	15.70
New Jersey	67,195	11.15
Michigan	37,687	6.25
Connecticut	33,514	5.56
Pennsylvania	26,007	4.31
Florida	24,079	3.99
Massachusetts	19,012	3.15
California	17,398	2.88
Ohio	13,372	2.22
Total in USA	638,059	

Source: Modern Language Association 2009, US Census Bureau 2007c.

Finally, the median Polish-American family income is $61,635 compared to the average $50,046.

As is common with European ancestry populations in the USA (see the chapters on German, French, and Italian in this volume), the majority of US residents of Polish ancestry do not speak Polish. The 2007 American Community Survey carried out by the US Census Bureau indicated that 638,059 individuals age 5 and older spoke Polish at home. This means that slightly less than 7 percent of the 8.5 million Americans of Polish origin speak Polish at home.

Table 15.4 indicates the ten states where the largest populations of Polish speakers are located. Despite recent increases in the Polish population in the western states, patterns of Polish settlement in the USA show remarkable consistency over the past seven generations. The first wave came to the rapidly growing industrial centers in the Midwest and the Northeast including Chicago, Detroit, Buffalo, New York and Pittsburgh They built churches and established parishes (administrative units in the Catholic Church) and neighborhoods, and subsequent generations of newcomers joined them to utilize the existing Polish infrastructure (Bukowczyk 1987). These are locations where the Polish language is maintained and spoken on a daily basis at home, at work, in shops, restaurants, businesses, and on the streets. This language maintenance is due to both intergenerational transmission (well-established heritage schools, presence of Polish classes in high schools, opportunities to use Polish in the community) and to continued immigration from Poland.

According to the 2005 American Community Survey (Stecuła 2007: 6), 78 percent of Polish Americans live in the thirteen states with the highest Polish populations. Ten of these thirteen states are in the Midwest and the Northeast (California, Florida and Texas are the exceptions), and nine of the ten have experienced a growth in the Polish population between 2000 and 2005 (New Jersey is the only exception).

Many older Polish Americans retired in Southwest states such as Colorado, California, and Nevada, as well as in Florida. Also, present-day immigrants and Polish-Americans have higher levels of education and are more likely to speak English and possess transferable professional skills (Pula 1995). They are thus free to move to places where job opportunities lead them outside of the established Polish areas. This is different from the past, when Polish-Americans and less-educated immigrants stayed in the Polish neighborhoods, close to their parish and their friends. As can be seen in Table 15.5, the top ten states with the highest percentage growth in the Polish population between 2000 and 2005 include primarily states in the West and South, which do not have a long history of extensive Polish immigration.

Table 15.5. *Ten states with the highest percentage growth in the Polish population*

	State	Percentage change, 2000 to 2005
1	Utah	+66
2	South Carolina	+42
3	Maine	+33
4	Idaho	+31
5	Alabama	+30
6	North Carolina	+30
7	Tennessee	+29
8	Louisiana	+29
9	Arizona	+28
10	Arkansas	+28

Source: Stecuła 2007.

Public presence of Polish

The previous section showed that Polish speakers are mostly concentrated in large metropolitan areas, predominantly in suburbs of former industrial centers of the Northeast and Midwest. There is a visible Polish presence in the cities and suburbs of Chicago, Pittsburgh, Buffalo, and New York, where one often sees stores selling Polish goods, window signs saying *mówimy po polsku* (we speak Polish), and churches offering masses in Polish. In those metropolitan areas, one can hear Polish spoken over the telephone and in person for some basic services including the Department of Motor Vehicles, County Treasurer's and Collector's offices, courts of law, hospitals, banks, and supermarkets. In this section we focus on the presence of Polish in the media, business, and education.

Media

In general, American media devote little time to Polish or Polish-American affairs. For example, neither the *Chicago Tribune* nor the *Chicago Sun Times* reported on the visit of Polish president Lech Kaczyński to the White House in October 2007. As an alternative source of information, major Polish-American communities have developed various types of media, most of which are available in Polish. For political reasons, US Poles have usually preferred media created in the USA because the ones in Poland were controlled by the communist state and viewed with distrust. Only recently have articles, radio and television programs produced in Poland been widely distributed, published, and broadcast in US-Polish communities. These include Polish TV channels available through satellite TV providers and the internet (e.g. *TV Polonia*, *Telewizja Polska*, *Polsat 2*, and many local TV stations from Poland), numerous radio stations (over fifty accessible at www.radiostacje.com), as well as all major and many local daily and weekly print publications available on the internet (e.g. *Gazeta Wyborcza*, *Rzeczpospolita*, *Polityka*, *Wprost*).

The first Polish language magazine in the USA appeared in Milwaukee in 1885. It was titled *Tygodnik Anonsowy* (The Weekly Announcer) and was later renamed *Kurier Polski* (The Polish Courier). In 1908, Chicago's Polish Daily, *Dziennik Związkowy* (Polish Daily News), made its debut. It is still published today by the Polish National Alliance and its weekend edition sells 30,000 copies. The longest running Polish weekly, published in Stevens Point, WI, is called *Gwiazda Polarna* (The Northern Star). It replaced *Rolnik* (The Farmer), established 1892, in 1908. According to Pula (1995: 143), the peak era for Polish periodical publications in America was between 1900 and 1920, when at least one such publication appeared in twenty-seven different states. 65 percent were located in the areas of high Polish-American population density: New York, Chicago, and Detroit were home to 43 percent of the publications, with the single largest number in Chicago. By 1974 there remained some 107 ethnic publications, of which 48 were in Polish, 27 in English, and 32 bilingual. The total circulation of these publications was estimated at 664,365 copies in forty-one cities in fourteen states and the District of Columbia. Today, Polish publications in the USA continue online as well as in print. The dailies, *Dziennik Związkowy* (Polish Daily News) from Chicago and *Nowy Dziennik*

(The New Daily) from New York, the biweekly *Gwiazda Polarna* (The Northern Star) from Stevens Point, WI, and the bilingual portal *Polish News Online* are some examples.

Polish language radio programs began in Ohio (1927), Illinois (1928), Indiana (1929), and later in Connecticut, Michigan, New York, Pennsylvania, Arizona, and California. According to Migala (1984), there are around 300 radio stations nationwide broadcasting programs in Polish that consist of local and international news, economic reports, cultural and artistic reviews, sports coverage, and weather. Polish language television operates in all major Polish-American centers with the advantage of satellite TV, which brings hundreds of hours of programming from Poland directly to Polish-American homes. There are also many local television programs reporting on community events in Polish. Some of the programs are broadcast via public access television stations. However, the readers, listeners and viewers of Polish media are mainly immigrants and visitors to the USA. It is quite common for a grandmother to come from Poland to care for her grandchildren, which motivates the immigrant or second generation family to order Polish TV via satellite.

Polish bookstores, art galleries, museums, and other forms of entertainment play an important role in cultivating the cultural interests of Polish immigrants and Polish-Americans. Every year, theater ensembles, variety shows, cabarets, and individual artists come to major Polish cities in America. For example, for over twenty years the Society for the Arts has been presenting the annual Polish Film Festival in Chicago and several other cities in the USA, where thousands of viewers have a chance to meet film directors, cinematographers, producers and movie stars from Poland.

Business

The opening of the Polish economy to foreign investors in the early 1990s provided an incredible boost for business (Sachs 1994). During fifty years of a state-planned and controlled economy, there was only a handful of companies from Poland doing business in the USA, such as LOT Polish Airlines and PEKAO Trading Corporation, a subsidiary of the only bank in the Soviet bloc facilitating retail transactions in US dollars and other Western currencies. Today, there is a multitude of big and small companies conducting business between Poland and the USA. During the period of transition to capitalism (1990–4) thousands of Polish professionals came to the USA to learn the rules and practices of a market economy. Polish translators and interpreters were charged with creating new vocabularies for banking, finance, securities, and other commercial operations as they assisted renowned scholars from the J. L. Kellogg Graduate School of Management at Northwestern University, as well as the instructors at the McDonald's University in Des Plains, in educating

Polish managers. International briefings for US managers going to Poland provided a unique opportunity for US-based Polish-speakers who had first-hand knowledge and experience working in Poland to educate their US counterparts in Polish business etiquette and cultural aspects of interacting in the workplace.

Community-based organizations such as the Economic Forum, the US–Poland Chamber of Commerce, and the Polish American Chamber of Commerce were established to promote business exchanges and investments in Poland. Each year a number of trade shows bring together businesspeople from Poland, Americans of Polish heritage, and others to help establish and foster business connections. There are thousands of local businesses catering to the Polish-American community, including insurance agencies, banks, beauty salons, bakeries, delis, supermarkets, restaurants, flower shops, funeral homes, medical clinics, car mechanics, and construction companies. They provide a diverse job market for Polish immigrants and play an important social function of a meeting place where one can exchange opinions on current Polish issues.

Education

Polish is taught both as a foreign language and as a heritage language in the USA. (See Chapter 1 of this volume for a definition of "heritage speaker" and a discussion of issues in heritage speaker education.) Teaching Polish as a foreign language in the USA is a relatively recent phenomenon, which spiked during the 1980s with heightened interest in Poland due to front-page news about the Polish Pope, John Paul II, and the *Solidarity* movement. Polish as a foreign language is taught mostly in colleges and universities as opposed to high schools. According to *NewPoland News* (2000), courses in Polish are offered at 191 schools of higher education, with forty located in New York, fourteen in Indiana, twelve in California, eleven in Massachusetts, nine in Pennsylvania, and seven in Illinois. The Polish Academic Information Center (2000) lists 143 US colleges and universities with some Polish offerings. As shown in Table 15.6, there has recently been an increase in the number of enrollments in Polish.

Table 15.6. *Enrollments in Polish-language courses in 2002 and 2006*

	2-Year Colleges		Undergraduate Programs		Graduate Programs		Total	
Year	2002	2006	2002	2006	2002	2006	2002	2006
Enrollment	80	155	935	1,177	38	47	1,053	1,379

Source: Furman *et al.* 2007.

There are several reasons why adults take courses in Polish as a foreign language, including a desire to communicate with their significant others or with family members, academic or professional interests, business reasons, etc. Recently Poland has become an attractive place to do business. Many multinational corporations and American companies have begun operations in Poland, hiring people who were willing to relocate and learn the language. A different, and increasingly popular, motivation involves the high cost of graduate education in medicine, dentistry, and pharmacy, paired with limited enrollment opportunities in the USA (Bednarek 1991). According to Bilanow (2007), there were 3,723 international students of Polish origin who had returned to study in Poland in the 2005–6 academic year (one third of the 10,000 total international students). Professional schools in Poland have a good enough reputation that some European nations, such as Norway, have intergovernmental agreements to educate their future doctors and dentists in Poland.

Other fields of interest attract smaller groups of individuals, mainly scholars, to study Polish. In the last century Poland had an unusually rich and varied experience in labor movements, models and transformations of political and economic structures, and Polish–Jewish relations. Literature, mainly poetry, has been recognized by two Nobel Prize awards in Literature for Czesław Miłosz (1980) and Wisława Szymborska (1996).

The limited offerings of Polish as a part of bilingual programs in public education mainly facilitate faster assimilation into mainstream English-speaking society, which is exactly what most immigrant parents and students want to accomplish. There are no dual immersion programs for Polish speakers in any public school system and Polish is very rarely taught as a foreign language in elementary or secondary schools, public or private. However, Polish has also long been taught as a heritage language in the USA. An elaborate parochial educational system was created through the initiative and support of the Roman Catholic hierarchy, which felt isolated in the overwhelmingly Protestant environment of the USA. The first and largest wave of Polish immigrants, estimated at over 3.5 million, had little or no formal education in the Polish language, due in part to restrictions imposed by the partitioning empires. Likewise, the poor and rural immigrants from the newly independent Poland between the two World Wars had limited access to schools. When they came to the USA, they wanted to replicate the familiar life of their villages, where the church played a dominant role. The number of Polish churches continued to grow and peaked at 540 in 1929 (Pula 1995). Along with these churches grew the parochial schools, which by 1927 exceeded 500 elementary schools administered by the Polish Roman Catholic Church. According to Cyganowski and Ziontz (1981), 85 percent of Polish-Americans who became adults in the postwar era lived in ethnic Polish neighborhoods and 74 percent attended parochial schools. Much has been written about the role of Polish parochial education in the USA.

Some argue that these institutions promoted Polish-language preservation to safeguard the national identity or *polskość* (Polishness). Others question their mediocre if not poor educational level and methodology, resulting in the Polish community in the USA being held back (Pula 1995).

The Polish language disappeared from parochial schools between 1930 and 1950 when church policy fostered integration, and the Polish parochial education system was finally dismantled by the 1950s. The shortage of priests in the second half of the twentieth century further eroded the opportunity to tie together Polish and Catholic education. At this point, both parents and professional educators who emigrated from Poland stepped in to build a remarkable network of Polish Saturday schools. These parents, belonging to the second wave of about a quarter million immigrants that arrived in the USA after World War II, were much better educated than their predecessors and sought to maintain their children's Polish identity through education. In the early 1950s they organized Polish schools and established or resurrected the Polish scout groups, dance groups, and sports clubs. For example, educators who came to Chicago established the first Polish Saturday schools – named after the two Polish-American revolutionary heroes Kościuszko and Pułaski – both founded in the early 1950s and still in operation today.

It is difficult to obtain precise statistics concerning current Polish Saturday schools. There is no single organization which compiles such data and the information found on websites is often outdated and inaccurate. Our figures are based on information from the three associations of heritage Polish teachers: Centrala Polskich Szkół Dokształcających (Headquarters of Polish Complementary Schools), which covers the East Coast, Forum Nauczycieli Polonijnych Zachodniego Wybrzeża (West Coast Polish Teachers Forum), located in Los Angeles, and Zrzeszenie Nauczycieli Polskich w Ameryce (The Association of Polish Teachers in America) based in Chicago. These professional associations provide support for Polish schools and educators and sponsor the publication of Polish textbooks designed for children growing up in the USA from grades one through eight. High school Polish education relies on books from Poland. We also consulted consular websites (New York, Chicago, and Los Angeles), and a list of Polish schools maintained by Wanda Mandecki (n.d.). Based on our findings from the above-mentioned sources (Nowicka McLees, in progress), we can say that at present there are over 120 Polish Saturday schools in the USA, including forty-two in Illinois, twenty-four in New York State, twenty-one in New Jersey, and seven in California. They are attended by over 26,000 children from kindergarten to twelfth grade. They are most numerous in the Midwest as a continuation of the Polish presence in the rust belt for almost 140 years.

One reason that the Polish Saturday schools continue to thrive despite all the forces affecting intergenerational transmission of immigrant languages (economic issues, acculturation and assimilation pressures, etc.) is the fact that the Polish partitions and the survival of the Polish language between 1772 and 1918 continue to play a large role in the Polish national psyche. Education in Poland stresses the importance of the preservation of the Polish language during the time when Poland did not officially exist as a country. Literary works about heroic struggles of Poles to maintain their language against all odds and restrictive laws passed by German, Russian, and Austrian authorities are a staple of the curriculum, and words like *germanizacja* "Germanization," *rusyfikacja* "Russification" and, more recently, *amerykanizacja* "Americanization" are highly charged, negative concepts. Thus Polish immigrants face enormous pressures and expectations to pass their language on to their children (as their ancestors did during the partitions), and this sense of obligation is often a motivating factor in their decision to enroll their children in the Saturday schools. Second generation Poles, born in the USA, have not been introduced into the Polish national ethos in such a fashion and thus do not feel similar pressures to enroll their children in heritage schools.

Evidence of language shift to English and of Polish maintenance

Signs of shift

Though comprehensive language-use studies documenting a shift to English do not exist for Polish as they do for many other languages in this volume (see, for example, Suro 2002 and Veltman 2000 for Spanish), several factors provide evidence of such a shift.

The first wave of Polonia began to "Americanize" in the second and third generation, and this affected their way of speaking Polish. One way, according to Pula (1995), was through affixing Polish endings to borrowed English words. For example, the Polish word *ulica* "street" was replaced by *strita*, an adaptation of the English word "street" spelled according to Polish orthography and with a Polish ending. It was common for Polish-Americans traveling to Poland to be negatively evaluated for these linguistic practices, a phenomenon described in Chapter 2 of the present volume. The post-World War II immigrants were also susceptible to the process of incorporating English words into Polish conversations, especially when Polish equivalents were not readily available due to new technological developments and social processes not known in Poland. This lead to the creation of "Polglish," a unique version of the Polish language as spoken by Polish-Americans (Furmanek 2000). These immigrants wanted to learn English and assimilate into mainstream US society and a once-common warning for those who tried too hard was that "one will never learn English well enough, but will forget the Polish language in the process."

The opening of Poland's borders and the resulting freedom to travel, which began gradually in the 1970s and flourished in the 1990s, transformed attitudes toward the English language. English became a key factor in professional success and social status. Today, the Polish language even in Poland is absorbing an array of English borrowings through business, popular culture, media, and the internet, as well as through personal contacts with English-speaking family and friends (Sękowska 2000).

The language of young Polish-Americans today exhibits many borrowings from English, as well as some morphosyntactic changes characteristic of heritage speakers. It seems that among the first grammatical features to disappear is the genitive of negation, an obligatory and completely grammaticalized rule of Polish which requires verbs which take accusative objects in affirmative sentences to take objects in the genitive when negated. Heritage Polish speakers often ignore this. They also ignore the use of instrumental case for predicate nouns (e.g. *He is a doctor/an American*), also obligatory in monolingual Polish. It could be argued that these are conventionalized aspects of language which do not contribute much to the meaning of the utterance (which are often omitted by heritage speakers of many languages), but what is interesting is that both of these features are present in the input the first generation of Polish-Americans receive from their parents and yet are completely disregarded. This might suggest that the transfer from English operates at a much deeper conceptual level than just surface lexicon/morphology/syntax. Other features of the heritage speakers' Polish, more obviously attributable to transfer, include the use of prepositional phrases where Polish uses case marking (especially the use of *dla* "for" or *do* "to" instead of dative case with goals, recipients and beneficiaries) and confusion regarding proper preposition use (Dziwirek and Cholewińska 2000; Dziwirek 2001).

It is important to note that 80 percent of the Polish-speaking respondents to the 2000 US Census declared that they spoke English "well" or "very well" (see Chapter 1).[1] This question, which attempts to assess the number of bilinguals among different populations, is crucial for evaluating language shift. As Romaine (1995: 5) points out: "It has often been said that bilingualism is a step along the road to linguistic extinction . . . Certainly, it is not hard to find cases where language death is preceded by bilingualism and extensive code-switching." In the case of Polish we need not perhaps fear language death as such, since Polish is alive and well in Poland, but for the fate of Polish in the USA the fact that 81 percent of Polish speakers see themselves as bilingual is an unmistakable sign of imminent language shift. Fishman's (1971) comment, as paraphrased by Romaine (1995: 19), suggests the reason why: "Any society which produced functionally balanced bilinguals who used both languages equally well in all contexts would soon cease to be bilingual because no society needs two languages for the same set of functions." As the set of functions for which Polish is essential in the USA (church, fraternal organizations, etc.) dwindles, so do the opportunities and reasons for using Polish. It is worth noting that, according to Rumbaut *et al.* (2006), while 35 percent of Mexicans in the USA retain strong language skills beyond the second generation, only 3 percent of European immigrants do, and, due to the reasons outlined above, Polish speakers can be safely assumed to follow this trend.

Signs of maintenance

Contact between Poles and their US relatives has increased dramatically after the fall of communism, and now many US-born children visit their families in Poland and spend summers there with their grandparents or participate in summer camps. This enhances Polish-language maintenance by giving these children an incentive to speak, read, and write Polish so they can effectively communicate with relatives and peers. An examination of the Polish Saturday-school system best illustrates ongoing efforts to maintain Polish in the first and second generations.

As mentioned above, based on our research, there are over 120 Polish Saturday schools in the USA today, and the total number of students attending is approximately 26,000 (Nowicka McLees, in progress). Saturday schools offer two to four hours of instruction in Polish about Polish literature, grammar, orthography, history, culture, geography, and traditions. These schools are usually located where there is a sympathetic Polish priest or local organization willing to rent the existing facilities for a reasonable price. Other schools rent space from the local public school system. One school in Chicago was able to buy its own building with the financial assistance from the Polish National Alliance. Annual fees per child vary from $100 to $700. Teachers are from diverse locations within Poland and with varied experience as educators. They share a passion for teaching Polish, which is also often their way of reaching the social status they gave up upon immigrating to the USA. Teaching, though not well paid, is a well-regarded occupation in Poland. Since Polish teachers find it difficult to obtain comparable jobs in the USA without additional education and certification, heritage schools provide them with a way of reclaiming their perceived lost prestige.

The thirty-four Polish Saturday schools in Chicago and its suburbs serve over 16,000 students. A survey of 115 students carried out at one school revealed that two thirds of the Polish Saturday-school students were born in the USA and almost 90 percent traveled to Poland during the summer (Nowicka McLees and Potowski, in progress). Less than one third attended Polish school solely because the parents wanted them to, with the rest specifying at least some intrinsic motivation to study Polish. Another positive sign was that 87 percent said they intended to teach Polish to their future children. However, only 4 percent of these students complete the final eleventh grade of Polish-school study. Most stop attending after eighth grade due to sports or other activities or because they work on Saturdays.

There are also three consular schools, in New York, Los Angeles, and Chicago, which were established and continue to be subsidized by the Ministry of Education from Poland. Their curriculum and teachers are subject to the Ministry's guidelines and classes meet for five to six hours each Saturday. These schools wish to maintain a high level of Polish fluency so the children returning to Poland will have an easier time catching up with their peers after an extended period abroad.

Conclusions

It is difficult to predict whether Polish will be in the group of the top dozen languages other than English spoken in the USA in the 2010 Census. On the one hand, data presented by Stecuła (2007) show that the number of Poles in the USA has increased by one million between 2000 and 2005. It is not clear whether this increase is due to increased immigration, underreporting in the 2000 Census or other causes. On the other hand, the number of Polish speakers declined 8 percent between 1990 and 2000 and another 4 percent between 2000 and 2007 (US Census Bureau 2000a, 2007c). It seems unlikely that Poles will want to keep coming to settle in the USA in quite the same numbers as before, now that employment opportunities in Europe are so much greater and the Polish economy keeps improving. The gradual decline in the number of immigrants, combined with the well-attested general pattern of a lack of intergenerational transmission of minority languages in the USA, suggests that Polish-language maintenance will be difficult. To some extent this may be compensated by frequent travels to and from Poland for familial, educational, and business exchanges. The current system of Polish Saturday schools will serve the community well for another generation or two, but without new teachers and pupils coming from Poland, the schools will empty and slowly diminish in scope and quality. Polish governmental subsidies and professional assistance might have a positive influence on prolonging the existence of the Polish Saturday-school system, but it is unlikely that the Polish government will have sufficient resources for this; most of their current funding efforts seem to target Polish communities in Europe, such as those in Ukraine and Belarus. Youth organizations and community based groups such as Polish scouting, folkdance ensembles, sports clubs, etc., may play an important role in maintaining Polish by sponsoring exchange programs with their counterparts in Poland. In many ways this is a bittersweet moment in the history of Polish in the USA. Poland has "graduated" to the group of "first world" countries and its people no longer need to seek a home in the USA to improve their lot in life, while at the same time this decrease in new immigration will eventually diminish the presence of Polish in the multilingual mosaic that is the USA.

DISCUSSION QUESTIONS

1. How is the role of religious institutions in the maintenance of Polish similar to or different than the role of religious institutions in the maintenance of other languages in this volume, such as French or Korean?

2. Poland's admittance to the European Union has had (and, the authors predict, will continue to have) dramatic effects on the maintenance of Polish in the USA. Describe the principal ways in which this political change has both favored and disfavored Polish maintenance.

---

16 Language policy in the USA

Terrence G. Wiley

In recent years, public policy debates regarding language in the USA have centered largely on the acquisition of English and the extent to which speakers of "other" languages should be accommodated if they do not speak English. The focus on English dominates public discourse so much that even the mere suggestion by a presidential candidate that there are advantages for Americans in learning languages such as Spanish has been met with ridicule (Sidoti 2008), although the presence of Spanish in North America predates that of English (Chapter 4, this volume) and the USA is the fifth largest Spanish-speaking country in the world (González and Wiley 2007). In its history, the USA has had many policies related to language. Many educational policies at the state level focus on the promotion of English, which is certainly important because it is the dominant language that is necessary for social, economic, and political participation. But the issue of the value of promoting other languages is rarely addressed. Thus, the country lacks a comprehensive policy for the promotion of languages other than English. This chapter addresses the need for a comprehensive national language policy and what such a policy might look like.

Within the specific domain of foreign language education, advocates have long noted the absence of policy. Several decades ago Rose Lee Hayden (1979), for example, lamented the need for a national *foreign* language policy. She quipped that "The United States can be characterized as the land of the monolingual" to which the late Senator Paul Simon added, "we should erect a sign at every port of entry . . . [which proclaims] 'Welcome to the United States, we cannot speak your language'" (Simon 1988: 1). These cynical remarks were aimed at the monolingual majority and were meant to decry the dominance of the ideology of English monolingualism, which was duly noted by other scholars around the same time (e.g. Macías 1985). But the claim of "we cannot speak your language" was not demographically correct, then or now. Despite the ideological and numerical dominance of English monolingualism, the characterization of the USA as the "land of the monolingual" never has been true, as the collective work of contributors to this volume documents.

Table 16.1. *Increasing language diversity in the USA*

Year	1980	1990	2000	2006
Number of LOTE speakers (millions)	23.1	31.8	46.9	54.9
Percent of population	11	13.8	17.9	19.7

Sources: McArthur 1993:43; US Census 2000, Summary File 3, Table DP-2 as reported in Wiley 2005b; and US Census Bureau 2006b.

Even as Hayden and Simon decried the weakness of US foreign educational language policy, multilingualism has thrived among the general population. In 1980, for example, about 11 percent residents of the USA could speak a language other than English. Today nearly 20 percent do (Table 16.1). Thus, there is a gap between the discursive construction of the USA as a monolingual nation and demographic reality.

The present volume provides a refreshing focus on our increasing multilingualism, and it provides a welcome closer look at some of the major languages used in this country. Multilingualism is a natural phenomenon throughout the planet and country, despite the imagined homogeneity dreamed of by some. Cultural assimilationists, for example, in many countries have long argued the benefits of monolingualism (see Kloss 1971; Wiley and Lukes 1996; Schmidt 2000 for discussion). Even though many countries have attempted to construct a national identity around one or more common languages, language diversity prevails. This is manifested by the plurality of languages, even in those countries with language academies that attempt to regulate and standardize national languages.

During the British colonial period, English achieved sufficient status to become the dominant language (Heath 1976). Thus, at the time of the founding of the republic, the USA had no need for an official language. The attempt to promote a standard "American" English language was the work of language strategists such as Noah Webster, who attempted to define and prescribe an *American language* that would be as distinct as possible from that of the English. He succeeded in regulating the spelling of much of American English; nevertheless, he failed to achieve his second goal, which was to eradicate regional and social dialects (Weinstein 1979, 1983; Lepore 2002; Wiley 2007a). Varieties of English persist, and other languages are widely spoken. Despite this, English has never been threatened, because most of those who speak other languages also speak English. Thus, to the extent that the country needs a comprehensive language policy, it is in need of one based on the demographic reality of multilingualism and the value of promoting not only English, but languages generally.

The value of case studies in developing a comprehensive national language policy

Case studies such as those in this volume, which are focused on specific languages and their speakers, provide an important starting point for thinking about a comprehensive language policy. Baseline and background information, such as that provided in these chapters, with reference to the history, demographics, and the public presence of languages in the government, media, businesses, and education, offer important lenses through which the linguistic vitality of languages and prospects for their maintenance and promotion can be assessed (Wiley 1999, 2003). The contributors herein demonstrate that there is very strong evidence for an *American bilingual tradition*, as Kloss (1998) previously proclaimed; perhaps more accurately, there continues to be evidence for an *American multilingual tradition*. Again, to the extent that the USA needs a comprehensive language policy, it needs to be predicated on that multilingual reality.

A comprehensive language policy would need to recognize that languages have different histories and functions. Historical and contemporary classification of languages and their speakers in the USA can be problematic (Wiley 2001). The dominant paradigm for this volume (with the exception of Chapter 3 on Native American languages) sees immigration as the principal source of language diversity. With this focus, we should remember that English too has been a major language of immigration, supported by immigration policies that between 1923 and 1965 were particularly favorable to the UK, Canada, and Western European countries. Thus, immigration helps to explain the dominance of English as well as the presence of non-English languages.

Even as immigration is a primary focus of this volume, it is also useful to complicate the focus by considering that major immigrant languages are not just the languages of immigrants. Languages such as Spanish (see Chapter 4) and French (Chapter 7) require multiple categories to determine their status and functions in time and place. Spanish and French, for example, are both *old colonial languages* (Molesky 1988), but they were also *indigenized* by native, colonial, and blended populations of the Americas and the Caribbean. Spanish and French are thus indigenous to many areas that ultimately became the present-day USA. Language minority peoples were incorporated into the USA not only through immigration, but also as a result of territorial expansion accomplished by means of purchase, annexation, and military conquest (Macías 2000; Wiley 2007a, 2007b). French can be multiply categorized as an old colonial, indigenized, and/or immigrant language, but it also can be the second or third language of immigrants from Vietnam, where it was a former colonial language. Similarly, Japanese is often a second language of elderly Taiwanese and Korean immigrants, who learned it under Japanese colonial rule. French also has creolized varieties such as Cajun and Haitian French, for example, as a result of language contact. Tagalog (see Chapter 6) was an indigenous language of the Philippines when it was colonized by the USA. Later, it was promoted as a national language in the Philippines under Marcos. For many Filipinos it is a second language, as they are likely to be speakers of Ilocano or numerous other languages. Also, Filipinos may or may not (based largely on their age) have acquired literacy in Tagalog. Perhaps, in the US context, Tagalog can be understood – based on time, status, function, and place – in several contexts: as a former indigenous, postcolonial national, and/or immigrant first or second language.

These examples demonstrate the importance of focusing on native language(s) *and* societal multilingualism in telling the stories of the people associated with a primary language minority group. The linguistic histories of people before they were incorporated through immigration, annexation, or conquest are often complex. Just as the USA should not be viewed as a monolingual English-speaking nation, neither should members of language minority communities *only* be viewed through the lens of immigration and bilingualism. Thus, a comprehensive educational language policy needs to embrace societal multilingualism as normative (Agnihotri 2007).

The challenges of language shift and loss

For advocates of maintaining and promoting heritage and community languages, the evidence cited by the contributors to this volume regarding language shift and loss is not encouraging. A number of language loss/shift studies have involved large data set analyses. Several of the authors in this collection, for example, have cited Veltman (2000), who contends that, "the rates of language shift to English are so high that all minority languages are routinely abandoned, depriving the United States of one type of human resource that may be economically and politically desirable both to maintain and develop" (p. 58). These conclusions are in line with findings from his previous studies (Veltman 1983, 1988). Further evidence of shift and loss have been noted by Portes and Rumbaut's (2001, 2005, 2006) longitudinal study of immigrants in San Diego and Miami, which also indicates rapid loss of minority languages and shift to English. Other studies, such as those done by López (1978) and more recently by the Pew Hispanic Center (2004), have reached similar conclusions. As Rumbaut (2009) notes, however, "a limitation of all those recent studies is that they are cross-sectional – that is, they are snapshots taken at one point in time, but do not follow specific individuals over time to ascertain the dynamics of acculturation and of bilingualism as they take place within a generation" (p. 10). To address this deficiency, he and his colleagues have undertaken and analyzed data from intergenerational longitudinal studies.

Table 16.2. *Non-English language use, proficiency, and preference, by generation cohort, greater Los Angeles, 2004*

Detailed generational cohorts	Growing up spoke a non-English language at home (%)	Speaks non-English language very well (%)	Prefers to speak English only at home (%)	*N*
1.0 generation (arrived 13 or older)	97.4	86.9	17.7	256
1.5 generation (arrive 0–12)	92.9	46.6	60.7	1,491
2.0 generation (2 foreign-born parents)	83.5	36.1	73.4	1,390
2.5 generation (1 foreign-born parent)	46.5	17.3	92.5	428
3.0 generation (3–4 foreign-born grandparents)	34.3	11.9	97.0	67
3.5 generation (1–2 foreign-born grandparents)	18.7	3.1	98.3	289
4+ generation (0 foreign-born grandparents)	10.4	2.0	99.0	859
Total	65.8	31.5	70.8	4,780

Source: Rumbaut *et al.* 2008

The Children of Immigrants Longitudinal Study (CILS) followed immigrant youth for over a decade. It focused on several dozen immigrant nationalities that had settled in San Diego and the Miami and Fort Lauderdale metropolitan areas. Over 5,000 youth were followed in the combined samples. Results from a second study, the *Immigration and Intergenerational Mobility in Metropolitan Los Angeles* (IIMMLA) survey, were compared. The IIMMLA collected similar data to that of the CILS on language and education from nearly 5,000 respondents in their 20s and 30s in southern California in the greater Los Angeles area. It surveyed youth across the 1.5 and second generations as well as the third, fourth, and later generations (Rumbaut, 2009). Based on Rumbaut's (in press) analysis of both these surveys, the analysis confirmed immigrant language loss by the third generation, as Table 16.2 illustrates. McCarty (Chapter 3, this volume), likewise presents dramatic evidence of the loss of indigenous languages.

Given the extent of language diversity in the USA, both immigrant and indigenous, a major question arises: Why has the loss of language been so rapid? Why, in the past, were some groups more likely to retain their languages longer than others? The case studies of languages in this volume suggest some of the answers we need to inform the development of policies that encourage language maintenance. There are numerous reasons for language shift, historically and presently, not the least of which relate to the dominance of English in this society. Most public and private education is mediated through English, and English facilitates economic and political access and social mobility. Nevertheless, other historical, contextual, and educational language policy factors need to be carefully examined to explain the rapidity of language shift and its implications for a comprehensive national language policy that would value and promote languages (Wiley 1999, 2003; Macías 2000).

Explaining language shift in the light of history

For each immigrant and indigenous ethnolinguistic group, we may ask: What was the *initial mode of incorporation*, and what was the *subsequent disposition* of the dominant majority population toward the language minority group that influenced each group's disposition toward the acquisition of English and retention of their heritage or community language(s)? And, *what efforts have the minority group made* on their own in spite of the disposition of the majority? The answers to these questions are group specific and have been addressed to some extent in this volume. An additional issue relates to the historical and contemporary policy context to which these questions also relate.

One of the first historians to systematically focus on language policies and their impact on minority bilingualism was Heinz Kloss. Kloss is a problematic figure because he began his work in Germany under Nazi state sponsorship during the 1930s, but in the post-World War II context, he championed language rights as a fundamental human right (regarding these concerns, see Hutton 1999; Wiley 2002). His work is referenced here because his extensive historical analyses have generally been considered foundational reading in understanding the history of US language policies and have been widely cited by American scholars. Kloss tended to focus on *official* policies or language-related laws that affected European immigrant groups and hypothesized about how they affected the continued use of native immigrant tongues. After a major historical review, he came to two major conclusions: First, there has always been an important minority tradition in the use of immigrant languages, which he called the *American bilingual tradition*. Second, with the exception of the World War I period, he argued that there generally has been a climate of tolerance toward immigrant language minorities; thus, language shift to English is the result of its so-called *absorbing power*. Certainly language minorities have always seen the utility of learning English, as it allows access to greater social, economic, and political participation, but there are definitely benefits to bi/multilingualism.

Although Kloss' cataloging of language policies is of value in helping us to understand the history of "official" policies, his notion of *absorbing power* was not explicated, and thus, explains little beyond the obvious fact that English is useful.

Language beliefs, ideologies, policies, practices and their connection to relations of status, legitimacy, and power all weigh on the language choices made by individuals and communities (Tollefson 1991, 1995, 2002). In social perception and popular discourse there are often connections between language, race, class, and national origin. Language differences may become the focal point or surrogate for societal competition and conflicts (Leibowitz 1969, 1971, 1974, 1976; Tatalovich 1995). Thus, it is important to note that when Kloss drew the conclusion that the policy climate toward the maintenance of minority languages was generally favorable, he made a distinction between what he termed *racial* laws and *language* laws. By so doing he failed to make the connection between language as a maker of, or surrogate for, race and ethnicity (Macías and Wiley 1998). Even though Kloss' work has been important in affirming a longstanding minority bilingual tradition in the USA, we also need to consider ways in which the flowering of that tradition has been thwarted by the ideological dominance of English monolingualism and often restrictive language policies and practices, which Kloss interpreted as being atypical.

If we focus on ethnic and racial minorities, who are often also language minorities, the alleged tradition of language tolerance has many exceptions that have influenced language loss and shift. We often forget that among the first language policies in the British colonies, which eventually became the USA, African languages were repressed and English illiteracy was compulsory (Weinberg 1995; Wiley 2005b). Language tolerance for native Americans ended with forced language shift as implemented through the boarding-school movement of 1880s–1930s (Chapter 3, this volume; McCarty 2004; McCarty and Watahomigie 2004). And, despite initial tolerance toward Hawaiian, it became restricted during the late nineteenth century when Hawaii was forced to submit to US control (Benham and Heck 1998). There was likewise general tolerance toward Spanish in the early histories of the formerly Spanish and Mexican territories, but Spanish became increasingly restricted after World War I through the 1960s (Hernández-Chávez 1994; Schiffman 1996; Macías 2000; Blanton 2004), and there are similar efforts to restrict the language today. In terms of tolerance toward European languages, a number of scholars have noted that the Americanization movement of the World War I period represented a major turning point toward European and other newer immigrant languages (Leibowitz 1969, 1971, 1982; Tamura 1993; Tatalovich 1995; Wiley 1998, 2000, 2004, 2007b; Pavlenko 2002).

The fate of German in the USA (Chapter 9, this volume) has sometimes been cited as the major case for the inevitability of language shift (e.g. Veltman

2000). During the late nineteenth and early twentieth centuries, German seemed to benefit from circumstances that were promising for language maintenance even though Germans were rapidly acquiring English. There was a steady supply of immigrants, German was used widely in churches and schools, and many German newspapers thrived. Within a century, however, German had declined significantly. As Veltman (2000: 60) notes, in the 1990 Census, of the "Americans who reported their ethnic ancestry, 58 million people claimed German ancestry in whole or part, whereas German was only spoken by 1.5 million people." Certainly, the fact that most people with German heritage no longer speak German represents a remarkable shift.

Again, however, particularly in the case of German, it is necessary to consider the historical, social, political, ideological, and policy contexts in order to explain not only the necessities and motivations for the acquisition of English, but also those factors that have worked against the retention of the language. Thus, German provides a major case in point regarding the impact of linguistic intolerance and restrictive policies. German thrived in the USA well into the twentieth century. Until World War I, the language was used widely in public and private schools, there were churches and local newspapers, and nearly one quarter of American high school students studied the language. But World War I and the gradual siding of the USA against Germany brought widespread xenophobia and a far reaching attack on all things German, especially the German language. By the war's end, German foreign language requirements for college had been dropped by most high schools, some university German-language departments were closed down, and German and/or foreign languages generally were restricted in elementary and/or middle schools by thirty-four states. German enrollments plunged from 324,000 high school students in 1915 to fewer than 14,000 by 1922 (Leibowitz 1971; Wiley 1998; Pavlenko 2002).

Not only was there a decline in the public use of German and other languages, but there was also a marked decline in the number of those who declared German ancestry in the 1920 US Census. Thus, it is important to note that even the accuracy of Census data can be affected by the general policy and ideological climate that the majority displays toward the minority (Wiley 1998). Interest in German never recovered from being stigmatized in World War I, and World War II drove the nail into its coffin. Other European and Asian languages were likewise greatly affected by the Americanization movement and the attack on German (Tamura 1993).

As the second major language of the USA, the situation of Spanish is somewhat demographically analogous to that of German a century ago. However, following several decades in which the federal government allowed the use of transitional bilingual education to accommodate mostly Spanish-speaking minority students, the country is now experiencing a return to the restrictive policy climate of the World War I era toward the use of heritage and community languages. This is evidenced by California's passage of Proposition 227, Arizona's Proposition 203, and Massachusetts' Question 2. Moreover, with the passage of the No Child Left Behind Act 2001 (NCLB) (Public Law 107–110), the federal policy climate for language minority students has changed significantly. Although NCLB does not ban bilingual education, any reference to "bilingual" disappeared from the legislation. According to García (2005), this represents a calculated change in discourse in which the new emphasis is only focused on the acquisition of English. The former Office of Bilingual Education and Minority Language Affairs (OBEMLA), for example, has become the Office of English Language Acquisition, Language Enhancement, and Academic Achievement (OELA). Similarly, the former National Clearinghouse on Bilingual Education (NCBE) was renamed the National Clearinghouse for English Language Acquisition (NCELA) (García 2005). Byrnes (2005) also notes that NCLB fails to promote foreign language education. Thus, as Wright (2007) has concluded, because federal educational policy fails to support the promotion of languages other than English, the burden of promoting heritage and community languages largely falls on language minority communities themselves.

A mixed bag of language policies

Much of the conflict regarding language policies results from a confusion regarding their goals and purposes. In his classic work *The American Bilingual Tradition*, Kloss (1998) attempted to categorize various types of official language laws and policies. As previously noted, he focused only on official policies and failed to understand how language laws can be manipulated as surrogates for racial laws (Macías and Wiley 1998; Wiley 2002). Subsequently, many scholars have noted that school and institutional *practices* regulating language use can likewise have the force of policy (Haas 1992; Corson 1999a, 1999b). Moreover, there can be *implicit* or *covert* policies that on the surface do not appear to be language policies but that may also regulate language behavior (Macías and Wiley 1998; Wiley 2004; Shohamy 2006). Thus, it is necessary to go beyond Kloss' original attempt to classify "formal" language policies by additionally analyzing informal, implicit, and tacit policies. The five major types of policies include (1) promotion-oriented; (2) accommodation/expediency-oriented; (3) tolerance-oriented; (4) restriction-oriented; and (5) repression-oriented policies (Wiley 2004).

Promotion-oriented policies imply the use of resources to further the use of a language or languages. English has generally been promoted as the primary language of schooling, and most governmental business is conducted through it. Occasionally, the government has put resources into promoting the study of foreign languages such as Arabic (Chapter 13, this volume) and Chinese

(Chapter 5, this volume), but only for "strategic" purposes (Wiley 2007b, 2007c; Bale 2008) rather than to promote them as languages of wider communication. In recent years, the federal government has given some endorsement to the preservation of native languages (Chapter 3, this volume), but, again, this is not promoting them for wider use outside of the community.

Accommodation policies (also known as expediency-oriented laws; *cf.* Kloss 1998) differ from promotion-oriented policies because they are not intended to advance the use of a minority language. In the USA there has been resistance to the use of other languages even for the purpose of accommodation. In some states, such as Alabama, bilingual driver's license testing has been prohibited. Some advocates of English-only policies argue that accommodation policies "coddle" minorities and, thereby, remove incentives to learn English. What is often not understood is that accommodation is intended to be a two-way street; it allows the government to communicate with those who do not speak English to promote compliance with laws and to facilitate such things as collecting tax revenue. Accommodation also ensures basic human and civil rights by facilitating access to education, voting, employment opportunities and legal protections through, for example, court interpretation (for example, see the reference to New York City's Executive Order 120 in Chapter 1 of this volume). Ironically, much of the controversy regarding bilingual education in recent years has been based on a confusion of accommodation with promotion.

Tolerance-oriented policies reflect the absence of governmental interference in the linguistic life of people. The preservation and use of minority languages is left to the members of the community themselves without any expectation that the government will provide support. As noted previously, currently and historically, US policies have demonstrated both tolerance and restrictionism toward minority languages. Restrictive language policies are those that constrain or disallow the use or teaching of certain languages. As previously noted, in the early twentieth century US immigration surged and xenophobia became widespread. Americanization indoctrination taught immigrants and their children that their ability to speak another language was cause for shame rather than pride. There was no appreciation that "they had a resource important to them personally and important to the nation [and] . . . the ideology of Americanization created this unusual, deep-seated phenomenon: a historical cultural barrier to the learning of another language in a land of great ethnic diversity" (Simon 1988: 12).

In the early twentieth century, the constitutionality of restrictive policies was challenged in two important US Supreme Court cases. The intention behind these restrictions was to thwart immigrant "foreign" language education during the years that children could best retain and develop their home languages. The Court's decisive ruling in the 1923 case of *Meyer* v. *Nebraska*, 262 US

390 (1923), held that states could not constitutionally prohibit the teaching of foreign languages to grade-school children. However, the *Meyer* ruling also affirmed the priority of English-medium instruction. During the 1920s, Chinese, Japanese, and Korean community language schools all became targets of restrictionism in Hawaii and California, similarly to what happened to German-language education across the nation (Leibowitz 1971; Tamura 1993). In the then territory of Hawaii, Governor Farrington targeted supplemental community-based language education. At first, he succeeded in the lower courts, but basing its decision on *Meyer*, the US Supreme Court in *Farrington* v. *Tokushige*, 273 US 284, 298 (1927) ruled that the governor could not prohibit community schools that teach "foreign" languages. *Farrington* v. *Tokushige* has significance for heritage and community-based education today because, as we have seen in this volume, communities are usually the prime movers in promoting languages other than English.

Finally, repression-oriented policies attempt to eradicate minority languages. The distinction between restrictive and repressive policies is one of degree. Repressive policies seek linguistic and cultural assimilation through deculturation and linguistic genocide. As noted above, the cases of enslaved Africans, through much of the colonial period until the end of the US Civil War, as well as that of Native-Americans, provide the most extreme examples of repressive polices. Enslaved Africans were prohibited from using their native languages and had to endure compulsory illiteracy laws, whereas Native-Americans experienced a half-century of language eradication efforts in boarding schools that resulted in devastating consequences as noted in Chapter 3 in this volume (see also Hernández-Chávez 1994; Spring 1994; Weinberg 1995; Baugh 1999).

In summary, throughout much of US history the major language-policy orientations have generally shifted between tolerance and restriction. The two major Supreme Court cases, *Meyer* v. *Nebraska* and *Farrington* v. *Tokushige*, have provided some relief from extreme restrictionism and allowed minority languages to be taught and promoted through private and community efforts. In recent years, however, some states have drifted back to restrictive policies, and English-only laws have been imposed in some workplace contexts. On the other hand, the federal government has stopped short of passing a nationwide English-only directive, and it has recognized the need to accommodate language minorities to ensure basic needs and civil rights protections, as well as the pragmatic need to promote some foreign language instruction for "strategic" purposes. Moreover, it has also provided some endorsement of Native language preservation, partly to redress its former repressive policies against Native peoples. Thus, the historical and contemporary landscape represents a mixed bag of tolerance-oriented and restrictive-oriented policies, thereby underscoring the need to develop a new comprehensive policy that both protects and promotes languages.

Toward a national language policy that embraces societal multilingualism

In many states, policy options have been presented to voters as false dichotomies, as if people must choose between native and ancestral tongues or English. Despite overwhelming evidence to the contrary, voters have been persuaded that English is under threat, so voter-approved efforts to restrict the use of native languages in bilingual education have been successful in California, Massachusetts, and Arizona. In the past, there have also been separate policy agendas for promoting English as a second language, bilingual education, and foreign language education. Thus, the need for a "comprehensive" national policy to promote languages is not new, but the discussion about language policy in the USA has rarely been framed comprehensively. In recent years, the movement to promote heritage and community language education has caught the attention of foreign language educators, who have increasingly had heritage speakers enrolled in traditional foreign language instruction. Over the past decade, there has been increasing recognition that heritage learners have both resources and special needs when engaged in formal study of their language (Kagan and Dillon, this volume; Valdés 2001; Wiley 2005a, 2007c, 2007d; Peyton *et al.* 2008). McGinnis (2005b) has also noted that in the teaching of some languages such as Chinese, community-based efforts have in certain respects been ahead of K-12 and university efforts. Accordingly, he has called for closer educational co-ordination and planning among these stakeholders. Increasing connections are now being made between foreign-language education and heritage language and community education, which now provide an opportunity to consider educational language policy more comprehensively. For example, several states now grant high school foreign-language credit for study in community heritage-language programs (ACTFL 2008).

Despite the evidence presented in a previous section related to language shift, there are other reasons for optimism. A number of surveys of language minority parents have demonstrated strong support for both bilingual and community-language education in Spanish, Chinese, Korean, and indigenous languages, when parents have the opportunity to choose them (see Chapter 3, this volume; Krashin 1996; Wiley 2005b; Wiley *et al.* 2008; Rumbaut, 2009), and many of the contributors to this volume have pointed to positive examples where community programs are demonstrating promising results. Thus, there is support within the communities themselves for the promotion of heritage and community languages. Again, what has been missing is a more comprehensive policy that links together those interested in the promotion of languages.

If we are to contemplate possibilities beyond the legacy of restrictive policies, what might a policy aimed at tapping and promoting the multilingual resources of the USA entail? Scholars have been giving this question serious consideration, especially given the demise of Title VII sponsored bilingual education (see Crawford 2007; González 2007). A number of perspectives have been offered. Spolsky's (2001, 2002b) suggestions are offered here as examples of principles to stimulate discussion for drafting a comprehensive language policy.

National Policy Statement on Heritage Language Development in the USA: Principles toward an agenda for action

(1) The development of policies that ensure there is no linguistic discrimination.
(2) The provision of adequate programs for the teaching of English to all.
(3) The development of respect for both plurilingual capacity and . . . diverse individual languages.
(4) The development of approaches that enhance the status and enrich the knowledge of heritage language and community languages.
(5) The development of a multibranched language-capacity program that strengthens and integrates a variety of language programs that assures the heritage programs connect with advanced training programs; builds on heritage, immersion and overseas-experience approaches to constantly replenish a cadre of efficient plurilingual citizens capable of professional work using their plurilingual skills; and provides rich and satisfying language programs that lead to a plurilingual population with knowledge of and respect for other languages and cultures.

Adapted from: Spolsky (2001)

The first two principles are closely linked. Regarding no linguistic discrimination, Macías (1979) has noted that there are two basic linguistic rights: the first is fundamentally the right to freedom from discrimination on the basis of language; the second is a right to language. Freedom from discrimination implies the need for policies of linguistic accommodation when language becomes a barrier to basic services and civil and human rights. Spolsky (2002b, 2004) has noted that in the USA, a good example of this is Executive Order (EO) 13166, which is entitled "Improving access to services for persons with limited English proficiency." Its purpose was to accommodate language minority individuals with translation services in places such as courts and hospitals. It is important to note, however, that EO 13166 is an executive order that can be rescinded; unfortunately, it does not have the same force as a constitutional right. This is a policy of linguistic accommodation rather than promotion.

The second principle, adequate instruction in English for all, is likewise related to freedom from discrimination because access to the dominant common language is necessary for social, economic, and political participation. This is both a policy of accommodation for language minorities and a policy of English promotion. Spolsky (2002b) has noted that by dropping bilingual education as a form of accommodation, NCLB has weakened the range of options for accommodation by not using the mother tongue.

Concerning "respect for both plurilingual capacity and diverse individual languages," Spolsky (2002b) and others (e.g. Crawford 2007; González 2007) have noted that the demise of the Bilingual Education Act has also reduced our capacity in this regard. Byrnes (2005) has similarly noted that NCLB's lack of emphasis on foreign language instruction likewise weakened the capacity to promote multilingualism; thus, considerable work is needed to reverse these negative policy trends. In particular, a new comprehensive policy initiative is needed that connects heritage language education with bilingual education, foreign language education, and Native language preservation.

The fourth principle addresses the need to "promote the status and enrich the knowledge of heritage language and community languages." Here promotion may be seen either as internal to language communities or aimed at promoting languages more widely. As Ruiz (1995) has noted, a distinction can be made among *endoglossic* policies that "are those that give primacy to, and promote an indigenous language of the community" (p. 75), *exoglossic* policies for the promotion of languages intended for wider communication, and *mixed* language policies, which would be applied differently depending on the disposition of the group toward its language. In the USA, indigenous language promotion efforts tend to be endoglossic, to promote language use mostly within the community. Some immigrant languages also tend not to be promoted as languages of wider communication, although they are valued by the community (see, for example, Chapter 6 on Tagalog in this volume). Thus, when considering policies aimed at status planning, it is important to consider the community's perspective about whether the intent is to promote the language within the community, or more broadly.

The fifth principle, which calls for the "building of a multibranched language-capacity network" to strengthen and integrate a variety of language programs, is the most ambitious and also the most needed. Again, this principle involves the development of a comprehensive language policy that could link communities with K-12 educational programs, and K-12 programs with university efforts. Such an agenda would require that schools and universities in population centers with high-density language minority populations partner in efforts to provide continuity between community-based instruction and that in schools and universities. Such linkages could also help to build community capacity in teacher training. Teacher training in the USA has largely been focused on English as a second language or generic bilingual education programs that sometimes default to a focus on Spanish. An emphasis on Spanish is necessary, given its position as the second major language of the USA, but there is also a need to develop awareness of languages more broadly in teacher training (Wiley 2008). University teacher training efforts are typically aimed at meeting state credentialing requirements; however, a few universities have also attempted to support community-based teacher training by developing programs for non-professional teachers who work in community-based programs, and there is much more that could be done (Pu 2008).

There are additional opportunities to develop more community-responsive programs. One, for example, is to create specially designed state certification programs for less commonly taught languages. Efforts in some states are far ahead of others in developing certificates for these languages. In addition, as Potowski and Carreira (2004) note, there is a need for official recognition of the special needs of heritage language learners in the form of state endorsements or credentials in *heritage* language teaching as differentiated from *foreign* language teaching. As Spolsky (2002b) has also noted, it is also possible to link language immersion programs and heritage programs to advanced training programs and overseas immersion experiences to enhance societal multilingual capacity and promote respect for languages and cultures. Although the pieces of such an approach exist, as Spolsky has observed, there is no overarching policy framework that links them together. Attempting to link them together necessitates engaging language minority communities to ensure that efforts to assist are not imposed, but are negotiated in a manner that is community-responsive. For most of the languages surveyed in this volume, formalized school-based curricula may be appropriate. Learners' prior educational experiences with their native languages may prove helpful in placing students into programs that are sensitive to their heritage language knowledge and abilities (Chapter 11, this volume). For those languages and dialects that have not traditionally been used as media of instruction, however, it may also be necessary to ensure that they are not merely morphed into academic languages that appear alien to their everyday lives (Action and Dalphinis 2000; Mercurio and Scarino 2005; Wiley 2005c). As Hakuta (1986: 229) noted: "Perhaps the rosiest future for bilingual education in the United States can be attained by dissolving the paradoxical attitude of admiration and pride for school-attained bilingualism on the one hand and scorn and shame for home-brewed immigrant bilinguals on the other."

Spolsky's principles provide a good starting point for a focused dialogue about developing a comprehensive national language policy. As McCarty (Chapter 3, this volume) and Ruíz (1995) have noted, however, the federal government has not always been a reliable partner and much of the effort has fallen on the communities themselves to form their own policies for practice.

In this regard, Spolsky (2002b) proposed an additional set of considerations that communities and parents need to consider if they are to provide the agency needed for heritage language preservation and development.

Principles for a language policy for a heritage language community in the USA

- The community recognizes the importance of plurilingual competence in its members.
- It supports programs that assure that everyone can develop full control of English for access to educational, economic, social, and cultural development.
- It supports efforts to assure that everyone can develop a high level of proficiency in the community language for the maintenance of tradition and culture. This involves:
  - raising children bilingually,
  - providing opportunities for developing oral and literacy skills in both languages,
  - ensuring the use of the community language in public domains as well as private,
  - assisting in the maintenance and cultivation of the community language,
  - providing ways of passing traditional language and culture between the generations,
  - providing community schools,
  - persuading public schools to respect and support community language maintenance,
  - encouraging and respecting efforts by other language groups to do the same.

(adapted from Spolsky 2001)

The strong involvement of parents and communities is a necessary ingredient in developing a comprehensive language policy. It is important to recognize, however, that this set of principles should not be seen as a top-down mandate, but rather as a guide for engagement and discussion. Promoting heritage languages requires what Hornberger (1996) has called bottom-up planning, as well as the community responsiveness urged by Corson (1999b), May (1999), McCarty and Watahomigie (1999), and McCarty (Chapter 3, this volume). It necessitates dialoging, negotiating roles, and working directly within the priorities of the communities themselves. There is an important role to play for universities and K-12 schools, and, hopefully, enlightened federal and state governments in supporting and linking with community-based programs, but that role must be negotiated, not imposed. There is much that we can accomplish together, if we get beyond the myth that this is the land of the monolingual.

DISCUSSION QUESTIONS

1. Make a chart listing each of Wiley's five types of language policies, along with its definition and an example. Does this categorization seem accurate? Can you think of a policy that spans more than one category? Then, choose a language profiled in one of the chapters of this book, and examine the language policies that have affected it in light of Wiley's typology. How can each policy be categorized? Why do certain types of policy predominate?

2. Hakuta (1986: 229) argues that "[p]erhaps the rosiest future for bilingual education in the United States can be attained by dissolving the paradoxical attitude of admiration and pride for school-attained bilingualism on the one hand and scorn and shame for home-brewed immigrant bilinguals on the other." Can these attitudes be changed? If so, what are some specific steps that could be taken by government or community groups? Be sure to consider Spolsky's (2001) "Principles for a language policy for a heritage language community."

Notes

NOTES ON CHAPTER 1

1 With thanks to Scott McGinnis
2 Bills proposed in Congress can be searched at http://thomas.loc.gov.
3 Hawaiian was declared a co-official language in Hawaii in 1978. In Louisiana, English and French are both legally recognized, although there is no official state language. New Mexico was declared "English plus" in 1989, with Spanish as the *de facto* second language.
4 This report states the following: "The pace of recent US economic growth would have been impossible without immigration. Since 1990, immigrants have contributed to job growth in three main ways: They fill an increasing share of jobs overall, they take jobs in labor-scarce regions, and they fill the types of jobs that native workers often shun. The foreign-born make up only 11.3 percent of the US population and 14 percent of the labor force. But amazingly, the flow of foreign-born is so large that immigrants currently account for a larger share of labor force growth than natives" (p. 16).
5 They also found that among the native-born in the USA, proficiency in an immigrant language in addition to English was associated with lower earnings. However, this is contradicted in the findings of Boswell (2000) in several major US cities that, among Hispanics, bilingualism in Spanish was associated with higher earnings than English monolingualism.
6 We accept Ruíz's framework, although Urcioli (2001) argues that "there is a false dichotomy between 'diversity-as-a-wonderful-garden' and 'diversity-as-polluting-and-dangerous.' It is false because it positions language as a 'thing' in a neat package that maps neatly onto ethnic, regional, racial, or national types of people." These debates have such teeth because "people can't leave them alone: they feel compelled to take and defend positions because these are not debates about language so much as they are about being 'American.' Hence the moral edge" (p. 191).
7 Of these, 176 are indigenous Native American languages.
8 This increase was not due to any significant change in the total number of non-citizen legal permanent residents, which was 11.8 million in 2005 and 11.5 million in 1995. Also, the number of unauthorized immigrants grew from 20% to 31% of the foreign-born between 1995 and 2005, so this ten-year period saw a growth "among both the most and the least rooted of immigrants" (Passel 2007).
9 As this chapter has sought to explain, there is a connection between immigration and language diversity. However, this book focuses on language issues and thus does

not describe in detail the deplorable problems faced by many immigrants, such as workplace abuse, factory raids, and immigrant-targeted homicides.

10 The EEOC stipulates that an employer can impose an English-only rule solely when necessary for conducting business.

11 Of related interest are groups that seek to promote linguistic diversity worldwide, such as Enduring Voices and Living Tongues.

12 More specifically, 24% of public elementary schools and 53% of private elementary schools offered foreign languages. It is notable that twice as many private schools offer foreign languages, reflecting the notion of foreign language study as more of an elitist pursuit.

13 Article 2 states thus: "Persons belonging to national or ethnic, religious and linguistic minorities . . . have the right to enjoy their own culture, to profess and practice their own religion, and to use their own language, in private and in public, freely and without interference or any form of discrimination."

14 For example, much has been written about African American Vernacular English (e.g. Smitherman 1977; Rickford 1999; Wolfram 1990, and others), which unfortunately falls outside the scope of this volume.

NOTES ON CHAPTER 3

1 Political incorporation into the USA has been different for American Indians, Alaska Natives, and Native Hawaiians, and among American Indian tribes themselves. The sovereignty of some tribes is recognized by states but not by the federal government; some tribes are not recognized either by states or the federal government. Native Hawaiians, whose internationally recognized sovereign kingdom was illegally overthrown by the US government in 1893 and who were officially incorporated into the USA upon Hawaiian statehood in 1959, are still fighting for federal recognition. The experience of Alaska Natives, who include American Indians and Aleut, Inupiat, and Yup'ik peoples, is different still. Nonetheless, all Native-Americans share a distinct status as Indigenous peoples and a singular legal–political relationship with the US government.

2 The US Census Bureau recognized Native Hawaiian homelands for the first time in 2000. In 1920, Congress established homelands using former government lands. At Hawaiian statehood, the federal government turned the administration of these lands over to the state, with one purpose being the betterment of those of 50 percent or more Native Hawaiian "blood" (individuals with at least one parent of Native Hawaiian descent). Unlike reservations, which are tribal lands held in trust by the federal government for tribal use, Hawaiian homelands are state-owned tracts of land leased to Native Hawaiians for state-authorized activity (US Census Bureau 2001a: 9).

3 Unlike the other languages examined in this volume, which are primarily languages of immigrant groups, the unique position of Native languages in US society, including the historical and political factors outlined above and the widely varying situations among the 175 Indigenous languages still spoken in the USA, does not lend itself well to the "Signs of shift"/"Signs of maintenance" dichotomy adopted elsewhere. As such, this section is slightly different in format from that of the other chapters.

NOTES ON CHAPTER 4

1 As shown in Table 4.2, Puerto Ricans are the second largest group of US Spanish speakers, but Puerto Rico is not included here because it is part of the USA.
2 There is, however, a considerable degree of undercounting in the Census, particularly of undocumented immigrants. For example, Lowell and Suro (2002) reported that there are 4.5 million undocumented Mexicans in the USA.
3 It is usually assumed that new immigrants revitalize the use of a minority language among US-born heritage speakers, but little empirical evidence has been collected about the degree of contact between these groups. For example, in Chicago, Gorman and Potowski (2009) found that less than 50% of second- and third-generation Latinos interact regularly with newly arrived Spanish-speaking immigrants, and less than 20% did so on a daily basis. It may be that frequent and prolonged periods of travel to Latin America do more to promote Spanish proficiency than does contact with new immigrants to the USA.
4 Several volumes have focused on Spanish in the USA including Elías-Olivares, Leone, Cisneros, and Gutiérrez (1985); Bergen (1990); Roca and Lipski (1993); Silva-Corvalán (1995); Roca (2000); Ortiz López and Lacorte (2005); Potowski and Cameron (2007); and Lipski (2008).
5 However, Alba *et al.* (2002) found that Spanish speakers are shifting to English at a slower rate than are Chinese speakers. Third generation Chinese speakers in that study were predominately English monolinguals, while fewer third generation Spanish speakers were.

NOTE ON CHAPTER 5

1 *Two-way* or *dual* immersion programs in the USA enroll children who are both foreign language learners and heritage speakers of the non-English language, and teach in both languages for significant parts of the school day.

NOTE ON CHAPTER 6

1 Filipinos are actually often *trilingual* in Tagalog, another Philippine language, and English, although like most heritage speakers, they often do not develop age-appropriate levels of literacy, vocabulary, and grammatical systems in their non-English languages.

NOTES ON CHAPTER 7

1 Note that these figures do not include French creoles, such as Haitian and Louisiana creoles, nor do they include what the Census calls "Patois" and "Cajun." Were these varieties included in the count, French would be the third most common non-English language with 1,984,824 speakers.
2 The term standard French refers to an idealized prestige variety of the language. It is based on the formal speech of educated and/or upper middle class Parisian speakers. In North American, especially Louisiana, it is termed International French.
3 During the colonial period, Saint-Domingue was the name given to the French-controlled western third of the island of Hispaniola (today Haiti). In fact, the

Saint-Domingue refugees had first fled to Cuba, and left for Louisiana after their expulsion from that Spanish-held territory.

4 Activists for the revitalization and maintenance of LF use the term *cadien* rather than that which more transparently reflects the pronunciation, *cadjin*. The former term is more suitable for a written representation of the language and also links it more closely to its etymon, *acadien*.

5 SF equivalents are provided in parentheses.

6 I am grateful to Cynthia Fox, SUNY-Albany, and Elaine Clément, Director of Community Relations for CODOFIL, for providing information about French-language media. The internet sites listed are: Radio CODOFIL: www.live365.com/stations/codofil; Radio Louisiane: www.radiolouisiane.com; French consulate website: www.espace.francophone.org.

7 I would like to thank Tamara Lindner, Indiana University, for recent information about immersion and advanced French-language classes in Acadiana high schools.

8 Caujolle (1972: 32) reports that one of her subjects indicated how pleased she was when her brother, who had participated in the liberation of France in World War II, came back with the word *ampoule* and, thus, enabled her to cast aside the borrowing *light bulb*.

9 The decreasing number of subjects in Henry's (1994) data as one proceeds to the younger generations suggests a decreasing pool of speakers, and hence another sign of language loss.

10 For the distinction between fluent and semispeakers see Dorian (1994).

NOTE ON CHAPTER 8

1 An interesting case resulted from two Vietnamese-American cousins who were co-valedictorians in a Louisiana high school in 2008. During their commencement speeches, one of the girls delivered a sentence in Vietnamese, roughly translated as "Be true to yourself." The other spoke at greater length in Vietnamese, expressing gratitude to her parents for the hardships they faced. This event prompted local school officials to pursue establishing a rule that English be the only language permitted during commencement ceremonies (Pleasant 2008).

NOTES ON CHAPTER 9

1 The apparent discrepancies for a few of the states between the two tables (9.2 and 9.3) are a result of data sourced from different years and reflect changing population trends discussed below. They are not relevant to the present discussion.

2 For a full review of Amish settlement patterns, see Crowley (1978) and Kraybill and Bowmann (2001).

NOTE ON CHAPTER 10

1 Students with transnational backgrounds, who went through international schooling in Asia, the South Pacific, or Europe and came to the USA for higher education, usually maintain good command of Korean because their families tend to be based in Korea.

NOTES ON CHAPTER 11

1 The Soviet Union was formed in 1924 and existed till December 1991, when it was dissolved by Boris Yeltsin and the former Soviet republics became independent countries. Russia's official name after the collapse of the Soviet Union is the *Russian Federation.*
2 The Slavic group has three main subdivisions: South Slavic, West Slavic, and East Slavic. For more information and for information on linguistic features, see Comrie and Corbett (2002) and Language Materials Project (n.d.).
3 The Pale of Settlement ceased to exist after the 1917 communist revolution.
4 The National Security Education Program (NSEP) began awarding grants to institutions in 2002 to create accelerated language training programs. Today Flagship programs are underway in Arabic, Chinese, Hindi/Urdu, Korean, Persian/Farsi, Russian, and Eurasian languages (Language Flagship 2008).
5 Andrews (1998) also examines loan words and borrowings, in such domains as (1) home/apartment/environs; (2) employment; (3) the automobile; (4) cuisine; (5) daily life; and (6) academia.
6 For more information about the Russkij Mir Foundation see www.russkiymir.ru/ru/rumir/ (in Russian).

NOTES ON CHAPTER 12

1 One of the criteria frequently invoked when classifying a language variety as a dialect of a common language is mutual intelligibility. However, in the Italian case, many among the Italian "dialects" are in fact not mutually comprehensible with the national language. The fact that these languages are still commonly referred to as "dialects" reflects a prejudice against linguistic varieties that do not conform to the prestige national language.
2 Although dialects are still widely spoken in Italy, especially in rural areas and certain regions such as the Veneto and Trentino in the north, and Calabria, Sicilia and Basilicata in the south (ISTAT 2007), their functions have been reduced, and monolingual dialect speakers are not as numerous as in the past. On the other hand, the use of dialects to mark regional identity witnessed a rise in the 1980s among northern separatist groups such as the Lega Nord (Tosi 2001).
3 Census statistics about Italian ancestry are based on one question about ancestry and ethnic origin contained in the questionnaire, while numbers from OSIA are estimates based on intermarriage data.
4 There is, however, scholarly discussion on the role of non-standard varieties in language shift. According to Clyne (2003) non-standard varieties tend to show less resistance to shift than standard ones. Likewise, Bettoni and Rubino (1996) and Rubino (2003) argue that in Italian-Australian communities, the standard has a greater chance of maintenance because of its higher prestige, its use as lingua franca, and its support by institutions. Conversely, Ferguson (1959) and Bettoni (1989) claim that in diglossic speech communities it is usually the High code that disappears first because its functions are taken over by the dominant language. On the other hand, the Low code tends to be maintained in family domains as the language of intimacy and affect.
5 By "Italianized archaic dialects" the author means dialects that have absorbed Italian traits, mainly in the area of the lexicon. Pidginized forms of Italian indicate a lingua

franca where forms have been simplified, with reduction of grammar and vocabulary and elimination of any irregularities or complexities (Trudgill 1983).

6 It is noteworthy how both older first and second generation participants (in their sixties and seventies) and younger third generation family members in their twenties, discussed by De Fina and Fellin respectively, displayed similar discursive strategies to mark their Italianness.

NOTES ON CHAPTER 13

1 According to Bagby, Perl, and Froehle (2001), 97% of mosques in the USA use English as the primary language for delivering the Friday Sermon, the most important religious gathering of the week. Of these mosques, 47% use one or more additional languages, with Arabic as the language of choice in most cases. The same report states that of the mosques that offer activities for their members, 57% teach Arabic regularly and 20% occasionally. Around 20% of US mosque members are of Arab descent.

2 The USA PATRIOT Act was passed by Congress in October 26, 2001. It stands for Uniting and Strengthening America by Providing Appropriate Tools Required to Intercept and Obstruct Terrorism Act. The main goal of the PATRIOT Act is to expand the authority of law enforcement agencies in order to increase their efficiency in the "war on terror."

NOTE ON CHAPTER 14

1 Thanks to Margo Milleret for pointing this out.

NOTE ON CHAPTER 15

1 This percentage falls more or less in the middle with German (95%), Tagalog (93%), French (92%), Italian (89%), and Arabic (89%) showing higher percentage of bilingualism, and Russian (75%), Chinese (73%), Korean (71%), Spanish (71%), and Vietnamese (69%) lower (US Census Bureau 2007c).

Media resources related to the top twelve non-English languages in the USA

Websites are included when available.

1 Native American languages in the USA

In the White Man's Image

PBS American Experience series. 1992. 60 min.
www.pbs.org/wgbh/americanexperience/IntheWhiteMansImage/
In 1875, Captain Richard Pratt began an ambitious experiment with a group of Indian warriors: he taught them to read and write, put them in uniform, and drilled them like soldiers. With the blessing of Congress, Pratt established the Carlisle School for Indian students to continue his "civilizing" mission. Indian students had their hair cut short, were forbidden to speak their Native languages or to visit home for up to five years. By 1902, there were twenty-six reservation boarding schools modeled after Carlisle. Native Americans who attended the schools help tell the story of the consequences for a generation of Native people.

A Weave of Time

1987. 60 min.
Anthropologist John Adair went to the Navajo Nation in the 1930s to study the art of Navajo silverwork. He was steered to the family of Mabel Burnside Meyers, a famous Navajo weaver, whose brother was one of the finest silver jewelry makers of the time. Adair lived with the family, shooting some of the first photographs of Navajo family life. This documentary, filmed 50 years later, is a powerful depiction of cultural, social, and linguistic change over the ensuing years, looking outward from the micro perspective of a single family to the larger Navajo cultural milieu and the influence of wider social, cultural, political, and economic forces. The footage is, literally, a "weave of

time," juxtaposing Adair's early photography with video of late twentieth-century family and community life, incorporating the theme of Mabel's breathtaking textile art. The film discusses the diminished use of the Navajo language even on the reservation, the decline of native crafts, and creeping modernization.

2 Spanish in the USA

Latino in America

2009. Multiple short segments.
www.cnn.com/SPECIALS/2009/latino.in.america/
By 2050, the US Latino population is expected to nearly triple. "CNN Presents: Latino in America" reported by Soledad O'Brien explores how Latinos are reshaping our communities and culture and forcing a nation of immigrants to rediscover what it means to be an American.

Mapa del corazón

KNME New Mexico. 1995. 30 min.
www.knme.org/footer/ColoresDVD.pdf
Documents the use of Spanish in Northern New Mexico and Southern Colorado through the eyes of trained researchers who interact with locals and collect speech samples. Explains the historical reasons why the Spanish of this region looks the way it does, how it varies from one town to another, and preserves stories, legends, and memories, revealing the link between language and culture.

3 Chinese in the USA

A Nation of Immigrants: The Chinese-American Experience

Films for the Humanities and Sciences. 1991. 21 min.
http://ffh.films.com/id/10629/A_Nation_of_Immigrants_The_Chinese-American_Experience.htm
Attracted to the USA by the need for farm and railroad laborers and by news of the California Gold Rush, the Chinese came by the hundreds of thousands, only to experience extremely hard work, low wages, and racial discrimination. In the West, they became the victims of race riots and discriminatory laws, and in 1882 the federal government created the Chinese Exclusion Act to restrict further immigration. Finally, after World War II, this

racist law was repealed and immigrants from China have since enriched the nation.

4 Tagalog in the USA

Filipino Americans: Discovering their Past for the Future

Wehman Video Distribution. 1994. VHS. 54 min.
http://distribution.asianamericanmedia.org/browse/film/?i=71
This is the first in-depth documentary produced about Filipinos in the USA. From the California coast in 1587 and Louisiana bayous in 1763, Filipino-American men and women in universities and colleges, Hawaiian plantations, California migrant farms, Alaskan fish canneries, labor organizations, US Navy and Army, and family, social, and cultural affairs have contributed significantly to the American way of life.

Dollar a Day, Ten Cents a Dance

1984. 24 min.
http://distribution.asianamericanmedia.org/browse/film/?i=59
Enticed by the promise of jobs and fair wages, 100,000 Filipinos immigrated to the USA between 1924 and 1935 to toil on California's farmlands. Because of the exclusion of Filipina women and US anti-miscegenation laws, they survived the loneliness of racial discrimination by creating close-knit bachelor societies where cockfights, poker games, and dance halls served as their entertainment, and by entering into common-law marriages.

5 French in the USA

Réveil: Waking up French

2003. 81 min.
www.wakingupfrench.com
This film explores the struggle for cultural survival among the Franco-American communities of New England. It traces the French heritage beginning with immigration from the Canadian provinces of Québec and Acadia through persecution by Ku Klux Klan and language loss, to cultural renaissance and heritage preservation. Through their determined loyalty to the French Catholic faith, language, and cultural values, the French of New England continue to discover new ways of renewal and cultural diversity through heritage language reacquisition.

6 Vietnamese in the USA

The New Generation: Vietnamese-Americans Today

2000. 33 min.
http://streaming.factsonfile.com/id/1187/The_New_Generation_Vietnamese-Americans_Today.htm
Through interviews with first and second generation Vietnamese-Americans, this film documents the process of assimilation into American culture of refugees from the former Republic of Vietnam. College students, professionals, and clergy explore what it means to be of Vietnamese descent in America today. Topics include stresses on the family unit caused by cultural and generational differences, gang membership and drug abuse among the young, anti-Vietnamese racial bias, and feelings about relations between the USA and Vietnam.

7 German in the USA

Germans in America

4 parts, 42 mins each.
www.engstfeldfilm.de/index_e.html
60 million Americans have their origins in German-speaking countries, forming America's largest ethnic group. Although their identity fell victim to feelings of shame and repression during and after the two world wars, their achievements are still the basis for much of American culture. In this landmark broadcast event, an epic of American history is told through a dramatic blend of contemporary personal stories and comprehensive historical reconstruction, rediscovering the German-Americans who have been at the heart of American enterprise on the land and in business. They profile those who have successfully struggled for the freedom of worship and the freedom of the press.

The Texas German Dialect Project

http://tgdp.org/index.php
In addition to useful information about Texas German language and culture, this site contains the Texas German Dialect Archive, an online digital repository of audio and textual materials documenting sociolinguistic interviews with native speakers of Texas German.

Devil's Playground

2002. 77 min.
They live in a strict society, under tight control of their family and close-knit community. But when they turn 16, Amish teenagers are allowed the freedom to explore the customs of the outside "English" world before deciding whether to join the Amish church for life or leave the community altogether. This documentary follows four Amish teens in LaGrange County, Indiana, during this tumultuous period, which the Amish call *rumspringa* – the Pennsylvania Dutch word for "running around."

8 Korean in the USA

Arirang: The Korean American Journey (Part 1) and The Korean American Dream (Part 2)

2002. 60 min. each.
http://distribution.asianamericanmedia.org/browse/film/?i=89
Part 1 begins the story of how and why more than 7,000 Koreans left their strife-torn homeland for new lives on the sugar plantations of Hawaii in the early 1900s. As American settlers, they organized around the cause of independence for Korea from Japan while simultaneously sinking roots deep into their new home. Part 2 continues with the dramatic renewal of migration as a result of the Korean War and subsequent changes in US immigration law. After 1970, the Korean-American population expanded rapidly. This is a story about distances: from Seoul to New Jersey; from storekeeper to Harvard graduate; and from the devastating Los Angeles riots of 1992 to a heightened involvement in the American scene.

9 Russian in the USA

No films have been located. Recommendations are welcome at kimpotow@uic.edu.

10 Italian in the USA

And they came to Chicago: Italian-Americans in the US

2007. 76 min.
www.italiansofchicago.com/DVD/index.html
Narrated by Tony Award winner Joe Mantegna, this film begins in Chicago in the 1850s, when Italian entrepreneurs first built thriving businesses. The

saga unfolds, including the struggle to gain acceptance on the factory floor, the establishment of Italian parishes, the anti-immigrant backlash, and the heroism of Italian-American servicemen and women during World War II even as their families' loyalty was being questioned in the USA. Finally, in the postwar era, it explores the contrasts between increased opportunity for Italian-Americans and urban renewal's devastating impact on inner-city Italian neighborhoods. Through rare archival photographs and footage and interviews, this is a tale of adversity and triumph, fierce individualism, and the strong bonds of community, celebrating the courage of Italian ancestors who first made the journey.

The Italian Americans

WLIW21 New York. 60 min.
Viewable online at www.wliw.org/productions/heritage/the-italian-americans/322/
This program celebrates the strength, resiliency and connectedness to family and community that enabled Italian immigrant families to bring Old World values to fruition on America's shores with extraordinary impact. As noted by Geraldine Ferraro, this passion for the possible stemmed from the sense that everyone "belonged to each other." As Stanley Tucci describes it, "everything always came back to being Italian." But perhaps Joe Mantegna says it best in his definition of *amore* in Italian families – "it's everything, it's what you feel about life."

10 Arabic in the USA

I speak Arabic

2003. 27 min.
www.ispeakarabic.org.
This presentation of the experiences of young Arab-Americans between the ages of fifteen and twenty five is an opportunity to enter into the world of Arabic speakers in the USA – their linguistic talents, difficulties and hopes for the future. Filmed in the homes, schools, and neighborhoods of Arab-Americans in the New York/New Jersey metropolitan area, it is rich with personal stories documenting the relationship that Arab-Americans have with their language. These immigrants share the same challenges as all immigrant families: how to balance the new with the old and come out whole. It also presents an outline for understanding how heritage speakers learn. The combination of community members and language-education specialists make it a valuable resource for both groups. Features the music of the award-winning Lebanese composer Marcel Khalife.

11 Portuguese in the USA

My Grandmother has a Video Camera

2007. 60 min.
http://grandmahasavideocamera.blogspot.com/
This documentary is about the use of home video by a family of Brazilian immigrants, which portrays their lives in the USA for over twenty years. From enchantment to disillusionment, from idealization to conformity, first-hand images and voices depict how newly arriving immigrants see their new world, and struggle to establish their final home.

12 Polish in the USA

The Polish Americans

WLIW21 New York. 2009. 1 hour 19 min.
Viewable online at www.wliw.org/productions/heritage/the-polish-americans/361/
Demonstrates the spirit, determination and solidarity of an immigrant success story. Using vintage film footage, family photos, personal recollections, and experiences, this documentary embodies Polish pride in a televised "family album" of the Polish-American experience.

References

ABS-CBN News Online. (2008, July 19). Tagalog set to be taught in New Zealand. Retrieved July 20, 2008 from www.abs-cbnnews.com/storypage.aspx?StoryId=125613.

Abraham, S. Y. & Abraham, N. (1981). *The Arab World and Arab-Americans: Understanding a Neglected Community*. Detroit: Wayne State University Center for Urban Studies.

Abshire-Fontenot, S. & Barry, D. (1979). *Cajun French*. Lafayette, LA: University of Southwestern Louisiana.

ACTFL. (2008). Legislative look. American Council on the Teaching of Foreign Languages. *The Language Educator* 3(4): 59.

Action, T. & Dalphinis, M. (2000). *Language, Blacks, and Gypsies: Languages without a Written Tradition and their Role in Education*. Salem, MA: Witing & Birch.

Adams, M. (2006). Unmasking the myths of structured English immersion. Gale Group. Retrieved August 8, 2008 from www.worldlanguage.com/Articles/59.htm.

Adams, W. P. (1993). *The German Americans*. Max Kade German-American Center, Bloomington, IN: University Press.

Agnihotri, R. K. (2007). Towards a pedagogical paradigm rooted in multilinguality. *International Multilingual Research Journal* 1(2), 79–88.

Aikhenvald, A. Y. (2006). Grammar in contact: A cross-linguistic perspective. In A. Y. Aikhenvald & R. M. W. Dixon (eds.), *Grammars in Contact: A Cross-Linguistic Typology* (pp. 1–66). Oxford: Oxford University Press.

Alaska Office of Economic Development. (n.d.) *Russian Heritage*. Retrieved April 1, 2008 from www.dced.state.ak.us/oed/student_info/learn/russianheritage.htm.

Alba, R. (2000). The twilight of ethnicity among Americans of European ancestry: The case of Italians. In F. Sorrentino and J. Krase (eds.), *Review of Italian American Studies* (pp. 41–74). Lanham, MD: Lexington.

(2004). Language assimilation today: Bilingualism persists more than in the past, but English still dominates. Lewis Mumford Center for Comparative Urban and Regional Research University at Albany. Retrieved September 12, 2007 from http://mumford.albany.edu/children/reports/language_assimilation/language_assimilation_brief.pdf.

Alba, R., Logan, J., Lutz, A., & Stults, B. (2002). Only English by the third generation? Loss and preservation of the mother tongue among the grandchildren of contemporary immigrants. *Demography* 39(3), 467–84.

Alba, R. & Nee, V. (2003). *Remaking the American Mainstream: Assimilation and Contemporary Immigration*. Cambridge, MA: Harvard University Press.

Allen, D. & Friedman, M. (2005). A deeper look into the US Hispanic market. In E. del Valle (ed). *Hispanic Marketing & Public Relations. Understanding and Targeting America's Largest Minority* (pp. 85–114). Boca Raton, FL: Poyeen Publishing.

Allen, R. (1992). Teaching Arabic in the United States: Past, present, and future. In A. Rouchdy (ed.), *The Arabic Language in America* (pp. 222–50). Detroit: Wayne State University Press.

Almeida, O. T. (2005). Portuguese-American literature: Some thoughts and questions. *Hispania* 88(4), 726–32.

Amella, G. M. (Producer). (2007, May 27). And they came to Chicago: The Italian-American legacy [Television broadcast]. Chicago: Modio Media.

American Association of Teachers of Korean. (2007). Colleges and universities offering Korean in the U.S. Retrieved October 25, 2007 from www.aatk.org/html/schools.html.

American Indian Policy Center. (2002). American Indian tribal sovereignty primer. Retrieved July 30, 2006 from www.airpi.org/pubs/indiansov.html.

Ancelet, B. J. (Arceneaux, J.) (1988). *Cris sur le Bayou: Naissance d'une Poésie Cadienne en Louisiane*. Montréal: Editions Intermèdes.

(1993). La politique socioculturelle de la transcription: la question du français louisianais. *Présence Francophone* 43, 47–61.

Andrews, D. R. (1998). *Sociocultural Perspectives on Language Change in Diaspora: Soviet Immigrants in the United States*. Amsterdam/Philadelphia: John Benjamins.

Anzaldúa, G. (1999). *Borderlands/La Frontera: The New Mestiza* (2nd edition). San Francisco: Aunt Lute Books.

Arab American Institute. (2007). Arab Americans: Demographics. Retrieved October 15, 2007 from www.aaiusa.org/arab-americans/22/demographics.

ARBC. (2006). *American-Russian Business Council*. American-Russian Business Council. Retrieved November 15, 2007 from www.russiancouncil.org/.

Arbitron. (2007). Hispanic Radio Today. Retrieved August 1, 2007 from www.arbitron.com.

Arviso, M. & Holm, W. (2001). Tséhootsooídi Ólta'gi Diné bizaad bíhoo'aah: A Navajo immersion program at Fort Defiance, Arizona. In L. Hinton & K. Hale (eds.), *The Green Book of Language Revitalization in Practice* (pp. 203–15). San Diego, CA: Academic Press.

Ash, A., Fermino, J. L. D., & Hale, K. (2001). Diversity in local language maintenance and restoration: A reason for optimism. In L. Hinton & K. Hale (eds.), *The Green Book of Language Revitalization in Practice* (pp. 19–35). San Diego, CA: Academic Press.

Asia Society & The College Board. (2008). Chinese in 2008: An expanding field. Retrieved July 28, 2008 from www.askasia.org/chinese/docs/Report2008.pdf.

Aspen Health Law Center. (1998). *Employment Discrimination in the Health Care Industry*. Maryland: Jones and Bartlett Publishing Co.

Au, T. K. & Romo, L. F. (1997). Does childhood language experience help adult learners? In H. C. Chen (ed.), *The Cognitive Processing of Chinese and Related Asian Languages* (pp. 417–41). Hong Kong: Chinese University Press.

Austin, A. D. (1984). *African Muslims in Antebellum America: A Sourcebook*. New York: Garland.

(1997). *African Muslims in Antebellum America: Transatlantic Stories and Spiritual Struggles*. New York and London: Routledge.
Azevedo, M. M. (2005). *Portuguese: A Linguistic Introduction*. Cambridge: Cambridge University Press.
Baetens-Beardsmore, H. (2003). Who's afraid of bilingualism? In J. M. Dewaele, L. Wei, & A. Housen (eds.), *Bilingualism: Beyond Basic Principles* (pp. 10–27). Clevedon: Multilingual Matters.
Bagby, I., Perl, P. M., & Froehle, B. T. (2001). The mosque in America: a national portrait. A report from the Mosque Study Project. Washington, DC: Council on American-Islamic Relations. Retrieved July 28, 2008 from www.cair.com/Portals/0/pdf/The_Mosque_in_America_A_National_Portrait.pdf.
Baker, C. & Prys Jones, S. (1998). *Encyclopedia of Bilingualism and Bilingual Education*. Clevedon: Multilingual Matters.
Bakker, P. & Mous, M. (eds.) (2003). *Mixed Languages: 15 Case Studies in Language Intertwining*. Den Haag: CIP-Gegevens Koninklijke Bibliotheek.
Bale, J. (2008). When Arabic is the "target" language: National security, Title VI, and Arabic language programs, 1958–1991. Doctoral Dissertation. Arizona State University, AZ: Tempe.
Bankston, C. L. III & Zhou, M. (1995). Effects of minority language literacy on the academic achievement of Vietnamese youths in New Orleans. *Sociology of Education* 68(1), 1–17.
(2002). Being well vs. doing well: Self esteem and school performance among immigrant and nonimmigrant racial and ethnic groups. *International Migration Review* 36(2), 389–415.
Baroni, W. (2001). Die deutschsprachige Presse in den USA. *VDA-Globus* 1, 22.
Baugh, J. W. (1999). *Out of the Mouths of Slaves: African American Language and Educational Malpractice*. TX: Austin, University of Texas Press.
Bautista, L. (1983). *Bata, Bata . . . Paano ka Ginawa?* Manila: Cacho Publishing House.
Bautista, M. L. (2004). Tagalog–English codeswitching as a mode of discourse. *Asia Pacific Education Review* 5(2), 226–33. Retrieved December 19, 2007 from www.eric.ed.gov/ERICDocs/data/ericdocs2sql/content_storage_01/0000019b/80/2a/25/c1.pdf.
Bayley, R. (2004). Linguistic diversity and English language acquisition. In E. Finegan & J. R. Rickford. (eds.), *Language in the USA: Themes for the Twenty-First Century* (pp. 268–89). Cambridge: Cambridge University Press.
Bean, F. D. & Stevens, G. (2003). *America's Newcomers and the Dynamics of Diversity*. New York: Russell Sage Foundation.
Bednarek, S. (1991). Foreign students in Poland: Their preparation and problems. *International Review of Education* 37(4), 489–91.
Benally, A. & Viri, D. (2005). *Diné bizaad* (Navajo language) at a crossroads: Extinction or renewal? *Bilingual Research Journal* 29(1), 85–108.
Benham, M. K. P. & Heck, R. H. (1998). *Culture and Education in Hawaii: The Silencing of Native Voices*. Mahwah, PA: Lawrence Erlbaum.
Benjamin, R., Pecos, R., & Romero, M. E. (1996). Language revitalization efforts in the Pueblo de Cochiti: Becoming "literate" in an oral society. In N. H. Hornberger (ed.), *Indigenous Literacies in the Americas: Language Planning from the Bottom Up* (pp. 115–36). Berlin: Mouton de Gruyter.

Benoit, V. (1975). Gentilly: A French-Canadian community in the Minnesota Red River Valley. *Minnesota History* 44(8), 278–89.

(1988). La présence franco-américaine dans le Midwest des Etats-Unis. *Études de Linguistique Appliquée* 70, 35–41.

Bensabat-Ott, M. (2000). Portuguese-English code-switching: The Brazilian community in greater Washington, DC. Doctoral dissertation, Georgetown University.

Bergen, John J. (ed.). (1990). *Spanish in the United States: Sociolinguistic Issues*. Washington, DC: Georgetown University Press.

Bettoni, C. (1989). Maintaining and developing Italian in Australia. *Vox* 3, 48–53.

Bettoni, C. & Gibbons, J. (1988). Linguistic purism and language shift: A guise-voice study of the Italian community in Sydney. *International Journal of the Sociology of Language* 72, 15–35.

Bettoni, C. & Rubino, A. (1996). *Emigrazione e comportamento linguistico. Un'indagine sul trilinguismo dei siciliani e dei veneti in Australia*. Galatina: Congedo Editore.

Bialystok, E., Craik, F. I. M., & Freedman, M. (2007). Bilingualism as a protection against the onset of symptoms of dementia. *Neuropsychologia* 45(2), 459–64.

Bialystok, E., Luk, G., & Kwan, E. (2005). Bilingualism, biliteracy, and learning to read: Interactions among languages and writing systems. *Scientific Studies of Reading* 9(1), 43–61.

Bilanow, K. (2007). *An International Education Policy for Poland*. Retrieved April 12, 2008 from www.iienetwork.org/page/116263/.

Blanton, C. K. (2004). *The Strange Career of Bilingual Education in Texas, 1836–1981*. College Station, TX: Texas A&M University Press.

Blejwas, S. (1996). Polonia and politics. In J. Bukowczyk (ed.), *Polish Americans and Their History: Community, Culture and Politics* (pp. 121–51). University of Pittsburgh Press.

Bloomfield, L. (1933). *Language*. New York: Holt.

Bonvillain, N. (1978). Linguistic change in Akwesasne Mohawk: French and English influences. *International Journal of American Linguistics* 44(1), 31–9.

Booth, C. (2001, June 24). Miami: the Capital of Latin America. *Time Magazine*. Retrieved July 3, 2007 from www.time.com/time/magazine/article/0,9171, 1101931202–162806,00.html.

Borges, D. (2008). Vozes do Povo: A comunicação social da língua portuguesa no estado da Califórnia – Uma possível leitura. Retrieved July 19, 2009, from www.comunidadesacorianas.org/artigo.php?artigo=20&idioma=PT.

(2009). Speaking and teaching Portuguese in California. Retrieved July 19, 2009, from www.comunidadesacorianas.org/artigo.php?id_artigo=67&id.

Boswell, T. (2000). Demographic changes in Florida and their importance for effective educational policies and practices. In A. Roca (ed.), *Research on Spanish in the United States: Linguistic Issues and Challenges* (pp. 406–31). Somerville, MA: Cascadilla Press.

Bougie, E., Wright, S. C., & Taylor, D. M. (2003). Early heritage-language education and the abrupt shift to a dominant-language classroom: impact on the personal and collective esteem of Inuit children in Arctic Quebec. *International Journal of Bilingual Education and Bilingualism* 6(5), 349–73.

Bourdieu, P. (1977). The economics of linguistic exchanges. *Social Science Information* 16, 645–68.

(1991). *Language and Symbolic Power*. Cambridge, MA: Harvard University Press.

Braga, L. J. & Jouët-Pastré, C. (2008). Introduction: Interdisciplinary perspectives on becoming Brazuca. In C. Jouët-Pastré & L. Braga (eds.), *Becoming Brazuca: Brazilian Immigration to the United States* (pp. 1–23). Cambridge, MA: Harvard University Press.

Brault, G. J. (1972). New England French Culture. *The French Review* 45(4), 831–37.

(1986). *The French Canadian Heritage of New England*. Hanover, NH: University Press of New England.

Brecht, R. D., with Caemmerer, J., & Walton, A. R. (1995). *Russian in the United States: A Case Study of America's Needs and Capacities*. Washington, DC: National Foreign Language Center.

Brecht, R. D. & Ingold, C. (2002). Tapping a national resource: heritage languages in the United States. Washington, DC: Center for Applied Linguistics. Retrieved October 31, 2007 from www.cal.org/resources/digest/0202brecht.html.

Brickson, B. (2007, July/August). Immersion programs: a parent's reflection. *Chinese Language Initiatives Newsletter*. New York: Asia Society. Retrieved July 28, 2008 from http://askasia.org/chinese/announcements/newsletter0707.htm.

Brittingham, A. & de la Cruz, G. P. (2005). We the people of Arab Ancestry in the United States. Census 2000 Special Reports. Washington, DC: US Census Bureau. Retrieved December 1, 2007 from www.census.gov/prod/2005pubs/censr-21.pdf.

Brod, R. & Welles, E. (2000). Foreign language enrollments in United States institutions of higher education. *Fall ADFL Bulletin* 31, 22–9.

Brown, B. (1988). Pronominal equivalence in a variable syntax. Unpublished doctoral dissertation, University of Texas at Austin.

Bukowczyk, J. (1987). *And My Children did not Know Me: A History of the Polish Americans*. Bloomington: Indiana University Press.

Bullock, B. & Gerfen, C. (2004). Frenchville French: Phonological convergence in a contracting language variety. *Bilingualism: Language and Cognition* 7(2, August), 95–104.

Burridge, K. (2006). Language contact and convergence in Pennsylvania German. In A. Y. Aikhenvald, & R. M. W. Dixon (eds.), *Grammars in Contact: A Cross-Linguistic Typology* (pp. 179–200). Oxford: Oxford University Press.

Business Editors. (2002, Sept. 27). EEOC Chair Cari Dominguez offers guidelines for success to Hispanic women on Wall Street; roundtable reveals obstacles, opportunities for advancement. *Business Wire*. Retrieved September 18, 2008 from http://findarticles.com/p/articles/mi_m0EIN/is_2002_Sept_27/ai_92128112.

Byers, B. (1988). Defining norms for a non-standardized language: A study of verb and pronoun variation in Cajun French. Unpublished doctoral dissertation, Indiana University.

Byrnes, H. (2005). Reconsidering the nexus of content and language: A mandate for NCLB legislation. *Modern Language Journal* 89, 277–82.

Calabrese, M. (2007, April 23). Usa, la rivincita dell'italiano è boom di corsi all'università. *La Repubblica*. Retrieved June 7, 2007 from www.repubblica.it/2006/a/sezioni/scuola_e_universita/servizi/americaoggi/italiano-record/italiano-record.html.

California State Department of Education. (1983). *A Handbook for Teaching Portuguese-Speaking Students*. Sacramento, CA. Office of Bilingual and Bicultural Education.

Calvet, L. & Chaudenson, R. (1988). *Saint-Barthélemy: Une Énigme Linguistique*. Paris: Diffusion Didier Érudition/CIRELFA-Agence Universitaire de la Francophonie.

Camarota, S. (2007). Immigrants in the United States, 2007: A profile of America's foreign-born population. Washington, DC: Center for Immigration Studies. Retrieved November 29, 2007 from http://graphics8.nytimes.com/packages/pdf/national/CIS1128ImmigStats.pdf.

Camarota, S. & McArdle, N. (2003). Where immigrants live: An examination of state residency of the foreign born by country of origin in 1990 and 2000. Washington, DC: Center for Immigration Studies. Retrieved December 10, 2007, from www.cis.org/articles/2003/back1203.pdf.

Campbell, G. (1995). *Concise Compendium of the World's Languages*. New York: Routledge.

Canyon Records. (2008). About Canyon. Retrieved July 8, 2008 from http://store.canyonrecords.com/index.php?app=ccp0&ns=display&ref=about=canyon.

CARLA. (n.d.) *LCTL Course Offerings*. Center for Advanced Research on Language Acquisition. Retrieved March, 24, 2008 from www.carla.umn.edu/lctl/db/index.html.

Carnevale, N. (2003). "No Italian spoken for the duration of the war": Language, Italian–American identity, and cultural pluralism in the World War II years. *Journal of American Ethnic History* 22(3), 3–33.

Carreira, M. M. (2002). Mass media, marketing, critical mass and other mechanisms of linguistic maintenance. *Southwest Journal of Linguistics* 21(4), 37–53.

(2007). SNS matters: Narrowing the Latino academic gap. *Heritage Language Journal* 5(1). Retrieved June 06, 2008 from www.heritagelanguages.org/.

Carreira, M., Jensen, L., Kagan, O., Tighearnain, S., & Abate, A. (2007). The heritage language learner survey: Report on the preliminary results. Los Angeles: National Heritage Language Resource Center. Retrieved July 14, 2008, from www.international.ucla.edu/languages/nhlrc/surveyreport/.

Carrière, J. M. (1937). *Tales from the French Folk-Lore of Missouri*. Evanston, IL: Northwestern University Press.

Carvalho, A. M. (2009). Introdução. In A. M. Carvalho (ed.), *Português em contato* (pp. 1–10). Madrid/Frankfurt: Iberoamericana Vervuert.

CASL. (n.d.). *Arabic Dialect Identification and Recognition*. Center for Advanced Study of Language. Retrieved July 28, 2008 from www.casl.umd.edu/work/ProjectDetail.cfm?project_id=166.

Caujolle, J. (1972). Esquisse d'une description du parler français de Frenchville. *The French Language in the Americas* (Newsletter of the French VIII Section of the Modern Language Association) 16, 26–32.

Center for Applied Linguistics. (1997). Foreign language instruction in the United States: A national survey of elementary and secondary schools. Washington, DC: Center for Applied Linguistics. Retrieved August 7, 2008 from www.cal.org/topics/fl/flsurvey97execsummary.pdf.

(2006a). Directory of foreign language immersion programs in U.S. schools. Retrieved Aug. 1, 2007 from www.cal.org/resources/immersion.

(2006b). Directory of two-way bilingual immersion. Retrieved Aug. 1, 2007 from www.cal.org/twi/directory/tables.htm#table3.

(2007). Directory of two-way bilingual immersion programs in the U.S. Retrieved April 5, 2008 from www.cal.org/jsp/TWI/SchoolSearch.jsp.

(2008). World language teaching in US schools: Preliminary results from the national K-12 foreign language survey. Washington, DC: Center for Applied Linguistics. Retrieved December 31, 2008 from www.cal.org/flsurvey/prelimbrochure08.pdf.

Center for Immigration Studies. (2003). *Where immigrants live: An examination of state residency of the foreign born by country of origin in 1990 and 2000*. Retrieved August 1, 2007 from www.cis.org/articles/2003/back1203.html.

CIA. (2008). *The World Factbook*. Central Intelligence Agency, Washington, DC: CIA.

Chang, H. (2006). Korean Wave washes over U.S.A. *Voice of America*, October 4, 2006. Retrieved October 29, 2007 from www.voanews.com/english/archive/2006–10/.

Chang, I. (2003). *The Chinese in America: A Narrative History*. New York Penguin.

Charbonneau, L. (1997). L'emprunt lexical et le transfert à l'anglais dans une communauté franco-américaine au nord du Vermont. Unpublished doctoral dissertation, State University of New York at Albany.

Charbonneau, H. & Guillemette, A. (1994). Provinces et habitats d'origine des pionniers de la vallée laurentienne. In C. Poirier, A. Boivin, C. Trépanier, & C. Verreault (eds.), *Langues, espaces, société: les variétés du français en Amérique du Nord* (157–83). Québec: Presses de l'Université Laval.

Cheng, L. & Yang, P. Q. (1996). Asians: The "model minority" deconstructed. In R. Waldinger & M. Bozorgmehr (eds.), *Ethnic Los Angeles* (pp. 305–44). New York: Russell Sage Foundation.

Chicago Council on Global Affairs. (2006). The United States and the rise of China and India: Results of a 2006 multination survey of public opinion. Chicago: Chicago Council on Global Affairs. Retrieved July 28, 2008 from www.asiasociety.org/publications/GlobalViews06.pdf.

Chinese American Data Center. (n.d.) City or borough with Chinese population more than 10,000, Census 2000. Retrieved August 16, 2008 from http://members.aol.com/chineseusa/00cen5.htm.

Chiswick, B. R. (1997). Language and Labour Market Adjustments. In N. Lewin-Erstein, Y. Ro'I, & P. Ritterband (eds.), *Russian Jews on Three Continents: Migration and Resettlement* (pp. 233–60). London: Frank Cass.

Chiswick, B. & Miller, P. (2007). *The Economics of Language: International Analyses*. New York: Routledge.

Cho, G. & Krashen, S. (1998). The negative consequences of heritage language loss and why we should care. In S. Krashen, L. Tse, & J. McQuillan (eds.), *Heritage Language Development* (pp. 3–13). Culver City, CA: Language Education Associates.

Chomsky, N. (1965). Aspects of the Theory of Syntax. Cambridge, MA: MIT Press.

CIC Research, Inc. (2007). German travelers to California (2006). San Diego, CA. Retrieved December 12, 2007, from www.visitcalifornia.com/media/uploads/files/2006GermanyReport-September182007.pdf.

Clyne, M. (2003). *Dynamics of Language Contact: English and Immigrant Languages.* Cambridge: Cambridge University Press.

College Board. (n.d.) 2006 Program summary report. Retrieved August 28, 2007 from http://apcentral.collegeboard.com/apc/public/repository/ap06_prog_summary_rptx.xls.

Committee on College and Pre-College Russian. (n.d.). Retrieved November 14, 2007 from www.american.edu/research/CCPCR/.

Comrie, B. & Corbett, G. (eds.). (2002). *The Slavonic Languages.* New York: Routledge.

Constantakos, C. & Spiradakis, J. (1997). Greek in New York. In O. Garcia & J. Fishman (eds.), *The Multilingual Apple: Languages in New York City* (pp. 143–66). New York: Mouton de Gruyter.

Conwell, M. & Juilland, A. (1963). *Louisiana French I: Phonology, Morphology, Syntax.* The Hague: Mouton & Co.

Conzen, K. N. (1985). German Americans and the invention of ethnicity. In F. Trommler & J. McVeigh (eds.), *America and the Germans: An Assessment of a Three-Hundred Year History* (Vol. I, pp. 131–47). Philadelphia: University of Pennsylvania Press.

Cooper, R. L. (1971). Degree of bilingualism. In J. A. Fishman, R. L. Cooper, & R. Ma (eds.), *Bilingualism in the Barrio* (pp. 273–309). Bloomington, IN: Indiana University Press.

Cordova, J. M. T. (2000). The language situation of Filipina/os: Diversity and complexity. In S. L. McKay & S. C. Wong (eds.), *New Immigrants in the United States: Readings for Second Language Education* (pp. 333–51). Cambridge: Cambridge University Press.

Cornell, C. (2008). "C'est important de garder sa langue aussi": The use of French among francophone African immigrants in Chicago. Unpublished manuscript.

Correa-Zoli, Y. (1980). The language of Italian Americans. In C. Ferguson, S. Brice-Heath & D. Hwang (eds.), *Foreign Language Instruction and Second Language Acquisition Research in the United States* (pp. 239–56). Washington, DC: National Foreign Language Center at Johns Hopkins.

Corson, D. (1999a). *Language Polices in Schools. A Resource for Teachers and Administrators.* Mahwah, NJ: Lawrence Erlbaum.

(1999b). Community-based education for indigenous cultures. In S. May (ed.), *Indigenous Community-Based Education* (pp. 85–108). Clevedon, UK: Multilingual Matters.

Cortelazzo, M. (1972). *Lineamenti di italiano popolare.* Pisa: Pacini.

Council of Europe. (2008). Common European Framework of Reference for Languages: Learning, Teaching, Assessment. Retrieved July 14, 2008, from www.coe.int/t/dg4/linguistic/CADRE_EN.asp.

Crawford, J. (1992). *Hold Your Tongue: Bilingualism and the Politics of "English Only."* Reading, MA: Addison Wesley.

(2006). Official English legislation: Bad for civil rights, bad for America's interests, and even bad for English. Testimony before the House Subcommittee on Education Reform, July 26, 2006. Retrieved August 8, 2008 from www.elladvocates.org/documents/englishonly/Crawford_Official_English_testimony.pdf

(2007). The decline of bilingual education: How to reverse a troubling trend. *International Multilingual Research Journal* 1(1), 33–8.

Creagh, R. (1988). *Nos Cousins d'Amérique*. Paris: Payot.

Crowley, W. K. (1978). Old Order Amish settlement: Diffusion and growth. *Annals of the Association of American Geographers* 68(2), 249–64.

Crystal, D. (1987). *The Cambridge Encyclopedia of Language*. Cambridge: Cambridge University Press.

(1997). *The Cambridge Encyclopedia of Language*. Cambridge: Cambridge University Press.

Cumings, B. (1997). *Korea's Place in the Sun: A Modern History*. New York: Norton.

Curtiss, R. H. (2004, December). Muslim-Americans gave qualified support to Kerry to "protest" Bush policies. *Washington Report on Middle East Affairs* 23(10), 26–7.

Cyganowski, M. & Ziontz, H. A. (1981). Survey: The Buffalo Polish-American legal experience. *Buffalo Law Review* 30(1), 161–84.

Dąbrowska, A. (2004). *Język Polski*. Wrocław: Wydawnictwo Dolnośląkie.

Dai, J.-h. E. & Zhang, L. (2008). What are the CHL learners inheriting: Habitus of the CHL learners. In A. W. He and Y. Xiao (eds.), *Chinese as a Heritage Language: Fostering Rooted World Citizenry* (pp. 35–50). Honolulu, HI: University of Hawaii, National Foreign Language Resource Center.

Daigle, J. O. (1984). *A Dictionary of the Cajun Language*. Ann Arbor, MI: Edwards Brothers.

Daly, G. E. (2002). "Dreaming" a language back to life. *Canku Ota* (Many Paths), April 6 (58), 1–5. Retrieved August 9, 2006 from www.turtletrack.org/Issues02/Co04062002/CO_04062002_Dreaming_Language.htm.

Dator, J. & Seo, Y. (2004). Korea as the wave of a future: The emerging Dream Society of icons and aesthetic experience. *Journal of Future Studies*, 9(1), 31–44.

Davis, J. (1969). *The Russian Immigrant*. New York: Arno Press and The New York Times.

De Fina, A. (2007a). Style and stylization in the construction of identities in an Italian American Club. In P. Auer (ed.), *Social Identity and Communicative Styles: An Alternative Approach to Variability in Language* (pp. 57–84). Berlin: Mouton de Gruyter.

(2007b). Code-switching and the construction of ethnic identity in an Italian American club. *Language in Society* 36(3), 371–92.

De Mauro, T. (1963). *Storia linguistica dell'Italia unita*. Bari: Laterza.

del Valle, J. (2006). US Latinos, la hispanofonía, and the language ideologies of high modernity. In C. Mar-Molinero & M. Stewart (eds.), *Globalization, Language and the Spanish-Speaking World* (pp. 27–46). London: Palgrave Macmillan.

Demmert, W. & Arnold, R. (Facilitators) (1996). Language Policy. In G. Cantoni (ed.), *Stabilizing Indigenous Languages* (Section II). Flagstaff, AZ: Center for Excellence in Education. Retrieved December 21, 2007 from www.ncela.gwu.edu/pubs/stabilize/ii-policy.

Di Stasi, L. (2001). *Una Storia Segreta: The Secret History of Italian American Evacuation and Internment during World War II*. Berkeley: Heyday Books.

Dickie, L. (2006). The Korean Wave. *The Seattle Times*, June 4, 2006. Retrieved October 27, 2007 from seattletimes.nwsource.com/html/opinion/2003036091_sundaykorea04.html.

Diehl, C. (2005). New research challenges notion of German "brain drain." Wiesbaden: German Federal Institute for Population Research. Retrieved December 16, 2007, from www.migrationinformation.org/Feature/display.cfm.

Dignam, C. (2006, June 1). Al-Jazeera sends its brand West. *World Business*. Retrieved August 1, 2008 from www.worldbusinesslive.com/article/560597/al-jazeera-sends-its-brand-west/.

Diouf, S. A. (1998). *Servants of Allah: African Muslims Enslaved in the Americas*. New York: New York University Press.

Ditchy, J. R. (1932). *Les Acadiens Louisianais et leur Parler*. Paris: Librairie E. Droz.

Dorian, N. C. (1994). Stylistic variation in a language restricted to private-sphere use. In D. Bibier & E. Finegan (eds.), *Sociolinguistic Perspectives on Register* (217–32). New York: Oxford University Press.

Dorrance, W. A. (1935). The survival of French in the Old District of Sainte-Geneviève. Unpublished doctoral dissertation, University of Missouri, Columbia.

Draper, J. B. & Hicks, J. H. (2002). Foreign language enrollments in public secondary schools, Fall 2000. Alexandria, VA: American Council on the Teaching of Foreign Languages. Retrieved August 15, 2007, from www.actfl.org/files/public/Enroll2000.pdf.

Dubois, S. (2000). *Final Report of the Cajun Project at LSU* (grant SBR-9514831). Washington, DC: National Science Foundation.

Dziwirek, K. (2001). Nauczanie języka polskiego na poziomie uniwersyteckim w Seattle. *Postscriptum* 37–8; 33–9.

Dziwirek, K. & Cholewińska, A. (2000). Teaching Polish in the US at the elementary and university levels. Paper presented at the Future of Poles Abroad Conference organized by the Council for Research on Poles Abroad of the Polish Academy of Sciences, Bydgoszcz, Poland.

Eichhoff, J. (1985). The Germans in America. In F. Trommler & J. McVeigh (eds.), *America and the Germans: An Assessment of a Three-Hundred Year History* (Vol. I, pp. 223–40). Philadelphia: University of Pennsylvania Press.

Elías-Olivares, L., Leone, E. A., Cisneros, R., & Gutiérrez, J. R. (eds.) (1985). *Spanish Language Use and Public Life in the United States*. Berlin: Mouton.

Erdmans, M. P. (1998). *Opposite Poles: Immigrants and Ethnics in Polish Chicago, 1976–1990*. University Park: Pennsylvania State University Press.

Evers, L., with Dozier, A., Lopez, D., Molina, F., Perkins, E. T., Sekaquaptewa, E., & Zepeda, O. (1983). *The South Corner of Time: Hopi, Navajo, Papago, Yaqui Tribal Literature*. Tucson: University of Arizona Press.

Farrington v. *Tokushige*. 273 U.S. 284, 298 (1927).

Faulk, J. D. (1977). *Cajun French I*. Crowley, LA: Cajun Press.

Faust, A. B. (1912). *Das Deutschtum in den Vereinigten Staaten* (Vols. I & II). Leipzig: B.G. Teubner.

Feldman, O. (2001). Inspired by a dream. *Spectrum, IIX* (2). Retrieved July 31, 2007 from http://web.mit.edu/giving/spectrum/spring01/inspired-by-a-dream.html.

Fellin, L. (2007). Lost tongues and reinvented repertoires: ideologies of language and creative communicative practices among 3rd generation Italian Americans. *Studi Italiani di Linguistica Teorica ed Applicata* 36(3), 443–62.

Ferguson, C. A. (1959). *Diglossia*. In P. Gilglioli (ed.), *Language in Social Context* (pp. 232–57). Middlesex, UK: Penguin.

Ferreira, F. (2005). That's not how my grandmother says it: Portuguese heritage language learners in southeastern Massachusetts. *Hispania* 88(4), 848–62.

(2007). Portuguese heritage language learners: Proficiency levels and sociolinguistic profiles. *Portuguese Language Journal*, 2. Retrieved July 19, 2009 from www.latam.ufl.edu/portugueselanguagejournal/index.html.

Field, M. (1998). Maintenance of indigenous ways of speaking despite language shift: Language socialization in a Navajo preschool. PhD dissertation. University of California, Santa Barbara.

Filipino-American Centennial Commemoration (2005). *Timeline: Filipino-American History*. Retrieved September 8, 2007, from www.apa.si.edu/filamcentennial/timeline.html.

Finnegan, E. & Rickford, J. (eds.) (2004). *Language in the USA*. New York: Cambridge University Press.

Finocchiaro, C. M. (2004). Language maintenance/shift of a three generation Italian family in three migration countries: An international comparative study. PhD dissertation. University of Melbourne.

Fishman, J. A. (1965). Who speaks what language to whom and when? *La Linguistique* 2, 67–88.

Fishman, J. A. (ed.). (1971). *Advances in the Sociology of Language*. The Hague: Mouton.

Fishman, J. A. (1985). Demographic and institutional indicators of German language maintenance in the United States, 1960–1980. In F. Trommler & J. McVeigh (eds.), *America and the Germans: An Assessment of a Three-Hundred Year History* (Vol. I, pp. 251–69). Philadelphia: University of Pennsylvania Press.

(1991a). An inter-polity perspective on the relationships between linguistic heterogeneity, civil strife, and per capita gross national product. *International Journal of Applied Linguistics* 1(1), 5–18.

(1991b). *Reversing Language Shift: Theoretical and Empirical Foundations of Assistance to Threatened Languages*. Philadelphia: Multilingual Matters.

(2004). Multilingualism and non-English mother tongues. In E. Finegan & J. R. Rickford (eds.), *Language in the USA: Themes for the Twenty-first Century* (pp. 115–23). Cambridge: Cambridge University Press.

Fishman, J. A., Gertner, M. H., Lowy, E. G. *et al.* (1985). *The Rise and Fall of Ethnic Revival*. Berlin: Mouton.

Fishman, T. C. (2004, July 4). The Chinese century. *The New York Times Magazine*. Retrieved August 16, 2008 from www.nytimes.com/2004/07/04/magazine/04CHINA.html.

Forbes, W. C. (1945). *The Philippine Islands*. London: Oxford University Press.

Fought, C. (2006). *Language and Ethnicity*. Cambridge: Cambridge University Press.

Foundation for Korean Language and Culture in the USA. (2007). List of schools offering Korean. Retrieved October 26, 2007 from www.klacusa.org/.

Fox, C. A. (1995). On maintaining a francophone identity in Cohoes, NY. *The French Review* 69(2), 264–74.

(1998). Le transfert linguistique et la réduction morphologique: le genre en français de Cohoes. In P. Brasseur (ed.), *Français d'Amérique: Variation, Créolisation, Normalisation* (61–74). Avignon: Centre d'Etudes Canadiennes, Université d'Avignon.

(2007). Franco-American voices: French in the Northeastern United States Today. *French Review* 80 (6), 1278–92.

Fox, C. A. & Smith, J. S. (2005). La situation du français franco-américain: aspects linguistiques et sociolinguistiques. In A. Valdman, J. Auger, & D. Piston-Hatlen (eds.), *Le Français en Amérique du Nord; État Présent* (117–41). Québec: Presses de l'Université Laval.

Freeman, D. & Freeman, Y. (1998). Sheltered English instruction. Washington, DC: ERIC Clearinghouse on Languages and Linguistics (ERIC Identifier: ED301070). Retrieved August 8, 2008 from www.ericdigests.org/pre-9210/english.htm.

Fuller, J. M. (1999). The role of English in Pennsylvania German development: Best supporting actress? *American Speech* 74(1), 38–55.

(2001). The principle of pragmatic detachability in borrowing: English-origin discourse markers in Pennsylvania German. *Linguistics* 39(2), 351–69.

Furman, N., Goldberg, D., & Lusin, N. (2007). Enrollments in languages other than English in United States institutions of higher learning, fall 2006. Modern Language Association. Retrieved November 24, 2007 from www.mla.org/pdf/06enrollmentsurvey_final.pdf.

Furmanek, O. (2000). Polglish: A valid sublanguage or a horrifying unacceptable deviation? *ATA Chronicle* 7, 50–52.

Galang, R. G. (2006). Heritage language maintenance in the US: The Filipino American experience. In S. Quakenbush & D. Dayag (eds.), *Sociolinguistics and Language Education in the Philippines and Beyond* (pp. 555–71). Manila: De La Salle University Press.

Galush, W. J. (1996). Polish Americans and religion. In J. Bukowczyk (ed.), *Polish Americans and Their History: Community, Culture and Politics* (pp. 80–92). Pittsburgh: University of Pittsburgh Press.

Gambhir, S. (2001). Truly less commonly taught languages and heritage language learners in the United States. In J. K. Peyton, D. A. Ranard, & S. McGinnis (eds.), *Heritage Languages in America: Preserving a National Resource* (pp. 207–28). McHenry, IL: The Center for Applied Linguistics and Delta Systems.

García, O. (2005). Positioning heritage languages in the United States. *The Modern Language Journal* 89(4), 601–5.

Gease, H. B. (2002). Oglala code talker last link to history. Canku Ota (Many Paths), 64, June 29. Retrieved December 11, 2007 from www.turtletrack.org/Issues02/Co06292002/CO_06292002_Oglala_Code_Talker.htm.

Gelhay, P. (1985). *Notre Langue Louisianaise: Our Louisiana Language*. Jennings, LA: Editions françaises de Louisiane.

German Information Center. (2008). *Book Culture in Germany*. Washington, DC: German Embassy. Retrieved, July 15, 2008 from www.germany.info/relaunch/info/publications/infocus/buchmesse/book_culture.html.

Gerstle, G. (1989). *Working-Class Americanism: The Politics of Labor in a Textile City, 1914–1960*. Cambridge: Cambridge University Press.

Gilbert, G. G. (1981). French and German: A comparative study. In C. A. Ferguson & S. B. Heath (eds.), *Language in the USA* (pp. 257–72). Cambridge: Cambridge University Press.

Giles, H., Bourhis, R. Y., & Taylor, D. M. (1977). Towards a theory of language in ethnic group relations. In H. Giles (ed.), *Language, Ethnicity and Intergroup Relations* (pp. 307–48). London: Academic Press.

Gitleman, Z. (1981). Soviet immigrants and American absorption efforts: A case study in Detroit. In D. N. Jacobs & E. F. Paul (eds.), *Studies of the Third Wave: Recent Migration of Soviet Jews to the United States* (pp. 11–28). Boulder: Co: Westview Press.

GLSC (n.d.). German Language Schools Conference. Retrieved September 13, 2008 from www.germanschools.org/.

Goddard, I. (1996). Introduction. In I. Goddard (Vol. ed.) & W. C. Sturtevant (Gen. ed.), *Handbook of North American Indians Vol. XVII: Languages* (pp. 1–16). Washington, DC: Smithsonian Institution.

Goldberg, D. & Welles, E. B. (2001). Successful college and university programs, 1995–1999: Part 1. *Profession* 2001, 171–210.

Gonzalez, J., III. (2001, Nov.). Christianity returns to America. *Filipina Magazine*. Retrieved March 5, 2008, from www.usfca.edu/TRIP/Gonzalez.pdf.

González, J. M. (2007). It's time to get another horse. *International Multilingual Research Journal* 1(1), 39–44.

González, J. M. & Wiley, T. G. (2007). In the shadow of English: The status and future of Spanish and Chinese as global languages in the United States. Paper presented at the Conference on Becoming a World Language: The Growth of Chinese, English, and Spanish. Hong Kong: City University of Hong Kong.

Gonzo, S. & Saltarelli, M. (1983). Pidginization and linguistic change in emigrant languages. In R. W. Andersen (ed.), *Pidginization and Creolization as Language Acquisition* (pp. 191–7). Rowley, MA: Newbury House.

Gordon, R. G., Jr. (ed.) (2005). *Ethnologue: Languages of the World* (15th edn.). Dallas: SIL International.

Gorman, L. & Potowski, K. (2009). Communicative contact between Spanish-speaking immigrants and US-born Latinos. Paper presented at the 22nd Meeting of Spanish in the USA, Miami, FL.

Graddol, D. (2000). *The Future of English?* London: The British Council.

Gravelles, M. U. de (Marcantel, D). (1979). *Mille misères–Laissant le bon temps rouler en Louisiane*. Québec: Projet Louisiane, Université Laval.

Grenoble, L. (2003). *Language Policy in the Soviet Union*. Dordrecht: Kluwer Academic Publishers.

Greymorning, S. (2001). Reflections on the Arapaho language project, or when Babmi spoke Arapaho and other tales of Arapaho language revitalization efforts. In L. Hinton & K. Hale (eds.), *The Green Book of Language Revitalization in Practice* (pp. 286–97). San Diego, CA: Academic Press.

Grimes, B. F. (1995). *Ethnologue: Languages of the World* (12th edn.). Dallas, TX: SIL International.

Grimes, B. F. (ed.) (1996). *Ethnologue Language Name Index to the Thirteenth Edition of the Ethnologue*. Dallas: Summer Institute of Linguistics.

Griolet, P. (1986). *Mots de Louisiane: Études Lexicales d'une Francophonie*. Romanica Gothoburgensia, 30. Götenborg: Acta Universitatis Gothenburgensis.

Grosjean, F. (1982). *Life with Two Languages: An Introduction to Bilingualism*. Cambridge, MA: Harvard University Press.

Haas, M. (1992). *Institutional Racism: The case of Hawai'i*. Westport, CT: Praeger.

Hagel, P. L. (1981). The Richford experience: French bilingual education as a "basic" approach to language competence. *The French Review* 54(3), 393–400.

Haiman, M. (1974). *Polish Past in America, 1608–1865*. Chicago: Polish Museum of America.

Hakuta, K. (1986). *Mirror of Language: The Debate on Bilingualism*. New York: Basic Books.

(1987). Degree of bilingualism and cognitive ability in mainland Puerto Rican children. *Child Development* 58, 1372–88.

(1989). Bilingualism and intelligence testing: An annotated bibliography. *BRG Working Papers 89–08*. Santa Cruz, CA: University of California, Santa Cruz, Bilingual Research Group.

Hale, K. (1997). Reasons to be optimistic about local language maintenance and restoration. Paper prepared for the Linguistic Association of the Southwest (LASSO) Conference.

Haller, H. (1987). Italian speech varieties in the United States and the Italian American lingua franca. *Italica* 64(3), 393–409.

(1993). *Una Lingua Perduta e Ritrovata*. Florence: La Nuova Italia.

Halter, M. (2005). Cape Verdeans in the United States. In I. Skoggard & C. R. Ember (eds.), *Encyclopedia of Diasporas: Immigrant and Refugee Cultures Around the World* (pp. 615–23). New York: Springer.

Ham, E. B. (1938). Journalism and the French survival in New England. *The New England Quarterly* 11(1), 89–107.

Hamilton, D. S. (2008). Creating the transatlantic marketplace. *AICGS Advisor (July 27, 2008)*. Washington, DC: American Institute for Contemporary German Studies. Retrieved July 16, 2008 from www.aicgs.org/documents/advisor/hamilton0608.pdf.

Hanley, D. C. (2004, September). Bush and Kerry may regret ignoring concerns of Muslim-, Arab-American voters. *Washington Report on Middle East Affairs*. Retrieved March 20, 2008 from http://wrmea.com/archives/Sept_2004/0409025.html.

Hardwick, S. W. (1993). *Russian Refuge: Religion, Migration, and Settlement on the North American Pacific Rim*. Chicago: The University of Chicago Press.

Haugen, E. (1953 [1969]). *The Norwegian Language in America: A Study in Bilingual Behavior*. Philadelphia: University of Pennsylvania Press. [Reprinted in 1969. Bloomington, IN: Indiana University Press]

Haugen, E. (1977). Norm and deviation in bilingual communities. In P. A. Hornby (ed.), *Bilingualism: Psychological, Social and Educational Implications* (pp. 91–102). New York: Academic Press.

Hayden, R. L. (1979). Toward a national foreign language policy. *Journal of Communication* 29(2), 93–102.

He, A. W. (2008). Chinese as a heritage language: An introduction. In A. W. He & Y. Xiao (eds.), *Fostering Rooted World Citizenry: Studies in Chinese as a Heritage Language* (pp. 1–12). Hawaii: NFLRC, University of Hawaii Press.

Heath, S. B. (1976). Colonial language status achievement: Mexico, Peru, and the United States. In A. Verdoodt & R. Kjolseth (eds.), *Language and Sociology* (pp. 49–91). Louvin: Peeters.

(1977). Language and politics in the United States. In M. Saville-Troike (ed.), *Linguistics and Anthropology* (pp. 267–96). Georgetown University Roundtable on Languages and Linguistics. Washington DC: Georgetown University Press.

Henry, J. (1994). Changement social et ethnicité en Louisiane: le CODOFIL dans le mouvement francophone. *Présence Francophone* 43, 25–46.

Hermes, M. & Roach, K. (2007, November). Creating Ojibwe movies: The idea of discourse and endangered languages. *Presentation at the Language, Education and Diversity Conference*. Hamilton, NZ: University of Waikato.

Hernández-Chávez, E. (1994). Language policy in the United States: A history of cultural genocide. In T. Skutnabb-Kangas & R. Phillipson (eds.), *Linguistic Human Rights; Overcoming Linguistic Discrimination* (pp. 141–58). Berlin: Mouton de Gruyter.

Highfield, A. R. (1979). *The French Dialect of St. Thomas, US Virgin Islands: A Descriptive Grammar with Texts and Glossary*. Ann Arbor, MI: Karoma Publishers.

Hill, J. H. (1995). Mock Spanish: A site for the indexical reproduction of racism in American English. Retrieved September 1, 2008 from http://web.archive.org/web/20021216220940/http://www.language-culture.org/colloquia/symposia/hill-jane/.

Hinton, L. (1998). Language loss and revitalization in California: Overview. *International Journal of the Sociology of Language* 132, 83–93.

(2001a). Sleeping languages: Can they be awakened? In L. Hinton & K. Hale (eds.), *The Green Book of Language Revitalization in Practice* (pp. 413–17). San Diego, CA: Academic Press.

(2001b). The master–apprentice language learning program. In L. Hinton & K. Hale (eds.), *The Green Book of Language Revitalization in Practice* (pp. 217–26). San Diego, CA: Academic Press.

Hinton, L. & Hale, K. (2001). (eds.). *The Green Book of Language Revitalization in Practice*. San Diego, CA: Academic Press.

Hinton, L. & Watahomigie, L. J. (eds.). (1984). *Spirit Mountain: An Anthology of Yuman Story and Song*. Tucson, AZ: Sun Tracks and the University of Arizona Press.

Hitti, P. (1924). *The Syrians in America*. New York: George H. Doran.

Holes, C. (1995). *Modern Arabic: Structures, Functions, and Varieties*. London: Longman.

Holm, W. (2006). The "goodness" of bilingual education for Native American children. In T. L. McCarty & O. Zepeda with V. H. Begay, S. Charging Eagle, S. C. Moore, L. Warhol, & T. M. K. Williams, *One Voice, Many Voices – Recreating Indigenous Language Communities* (pp. 1–46). Tempe: Arizona State University Center for Indian Education.

Holm, A. & Holm, W. (1995). Navajo language education: Retrospect and prospects. *Bilingual Research Journal* 19(1), 141–67.

Hornberger, N. H. (ed.). (1996). *Indigenous Literacies in the Americas: Language Planning from the Bottom Up*. Berlin: Mouton de Gruyter.

Hostetler, J. A. (1980). *Amish Society*. Baltimore, MD: Johns Hopkins University Press.

Hudson-Edwards, A., Hernández Chávez, E., & Bills, G. D. (1995). The many faces of language maintenance: Spanish language claiming in five southwestern states. In

C. Silva-Corvalán (ed.), *Spanish in Four Continents: Studies in Language Contact and Bilingualism* (pp. 165–83). Washington, DC: Georgetown University Press.

Huffines, M. L. (1985). Language maintenance efforts among German immigrants and their descendants in the United States. In F. Trommler & J. McVeigh (eds.), *America and the Germans: An Assessment of a Three-Hundred Year History* (Vol. I, pp. 241–50). Philadelphia: University of Pennsylvania Press.

Huntingdon, S. P. (2004). *Who are We?: The Challenges to America's National Identity*. New York: Simon and Schuster.

Hurh, W. M. (1998). *The Korean Americans*. Westport, CT: Greenwood.

Hutton, C. M. (1999). *Linguistics and the Third Reich: Mother-Tongue Fascism, Race, and the Science of Language*. London: Routledge.

Ilano-Tenorio, B. (1997). Filipino Americans, children of immigrants: A participatory research of language and identity. Doctoral Dissertation, 9726480. Michigan: UMI.

Ingold, C. W., Rivers, W., Tesser, C. C., & Ashby, E. (2002). Report on the NFLC/AATSP survey of Spanish language programs for native speakers. *Hispania* 85, 324–9.

Internet World Stats. (2008). *Internet World Users by Language: Top 10 Languages*. Retrieved October 10, 2008 from http://internetworldstats.com/stats7.htm.

Institute of International Education. (2007). Open doors 2007: International Students in the U.S. Retrieved April 5, 2008 from http://opendoors.iienetwork.org/?p=113743.

ISTAT. (2007). La lingua italiana, i dialetti e le lingue straniere: Anno 2006. Istituto Nazionale di Statistica. Retrieved February 14, 2008 from www.istat.it/salastampa/comunicati/non_calendario/20070420_00/testointegrale.pdf.

Jackson, F. H. & Kaplan, M. A. (1999). Lessons learned from fifty years of theory and practice in government language teaching. *Georgetown University Round Table on Languages and Linguistics*. Retrieved February 13, 2010 from http://dspace.wrlc.org/bitstream/1961/3455/8/gurt_1999_07.pdf.

Jacobs, D. N., Paul, E. F., & Frankel, E. (eds.). (1981). *Studies of the Third Wave: Recent Migration of Soviet Jews to the United States*. Boulder, CO: Westview Press.

Jacobson, P. L. (1984). The social context of Franco-American schooling in New England. *The French Review* 57(5), 641–56.

Jacoby, T. (ed.). (2004). *Reinventing the Melting Pot: The New Immigrants and What it Means to be American*. New York: Basic Books.

Jaspaert, K. & Kroon, S. (1992). From the typewriter of A. L.: A case study in language loss. In W. Fase, K. Jaspaert, & S. Kroon (eds.), *Maintenance and Loss of Minority Languages* (pp. 137–47). Amsterdam: John Benjamins.

Jeon, M. (2008). Korean heritage language maintenance and language ideology. *Heritage Language Journal* 6(2), 54–72.

Jia, G. (2008). Heritage language maintenance and attrition among first generation Chinese immigrants in New York City. In A. W. He & Y. Xiao (eds.), *Fostering Rooted World Citizenry: Studies in Chinese as a Heritage Language* (pp. 189–204). Hawaii: NFLRC, University of Hawaii Press.

Jia, L. & Bayley, R. (2008). The (re)acquisition of perfective aspect marking by Chinese heritage language learners. In A. W. He & Y. Xiao (eds.), *Fostering Rooted World Citizenry: Studies in Chinese as a Heritage Language* (pp. 205–24). Hawaii: NFLRC, University of Hawaii Press.

Jim, R. L. (1998). *Dúchas/Táá kóó Diné: A Trilingual Poetry Collection in Navajo, Irish, and English*. Diarmuid O'Breaslin, Irish trans. Belfast: An Clochán.

Jo, J. O. (To appear). Journey of language: US Korean youths' life histories and language experiences. In C. C. Park, S. J. Lee, X. L. Rong, & R. Endo (eds.), *Research Anthology on the Education of Asian and Pacific Americans* (Vol. 4) (pp. 55–75). Greenwich, CT: Information Age Publishing.

Jongh, E. M. (1990). Interpreting in Miami's federal courts: code-switching and Spanglish. *Hispania* 73(1), 274–8.

Johnson, F. L. (2000). *Speaking Culturally: Language Diversity in the United States*. London: Sage Publications.

Johnson, F. T. & Legatz, J. (2006). Tséhootsooí Dine Bi'ólta'. *Journal of American Indian Education* 45(2), 26–33.

Johnson-Weiner, K. (1998). Community identity and language change in North America Anabaptist communities. *Journal of Sociolinguistics* 2/3, 375–94.

Jordan, H. (1999, February 17). Latino lawmakers study their Spanish: Some were fluent as kids but stumble today. *San Jose Mercury News*. Retrieved September 23, 2004 from www.stanford.edu/dept/SUSE/Spencer_PRproject/indexSJMNarticle.htm.

Jouët-Pastré, C. & Braga, L. (2005). Community-based learning: A window into the Portuguese-speaking communities of New England. *Hispania* 88(4), 863–72.

Jouët-Pastré, C. & Braga, L. (eds.) (2008). *Becoming Brazuca. Brazilian Immigration to the United States*. Cambridge, MA: Harvard University Press.

Kagan, O. (2005). In support of a proficiency-based definition of heritage language learners: A case of Russian. *International Journal of Bilingual Education and Bilingualism* 8(2&3), 213–21.

Kagan, O. & Dillon, K. (2001/2002). A new perspective on teaching Russian: Focus on the heritage learner. *Slavic and East European Journal* 45(3), 507–18. Rpt. in *Heritage Language Journal* 1.1 (www.heritagelanguages.org).

(2006). Russian heritage learners: So what happens now? *Slavic and East European Journal* 50(1), 83–96.

Kagan, O., Akishina, T., & Robin, R. (2003). *Russian for Russians: Textbook for Heritage Speakers*. Bloomington, IN: Slavica.

Karandash. (2007). Retrieved November 16, 2007 from www.karandash.us/pr/russian/info/default.asp.

Katzner, K. (2002). *The Languages of the World*. New York: Routledge.

Kavé, G., Eyal, N., Shorek, A., & Cohen-Mansfield, J. (2008). Multilingualism and cognitive state in the oldest old. *Psychology and Aging* 23(1), 70–8.

Kim, B. H. (1984). *Hangugŏ-üy kyethong (Geneology of Korean)*. Seoul: Minŭmsa.

Kim, R. Y. (2002). Ethnic differences in academic achievement between Vietnamese and Cambodian children: Cultural and structural explanations. *The Sociological Quarterly* 43(2), 213–35.

(2006). *God's New Whiz Kids: Korean American Evangelicals on Campus*. New York: New York University Press.

King, R. (1998) Korean as a Heritage Language (KHL) vs. Korean as a Foreign Language (KFL) in North America and the Former USSR: Ambiguous Priorities and Insufficient Resources. *Acta Koreana* 1, 27–40.

(2000). *The Lexical Basis of Grammatical Borrowing: A Prince Edward Island French Case Study*. Amsterdam: John Benjamins.

Kiser & Associates. (n.d.). The market. Retrieved July 5, 2008 from www.kiserassociates.com/market.html.

Kishinevsky, V. (2004). *Russian Immigrants in the United States: Adapting to American Culture*. New York: LFB Scholarly Publishing LLC.

Klemensiewicz, Z. (1980). *Historia Języka Polskiego*. Warszawa: Państwowe Wydawnictwo Naukowe.

Klingler, T. A. (2003). *"If I could Turn my Tongue like That": The Creole Language of Pointe Coupee Parish, Louisiana*. Baton Rouge: Louisiana State University.

Kloss, H. (1963 [1998]). *Das Nationalitätenrecht der Vereinigen Staaten*. McHenry, IL: CAL.

(1971). Language rights of immigrant groups. *International Migration Review* 5, 250–68.

(1998). *The American Bilingual Tradition*. Washington, DC: Center for Applied Linguistics.

Koda, K., Zhang,Y., & Yang, C. L. (2008). Literacy development in Chinese as a heritage language. In A. W. He & Y. Xiao (eds.), *Fostering Rooted World Citizenry: Studies in Chinese as a Heritage Language* (pp. 125–36). Hawaii: NFLRC, University of Hawaii Press.

Koehn, P. H. & Yin, X. H. (2002). Chinese American transnationalism and U.S.–China relations: Presence and promise for the trans-Pacific century. In P. H. Koehn & X. H. Yin (eds.), *The Expanding Roles of Chinese Americans in U.S.–China Relations: Transnational Networks and Trans-Pacific Interactions* (pp. xi–xxxx). Armonk, NY: M. E. Sharpe, Inc.

Kondo-Brown, K. (ed.). (2006). *Heritage Language Development: Focus on East Asian Immigrants*. Amsterdam/Philadelphia: John Benjamins Publishing Company.

Korean-American Education Commission. (2007). USEC Newsletter Volume 132. Retrieved April 5, 2008 from www.fulbright.or.kr/bbs/zboard.php?id=newsletter.

Kotlovitz, A. (2007, August 5). Our town. *New York Times Magazine*. Retrieved October 16, 2007 from www.nytimes.com/2007/08/05/magazine/05Immigration-t.html?_r=1&emc=eta1&oref=slogin.

Krashen, S. D. (1996). *Under Attack: The Case Against Bilingual Education*. CA: Culver City, Language Education Associates.

Krashen, S. D. (1998). Heritage language development: Some practical arguments. In K. Stephen, L. Tse, & J. McQuillan (eds.), *Heritage Language Development* (pp. 3–13). Culver City, CA: Language Education Associates.

Krauss, M. (1998). The condition of Native North American languages: The need for realistic assessment and action. *International Journal of the Sociology of Language* 132, 9–21.

Kraybill, D. B. (2003). *Who are the Anabaptists? Amish, Brethren, Hutterites, and Mennonites*. Scottdale, PA: Herald Press.

Kraybill, D. B. & Bowman, C. F. (2001). *On the Backroad to Heaven*, Baltimore, MD: Johns Hopkins University Press.

Kroskrity, P. V. (1993). *Language, History, and Identity: Ethnolinguistic Studies of the Arizona Tewa*. Tucson, AZ: University of Arizona Press.

(2000). Language ideologies in the expression and representation of Arizona Tewa identity. In P. V. Kroskrity (ed.), *Regimes of Language: Ideologies, Polities, and Identities* (pp. 329–59). Santa Fe, NM: School of American Research Press.

Lagarde, F. (2007). *Français aux Etats-Unis (1990–2005)*. New York: Peter Lang.

Language Flagship. (2008). *Language Flagship*. Retrieved July 7, 2008 from www.thelanguageflagship.org/index.html.

Language Materials Project. (n.d.). *Language Profiles*. Los Angeles: UCLA Language Materials Project. Retrieved September 14, 2008 from www.lmp.ucla.edu/Profile.aspx?menu=004.

Lavandera, B. R. (1978). The variable component in bilingual performance. In J. E. Alatis (ed.), *International Dimensions of Bilingual Education* (pp. 391–409). Washington, DC: Georgetown University Press.

Lavaud-Grassin, M. (1988). Particularités lexicales du parler cadjin en Louisiane (Etats-Unis). Enquête, dictionnaire et documentation bibliographique (4 vols.). Unpublished doctoral dissertation (doctorat d'Etat), University of Paris III – Sorbonne Nouvelle.

Lavretsky, E., Meland, D., & Plotkin, D. A. (1997). Children from the former Soviet Union. In G. Johnson-Powell & J. Yamamoto (eds.), *Transcultural Child Development* (pp. 328–46). New York: John Wiley & Sons.

Lazin, F. A. (2005). Refugee resettlement and "freedom of choice": The case of Soviet Jewry. Center for Immigration Studies. Retrieved October 27, 2007 from www.cis.org/articles/2005/back705.html.

Lee, E. (2004). Korean immigrant women's work in the nail salon industry: gender, race and class in the service sector. In I. J. Kim (ed.), *Korean-Americans: Past, Present and Future* (pp. 75–89). Elizabeth, NJ: Holly International Corp.

Lee, J. & Bean, F. D. (2003). Beyond black and white: Remaking race in America. *Contexts* 2(3), 26–33.

Lee, J. S. (2002). The Korean language in America: The role of cultural identity in heritage language learning. *Language, Culture and Curriculum* 15(2), 111–33.

(2006). Exploring the relationship between electronic literacy and heritage language maintenance. *Language, Learning, and Technology* 10(2), 93–113.

Lee, J. S. & Kim, H.-Y. (2008). Heritage language learners' attitudes, motivations and instructional needs: The case of post-secondary Korean language learners. In K. Kondo-Brown & J. D. Brown (eds.), *Teaching Chinese, Japanese, and Korean Heritage Students: Curriculum, Needs, Materials, and Assessment* (pp. 159–85). Philadelphia: Lawrence Erlbaum.

Lee, K. M. (1976). *Kaejŏng kugŏsa kaesŏl* [A revised introduction to the history of Korean]. Seoul: Minjungsŏgwan.

Leibowitz, A. H. (1969). English literacy: Legal sanction for discrimination. *Notre Dame Lawyer* 25(1), 7–66.

(1971). Educational policy and political acceptance: The imposition of English as the language of instruction in American Schools. Eric No. ED 047 321.

(1974). Language as a means of social control. Paper presented at the VIII World Congress of Sociology. University of Toronto, Toronto, Canada, August 1974.

(1976). Language and the law: The exercise of political power through the official designation of language. In O'Barr & O'Barr (eds.), *Language and politics* (pp. 449–66). The Hague: Mouton.

Leibowitz, A. H. (1982). *Federal Recognition of the Rights of Minority Language Groups*. Rosslyn, VA: National Clearinghouse of Bilingual Education.

Leonard, W. Y. (2008). When is an "extinct language" not extinct? Miami, a formerly sleeping language. In K. A. King, N. Schilling-Estes, L. Fogle, J. J. Louo,

& B. Soukup (eds.), *Sustaining Linguistic Diversity: Endangered and Minority Languages and Language Varieties* (pp. 23–33). Washington, DC: Georgetown University Press.

Lepore, J. (2002). *A is for American: Letters and other Characters in the Newly United States*. New York: Alfred Knopf.

Levine, B. (2003). *Réveil: The Repression and Renaissance of the French in New England* [Motion Picture]. USA: Watching Place Productions.

Li, G. F. (2003). Literacy, culture, and politics of schooling: Counternarratives of a Chinese Canadian family. *Anthropology and Education Quarterly* 34(2), 182–204.

(2006a). *Culturally Contested pedagogy: Battles of Literacy and Schooling Between Mainstream Teachers and Asian Immigrant Parents*. SUNY series, Power, Social Identity, and Education. Albany, NY: State University of New York Press.

(2006b). The role of parents in heritage language maintenance and development. In K. Kondo-Brown (ed.), *Heritage Language Development: Focus on East Asian Immigrants* (pp. 15–32). Amsterdam/Philadelphia: John Benjamins.

Li, S. (2002). Navigating U.S.–China waters: The experience of Chinese students and professionals in science, technology, and business. In P. H. Koehn & X. H. Yin (eds.), *The Expanding Roles of Chinese Americans in U.S.–China Relations: Transnational Networks and Trans-Pacific Interactions* (pp. 20–35). Armonk, NY: M. E. Sharpe, Inc.

Lieberson, S., Dalto, G., & Johnston, M. E. (1975). The course of mother-tongue diversity in nations. *American Journal of Sociology* 81, 34–61.

Lindenfeld, J. (2000). *The French in the United States*. Westport, CT and London: Bergin and Garvey.

Lipski, J. M. (1993). Creoloid phenomena in the Spanish of transitional bilinguals. In A. Roca & J. M. Lipski (eds.), *Spanish in the United States: Linguistic Contact and Diversity* (pp. 155–82). Berlin: Mouton de Gruyter.

(2008). *Varieties of Spanish in the United States*. Washington, DC: Georgetown University Press.

L'Italo-Americano. (2003). About Us. Retrieved July 9, 2008 from www.italoamericano.com/about%20us.htm.

Liu, H. (2002). Historical connections between the Chinese trans-Pacific family and U.S.–China relations. In P. H. Koehn & X. H. Yin (eds.), *The Expanding Roles of Chinese Americans in U.S.–China Relations: Transnational Networks and Trans-Pacific Interactions* (pp. 3–19). Armonk, NY: M. E. Sharpe, Inc.

Liu, H., Bates, E., & Li, P. (1992). Sentence processing in bilingual speakers of English and Chinese. *Applied Psycholinguistics* 13, 451–84.

Locke, W. N. (1946). Notes on the vocabulary of the French-Canadian dialect spoken in Brunswick, Maine, *French Review* 19(6), 416–22.

Lokensgard, M. (2007). A presença da língua portuguesa nos EUA. *Revista Espaço Acadêmico* 73, 1–3.

Lomawaima, K. T. (1994). *They called it Prairie Light: The Story of Chilocco Indian School*. Lincoln and London: University of Nebraska Press.

Lomawaima, K. T. & McCarty, T. L. (2006). *"To Remain an Indian": Lessons in Democracy from a Century of Native American Education*. New York, NY: Teachers College Press.

López, D. E. (1978). Chicano language loyalty in an urban setting. *Sociology and Social Research* 62, 267–78.
(1991). The emergence of language minorities in the United States. In J. R. Dow (ed.), *Focus on Language and Ethnicity*. Amsterdam: John Benjamins.
Lovato, R. (2007, September 10). Univision presidential debate: Media, migrants, translating power. *Of America*. Retrieved March 29, 2008 from http://ofamerica.wordpress.com/2007/09/10/univision-presidential-debate-media-and-migrants-translating-power/.
Lowell, B. L. & Suro, R. (2002). How many undocumented – The numbers behind the US–Mexico migration talks. Pew Hispanic Center. Accessed February 7, 2010 at http://pewhispanic.org/reports/report.php?ReportID=6.
Luebke, F. C. (1990). *Germans in the New World*. Urbana, IL; University of Illinois Press.
Macías, R. F. (1979). Choice of language as a human right: Public policy implications in the United States. In R. V. Padilla (ed.), *Bilingual Education and Public Policy in the United States* (pp. 39–75). Ypsilanti, MI: Eastern Michigan University.
(1985). Language and ideology in the United States. *Social Education* (February), 97–100.
(2000). Language politics and the historiography of Spanish in the United States. In J. K. Peyton, P. Griffin & W. Wolfram (eds.), *Language in Action: New Studies of Language in Society Essays in Honor of Roger W. Shuy* (pp. 52–83). Cresskill, NJ: Hampton Press.
Macías, R. F. & Wiley, T. G. (1998). Introduction. In H. Kloss, *The American Bilingual Tradition* (pp. vii–xiv). Washington, DC & McHenry, IL: Center for Applied Linguistics & Delta Systems.
MacSwan, J. (2000). The architecture of the bilingual language faculty: evidence from codeswitching. *Bilingualism, Language and Cognition* 3(1), 37–54.
Mandecki, W. (n.d.). *Wykaz polskich szkół w USA*. Retrieved April 12, 2008, from http://home.comcast.net/~wmandecki/wykazpolskichszkol/index1.html.
Margolis, M. L. (1994). *Little Brazil: An Ethnography of Brazilian Immigrants in New York City*. Princeton: Princeton University Press.
(2008). Brazilian immigration to the United States: Research and issues for the new millennium. In C. Jouët-Pastré & L. Braga (eds.), *Becoming Brazuca. Brazilian Immigration to the United States* (pp. 339–63). Cambridge, MA: Harvard University Press.
(2009). *An Invisible Minority: Brazilians in New York City*. Gainesville: University Press of Florida.
Martes, A. C. (2008). The commitment of return: Remittances of Brazilian émigrés. In C. Jouët-Pastré & L. Braga (eds.), *Becoming Brazuca. Brazilian Immigration to the United States* (pp. 125–50). Cambridge, MA: Harvard University Press.
Matras, Y. & Bakker, P. (eds.). (2003). *The Mixed Language Debate*. Berlin: Mouton de Gruyter.
May, S. (ed.). (1999). *Indigenous Community-Based Education*. Clevedon, UK: Multilingual Matters.
Mayes, F. (1998). *Under the Tuscan Sun*. Broadway Books: New York.
Mayle, P. (1989). *A Year in Provence*. New York: Random House.

McArthur, E. K. (1993). *Language Characteristics and Schooling in the United States, A Changing Picture: 1979 and 1989*. Washington, DC: US Department of Education, Office of Educational Research and Improvement, National Center for Educational Statistics. (NCES Report 93–699)

McCarthey, S. J. (1997). Connecting home and school literacy practices in classroom with diverse population. *Journal of Literacy Research* 29(2), 145–82.

McCarthy, J. A. (1985). The German language in America: An open forum. In F. Trommler & J. McVeigh (eds.), *America and the Germans: An Assessment of a Three-Hundred Year History* (Vol. I, pp. 270–9). Philadelphia: University of Pennsylvania Press.

McCarty, T. L. (2002). *A Place to be Navajo – Rough Rock and the Struggle for Self-Determination in Indigenous Schooling*. Mahwah, NJ: Lawrence Erlbaum.

(2004). Dangerous difference: A critical-historical analysis of language education policies in the United States. In J. W. Tollefson & A. B. M. Tsui (eds.), *Medium of Instruction Policies: Which Agenda? Whose Agenda?* (pp. 71–93). Mahwah, NJ: Lawrence Erlbaum.

(2008). Evaluating images of groups in your curriculum. In M. Pollack (ed.), *Everyday Antiracism: Getting Real about Race in School* (pp. 180–5). New York: The New Press.

McCarty, T. L. & Watahomigie, L. J. (1999). Community-based indigenous language education in the USA. In S. May (ed.), *Indigenous Community-Based Education* (pp. 79–96). Clevedon, UK: Multilingual Matters.

McCarty, T. L. & Watahomigie, L. J. (2004). Language and literacy in American Indian and Alaska Native communities. In B. Pérez (ed.), *Sociocultural Contexts of Language and Literacy* (pp. 79–110). Mahwah, NJ: Lawrence Erlbaum.

McCarty, T. L. & Zepeda, O. (eds.) with Begay, V. H., Charging-Eagle, S., Moore, S. C., Warhol, L., & Williams, T. M. K. (2006). *One Voice, Many Voices – Recreating Indigenous Language Communities*, Tempe: Center for Indian Education, Arizona State University.

McCarus, E. (1992). History of Arabic study in the United States. In A. Rouchdy (ed.), *The Arabic Language in America* (pp. 207–21). Detroit: Wayne State University Press.

McDermott, J. F. (1941). *A Glossary of Mississippi Valley French 1673–1850*. Saint Louis, MO: Washington University Studies.

McGinnis, S. (1994). The less common alternative: A report from the Task Force for Teacher Training for the Less Commonly Taught Languages. *ADFL Bulletin* 25(2) (Winter 1994), 17–22.

(2005a). *Statistics on Chinese language enrollment*. Washington, DC: Chinese Language Teachers Association. Retrieved September 10, 2007 from http://clta-us.org/flyers/enrollment_stats.htm.

(2005b). From mirror to compass: The Chinese heritage language education sector in the United States: Paper presented at the *AILA Conference*. Madison, WI.

McKay, S. L. & Wong, S. C. (eds.) (2000). *New Immigrants in the United States*. Cambridge: Cambridge University Press.

McLaughlin, D. (1992). *When Literacy Empowers: Navajo Language in Print*. Albuquerque: University of New Mexico Press.

Medicine, B. (2001). Bilingual education and public policy: The cases of the American Indian. In B. Medicine & S.-E. Jacobs (eds.), *Learning to be an Anthropologist and Remaining "Native": Selected Writings* (pp. 50–7). Urbana: University of Illinois Press.

Meihy, J. C. S. (2004). *Brasil fora de si. Experiências de brasileiros em Nova York*. São Paulo: Parábola.

Menezes, G. H. (2003). Filhos da imigração: A segunda geração de brasileiros em Connecticut. In A. C. B. Martes & S. Fleischer (eds.), *Fronteiras Cruzadas. Etnicidade, Gênero e Redes Sociais* (pp. 1157–73). São Paulo: Paz e Terra.

Mercurio, A. & Scarino, A. (2005). Heritage languages at upper secondary level in South Australia: A struggle for legitimacy. *International Journal of Bilingual Education and Bilingualism* 8(2&3), 145–59.

Meyer v. *Nebraska*. 262 US 390 (1923).

Meyers, C. & Yau, J. (2004). Legal immigration to US still declining. *Immigration Facts 9*. Washington, DC: Migration Policy Institute. Retrieved Jan 18, 2008 from www.migrationpolicy.org/pubs/Factsheet_102904.pdf.

MA-RBC. (2007). *Mid-Atlantic – Russia Business Council*. Mid-Atlantic - Russia Business Council Retrieved November 15, 2007 from www.ma-rbc.org/.

Migala, J. (1984). *Polskie programy radiowe w Stanach Zjednoczonych*. Warszawa: Wydawnictwa Radia i Telewizji.

Migliorini, B. (1987). *Storia della Lingua Italiana*. Florence: Sansoni.

Miller, M. K. (1969). Bilingualism in northern New England. *Publications of the American Dialect Society* 52, 1–23.

Miller, R. A. (1979). Some Old Packche fragments. *Journal of Korean Studies* 1, 3–69.

Miller Maloof, V., Rubin, D., & Neville Miller, A. (2006). Cultural competence and identity in cross-cultural adaptation: The role of a Vietnamese heritage language school. *International Journal of Bilingual Education and Bilingualism* 9(2), 255–73.

Min, P. G. (2000). Korean Americans' language use. In S. L. McKay and S. C. Wong (eds.), *New Immigrants in the United States* (pp. 306–32). Cambridge: Cambridge University Press.

(2001). Koreans: An "institutionally complete community" in New York. In N. Foner (ed.), *New Immigrants in New York* (second edition) (pp. 173–200). New York: Columbia University Press.

(2006). Korean Americans. In P. G. Min (ed.), *Asian Americans: Contemporary Trends and Issues* (second edition) (pp. 230–59). Thousand Oaks, CA: Sage.

Ming, T. & Tao, H. Y. (2008.). Developing a Chinese heritage language corpus: Issues and a preliminary report. In A. W. He & Y. Xiao (eds.), *Fostering Rooted World Citizenry: Studies in Chinese as a Heritage Language* (pp. 167–88). Hawaii: NFLRC, University of Hawaii Press.

Ministério das Relações Exteriores. (n.d.) Brasileiros no mundo: Portal das comunidades Brasileiras no exterior. Retrieved July 19, 2009, from www.brasileirosnomundo.mre.gov.br.

Mischner-Bang, S. (2005). *Background Survey of the German Language Saturday Schools*. New Brunswick, NJ: German Language School Conference.

Modern Language Association. (2007). New MLA survey shows significant increases in foreign language study at U.S. colleges and universities. Retrieved August 7, 2008 from www.mla.org/enroll_survpr06_fin.

(2008). *The Modern Language Association Language Map*. Retrieved August 28, 2008 from www.mla.org/map_main.

(2009). *MLA Language Map Data Center*. Retrieved June 19, 2009 from www.mla.org/map_data.

Molesky, J. (1988). Understanding the American linguistic mosaic: A historical overview of language maintenance and language shift. In S. L. McKay & S. C. Wong (eds.), *Language Diversity: Problem or Resource?* (pp. 29–68). Cambridge, MA: Newbury House.

Moltmann, G. (1985). The Germans in America. In F. Trommler & J. McVeigh (eds.), *America and the Germans: An Assessment of a Three-Hundred Year History* (Vol. I, pp. 14–24). Philadelphia: University of Pennsylvania Press.

Montrul, S. (2002). Incomplete acquisition and attrition of Spanish tense/aspect distinctions in adult bilinguals. *Bilingualism: Language and Cognition* 5(1), 39–68.

(2005). Second language acquisition and first language loss in adult early bilinguals: Exploring some differences and similarities. *Second Language Research* 21(3), 199–249.

(2007). Interpreting mood distinctions in Spanish as a heritage language. In K. Potowski & R. Cameron (eds.), *Spanish in Contact: Educational, Linguistic and Social Perspectives* (pp. 23–40). New York: John Benjamins.

Moon, S. (2005). *Militarized Modernity and Gendered Citizenship in South Korea*. Durham: Duke University Press.

Mora, M. T., Villa, D., & Dávila, J. (2006). Language shift and maintenance among the children of immigrants in the US: Evidence in the Census for Spanish speakers and other language minorities. *Spanish in Context* 3(2), 239–54.

Morales, E. (2002). *Living in Spanglish: The Search for Latino Identity in America*. New York: L. A. Weekly Books.

Moreau, M.-L. (2000). Pluralité des normes dans la francophonie. In P. Dumont & C. Santodomingo (eds.), *La Coexistence des Langues dans l'Espace Francophone. Approche Macrosociolinguistique* (pp. 137–51). Paris: Aupelf-Uref.

Mota, K. M. S. (2002). Imigrantes brasileiros: esforços de preservação da língua materna. *Revista do Grupo de Estudos Lingüísticos do Nordeste* 4(2). Retrieved July 19, 2009 from www.gelne.ufc.br/revista_ano4_no2_sum.htm.

(2008). Two languages at play: Language boundaries in the speech of second-generation immigrants. In C. Jouët-Pastré & L. Braga (eds.), *Becoming Brazuca: Brazilian Immigration to the United States* (pp. 313–37). Cambridge, MA: Harvard University Press.

Multilingual Chicago. (n.d.) Multilingual Chicago. Retrieved August 28, 2008 from http://multilingualchicago.org.

Murray, N. (2004). Arabs, Muslims and the post 9/11 hunt for the "enemy within." In E. C. Hagopian (ed.), *Civil Rights in Peril: The Targeting of Arabs and Muslims* (pp. 27–70). Chicago: Haymarket.

Muysken, P. (2000). *Bilingual Speech: A Typology of Code-Switching*. Cambridge: Cambridge University Press.

Myers-Scotton, C. (2003). *Contact Linguistics: Bilingual Encounters and Grammatical Outcomes*. Oxford: Oxford University Press.

Nadell, P. S. (1990). En route to the promised land. In K. M. Olitzky (ed.), *We Are Leaving Mother Russia* (pp. 11–24). Cincinnati: The American Jewish Archives.

National Center for Education Statistics. (2002a). Digest of Education Statistics, 2002. Washington, DC: US Department of Education. Retrieved August 7, 2008 from www.ncela.gwu.edu/expert/faq/17foreign.html.

(2002b). Digest of Education Statistics Tables and Figures 2002. Washington, DC: US Department of Education. Retrieved Aug. 1, 2007 from http://nces.ed.gov/programs/digest/d02/dt057.asp.

(2008). National Indian education study 2007. Part I. Washington, DC: Institute of Education Sciences, US Department of Education. Retrieved July 14, 2008 from http://nces.ed.gov/nationsreportcard/nies.

National Heritage Language Resource Center. (2007). The alliance for the advancement of heritage languages. Los Angeles: University of California, Los Angeles. Retrieved August 28, 2008 from www.international.ucla.edu/languages/nhlrc/article.asp?parentID=77668.

National Foreign Language Center. (2008). *STARTALK*. College Park, MD: University of Maryland. Retrieved August 4, 2008 from www.nflc.org/projects/current_projects/startalk/.

National Middle East Language Resource Center (NMLRC). (2002). Report on Arabic, Hebrew, Persian, and Turkish Learner Surveys: Profiles, Motivation and Enrollments. Retrieved November 1, 2007 from http://nmelrc.byu.edu.

National Security Education Program. (2005). National Flagship Language Initiative: Chinese K-16 Pipeline Project. Retrieved July 28, 2008 from www.committee100.org/initiatives/education/NFLI.pdf.

NBC11.com (2006, August 31). Oakland-bound passenger barred for Arabic t-shirt. Retrieved August 31, 2008 from www.nbc11.com/news/9769544/detail.html.

NCELA. (2002). How many indigenous American languages are spoken in the United States? By how many speakers? National Clearinghouse on English Language Acquisition. Retrieved July 16, 2007 from www.ncela.gwu.edu/expert/faq/20natlang.html.

Neundorf, A. (1987). Bilingualism: A bridge to power for interpreters and leaders in the Navajo Tribal Council. PhD dissertation, Department of Educational Foundations, University of New Mexico.

Nelli, H. S. (1983). *From Immigrants to Ethnics: The Italian Americans*. Oxford: Oxford University Press.

NewPoland News. (2000). Universities/Colleges (USA). Retrieved July 9, 2008 from www.newpoland.com/schools_universities_usa.htm.

New York State Education Department. (2004). The teaching of language arts to limited English proficient/ English language learners: Learning standards for Native language arts. Retrieved August 1, 2007 from www.emsc.nysed.gov/biling/resource/NLA.html.

Nicholas, S. E. (2008). Becoming "fully" Hopi: The role of the Hopi language in the contemporary lives of Hopi youth – A Hopi case study of language shift and vitality. PhD dissertation, American Indian Studies Program, University of Arizona, Tucson.

Niznik, M., Vinokurova, A., Kagan, O. & Cherp, A. (2009). *Russkij bez granic* [Russian without borders] (Pts. 1–3). Old City of Jaffa, Israel: Mannsohn House Press.

No Child Left Behind Act (NCLB). (2001). US Public Law 107–110.

Nowicka McLees, B. (In progress). Polish Saturday Schools in the USA.

Nowicka McLees, B. & Potowski, K. (In progress). Polish Saturday Schools in Chicago.

Office of the High Commissioner for Human Rights. (1992). Declaration on the rights of persons belonging to national or ethnic, religious and linguistic minorities. Retrieved September 3, 2008 at www.ohchr.org/Documents/Publications/GuideMinoritiesDeclarationen.pdf.

Office of Travel & Tourism Industries. (2007). International arrivals to the United States for fourth quarter and annual 2006. Washington, DC: US Dept. of Commerce. Retrieved December 31, 2008 from http://tinet.ita.doc.gov/view/a-2006–400/index.html.

Ogbu, J. U. (1977). *Minority Education and Caste: The American System in Cross-Cultural Perspective*. New York: Academic Press.

Okamura, J. (1998). *Asian American: Reconceptualizing Culture, History, Politics*. New York: Garland Publishing, Inc.

Omaggio, A. C. (2001). *Teaching Language in Context: Proficiency-Oriented Instruction* (3rd edn.). Boston, MA: Heinle & Heinle Publishers.

Opoku, K. (2006). *Profile deutschstämmiger "heritage learners" in den Samstagsschulen der USA*. Bayreuth, Germany: Bayreuth University.

O'Rahilly, T. F. (1932). *Irish Dialects Past and Present: With Chapters on Scottish and Manx*. Dublin: Dublin Institute for Advanced Studies.

Order of the Sons of Italy in America. (2003). *A Profile of Today's Italian Americans*. Washington, DC: OSIA. Retrieved September 10, 2007 from www.osia.org/public/pdf/IA_Profile.pdf.

(2007). Italian American culture & history. Retrieved, August 30, 2007 from www.osia.org/public/culture/culture_intro.asp.

Orrenius, P. M. (2003). US Immigration and economic growth: Putting policy on hold. *Southwest Economy* 6, November/December. Dallas, TX: Federal Reserve Bank of Dallas. Retrieved August 8, 2008 from www.dallasfed.org/research/swe/2003/swe0306a.html.

Ortiz López, L. & Lacorte, M. (eds.). (2005). *Contactos y contextos lingüísticos: El español en los Estados Unidos y en contacto con otras lenguas*. Madrid: Lingüística Iberoamericana.

Otheguy, R. (1993). A reconsideration of the notion of loan translation in the analysis of US Spanish. In A. Roca & J. Lipski (eds.), *Spanish in the United States: Linguistic Contact and Diversity* (pp. 31–45). New York: Mouton de Gruyter.

Otheguy, R. & Zentella, A. C. (2007). Apuntes preliminares sobre el contacto lingüístico y dialectal en el uso pronominal del español en Nueva York. In K. Potowski & R. Cameron (eds.), *Spanish in Contact: Policy, Social and Linguistic Inquiries* (pp. 275–95). Amsterdam: John Benjamins.

Overseas Koreans Foundation. (2007). Overseas Koreans (status); Korean language school; Press. Retrieved October 28, 2007 from www.korean.net/morgue/.

Pacheco, D. G. (2008). Portuguese out of the shadow of Spanish in the USA: Prophecy or utopia? Paper presented at the Fifth Annual UCLA Department of Spanish and Portuguese Graduate Student Conference. University of California Los Angeles.

Papen, R. (2005). La survivance du français dans le Midwest américain: le franco-minnesotain. In A. Fauchon (ed.), *L'Ouest: Directions, dimensions et destinations:*

Actes du Colloque du Centre d'Etudes françaises-canadiennes de l'Ouest. Winnepeg, Manitoba: Presses universitaires de Saint-Boniface.

Park, E. (2006). Grandparents, grandchildren, and heritage language. In K. Kondo-Brown (ed.), *Heritage Language Development: Focus and East Asian Immigrants* (pp. 57–87). Amsterdam/Philadelphia: John Benjamins.

Park, H. S. (2002). *North Korea: The Politics of Unconventional Wisdom*. Boulder, CO: Lynne Rienner Publishers.

Park, J.-S. (2006). The Korean wave: Transnational cultural flows in East-Asia. In C. K. Armstrong, G. Rozman, S. S. Kim, & S. Kotkin (eds.), *Korea at the Center: Dynamics of Regionalism in Northeast Asia* (pp. 244–56). Armonk, NY: M.E. Sharpe.

Parodi, C. (2003). Contacto de dialectos del español en Los Ángeles. In G. Perissinotto (ed.), *Ensayos de lengua y pedagogía* (pp. 23–38). Santa Barbara: University of California, Linguistic Minority Research Institute.

Pasquandrea, S. (2007). Code-switching e identità: pratiche discorsive di famiglie italiane in paesi anglofoni. PhD thesis, Università degli Studi di Pisa. Retrieved September 5, 2007 from http://etd.adm.unipi.it/theses/available/etd-09052007–125152/unrestricted/Tesi_di_dottorato_Sergio_Pasquandrea.pdf.

Passel, J. (2005). Unauthorized migrants: Numbers and characteristics. Washington, DC: Pew Hispanic Center. Retrieved July 12, 2008 from http://pewhispanic.org/files/reports/46.pdf.

(2007). Growing share of immigrants choosing naturalization. Washington, DC: Pew Hispanic Center. Retrieved July 10, 2008 from http://pewhispanic.org/reports/report.php?ReportID=61.

Pavlenko. (2002). We have room for but one language here: Language and national identity in the US at the turn of the 20th century. *Multilingua – Journal of Cross-Cultural and Interlanguage Communication* 21(2–3), 163–96.

Pease-Alvarez, L. (2002). Moving beyond linear trajectories of language shift and bilingual language socialization. *Hispanic Journal of Behavioral Sciences* 24(2), 114–37.

Pease-Alvarez, L., Garcia, E. E., & Espinosa, P. (1991). Effective instruction for language-minority students: An early childhood case study. *Early Childhood Research Quarterly* 6, 347–61.

Penny, R. (2002). *A History of the Spanish Language*. Cambridge: Cambridge University Press.

Peterson, M. P. & Sosnowski, B. (1985). Preparing refugee youth for American secondary school: The PASS program. *Passage* 1(3), 8–12.

Pew Hispanic Center. (2004). Assimilation and language. *Survey Brief (March 2004)*. Washington, DC: Pew Hispanic Center. Retrieved September 14, 2008 from http://pewhispanic.org/files/reports/15.10.pdf.

(2007). A statistical portrait of Hispanics at mid-decade. Retrieved July 1, 2007 from http://pewhispanic.org/reports/middecade.

Pew Hispanic Center/Kaiser Family Foundation. (2004). National survey of Latinos: Education. Retrieved Feb. 3, 2004 from www.pewhispanic.org.

Peyton, J. K., Carreira, M., Wang, S., & Wiley, T. G. (2008). Heritage language education in the United States: A need to reconceptualize and restructure. In K. A. King, N. Schilling-Estes, L. W. Fogle, J. J. Lou, & B. Soukup (eds.), *Sustaining Linguistic*

Diversity: Endangered and Minority Languages and Language Varieties (pp. 173–86). Washington, DC: Georgetown University Press.

Picone, M. D. (1996). Stratégies lexicogénétiques franco-louisianaises. *Plurilinguismes* 11, 63–99.

Picone, M. D. & Valdman, A. (2005). La situation du français en Louisiane. In A. Valdman, J. Auger, & D. Piston-Hatlen (eds.), *Le Français en Amérique du Nord; État présent* (143–66). Québec: Presses de l'Université Laval.

Pienkos, D. (1984). *PNA: A Centennial History of the Polish National Alliance of the United States of North America*. New York: Columbia University Press.

Pienkos, D. & Pienkos, A. (2003). *"In the Ideals of Women is the Strength of a Nation": A History of the Polish Women's Alliance of America*. New York: Columbia University Press.

Pires, A. & Rothman, J. (2009). Disentangling contributing variables to incomplete acquisition competence outcomes: What differences across Brazilian and European Portuguese heritage speakers tell us. *International Journal of Bilingualism* 13(2), 1–28.

Platero, P. (2001). Navajo Head Start language study. In L. Hinton & K. Hale (eds.), *The Green Book of Language Revitalization in Practice* (pp. 87–97). San Diego, CA: Academic Press.

Pleasant, M. (2008, June 29). Valedictorian's speech sets off call for English-only at graduations. *The Courier* (Houma, LA). Retrieved August 29, 2008 from www.wwltv.com/local/lafourche/stories/wwl062908tpenglishonly.87fd056.html.

Polinsky, M. (2000). A composite linguistic profile of a speaker of Russian in the US. In O. Kagan & B. Rifkin, with S. Bauckus (eds.), *The Learning and Teaching of Slavic Languages and Cultures* (pp. 437–65). Bloomington, IN: Slavica Publishers.

Polish Academic Information Center. (2000). Polish Studies in the United States. Retrieved July 9, 2008 from http://info-poland.buffalo.edu/polstud/plist.html.

Pons, C. R. (1990). Language death among Waldensians of Valdese, North Carolina. Unpublished doctoral dissertation, Indiana University.

Pons, T. G. (1973). *Dizionario del dialetto valdese della valle Germanesca (Torino). Note fonetiche e morphologiche di A Genre*. Torre Pellice: Collana della Società di Studi Valese.

Portes, A. & Hao, L. (1998). E pluribus unum: Bilingualism and loss of language in the second generation. *Sociology of Education* 71, 269–94.

(2004). The schooling of children of immigrants: Contextual effects on the educational attainment of the second generation. *Proceedings of the National Academy of Sciences* 101(33), 11920–7.

Portes, A. & Rumbaut, R. G. (1996). *Immigrant America: A portrait*. Berkeley: University of California Press.

(2001) *Legacies: The Story of the Immigrant Second Generation*. Berkeley and New York: University of California Press and Russell Sage Foundation.

(2005) The second generation and the children of immigrants longitudinal study. *Ethnic and Racial Studies* 28(6), 983–99.

(2006) *Immigrant America: A Portrait* (3rd edn.). Berkeley, CA: University of California Press.

Portes, A. & Rumbaut, R. G. (2008). Children of Immigrants Longitudinal Study (CILS), 1991–2006 [Computer file]. ICPSR20520-v1. Ann Arbor, MI:

Inter-university Consortium for Political and Social Research [distributor], 2008-01-07. doi:10.3886/ICPSR20520.

Portes, A. & Schauffler, R. (1996). Language and the second generation: Bilingualism yesterday and today. In A. Portes (ed.), *The New Second Generation* (pp. 8–29). New York: Russell Sage Foundation.

Posadas, B. (1999). *The Filipino Americans*. Westport, CT: Greenwood Press.

Potowski, K. (2008). "I was raised talking like my mom": The influence of mothers in the development of MexiRicans' phonological and lexical features. In J. Rothman & M. Niño-Murcia (eds.), *Linguistic Identity and Bilingualism in Different Hispanic Contexts* (pp. 201–20). New York: John Benjamins.

Potowski, K. & Cameron, R. (eds.) (2007). *Spanish in Contact: Educational, Linguistic, and Social Inquiries*. Selected proceedings from the 20th Conference on Spanish in the United States and the 5th Conference on Spanish in Contact with Other Languages. New York: John Benjamins.

Potowski, K. & Carreira, M. (2004). Towards teacher development and national standards for Spanish as a heritage language. *Foreign Language Annals* 37(3), 421–31.

Potowski, K., Berne, J., Clark, A., & Hammerand, A. (2008). Spanish for K-8 heritage speakers: A standards-based curriculum project. *Hispania* 91(1), 25–41.

Press Guide. (2007). Auslandsdeutsche Zeitungen weltweit. Retrieved Dec. 10, 2007 from www.press-guide.com.

Price, J. E. (2007). The status of French among youth in a bilingual American–Canadian border community: The case of Madawaska, Maine. Unpublished doctoral dissertation, Indiana University.

Pu, Chang (2008). Chinese American children's bilingual and biliteracy development in heritage language and public schools. Doctoral Dissertation. University of Texas, TX: San Antonio.

Pula, J. (1995). *Polish Americans: An Ethnic Community*. New York: Twayne Publishing.

Quintal, C. & Cotnoir, M.-M. (1983). *La situation du Français aux Etats-Unis*. Québec: Conseil de la langue française.

Read, W. A. (1931). *Louisiana-French*. Baton Rouge: Louisiana State University Press.

Refugee Act of 1980. Pub. L. No. 96–212, 94 Stat. 102–103 (1980).

Reid, T. R. (2005, Dec. 9). Spanish at school translates to suspension. *Washington Post*. Retrieved January 1, 2008 from www.washingtonpost.com/wp-dyn/content/article/2005/12/08/AR2005120802122.html.

Revilla, L. (1996). Filipino Americans: Historical perspective. In G. Y. Mark, D. P. McGregor, and L. Revilla (eds.), *Our History, Our Way* (pp. 276–94). Dubuque, IA: Kendall/Hunt Publishing Co.

Reyhner, J. & Eder, J. (2002). *American Indian Education: A History*. Norman: University of Oklahoma Press.

Richard, S. (2002). American perspectives on La fièvre aux Etats-Unis, 1860–1930: A historiographical analysis of recent writings on the Franco-Americans of New England, *Canadian Review of American Studies/Revue canadiennes d'études américaines* 32(1), 105–32.

Richards, D. (1999). *Italian American. The Racializing of an Ethnic Identity*. New York: New York University Press.

Rickford, J. (1999). *African American Vernacular English*. Oxford: Blackwell.

Rivera-Mills, S. (2001). Acculturation and communicative need: Language shift in an ethnically diverse Hispanic community. *Southwest Journal of Linguistics* 20, 211–23.

Rhodes, N. & Branaman, L. (1999). *Foreign Language Instruction in the United States: A National Survey of Elementary and Secondary Schools*. McHenry, IL: Delta Systems and the Center for Applied Linguistics.

Roberts, C. A. (1994). Transferring literacy skills from L1 to L2: From theory to practice. *The Journal of Educational Issues of Language Minority Students* 13, 209–21.

Roca, A. (ed.) (2000). *Research on Spanish in the United States: Linguistic Issues and Challenges*. Somerville, MA: Cascadilla Press.

Roca, A. & Lipski, J. M. (eds.) (1993). *Spanish in the United States: Linguistic Contact and Diversity*. Berlin: Mouton de Gruyter.

Rodriguez, Rey. (2007). Won't your Spanish hurt their English? *LA Language World*. www.lalamag.ucla.edu/features/article.asp?parentid=74511.

Rodriguez, Richard. (1982). *Hunger of Memory: The Education of Richard Rodriguez*. New York: Bantam Books.

Rodríguez-Martín, N. (2006, October 15). Who's who in US Spanish-language publishing: The international players. *Críticas*. Retrieved March 29, 2008 from www.criticasmagazine.com/article/CA6382599.html.

Romaine, S. (1995). *Bilingualism* (2nd edition). Oxford: Blackwell.

(1996). Pidgins and creoles as literary languages: Ausbau and Abstand. In M. Hellinger & U. Ammon (eds.), *Constrastive Sociolinguistics* (pp. 271–89). Berlin: Mouton de Gruyter.

(2001). Contact between English and other languages. In J. Algeo (ed.), *Cambridge History of the English Language*. Vol. VI: *English in North America* (pp. 154–83). Cambridge: Cambridge University Press.

Romero, M. E. (2003). Perpetuating the Cochiti way of life: A study of child language socialization and language shift in a Pueblo community. PhD dissertation, Graduate School of Education, University of California, Berkeley.

Roosevelt, T. (1919). Americanism and Americanization: Selections from the writings of Theodore Roosevelt. *Monthly Bulletin of the Carnegie Library of Pittsburgh* 24(2), 82.

Rothman, J. (2007). Heritage speaker competence differences, language change and input type: Inflected infinitives in heritage Brazilian Portuguese. *International Journal of Bilingualism* 11(4), 359–89.

Rothman, J. & Rell, A. B. (2005). A linguistic analysis of Spanglish: Relating language to identity. *Linguistics and the Human Sciences* 1(3), 515–36.

Rottet, K. J. (2001). *Language Shift in the Coastal Marshes of Louisiana*. New York: Peter Lang.

(2005). Variation et étiolement en français cadien: perspectives comparées. In A. Valdman, J. Auger, & D. Piston-Hatlen (eds.), *Le Français en Amérique du Nord; État présent* (pp. 207–28). Québec: Presses de l'Université Laval.

Rouchdy, A. (ed.). (1992). *The Arabic Language in America*. Detroit: Wayne State University Press.

Rúa, M. (2001). Colao subjectivities: PortoMex and MexiRican perspectives on language and identity. *Centro Journal* 13(2), 117–33.

Rubino, A. (2003). Prospettive di mantenimento linguistico: fase di vita e di comunità come fattori di variabilità tra gli italiani in Australia. In A. Valentini, P. Molinelli, P. Cuzzolin, & G. Bernini (eds.), *Ecologia linguistica. Atti del XXXVI Congresso Internazionale di Studi della Società di Linguistica Italiana Bergamo 26–28 settembre 2002–2003* (pp. 309–29). Roma: Bulzoni.

(2006). Linguistic practices and language attitudes of second-generation Italo-Australians. In S. Kipp & C. Norrby (eds.), *Community Languages in Practice: The Case of Australia. Special Issue of The International Journal of the Sociology of Language* 180, 71–88.

Rubinstein-Avila, E. (2002). Problematizing the "dual" in a dual-immersion program: A portrait. *Linguistics and Education* 13(1), 65–87.

(2005). Brazilian Portuguese in Massachusetts' linguistic landscape: A prevalent yet understudied phenomenon. *Hispania* 88(4), 873–80.

Rubrico, J. G. (2007). The metamorphosis of Filipino as a National Language. Retrieved Dec 19, 2007, from www.languagelinks.org/onlinepapers/fil_met.

Ruggles, S., Sobek, M., Alexander, T. *et al.* (2009). *Integrated Public Use Microdata Series: Version 3.0.* [Machine-readable database] Mineapolis, MN: Minnesota Population Center [producer and distributor].

Ruíz, R. (1984). Orientations in language planning. *NABE Journal* 8(2), 15–34.

(1995). Language planning considerations in indigenous communities. *Bilingual Research Journal* 19(1), 71–81.

Rumbaut, R. G. (1995). The new Californians: Comparative research findings on the educational progress of immigrant children. In R. G. Rumbaut & W. A. Cornelius (eds.), *California's Immigrant Children: Theory, Research, and Implications for Educational Policy* (pp. 17–69). San Diego: University of California, San Diego, Center for US–Mexican Studies.

(2007). Vietnam. In M. C. Waters & R. Ueda with H. B. Marrow (eds.), *The New Americans: A Guide to Immigration since 1965* (pp. 652–73). Cambridge, MA: Harvard University Press.

(2009). A language graveyard? The evolution of language competencies, preferences and use among young adult children of immigrants. In T. G. Wiley, J. S. Lee, & R. Rumberger (eds.), *The Education of Immigrant Language Minorities in the United States*. Bristol: Multilingual Matters.

Rumbaut, R. G., Bean, F. D., Chávez, L. R. *et al.* (2008). Immigration and intergenerational mobility in Metropolitan Los Angeles (IIMMLA), 2004 [Computer File]. ICPSR22627-v1. Ann Arbor, MI: Inter-University Consortium for Political and Social Research [distributor], 2008–07–01. doi:10.3886/ICPSR22627. Retrieved from www.icpsr.umich.edu/cocoon/ICPSR/STUDY/22627.xml.

Rumbaut, R. G., Massey, D. S., & Bean, F. D. (2006). Linguistic life expectancies: Immigrant language retention in Southern California. *Population and Development Review* 32(3), 447–60.

RABAC. (2008). *Russian-American Business and Arts Council.* Russian-American Business and Arts Council. Retrieved July 7, 2008 from www.russianamericancouncil.org/.

RAMA and RADA. (n.d.) *Russian American Medical Association.* Russian American Medical Association and Russian American Dental Association. Retrieved November 15, 2007 from www.russiandoctors.org/.

Russian Yellow Pages: All States. (2008). Retrieved July 6, 2008 from www.rususa.com/business/.

Russkij Jazyk Publishers. (n.d.) Retrieved July 6, 2008 from www.rus-lang.ru/.

Russo, M. & Roberts, J. (1999). Linguistic change in endangered dialects: The case of alternation between avoir and être in Vermont French. *Language Variation and Change* 11(1), 67–85.

Ryman, A. & Madrid, O. (2004, Jan. 16). State investigating teacher accused of hitting student. *The Arizona Republic*. Retrieved January 1, 2008 from www.azbilingualed.org/AABE%20Site/AABE–News%202004/state_investigating_teacher_accu.htm.

Rytina, N. F. (2006). Estimates of the legal permanent resident population and population eligible to naturalize in 2004. Washington, DC: Office of Immigration Statistics, Dept. Homeland Security. Retrieved December 18, 2007, from www.dhs.gov/xlibrary/assets/statistics/publications/LPRest2004.pdf.

Sachs, J. (1994). *Poland's Jump to the Market Economy (Lionel Robbins Lectures)*. Cambridge, MA: The MIT Press.

Saito, L. T. (1999). Socio-cultural factors in the educational achievement of Vietnamese American students. EdD. Dissertation, University of California, Irvine.

Sales, T. & Loureiro, M. (2008). Between dream and reality: Adolescent and second-generation Brazilian immigrants in Massachusetts. In C. Jouët-Pastré & L. Braga (eds.), *Becoming Brazuca. Brazilian Immigration to the United States* (pp. 287–311). Cambridge, MA: Harvard University Press.

Sampson, G. (1985). *Writing Systems: A Linguistic Introduction*. London: Hutchinson.

San Buenaventura, S. (1996). Filipino Immigration to the United States. In F. Ng (ed.), *The Asian American Encyclopedia* (pp. 439–53). New York: Marshall Cavendish.

Santos, F. (2007a, Feb. 27). Demand for English lessons outstrips supply. *New York Times*. Retrieved August 7, 2008 from www.nytimes.com/2007/02/27/education/27esl.html?pagewanted=1&_r=1.

(2007b, May 7). Students search for the words to go with their cultural pride. *New York Times*. Retrieved August 7, 2008 from www.nytimes.com/2007/05/07/nyregion/07heritage.html.

(2008, July 23). Mayor orders New York to expand language help. *New York Times*. Retrieved August 7, 2008 from www.nytimes.com/2008/07/23/nyregion/23translate.html.

Sauerwein, K. (2003, Oct. 20). San Bernardino schools see the future: 2-language graduates. *Los Angeles Times*. Retrieved August 8, 2008 from http://articles.latimes.com/2003/oct/20/local/me-bilingual20.

Sawaie, M. (1986). The present and future status of a minority language: The case of Arabic in the United States. *Journal of Multilingual and Multicultural Development* 7(1), 31–40.

(1992). Arabic in the melting pot: Will it survive? In A. Rouchdy (ed.), *The Arabic Language in America* (pp. 83–99). Detroit: Wayne State University Press.

Sawaie, M. & Fishman, J. A. (1985). Arabic-language maintenance efforts in the United States. *Journal of Ethnic Studies* 13(2), 33–49.

Schaengold, C. C. (2004). Bilingual Navajo: Mixed codes, bilingualism and language maintenance. PhD dissertation. The Ohio State University.

Schiffman, H. (1996). *Linguistic Culture and Language Policy*. London: Routledge.

(1998). *Language loyalty in the German-American church: The case of an over-confident minority*. Retrieved June 9, 2008 from http://ccat.sas.upenn.edu/~haroldfs/540/handouts/gachurch/index.html.

(2005). Language policy and linguistic culture. In T. Ricento (ed.), *An Introduction to Language Policy: Theory and Method* (pp. 111–24). Malden, MA: Blackwell.

(2008). Language, policy and citizenship: Three views. In J. V. Ciprut (ed.), *The Future of Citizenship* (pp. 75–96). Cambridge, MA: MIT Press.

Schmid, A. (2002). *Korea between Empires, 1895–1919*. New York: Columbia University Press.

Schmidt, R. (2000). *Language Policy and Identity Politics in the United States*. Philadelphia: Temple University.

Schneider, E. W. (2000). The dynamics of new Englishes: From identity construction to dialect birth. *Language* 79, 2.

SEAsite. (n.d.). Tagalog. Dekalb, IL: Center for Southeast Asian Studies, Northern Illinois University. Retrieved July 18, 2008 from www.seasite.niu.edu/tagalog.

Sękowska, E. (2000). Wpływ języka angielskiego na słownictwo polszczyzny ogólnej. *Poradnik Językowy* 5, 44–53.

Sheldon, E. S. (1887). Some specimens of a Canadian French dialect spoken in Maine. *PMLA* 3, 210–18.

Shim, D. (2006). Hybridity and the rise of Korean popular culture in Asia. *Media, Culture and Society* 28, 25–44.

Shin, S. J. (2005). *Developing in Two Languages: Korean Children in America*. Clevedon, UK: Multilingual Matters.

(2006). High-stakes testing and heritage language maintenance. In K. Kondo-Brown (ed.), *Heritage Language Development: Focus on East Asian Immigrants* (pp. 127–44). Amsterdam/Philadelphia: John Benjamins.

Shiri, S. (2002). Speak Arabic please!: Tunisian Arabic speakers' linguistic accommodation to Middle Easterners. In A. Rouchdy (ed.), *Language Contact and Language Conflict in Arabic* (pp. 149–74). London: Routledge Curzon.

Shmelev, A. (2006). Russians in the Repositories. In A. Shmelev (ed.), *Tracking a Diaspora: Émigrés from Russia and Eastern Europe in the Repositories*. New York and London: The Haworth Information Press.

Shohamy, E. (2006). *Language Policy: Hidden Agendas and New Approaches*. London: Routledge.

Sidoti, L. (2008, July 12). Obama defends comment about learning foreign languages. *The Associated Press*. Retrieved August 13, 2008 from www.northjersey.com/news/nationalpolitics/Obama_defends_comment_about_learning_foreign_languages.html.

Silva, G. (2008). Heritage language learning and the Portuguese subjunctive. *Portuguese Language Journal* 3. Retrieved July 19, 2009 from www.latam.ufl.edu/portugueselanguagejournal/index.html.

Silva, H. (2006). Brazilian immigration to Utah: An oral history. Paper presented at the National Conference on Undergraduate Research (NCUR), University of North Carolina, Asheville.

Silva-Corvalán, C. (1994). *Language Contact and Change: Spanish in Los Angeles*. Oxford: Oxford University Press.

(ed.). (1995). *Spanish in Four Continents: Studies in Language Contact and Bilingualism*. Washington, DC: Georgetown University Press.

Silverstein, M. (1996). Monoglot "standard" in America: Standardization and metaphors of linguistic hegemony. In L. Brenneis & R. Macaulay (eds.), *The Matrix of Language: Contemporary Linguistic Anthropology* (pp. 284–306). Boulder: Westview Press.

Simon, P. (1988). *The Tongue-Tied American: Confronting the Foreign Language Crisis*. New York: Continuum.

Simon, R. J. (1997). *In the Golden Land: A Century of Russian and Soviet Jewish Immigration in America*. Westport, Co: Praeger.

Sims, C. P. (1998). Community-based efforts to preserve Native languages: A descriptive study of the Karuk Tribe of northern California. *International Journal of the Sociology of Language* 132, 95–113.

(2001). Navajo language planning: A pilot process in the Acoma Pueblo community. In L. Hinton & K. Hale (eds.), *The Green Book of Language Revitalization in Practice* (pp. 63–73). San Diego, CA: Academic Press.

Siqueira, S. (2008). Emigrants from Governador Valadares: Projects of return and investment. In C. Jouët-Pastré & L. Braga (eds.), *Becoming Brazuca: Brazilian Immigration to the United States* (pp. 175–94). Cambridge, MA: Harvard University Press.

Siqueira, C. E. & Jansen, T. (2008). Updating demographic, geographic, and occupational data on Brazilian Massachusetts. In C. Jouët-Pastré & L. Braga (eds.), *Becoming Brazuca. Brazilian Immigration to the United States* (pp. 1105–24). Cambridge, MA: Harvard University Press.

Slate, C. (2001). Promoting advanced Navajo language scholarship. In L. Hinton & K. Hale (eds.), *The Green Book of Language Revitalization in Practice* (pp. 389–410). San Diego, CA: Academic Press.

Smitherman, G. (1977). *Talkin' and Testifyin': The Language of Black America*. Boston: Houghton Mifflin Co. [Reissued 1986: Detroit: Wayne State University Press]

Snipp, C. M. (2002). *American Indian and Alaska Native Children in the 2000 Census*. Baltimore, MD and Washington, DC: The Annie E. Casey Foundation and the Population Reference Bureau.

Sohn, H.-M. (1999). *The Korean Language*. Cambridge: Cambridge University Press.

(2000). Migŭk esŏŭy hangŭgŏ kyoyuk (Teaching of Korean in the USA). In D. J. Lee, S. Cho, M. Lee, M. S. Song, & W. O'Grady (eds.), *Studies on Korean in Community Schools* (pp. 3–24). Second Language Teaching & Curriculum Center. Honolulu: University of Hawaii Press.

Song, J. J. (2005). *The Korean Language: Structure, Use and Context*. London: Routledge.

Souza, H. (2000). Language loss and language gain in the Brazilian community: The role of schools and families. In A. F. Beykont (ed.), *Lifting Every Voice: Pedagogy and Politics of Bilingualism* (pp. 7–20). Cambridge, MA: Harvard University Press.

Special Eurobarometer. (2006). Europeans and their languages. European Commission, Directorate-General Press and Communication. Retrieved August 15, 2007, from http://ec.europa.eu/public_opinion/archives/ebs/ebs_243_en.pdf.

Spicer, E. H. (1962 [1976]). *Cycles of Conquest: The Impact of Spain, Mexico, and the United States on the Indians of the Southwest, 1533–1960* (6th printing). Tucson: University of Arizona Press.

Spolsky, B. (2001). Heritage languages and national security: an ecological view. In S. J. Baker (ed.), *Language Policy: Lessons from Global Models* (pp. 103–14). Monterey, CA: Monterey Institute of International Studies.

(2002a). Prospects for the survival of the Navajo language: A reconsideration. *Anthropology and Education Quarterly* 33(2), 139–62.

(2002b). National policy statement on heritage language development: Toward an agenda for action. Paper presented at the Heritage Languages in America: Building on Our National Resources conference. Tysons Corner, VA. October, 2002.

(2004). *Language Policy*. Cambridge: Cambridge University Press.

Spring, J. (1994). *Deculturation and the Struggle for Equality: A Brief History of the Education of Dominated Cultures in the United States*. New York: McGraw-Hill.

Statistisches Bundesamt Deutschland (German Federal Statistical Office). (2006). Wanderungen zwischen Deutschland und den Vereinigten Staaten 1952 bis 2006 [Unpublished data file]. Wiesbaden, Germany: Statistisches Bundesamt Deutschland.

Stavans, I. (2003). *The Making of a New American Language*. New York: Harper-Collins Publishers.

Stearns, C. and Watanabe, S. (2002). *Hispanic Serving Institutions: Statistical Trends from 1990–1999, NCES, 2002-051*. US Department of Education. National Center for Education Statistics: Washington DC.

Stecuła, D. (2007). *Polonia in Numbers: Report on the Polish Population in the United States*. Hamtramck: Piast Institute.

Stephens, T. (1989). Language maintenance and ethical survival: The Portuguese in New Jersey. *Hispania* 72(3), 716–20.

Stevens, G. (1999). A century of US Censuses and the language characteristics of immigrants. *Demography* 36(3), 387–97.

Stewart, V. & Wang, C. S. (2005). Expanding Chinese-language capacity in the United States. New York: Asia Society. Retrieved July 28, 2008 from www.askasia.org/teachers/essays/essay.php?no=109.

Stowe, L. A. & Sabourin L. (2005). Imaging the processing of a second language: Effects of maturation and proficiency on the neural processes involved. *International Review of Applied Linguistics in Language Teaching* 43(4), 329–53.

Supahan, T. & Supahan, S. (2001). Teaching well, learning quickly: Communication-based language instruction. In L. Hinton & K. Hale (eds.), *The Green Book of Language Revitalization in Practice* (pp. 195–7). San Diego, CA: Academic Press.

Suro, R. (2002). National survey of Latinos. Pew Hispanic Center/Kaiser Family Foundation. Retrieved May 17, 2004 from www.pewhispanic.org.

Takaki, R. (1989). *Strangers from a Different Shore: A History of Asian Americans*. New York: Penguin Books.

Tamura, E. H. (1993). The English-only effort, the anti-Japanese campaign, and language acquisition in the education of Japanese Americans in Hawaii, 1915–1940. *History of Education Quarterly* 33, 37–58.

Tannenbaum, M. (2003). The multifaceted aspects of language maintenance: a new measure for its assessment in immigrant families. *International Journal of Bilingual Education and Bilingualism* 6(5), 374–93.

Tatalovich, R. (1995). *Nativism Reborn? The Official English Language Movement and the American States*. Lexington, KY: University Press of Kentucky.

Tayash, F. A. & Ayouby, K. K. (1992). Arab-American media: Past and present. In A. Rouchdy (ed.), *The Arabic Language in America* (pp. 162–83). Detroit: Wayne State University Press.

Tesser, C. (2004). Brazilian Portuguese for Spanish speakers: Back to the future. In A. Simões, A. M. Carvalho, & L. Wiedemann (eds.), *Português para falantes de espanhol. Portuguese for Spanish Speakers* (pp. 37–47). Campinas, Brazil: Pontes.

Thibault, A. (2003). Histoire externe du français au Canada, en Nouvelle-Angleterre et à Saint-Pierre et Miquelon. In G. Ernst, M. Gleßgen, C. Schmitt, & W. Schweickard (eds.), *Romanische Sprachgeschichte – Histoire linguistique de la Romania* (pp. 895–911). Berlin: Walter de Gruyter.

Thogmartin, C. (1970). The French dialect of Old Mines, Missouri. Unpublished doctoral dissertation, University of Michigan.

(1979). Old Mines, Missouri et la survivance du français dans la haute vallée du Mississippi. In A. Valdman (ed.), *Le français hors de France* (111–18). Paris: Editions Honoré Champion.

Thomas, R. H. (1981). *It's Good to Tell You. French Folktales from Missouri*. Columbia, MO/London: University of Missouri Press.

Thomason, S. G. (2001). *Language Contact: An Introduction*. Edinburgh: Edinburgh University Press.

Thompson, R. (2003). *Filipino English and Taglish: Language Switching from Multiple Perspectives*. Varieties of English Around the World Series. Amsterdam: John Benjamins.

Thornton, R. (1987). *American Indian Holocaust and Survival: A Population History since 1492*. Norman: University of Oklahoma Press.

Tirado, M. (2001, September). Left behind: Are public schools failing Indian kids? *American Indian Report* 12–15.

Tollefson, J. (1991). *Planning Language, Planning Inequality*. New York: Longman.

Tollefson, J. (ed.) (1995). *Power and Inequality in Language Education*. Cambridge: Cambridge University Press.

Tollefson, J. (2002). *Language Policies in Education: Critical Issues*. Mahwah, NJ: Lawrence Erlbaum.

Tolts, M. (1997). The interrelationship between emigration and the socio-demographic profile of Russian Jewry. In N. Lewin-Erstein, Y. Ro'I, & P. Ritterband (eds.), *Russian Jews on Three Continents: Migration and Resettlement* (pp. 147–76). London: Frank Cass.

Tornquist, L. (2000). Attitudes linguistiques vis-à-vis du vernaculaire franco-louisianais dans le programme d'immersion en Louisiane. Unpublished doctoral dissertation, University of Louisiana at Lafayette.

Torres, L. & Potowski, K. (2008). A comparative study of bilingual discourse markers in Chicago Mexican, Puerto Rican, and MexiRican Spanish. *International Journal of Bilingualism* 12(4), 263–79.

Tosi, A. (2001). *Language and Society in a Changing Italy*. Clevedon: Multilingual Matters.

Tosta, L. A. (2005). Between heaven and hell: Perceptions of Brazil and the United States in Brazuca literature. *Hispania* 88(4), 713–25.

Totten, C. M. (1983). *Roots in the Rhineland*. New York: German Information Center.

Trade Act. 19 U.S.C. § 2432 (1974). Retrieved July 21, 2008, from http://frwebgate.access.gpo.gov/cgibin/getdoc.cgi?dbname=browse_usc&docid=Cite:=19USC2432.

Trépanier, C. (1993). La Louisiane française au seuil du XXIe siècle: La commercialisation de la culture. In G. Bouchard & S. Courville (eds.), *La Construction d'une culture: Le Québec et l'Amérique française* (361–94). Québec: Presses de l'Université Laval.

Trudgill, P. (1983). *Sociolinguistics: An Introduction to Language and Society*. Harmondsworth: Penguin.

Tse, L. (2001a). *Why don't they Learn English? Separating Fact from Fallacy in the US Language Debate*. New York: Teachers College Press.

(2001b). Resisting and reversing language shift: Heritage-language resilience among US native biliterates. *Harvard Educational Review* 71(4), 676–706.

Tucker, J. T. (2006). Waiting times for adult ESL classes and the impact on English learners. National Association of Latino Elected and Appointed Officials Education Fund. Retrieved September 3, 2008 at http://renewthevra.civilrights.org/resources/ESL.pdf.

Tursi, J. (1983). L'emigrazione e l'insegnamento dell'italiano negli Stati Uniti. In *L'italiano come Lingua Seconda in Italia e all'Estero* (pp. 396–400). Rome: Istituto Poligrafico e Zecca dello Stato.

Urcioli, B. (2001). The complex diversity of language in the United States. In I. Susser & T. C. Patterson (eds.), *Cultural Diversity in the United States* (pp. 190–205). Oxford: Blackwell.

Uritescu, D. & Mougeon, F. (2003). Les derniers Français de Frenchville. Paper presented at the Conference Le français aux États-Unis, Indiana University, Bloomington.

US Census Bureau. (1993). We the American: Foreign born. Washington, DC: US Department of Commerce. Retrieved August 22, 2007 from www.census.gov/apsd/wepeople/we-7.pdf.

(2000a). US Census 2000. Washington, DC: US Department of Commerce, Economics and Statistics, US Census Bureau. Available at www.census.gov.

(2000b). *Census 2000, Summary File 3 and 2000 County and County Equivalent Areas Cartographic Boundary File*. Washington, DC: US Department of Commerce, Economics and Statistics, US Census Bureau.

(2000c). Profile of general demographic characteristics: 2000 (California). Retrieved March 5, 2008, from http://factfinder.census.gov/servlet/QTTable?_bm=n&_lang=en&qr_name=DEC_2000_SF1_U_DP1&ds_name=DEC_2000_SF1_U&geo_id=04000US06.

(2001a). *The Native Hawaiian and Other Pacific Islander population: 2000*. Washington, DC: US Department of Commerce, Economics and Statistics, US Census Bureau.

(2001b). *Profile of General Demographic Characteristics: 2000*. Retrieved October 20, 2007 from www.census.gov/Press-Release/www/2001/demoprofile.html/2khus.pdf.

(2002). *The American Indian and Alaska Native Population: 2000*. Washington, DC: US Department of Commerce, Economics and Statistics Administration, US Census Bureau.

(2003a). *The Hispanic Population in the United States: March 2002*. Current Population Report P20–545. Washington, DC.

(2003b). The Arab Population: 2000. Washington, DC: US Census Bureau. Retrieved November 5, 2007 from www.census.gov/prod/2003pubs/c2kbr-23.pdf.

(2006a). *We the People: American Indians and Alaska Natives in the United States. Census 2000 Special Reports*. Washington, DC: US Department of Commerce, Economics and Statistics Administration, US Census Bureau.

(2006b). *American Community Survey 2006*. Washington, DC: US Census Bureau.

(2007a). *The American Community – American Indians and Alaska Natives: 2004*. Washington, DC: US Department of Commerce, Economics and Statistics Administration, US Census Bureau.

(2007b). Country summary: Korea, South. *International Data Base*. Retrieved October 29, 2007 from www.census.gov/ipc/www/idb/country/ksportal.html.

(2007c). *American Community Survey 2007*. Washington, DC: US Census Bureau.

(2008). American Community Survey. Retrieved Feb. 7, 2010 at http://quickfacts.census.gov/qfd/states/06/06037.html.

(2009). Census 2010 activity update. Washington, DC: US Census Bureau. Retrieved July 19, 2009, from www.census.gov/robos/www/2010-Activities-Update-June09.pdf.

US Citizenship and Immigration Services (USCIS). (n.d.1). Preference system (Immigration Act of 1990). Retrieved May 29, 2008, from www.uscis.gov/portal/site/uscis/menuitem.5af9bb95919f35e66f614176543f6d1a/?vgnextoid=4b7e8fa29935f010VgnVCM1000000ecd190aRCRD&vgnextchannel=b328194d3e88d010VgnVCM10000048f3d6a1RCRD.

(n.d.2). Legislation from 1941–1960. Retrieved July 19, 2008 from www.uscis.gov/files/nativedocuments/Legislation%20from%201941–1960.pdf.

US Department of Defense. (2005). Defense language transformation roadmap. Retrieved November 12, 2007 from www.defense.gov/news/Mar2005/d20050330roadmap.pdf.

US Department of Education (2005). Office of Vocational and Adult Education. Enrolment and participation in the state-administered adult education program. Retrieved February 7, 2010 at www2.ed.gov/about/offices/list/ovae/pi/AdultEd/aedatatables.html.

(2007, June 14). $8.7 Million in grants awarded for critical foreign language instruction. Washington, DC: US Department of Education. Retrieved on March 23, 2008 from www.ed.gov/news/pressreleases/2007/06/06152007.html.

US Department of the Interior. (2004). *"Learn today lead tomorrow": Fingertip facts 2004*. Washington, DC: US Department of the Interior, Bureau of Indian Affairs, Office of Indian Education Programs.

US Department of Homeland Security. (2007). 2006 yearbook of immigration statistics. Washington, DC. Retrieved 17 December 2007, from www.dhs.gov/xlibrary/assets/statistics/yearbook/2006/OIS_2006_Yearbook.pdf.

US State Department. (2006). National security language initiative. Retrieved November 12, 2007 from http://exchanges.state.gov/NSLI/.

US–China Business Council. (2008). US–China trade statistics and China's world trade statistics. Washington, DC: US–China Business Council. Retrieved December 31, 2008 from www.uschina.org/statistics/tradetable.html.

Valdés, G. (2001). Heritage language students: Profiles and possibilities. In J. K. Peyton, D. A. Ranard, & S. McGinnis (eds.), *Heritage Languages in America: Preserving a National Resource* (pp. 37–80). Washington, DC & McHenry, IL: Center for Applied Linguistics and Delta Systems.

(forthcoming). Ethnolinguistic identity: The challenge of maintaining Spanish–English bilingualism in American schools. In K. Potowski & J. Rothman (eds.), *Child Spanish Speakers in English-Speaking Societies: Linguistic Identity Construction and Performance*.

Valdman, A. (1979). Créolisation, français populaire et le parler des isolats francophones d'Amérique du Nord. In A. Valdman (ed.), *Le français hors de France* (191–7). Paris: Éditions Honoré Champion.

Valdman, A., Rottet, K. J., Ancelet, J. B. *et al.* (2009). *Dictionary of Louisiana French as Spoken in the Cajun, Creole, and American Indian Communities*. Oxford, MS: University Press of Mississippi.

Valenti, C. (2003, Dec. 11). When the boss says English only. *ABC News*. Retrieved January 1, 2008 from http://azbilingualed.org/AABE%20Site/AABE%20NEWS%202003/when_the_boss_says_english_only.htm.

Veltman, C. (1983). *Language Shift in the United States*. Berlin: Mouton.

(1988). *The Future of the Spanish Language in the United States*. Washington, DC: Hispanic Policy Development Project.

(2000). The American linguistic mosaic: Understanding language shift in the United States. In S. L. McKay & S. C. Wong (eds.), *New Immigrants in the United States* (pp. 58–93). Cambridge: Cambridge University Press.

Verhovek, S. (1995). Mother scolded by judge for speaking in Spanish, *New York Times*, Aug. 30, 1995. Retrieved February 7, 2010 at www.nytimes.com/1995/08/30/us/mother-scolded-by-judge-for-speaking-in-spanish.html?pagewanted=1.

Vermette, D. (2006). Ku Klux Klan activity in Brunswick, Maine. Retrieved August 8, 2008 from www.i-dont-know.com/vermette/KKK%20in%20Brunswick.html.

Vicente, A. L. & Pimenta, M. (2008). *Promoção da língua portuguesa no mundo*. Lisboa: Fundação Luso-Americana.

Vieira, N. (1980). Bilingual–bicultural education for Portuguese-Americans: An overview. In D. Macedo (ed.), *Issues in Portuguese Bilingual Education* (pp. 1–21). Cambridge, MA: National Assessment and Dissemination, Center for Bilingual/Bicultural Education.

Wachtel, K. (1913). *Z.P.R. K.: Dzieje Zjednoczenia Polskiego Rzym.-Kat. w Ameryce*. Chicago: L. J. Winiecki.

Wagner, H. (1929). *Spanish Voyages to the Northwest Coast of America in the Sixteenth Century*. San Francisco: California Historical Society in San Francisco.

Wang, C. S. (2004). Biliteracy resource eco-system of intergenerational language and culture transmission: An ethnographic study of a Chinese-American community. Doctoral Dissertation, University of Pennsylvania.

Warner, S. L. N. (1999). Kuleana: the right, responsibility, and authority of Indigenous peoples to speak and make decisions for themselves in language and culture revitalization. *Anthropology and Education Quarterly* 30(1), 68–93.

(2001). The movement to revitalize Hawaiian language and culture. In L. Hinton & K. Hale (eds.), *The Green Book of Language Revitalization in Practice* (pp. 133–44). San Diego, CA: Academic Press.

Wei, L., Milroy, L., & Pong, S. C. (1992). A two-step sociolinguistic analysis of code-switching and language choice. *International Journal of Applied Linguistics* 2(1), 63–86.

Weinberg, M. (1995). *A Change to Learn: A History of Race and Education in the United States* (2nd edition). Long Beach, CA: California State University, Long Beach Press.

Weinreich, U. (1968). *Languages in Contact*. The Hague: Mouton. [First edition 1953. New York: Linguistic Circle of New York Publication No. 2]

Weinstein, B. (1979). Language strategists: Redefining political frontiers on the basis of linguistic choices. *World Politics* 20, 344–64.

(1983). *The Civic Tongue: Political Consequences of Language Choices*. New York: Longman.

Welles, E. (2004). Foreign language enrollments in the United States institutions of higher education, fall 2002. *ADFL Bulletin* 35(2–3), 8–22.

Wharry, C. (1993). Bilingualism and ancestral language maintenance among Native American, Vietnamese American, and Hispanic American college students. *The Bilingual Research Journal* 17(3 & 4), 117–33.

Whistler, K. (2007). Hispanic print continues to show significant growth in 2006. *Latino Print Network*. Retrieved March 30, 2008 from www.latinoprintnetwork.com/assets/StateofHispanicPrint.pdf.

Whittaker, Robert. (2006). The Tolstoy Foundation: Library and archives. In A. Shmelev (ed.), *Tracking a Diaspora: Émigrés from Russia and Eastern Europe in the Repositories* (pp. 49–70). New York and London: The Haworth Information Press.

Wiley, T. G. (1998). The imposition of World War I era English-only policies and the fate of German in North America. In T. Ricento & B. Burnaby (eds.), *Language and Politics in the US and Canada: Myths and Realities* (pp. 211–24). Mahwah, NJ: Lawrence Earlbaum Associates.

(1999). Comparative historical analysis of US language policy and language planning: Extending the foundations. In T. Huebner & K. A. Davis (eds.), *Sociopolitical Perspectives on Language Policy and Planning in the USA* (pp. 17–37). Amsterdam: John Benjamins.

(2000). Continuity and change in the function of language ideologies in the United States. In T. Ricento (ed.), *Ideology, Politics, and Language Policies: Focus on English* (pp. 67–86). Amsterdam, Netherlands: John Benjamins.

(2001). On defining heritage Languages and their speakers. In J. K. Peyton, D. A. Ranard, & S. McGinnis (eds.), *Heritage languages in America: Preserving a National Resource* (pp. 29–36). Washington, DC & McHenry, IL: Center for Applied Linguistics and Delta Systems.

(2002). Heinz Kloss revisited: National Socialist ideologue or champion of language-minority rights? *International Journal of Sociology of Language* 154, 83–97.

(2003). Learning from history. In R. N. Campbell & D. Christian (eds.), Directions in research: Intergenerational transmission of heritage languages, *Heritage Language Journal* 1(1). Retrieved September 14, 2008 from www.heritagelanguages.org.

(2004). Language policy and English-only. In E. Finegan & J. R. Rickford (eds.), *Language in the USA: Perspectives for the Twenty-First Century* (pp. 319–38). Cambridge: Cambridge University Press.

(2005a). The reemergence of heritage and community language policy in the US national spotlight. *The Modern Language Journal* 89(4), 594–601.

(2005b). *Literacy and Language Diversity in the United States*. McHenry, IL & Washington, DC: Delta Systems and Center for Applied Linguistics.

(2005c). Discontinuities in heritage and community language education: Challenges for educational language policies. *The International Journal of Bilingual Education and Bilingualism* 8(2&3), 222–9.

(2007a). Immigrant minorities: USA. In M. Hellinger & A. Pauwels (eds.), *Handbooks of Applied Linguistics*, Vol. IX: *Language and Communication: Diversity and Change* (pp. 53–85). Berlin: Mouton de Gruyter.

(2007b). Accessing language rights in education: A brief history of the US context. In O. Garcia & C. Baker (eds.), *Bilingual Education: An Introductory Reader* (pp. 89–109). Clevedon, UK: Multilingual Matters. Reprint of: Wiley, T. G. (2002). Accessing language rights in education: A brief history of the US context. In J. Tollefson (ed.), *Language Policies in Education: Critical Readings* (pp. 39–64). Mahwah, NJ: Lawrence Erlbaum.

(2007c). Beyond the foreign language crisis: Toward alternatives to xenophobia and national security as bases for US language policies. *Modern Language Journal* 91(2), 252–5.

(2007d). The foreign language "crisis" in the US: Are heritage and community languages the remedy? *Critical Inquiry in Language Studies* 4(2–3), 179–205.

(2008). Language policy and teacher education. In S. May & N. Hornberger (eds.), *Language Policy and Political Issues in Education* (Vol. 1, pp. 229–42). N. Hornberger (General Editor), *Encyclopedia of Language and Education* (2nd edition). New York: Springer.

Wiley, T. G. & Lukes, M. (1996). English-only and standard English ideologies in the United States. *TESOL Quarterly* 30(3), 511–35.

Wiley, T. G., De Klerk, G., Li, M.-Y, Liu, N., Teng, Y., & Yang, P. (2008). Language attitudes toward Chinese "dialects" among Chinese immigrants and international students. In A. He & Y. Xiao (eds.), *Chinese as a Heritage Language in the United States* (pp. 67–88). National Foreign Language Resource Center, University of Hawaii at Manoa. Honolulu, HA: University of Hawaii Press.

Williams, F. G. (1980). Portuguese bilingualism among Azoreans in California. *Hispania* 63(4), 724–30.

Wilson, W. H. (1998). I ka 'ölelo Hawai'i ke ola, "Life is found in the Hawaiian language," *International Journal of the Sociology of Language* 132, 123–37.

Wilson, W. H. & Kamanä, K. (2001). "Mai loko mai o ka 'I'ii: Proceeding from a dream." The 'Aha Pünana Leo connection in Hawaiian language revitalization. In

L. Hinton & K. Hale (eds.), *The Green Book of Language Revitalization in Practice* (pp. 147–76). San Diego, CA: Academic Press.

Wittke, C. (1973). *The German Language Press in America*. Lexington, KY: University of Kentucky Press.

Wolfram, W. (1990). Re-examining Vernacular Black English. *Language* 66(1), 121–34.

Wong-Fillmore, L. (1991). When learning a second language means losing the first. *Early Childhood Research Quarterly* 6, 323–46.

Worthy, L. (n.d.). The *Cherokee Phoenix* (and *Indian Advocate*). Retrieved December 20, 2007 from http://ngeorgia.com/history/phoenix.html.

Wright, W. E. (2007). Heritage language programs in the era of English-only and No Child Left Behind. *Heritage Language Journal* 5(1). Retrieved September 14, 2008 from www.heritagelanguages.org/.

Wu, Y. C. (1978). *WenZi Gao ge Wen Qi*. Beijing, China: People's University Press.

Xiao, Y. (2007). Early exposure to home language on advanced learning. Paper presented at ACTFL, Nov. 16–18, San Antonio, TX.

(2008a). Charting the CHL development. In A. W. He & Y. Xiao (eds.), *Fostering Rooted World Citizenry: Studies in Chinese as a Heritage Language* (pp. 256–66). Hawaii: NFLRC, University of Hawaii Press.

(2008b). Home literacy environment in Chinese as a heritage language. In A. W. He & Y. Xiao (eds.), *Fostering Rooted World Citizenry: Studies in Chinese as a Heritage Language* (pp. 151–66). Hawaii: NFLRC, University of Hawaii Press.

Xu, H. (1999). Young Chinese ESL children's home literacy experiences. *Reading Horizons* 40(1), 47–64.

Yi, Y. (2008). Voluntary writing in the heritage language: A study of biliterate Korean-heritage adolescents in the US. *Heritage Language Journal* 6(2), 72–93.

Yoon, I. J. (1997). *On my Own: Korean Businesses and Race Relations in America*. Chicago: University of Chicago Press.

You, C. (2001). Heritage vs. non-heritage issues revisited. In J. J. Ree (ed.), *Korean Language in America 6* (the 2001 AATK conference proceedings) (pp. 275–84). Honolulu, HI: The American Association of Teachers of Korean.

YCAPS. (2008). *Amish Population by State (2008)*. Young Center for Anabaptist and Pietist Studies. Elizabethtown, PA: Elizabethtown College. Retrieved September 14, 2008 from www2.etown.edu/amishstudies/Population_by_State_2008.asp.

Young, R. L. & Tran, M. T. (1999). Vietnamese parent attitudes toward bilingual education. *Bilingual Research Journal* 23, 225–33.

Zehr, M. A. (2004, May 16). Arabic Offerings Rare in Schools. *Education Week* 23, 1–2.

Zemskaia, E. A. (ed.). (2001). *Iazyk russkogo zarubezh'ia: Obschie processy i rechevye Portrety* [The language of the Russian diaspora: General processes and speech portraits]. Moscow/Vienna: Wiener Slawistischer Almanach (in Russian).

Zentella, A. C. (1997). *Growing up Bilingual: Puerto Rican Children in New York*. Malden, MA: Blackwell.

Zepeda, O. (1995). *Ocean Power: Poems from the Desert*. Tucson and London: University of Arizona Press.

(1997). *Jewed 'I-hoi: Earth Movements*. Tucson, AZ: Kore Press.

Zéphir, F. (2005). Les rôles respectifs du créole et du français dans l'identité culturelle de la diaspora haïtienne. In A. Valdman, J. Auger, & D. Piston-Hatlen (eds.),

Le Français en Amérique du Nord; État présent (455–78). Québec: Presses de l'Université Laval.

Zhao, X. J. (2002). Chinese Americans' views on US–China relations: An analysis based on Chinese-community newspapers published in the US. In P. H. Koehn & X. H. Yin (eds.), *The Expanding Roles of Chinese Americans in US–China Relations: Transnational Networks and Trans-Pacific Interactions* (pp. 125–42). Armonk, NY: M. E. Sharpe, Inc.

Zhou, M. (2004). Assimilation, the Asian way. In T. Jacoby (ed.), *Reinventing the Melting Pot: The New Immigrants and What it Means to be American*. New York: Basic Books.

Zhou, M. & Bankston, C. L. III. (1998). *Growing up American: How Vietnamese Children Adapt to Life in the United States*. New York: Russell Sage Foundation Press.

(2000a). The biculturation of Vietnamese students. *ERIC/CUE Digest* no. 152. New York: ERIC.

(2000b). *Straddling Different Social Worlds: The Experience of Vietnamese Refugee Children in the United States*. New York: ERIC Clearinghouse on Urban Education, Institute for Urban and Minority Education, Teachers College, Columbia University.

新1326;词典. *Xinhua Cidan*, The New Chinese Dictionary. (2001). Reprinted. 1271;京: 商务1360;书馆2290; 中2269;语言文字使用情况调查总2467; 2298;中2269;语言文字2593;》 www.cchina-language.gov.cn.

Index